CELEBRATING CUENTOS

Recent Titles in the
Children's and Young Adult Literature Reference Series
Catherine Barr, Series Editor

Historical Fiction for Young Readers (Grades 4–8): An Introduction
John T. Gillespie

Twice Upon a Time: A Guide to Fractured, Altered, and Retold Folk and Fairy Tales
Catharine Bomhold and Terri E. Elder

Popular Series Fiction for K–6 Readers: A Reading and Selection Guide. 2nd Edition
Rebecca L. Thomas and Catherine Barr

Popular Series Fiction for Middle School and Teen Readers: A Reading and Selection Guide. 2nd Edition
Rebecca L. Thomas and Catherine Barr

Best Books for High School Readers, Grades 9–12. 2nd Edition
Catherine Barr and John T. Gillespie

Best Books for Middle School and Junior High Readers, Grades 6–9. 2nd Edition
Catherine Barr and John T. Gillespie

Green Reads: Best Environmental Resources for Youth, K–12
Lindsey Patrick Wesson

Best Books for Children: Preschool Through Grade 6. 9th Edition
Catherine Barr and John T. Gillespie

Literature Links toWorld History, K–12: Resources to Enhance and Entice
Lynda G. Adamson

A to Zoo: Subject Access to Children's Picture Books. 8th Edition
Carolyn W. Lima and Rebecca L. Thomas

Literature Links to American History, 7–12: Resources to Enhance and Entice
Lynda G. Adamson

Literature Links to American History, K–6: Resources to Enhance and Entice
Lynda G. Adamson

CELEBRATING CUENTOS

PROMOTING LATINO CHILDREN'S LITERATURE AND LITERACY IN CLASSROOMS AND LIBRARIES

Jamie Campbell Naidoo, Editor

Children's and Young Adult Literature Reference
Catherine Barr, Series Editor

AN IMPRINT OF ABC-CLIO, LLC
Santa Barbara, California • Denver, Colorado • Oxford, England

Library of Congress Cataloging-in-Publication Data

Celebrating cuentos : promoting Latino children's literature and literacy in classrooms and libraries / Jamie Campbell Naidoo, editor.
   p. cm. — (Children's and young adult literature reference)
  Includes bibliographical references and index.
  ISBN 978-1-59158-904-4 (acid-free paper) 1. Children's libraries—Services to Hispanic Americans. 2. School libraries—Services to minorities—United States. 3. Hispanic Americans—Juvenile literature—Bibliography. 4. Children's literature, Spanish American—Bibliography. 5. Tales—Latin America—Bibliography. 6. Hispanic American children—Books and reading. 7. Hispanic American children—Education. 8. Multicultural education—United States. 9. Literacy—United States. I. Naidoo, Jamie Campbell.
  Z718.2.U6C46 2011
  027.6'3—dc22
                        2010040790
ISBN: 978-1-59158-904-4
EISBN: 978-1-59158-905-1

15 14 13 12 11   1 2 3 4 5

This book is also available on the World Wide Web as an eBook.
Visit www.abc-clio.com for details.

Libraries Unlimited
An Imprint of ABC-CLIO, LLC

ABC-CLIO, LLC
130 Cremona Drive, P.O. Box 1911
Santa Barbara, California 93116-1911

This book is printed on acid-free paper ∞
Manufactured in the United States of America

CONTENTS

PART 1. EDUCATIONAL, DEVELOPMENTAL, AND LITERACY NEEDS OF LATINO CHILDREN

PART 2. LATINO CHILDREN'S LITERATURE: THEN AND NOW

Splendid Treasures of *Mi Corazón*

I am only an expert about my own sentiments. That is why when asked about the value of Latino children's literature, I have an urge to point in the direction of my own head, my two hands, and my throbbing chest to say that high-quality Latino literature is a beating and sacred heart, the shaman's ancient magic, the much-sought-after El Dorado, Moctezuma's lost treasure, Quetzalcoatl returning, the fifth sun. Yes, high-quality Latino children's literature is a roaring fire lighting people's path—but what do I know besides my own *corazón*?

Let me say that to me, the United States is a country of surprises. Since I crossed to "the other side" from Mexico in 1994 to make this place my home, I have learned that anything unexpected can happen here. I came to the United States as a new mother and, like most emigrants, having left behind my country, my family, my language, and all that was familiar to me, I felt thrown into what I perceived as a land of strange costumes and solitude—an almost unimaginable world. To me the United States posed a challenge that I felt ill equipped to take on; I had a minimal knowledge of the English language and a strong belief, rooted in my family's culture for generations, that all things white and foreign were better than me. But, to my surprise, it was here in this strange country of the unexpected that I would come to find art and books as the path I had been looking for in my life, while also building a new perception of my own identity—one that for the first time honored such things as the color of my skin, the complexity of my language, and the story of my ancestors. What was even more surprising to me was that all of this I discovered through children's books.

This is how it all began. Growing up in Mexico I had already loved the books and stories that I found on my parents' bookshelf. They were mostly adult books—many of which I barely understood. Yet many of them were jewels that marked me forever as a reader; they were books such as *La increíble y triste historia de la Candida Erendira y su Abuela Desalmada* written by Gabriel García Márquez, *La vispera del trueno* and *La carcajada del gato* by the Mexican novelist Luis Spota, as well as comic magazines such as *La familia Burron,* by Gabriel Vargas, which depicted the incredible adventures and struggles for survival of the members of the Burron family living in the slums of Mexico City. These books took me to places that often felt familiar, portraying things that could have happened to me or to people I knew. But at the same time these stories—the works of creative minds with visions others than mine—offered me worlds beyond my imagination.

Children's books were not part of my childhood. Instead they were a wonder I would come to discover when, as an adult, I stepped with my infant son for the first time inside one of the public libraries of California. Standing in front of the children's book section, I marveled at what I found. Here was row after row of books printed on bright, thick paper, bound between sturdy covers, recounting fascinating narratives, and brandishing the most extraordinary illustrations I have ever seen. These were true works of art, and they were all made for children. I had never before seen anything like it.

Yet the most significant surprises came when I began finding my first Latino books. From the shelves of the library, I pulled the story of *Mother Scorpion Country / La tierra de la madre escorpion,* a bilingual book by Harriet Rohmer, Dorminster Newton Wilson, and Virginia Stearns that mesmerized me with the uncanny Miskito Indian legend of a man who loved his wife so much that he asked to be buried alive with her so that he could follow her to the land of the dead. In *Family Pictures / Cuadros de familia,* I read and explored the images so meticulously painted by Carmen Lomas Garza as she poured out her memories and her pride about growing up in a Mexican American family, much like the one I came from. Suddenly I wondered why I had never before considered it an honor to have grown up eating *nopalitos,* using *remedios* instead of medicines, and dancing to ranchero music. *La mujer que brillaba aún más que el sol / The Woman Who Outshone the Sun,* from a poem of Alejandro Cruz Martinez and illustrated by Fernando Oliver, states in its narrative that Lucia Zenteno—a Zapotec Indian woman pictured with a broad body, long black hair, and brown skin—was a person so beautiful that she outshone the sun, bringing to me an idea of beauty I had never accepted before. *Chato's Kitchen* by Gary Soto and Susan Guevara opened my eyes to the richness of cultural humor and the validity of the barrio hero. I was in awe. Could it be true that here in the mythical USA—the land of the rich and the powerful, where I had felt without a rightful place—there was emerging a body of books that took pride and honor in what it means to be bilingual, to speak Spanish or Spanglish, to have an accent, to be multicolored, to play with *tíos* and *tías,* to listen to *abuelitas,* to be a *niño* or a *niña?*

It was here, inside the pages of these remarkable children's books that people like me and my son, Latinos, were finally just as smart, beautiful, complex, powerful, and human as any other person in the world—and this was not a favor handed down to us; it was an undeniable truth, and our right. The irony of having to come to a foreign land to be exposed to this truth for the first time does not escape me.

I have been in a passionate relationship with children's books ever since. They are what I think about most of my day, what I dream about at night, and what my work explores tirelessly. I have no choice; I am under a spell. And who wouldn't be? I find myself constantly amazed by how these books, turned works of art, urge both their creators and readers to explore, remember, question, understand, and also to share and celebrate that we have living roots in the countries we have left, ancestors who whisper their wisdom to us in our language, memories that recount our stories as people and as a community, and dreams to make true.

My friend Isabel Campoy wrote once that there are no Latinos in Mexico, or El Salvador, or Cuba, or in any of the twenty Hispanic countries for that matter, because *Latinos* is actually the term used to refer to the Spanish-speaking population (and their descendants) of the United States. For the same reason, I realize now, I had to come to a foreign country to become who I am: a *Latino* author and illustrator. I have learned that to be labeled *Latino* also defines such things as the shelves where my work will be displayed. I sense danger in any term that specifies ethnicity, as if being Latino, or African American, or indigenous suggests the possession of a monolingual voice and a specific vision meant to be understood only by those who are already familiar with these. I must say that I do not fear this label. In my path through schools and in visiting my readers, I have learned that children take from our work what they need the most. The Latino child recognizes himself or herself in the stories, finds in the illustrations things that he has at home, sees foods that she eats with her family, cherishes celebrations that his loved ones taught him about, understands habits that exist within her community. The non-Latino children, the ones not yet familiar with the culture, open the book and encounter surprises, those that we, like all other ethnic groups, have to offer from the most precious gifts of our culture. And, how could we, *Latinos*, not share our legacy with others? After all, our treasures are splendid.

Yuyi Morales

❀ INTRODUCTION

Latino Children's Literature in Today's Classrooms and Libraries

Jamie Campbell Naidoo

> Thank you especially to Pura Belpré, whose life's work—as a children's librarian, storyteller, and author—is a beautiful, brilliant example of creating light to illuminate, and thus empower, a previously ignored, unappreciated, and misunderstood culture and people, through the magic of telling their stories. Her spirit still shines, both upon the Latino community—strengthening our children with self pride and the possibilities for living compelling, fulfilling lives—and upon this nation, this whole world, really, by introducing and sharing with others the wonders and riches of our cultural traditions, our treasures (Canales 2006, p. 16).

I cannot think of a more fitting way to begin a book on the power, potential, and importance of incorporating Latino (see note on p. xix) children's literature into classrooms and libraries than with an accolade to the lifetime achievement of *the* pioneer of library services to Latino children and their families. At a time when the Puerto Rican immigrant population was vastly growing in New York, Belpré recognized the importance of the library and of culturally relevant books in the lives of children who longed to find a warm, secure place where someone could speak Spanish and share stories from their homeland.

Indeed, Belpré's passion for serving Latino families is just as relevant today as it was almost 90 years ago when she began her career. Latinos represent the largest and fastest-growing ethnic minority in the United States with the most recent estimates indicating that more than 48 million Latinos reside in the country in addition to the 4 million residents of Puerto Rico (U.S. Census Bureau 2010). In 2009, 1 in 4 children under the age of five and 22 percent of all children under the age of eighteen identified as Latino (U.S. Census Bureau 2010). Along with this growth in the Latino population comes the opportunity for librarians, teachers, and other educators to serve the informational, cultural, literary, and literacy needs of Latino children and their families. You may ask: How can I as a teacher reach out to Latino children in my classroom? How can I as a librarian exemplify Belpré's passion in my outreach to Latino children and their families when I don't speak Spanish or have a working understanding of Latino children's literature? Answers to these questions can be found in this book. What follows are just two examples of how current librarians and teachers are using Latino children's literature in their classrooms and libraries.

It's a bright, sunny afternoon in Redlands, California, when Latina author Pat Mora begins to cry. These are not tears of frustration or sorrow—they are tears of joy! For the past hour, a group of approximately fifty, predominantly Latino, third grade students have presented the award-winning author with a collection of rich responses to her poetry and books for children. They have shared their drawing, oral, dramatic, written, and creative reactions to Mora's *A Birthday Basket for Tía* (1992), *Rainbow Tulip* (1999), *Pablo's Tree* (1994), *Gracias Thanks* (2009), *Abuelos* (2008), *The Bakery Lady/La señora de la panadería* (2001), *The Gift of the Poinsettia/El regalo de la flor de nochebuena* (1995), and *Tomás and the Library Lady* (1997). These responses, indicative of the aesthetic responses that Louise Rosenblatt (1993) describes in her idea of reader response theory, included a class-made big book, *An Author Basket for Pat Mora*, which highlighted their drawing and creative responses to Mora's various books. Additionally the students wrote thank you notes to the author as a response to her book *Gracias/Thanks*, read and recited their poems sparked by her work, created Abuelos masks to accompany her book *Abuelos*, performed a dramatic response to her poem "Library Magic," and produced both written and drawing responses to the writing prompt "The library is a special place because . . ." in association with her book *Tomás and the Library Lady*. Finally, the students presented the author with an actual basket filled with handmade *pan dulce*, chocolate, an embroidered poinsettia kerchief, and an Abuelos mask. All of these gifts, mementos representing her various books, were the students' way of honoring the author for crafting books that allow them to see reflections of themselves—their languages and cultures. Mora, wiping away her tears of joy, reinforces the purpose of her work when she tells the children, "I want you to see pictures of you in books. . . . Be proud of being bilingual. Be proud of being readers."

This vignette is a vivid example of the potential for using high-quality Latino children's literature in classrooms to address the literacy needs of Latino children. Through a collection of books by a notable Latina author, two teachers helped their Latino students make lasting connections across the curriculum while also strengthening their cultural pride. At the same time, these astute teachers opened a window into the Latino culture for non-Latino students who want to know more about the heritage of their classmates. Both groups of students had the opportunity to develop critical literacy skills that will help them in the future.

I had the fortune to watch this scene unfold during the 2010 Charlotte Huck Children's Literature Conference. It was gratifying to see how a group of children and their teachers could use Latino children's literature to make cultural connections. An equally fulfilling experience occurred at the 2010 National Latino Children's Literature Conference in Tuscaloosa, Alabama, when a group of approximately 80 Latino and non-Latino children and their families interacted with Latino children's book artists Carmen Tafolla, Monica Brown, and Rafael López during a dual *Noche de cuentos* (Evening of Stories) and *El día de los niños/El día de los libros* (Children's Day/Book Day) storytelling event at the local public library. Some of the Latino children and families were attending the library for the first time and had a unique opportunity to meet authors and illustrators who were celebrating stories the reflected *their* own cultural experience. Non-Latino children and families played alongside their Latino counterparts as cultural folktales and *cuentos*[1] were shared in English and Spanish. Bright smiles and shining eyes abounded throughout the library as each child left with a signed copy of Pat Mora's and Rafael López's bilingual picture book *Book Fiesta* (2009) and with the knowledge that Spanish and Latino cultures are honored at the public library.

Both of these experiences reinforce the importance of incorporating Latino children's literature in classrooms and libraries. In both instances, Latino children had the opportunity to see reflections of their culture and non-Latino children had the opportunity to celebrate the culture of their peers. Positively acknowledging Latino cultures is integral in helping children navigate our culturally pluralistic society. Children of all cultures in the United States will inevitably interact with Latino peers at some point in their lives, and it is important that they understand and respect the Latino culture. Latino children's literature is a great way to foster this appreciation. In fact, Canales (2006) asserts

---

1   The term *cuentos* is used throughout this book to represent stories told by librarians, storytellers, teachers, and others. At times the word is also used to mean tales, short stories, and sometimes books. Although the Spanish word for book is *libro*, the term *cuento* is sometimes employed in this book to mean a culturally relevant story book either in Spanish or about Latinos.

it is "through the telling and the sharing of stories—everyone's stories—[that] we come to see how we're really all in this together. In a time when far too many think we should be erecting bigger and bigger walls to close our borders, it is literature that inspires us to build broader bridges instead—ones that open our eyes, our minds, our hearts" (p. 17).

Unfortunately, compared with other children's books being published, there are not that many Latino children's books available. A teacher or librarian wanting to introduce her students to Latino authors, cultures, and life must be selective when choosing books to share. Some books reinforce stereotypes through cultural inaccuracies and contain Spanish that is grammatically incorrect. How and where can teachers and librarians find the best books to use with their students? Also, in addition to simply reading books aloud to children, how can librarians and teachers create and implement activities that will foster cultural understanding and pride? Answers to these questions and more can be found throughout this book.

The first section of *Celebrating Cuentos* is intended to describe how Latino children's literature can influence the lives and development of both Latino and non-Latino children. Dr. Robert Ream and Lillia Vazquez give a brief historical overview of the education of Latino children to frame the struggles faced by Latinos seeking high-quality education and to reinforce the importance of reflecting their culture in teaching materials. In the following chapter, I describe the role of culturally accurate, high-quality Latino children's literature in the development of a Latino children's positive ethnic identity and detail how both Latino and non-Latino children are influenced by Latino children's books.

The second section of the book presents an overview of the development of Latino children's literature in the United States. I begin by highlighting some of the milestones in Latino children's book publishing and follow the literature from its beginnings as a body of stereotyped books to a wide variety of books representing multiple Latino cultures. In the next chapter, I provide a literature review of the various studies of Latino children's books, supplying additional examples of the triumphs and plights of this body of literature. Dr. Jennifer Battle, Oralia Garza de Cortes, and I then round out this section with a discussion of the three major awards for Latino children's literature, emphasizing some of the more notable titles.

In the third section, the authors and I detail resources for developing collections and highlight the must-have Latino and Spanish-language materials for children. Dr. Ruth Quiroa describes how she was able to attend Feria internacional del libro (FIL) in Guadalajara, Mexico, in December 2008 through the American Library Association Free Pass Program and how she became involved in the Américas Collection, which is a valuable list of high-quality books in Spanish organized by grade levels. Hope Crandall and I provide an extensive list of recommended titles organized according to the subjects that teachers and librarians will most likely use when incorporating Latino-oriented materials into the curriculum or a library program. In addition to books, this list includes films, puppets, audiobooks, music, magazines, and more!

The concluding section of the book provides an extensive overview of the various types of programs and lessons that can be used to incorporate Latino children's books into both classroom and library settings. It is designed in such a way that readers can pick and choose what is most useful to them in their current situation. Some of the chapters provide additional book suggestions while highlighting Web and print resources, and other chapters describe specific types of programming for libraries such as bilingual storytimes and Día programs. Still other chapters record the rich responses of Latino children to books authentically representing their cultural experiences. Dr. Maria Arroyo and Gigi Towers begin the section by describing their early literacy program for Latino preschool children and their families. Katie Cunningham then describes how early literacy principles can be taught to Latino families in the library through bilingual storytime programs. Amy Olson also discusses early literacy strategies for working with young children but within the context of using bilingual music. Irania Patterson provides specific suggestions on how libraries can create their own Día programs. In the subsequent chapter, storyteller and Latina author Lucía González explains the power that storytelling holds for Latino children, particularly when the stories feature Latino topics and themes. Next, I describe how public libraries and school libraries can collaborate to meet the literacy needs of Latino families and suggest a variety of useful planning resources for programs and services. The next two chapters highlight the work of Drs. Ruth Quiroa, Carmen Medina, and Carmen Martinez as they describe how Latino children develop deeper connections in their learning when Latino children's books are used in the classroom. These chapters are followed by Amy Olson's description of types of Latino folklore and the value that they hold for all children. In her chapter, she provides many examples of craft activities and programs that incorporate Latino folklore. I end the section by describing how Latino children's literature, particularly in digital format, can be used to encourage children to navigate the new literacies in classrooms and libraries (Web literacy, visual literacy, informational literacy, cultural literacy, and so forth).

The book begins and ends with individual accounts of the power of culturally authentic Latino children's literature in the lives of Latinos. Yuyi Morales and Maya Christina Gonzalez, both award-winning Latino children's book creators, describe their personal relationships with Latino children's literature as well as how these books led them on creative journeys of self-discovery.

Throughout the book, I have provided interviews with notable Latina authors and illustrators that further reinforce the importance of celebrating Latino cuentos. Additionally, I offer evaluation criteria to assist in the selection of Latino children's materials as well as a comprehensive bibliography of online and print resources relating to Latino children's literature. Also included in the bibliography are links to common publishers of Latino books, Web pages of Latino authors and illustrators, and online resources for planning Latino-themed literacy programs. I hope that you find something within each chapter and throughout the book that will inspire you to choose the best Latino literature to help children connect cultures and celebrate cuentos!

I am dedicated to helping educators and librarians find the right book for the right reader that can be given at the right time. Now is the right time to ensure that all children discover the beauty of the Latino cultures through high-quality, culturally accurate books. To help guarantee that high-quality children's books are published, a portion of my author proceeds will be donated to the nonprofit, multicultural publisher Children's Book Press. The remainder of the proceeds will support the National Latino Children's Literature Conference, which prepares librarians and educators to serve the informational and literacy needs of the fastest-growing minority in the United States.

I would like to thank editors Catherine Barr and Barbara Ittner at Libraries Unlimited for their unwavering support and encouragement. A special thanks also goes to Christine McNaull and Jane Higgins for their assistance with the designing, proofing, and typesetting of the book, and to Jamaica Pouncy and Michelle Harper for their work compiling and formatting the *grande* bibliography. My deepest gratitude goes out to all the talented authors and illustrators (as well as their publishers) who create the beautiful manuscripts and illustrations for the many wonderful Latino children's books available to children throughout the country. Finally, thank you to Pura Belpré, Oralia Garza de Cortes, Lucía González, Rose Treviño, Sandra Ríos Balderrama, Irania Patterson, and countless other librarians for all that you have done to promote library services to Latino children and their families.

NOTE

The terms *Latino* and *Hispanic* are labels often used interchangeably in U.S. society to refer to the same population of people who live in Mexico, Central and South America, Puerto Rico, Cuba, and the Caribbean. Each term is loaded with both social and political implications and is accepted/rejected in various degrees by the people they purport to describe. Gracia (2000) provides a lengthy discussion on the issues and politics behind each term and describes the rationalizations used by the people who adopt one label over the other to describe themselves. Similarly, Oboler (2002) describes the resistance of Latino people to the labels *Hispanic* and *Latino*, stating that this minority of more than 40 million interprets the labels as derogatory terms used by white Americans (Anglos) to describe the group as dirty and low class. Oboler also asserts that the terms create social barriers and lower the self-worth of this diverse cultural group. She acknowledges that the group prefers to identify itself in terms of national origin—Mexican, Cuban, Puerto Rican, etc.—rather than by race or language. Acuña (2003) also discusses how U.S. Latinos described themselves in the 2000 U.S. Census, asserting that the U.S. Census defines *Latino* as an ethnic group rather than as a race, because it cannot decide how to use the label. According the U.S. Census Bureau (2010), the government treats Hispanic origin and race as two separate concepts.

"People of Hispanic, Latino, or Spanish origin are those who trace their origin or descent to Mexico, Puerto Rico, Cuba, Spanish-speaking countries of Central or South America, and other Spanish cultures. Origin can be considered as the heritage, nationality group, lineage, or country of birth of the person or the person's parents or ancestors before their arrival in the United States. People of Hispanic, Latino, or Spanish origin may be of any race" (p. 26).

To determine whether Latino children accept or reject the label *Hispanic*, Portes and MacLeod (1996) studied second-generation children whose parents immigrated to the United States from Latin America and report, "Children who adopt the Hispanic label are the least well assimilated: they report poorer English skills, lower self-esteem and higher rates of poverty than their counterparts who identify themselves as Americans or as hyphenated Americans [Cuban-American, Mexican-American, etc.]" (p. 523). Further, Ada (2003), recognizing that the United States likes neat labels to describe the population, explains her rationalization for choosing the term *Latina* to describe herself. The words *Latino* and *Latina* are from her native Spanish language, express both masculine and feminine forms that affirm gender, and signify recognition of her *mestizo* (a mixture of Indian and European ancestries) nature, which she feels is essential to accepting the fullness of one's own self. Finally, Kibler (1996) suggests that the term *Hispanic* is linked to conservative policy issues while *Latino* is linked to liberal policy issues. He also reiterates that the labels are only used in the United States.

Throughout this book you will find the two terms used interchangeably, depending on the research being cited or the author writing the chapter. The labels are used for clarity purposes only; I fully respect the rights of each individual to adopt the term she feels best describes her individual life and culture.

REFERENCES

Acuña, Rudolfo F. *U.S. Latino Issues*. Westport, CT: Greenwood, 2003.

Ada, Alma Flor. *A Magical Encounter: Latino Children's Literature in the Classroom* (2nd ed.). Boston, MA: Allyn and Bacon, 2003.

Canales, Viola. "Belpré Author Award Acceptance Speech: The Beauty of Us All, Together." *Children and Libraries*, 4 (Summer/Fall 2006): 16–17.

Gracia, Jorge J. E. *Hispanic/Latino Identity: A Philosophical Perspective*. Malden, MA: Blackwell, 2000.

Kibler, John M. "Latino Voices in Children's Literature: Instructional Approaches for Developing Cultural Understanding in the Classroom." In *Children of La Frontera: Binational Efforts to Serve Mexican Migrant and Immigrant Students*, ed. by Judith LeBlanc Flores, 239–268. Charleston, WV: ERIC, 1996.

Oboler, Suzanne. "The Politics of Labeling." In *Transnational Latina/o Communities: Politics, Processes, and Culture*, ed. by C. Vélez-Ibáñez and A. Sampio, 73–89. New York: Rowan & Littlefield, 2002.

Portes, Alejandro, and Dag MacLeod. "What Shall I Call Myself? Hispanic Identity Formation in the Second Generation." *Ethnic and Racial Studies*, 19 (1996): 523–547.

Rosenblatt, Louise. "The Literary Transaction: Evocation and Response." In *Journeying: Children Responding to Literature*, ed. by K. Holland, R. Hungerford, and S. Ernst, pp. 6–23. Portsmouth, NH: Heinemann, 1993.

U.S. Census Bureau. "Hispanic Heritage Month 2010: September 15–October 15." http://www.census.gov/newsroom/releases/archives/facts_for_features_special_editions/cb10-ff17.html (accessed October 1, 2010).

———. "2010 Census Questionnaire Reference Book." http://2010.census.gov/partners/pdf/langfiles/qrb_English.pdf (accessed October 1, 2010).

PART 1

EDUCATIONAL, DEVELOPMENTAL, AND LITERACY NEEDS OF LATINO CHILDREN

CHAPTER 1

Overview of Latino Children and U.S. Public Education

Robert K. Ream and Lillia Vazquez

The history of Latinos[1] in U.S. public education is fraught with contradictions, none of them more basic than this: schooling serves both as the pathway to the proverbial American Dream and as the threshing floor on which Hispanic students' cultural and linguistic knowledge is so often separated and then swept aside. A recent study based on data gathered by the U.S. Census Bureau reveals impressive advances over the course of the 20th century in Hispanic educational attainment from generation to generation. Mexican immigrants born between 1905 and 1909 averaged only 4.3 years of schooling. Their American-born sons, averaging 9.3 years of schooling, doubled the years of schooling, and their grandsons were high school graduates, averaging 12.2 years of schooling (Smith 2003). These gains notwithstanding, the rates of socioeconomic progress for many U.S. Hispanics over successive generations have been decidedly slower than the rates for European immigrants of the 19th and early 20th centuries (Chapa 1988; Gans 1992; National Research Council 2006). So while there is some merit to the notion of public education as "the great leveler of the social hierarchy" (McMurrer and Sawhill 1998), Hispanics count disproportionately among exceptions by almost any measure of the American Dream narrative popularized in the 19th century in Horatio Alger's hackneyed tales of self-made success (Pew Hispanic Center 2009).

---

1   On the West Coast the meta-categorical term *Latino* is generally preferred to *Hispanic*—the latter adopted in the 1970s and first employed in the 1980 U.S. Census (Bean and Tienda 1987). Yet if U.S. Latinos/Hispanics are asked to choose between the panethnic terms, Hispanic is preferred to Latino by a 3 to 1 margin (National Research Council 2006). We use both terms interchangeably. As mere labels, however, neither adequately describes the diverse ethnic and cultural heritage of the populations in question.

Widespread disaffection with schooling among Hispanic youth can be traced not only to historical burdens of poverty and nativist hostility, but also to longstanding subtractive schooling practices (Valenzuela 1999). By the term *subtractive schooling* we refer to the practice of many U.S. schools of divesting the children of immigrants of the cultures and languages they bring to school from home, and thus on a basic level of the formative experiences, imaginative resources, and rudimentary identity derived through family life and tradition (Moll 2001; Portes and Rumbaut 2001). Dropout rates among Hispanic students are three times those of non-Hispanic whites (National Center for Education Statistics 2005). Notably, schools employing subtractive practices are implicated in, though by no means entirely responsible for,[2] our country's continuing history of racialized inequality, as measured by educational inputs and outcomes (Gibson, Gándara, and Koyama 2004; Ream 2005; Valenzuela, 1999).

Perhaps the best evidence regarding racialized gaps in test score outcomes is derived from the National Assessment of Educational Progress (NAEP), widely known as the nation's report card. NAEP trend data demonstrate persistent, if fluctuating, test score gaps running back to 1971. According to the 2007 NAEP data, by the time they are in fourth grade Hispanic students are already lagging one year behind their non-Hispanic counterparts in both mathematics and reading (Ream, Espinoza, and Ryan 2009). For too long these patterned differences have been referred to as "achievement gaps," a term that is considered by many to be a problematic misnomer. Indeed, by reframing outcome gaps as the shameful product of a long history of discriminatory gaps in educational inputs, Gloria Ladson-Billings argued in her 2005 presidential address to the American Educational Research Association that the "achievement gap" could

---

2   James Coleman was a sociologist at Johns Hopkins University when his controversial 1966 report to the U.S. Congress, *Equality of Educational Opportunity*, became the first national study to offer a systemic description of ethnoracial differences in academic achievement among children of various ages. To his surprise, Coleman found that (1) while schools certainly influence student achievement—much of what tests measure must be learned in schools—and (2) although school quality varies widely in the United States, the large documented differences in the quality of schools attended by Hispanic versus white children fail to explain most of the difference in average levels of achievement between Hispanics and whites (Miller 1997). These rather controversial findings have been cross-examined by many researchers. Few, if any, dispute Coleman's fundamental claims (Rothstein 2004).

be more accurately understood as a historically accumulated "educational debt" that the United States owes to minority and poor students who have been inadequately served by the education system (Ladson-Billings 2006). In the sections that follow we look back at one of the earliest school desegregation cases in U.S. history, specifically the 1931 Lemon Grove Incident, and then consider a series of subsequent judicial rulings and legislative events that lend support to Ladson-Billing's perception of a longstanding educational debt. Although we would have liked to cover more ground, we can account here for only a fraction of the many events in history that have influenced education outcomes for U.S. Hispanics. In our closing remarks, however, we take a look at an emergent new and potentially historic chapter in the making, one that seems especially suited to a book designed to celebrate Latino children's literature and literacy.

In her essay "Reading Trauma and Violence in U.S. Latina/o Children's Literature," cultural studies scholar Tiffany Ana Lopez perceives a renaissance in children's literature, spurred in large part by Latino authors such as Luis Rodriguez, Gloria Anzaldúa, Roberto Gonzalez, and Julia Alvarez, who are better known for their contributions to literature for adults (Lopez 2009). As part of an effort to give back to their community, these writers are fashioning stories that can help counter the histories, policies, and educational practices that have so often culminated in subtractive cultural assimilation and have thus promoted racialized gaps in achievement. In Lopez's view, stories for children partake of a cultural project of documenting Latino experiences, what Lopez refers to as an act of "critical witnessing," which we believe is itself part of an ambitious project of history-making. In this sense, the critical witness (as performed by children's literature) describes a way of being "so moved or inspired by the experience of encountering a text as to embrace a specific course of action avowedly intended to forge a path toward change" (Lopez 2009, p. 1). In writing about past and present injustices, these writers figure them as part of a hopeful expectation, as a prologue to a history of Hispanics yet to be written, and for this reason we highlight the educational implications of their history-making work in our concluding remarks.

COLLECTIVE VIGILANCE

Alvarez v. Lemon Grove School District (1931)

In the midst of the Great Depression, the Lemon Grove School Board met in the summer of 1930, ostensibly to discuss the issue of overcrowding in the local elementary school. In fact, board members sought to appease the predominantly non-Hispanic white community located in eastern San Diego County by approving the construction of a two-room schoolhouse for Mexican Americans only. This "new" school would serve effectively as a pretext to deny Mexican Americans access to the common school they had previously attended, on the grounds that these children "did not speak English and were unsanitary" (Ladson-Billings 2004, p. 5). Standing before the entrance to the Lemon Grove Grammar School on January 5, 1931, the principal prevented the Hispanic children from returning to the classroom in which they had been educated only weeks earlier, redirecting them to the segregated two-room school site later to become known as *La Caballeriza*—"the stable" (Valencia 2008). No National Guard troops were called in to enforce desegregation in Depression-era Lemon Grove, because there were as yet no federal laws to make the actions of the board obviously illegal. Nevertheless, in defiance of the district's separatist solution to the problem of overcrowding, the parents of the affected children boycotted the school, galvanizing support from the larger Mexican American community. The *Comité de Vecinos de Lemon Grove* (Lemon Grove Neighborhood Committee) subsequently sued the school board in the name of Roberto Alvarez, one of the aggrieved schoolchildren (Valencia, Menchaca, and Donato 2002). In their petition they noted that California, unlike Arizona and Texas at that time, had "no statute allowing for the segregation of Mexican American children based on race" (Valencia 2008, p. 20).[3]

If the school board justified its decision by citing the need to Americanize "Mexican" students, and to attend specially and separately to their English-language developmental needs, the arguments were riddled with double standards, especially as no such remedy was offered to children who were not of Mexican origin but demonstrated similar needs. In his decision, the judge instructed the district to readmit all students to Lemon Grove Grammar School. For the most part the ruling was considered a local event, setting no immediate precedent for legal struggles against segregation practices in the Southwest (Alvarez 1986). Nevertheless, the Lemon Grove Incident came to be known as the first case of its kind in the United States, a successful class-action lawsuit regarding school desegregation, and an antecedent to the 1946 *Méndez v. Westminster* case—the first to call into question the High Court's "separate

---

3   Essentialist laws allowing the segregation of "Oriental," "Negro," and "Indian" children did not apply to Mexican Americans, who were at that time considered in California to be "of the Caucasian race" (Valencia 2008).

but equal" doctrine handed down a half century earlier in *Plessy v. Ferguson* (1896).

Méndez v. Westminster (1946)

While the limited reach of the district court ruling constrained the impact of the Lemon Grove Incident, some fifteen years later the Ninth Circuit Appeals Court established in *Méndez v. Westminster* a nationwide precedent for the cessation of segregated "Mexican schools." In 1944 the Méndez family resided in the Southern California town of Westminster, where the local elementary school officially admitted only Anglo students. Despite this restriction, fair-skinned Soledad Vidaurri—the Méndez siblings' aunt—had managed to enroll her own children in Westminster Elementary. The advantages of light complexion and a French-origin surname did not extend to the Méndez children, however. When his children's enrollment application was denied, Gonzalo Méndez joined cause with other parents in the region who were determined to confront public schools designed for whites only (Valencia 2008; Wollenberg 1974). The group of parents retained the services of civil rights attorney David C. Marcus, who filed suit on behalf of the Méndez group against four Orange County school districts. Although previous segregation cases, such as the Lemon Grove Incident, had proceeded partially on racial grounds, *Méndez* was the first case to assert that the rationale of "separate but equal" did not square with the Fourteenth Amendment of the U.S. Constitution.

Deploying expert testimony from social scientists, Marcus contended with the logic of segregation itself. Rather than facilitating "Americanization," as the Lemon Grove School Board had maintained, segregation actually posed barriers to English language acquisition as well as to the assimilation of Mexican Americans (Diaz 2007; Galicia 2007). The introduction of empirical data for the court's deliberations was a key aspect of this case, facilitating in effect a reinterpretation of the law. In his decision, Judge Paul J. McCormick had obviously been swayed:

> The "equal protection of the laws" pertaining to the public school system in California is not provided by furnishing in separate schools the same technical facilities, text books and courses of instruction to children of Mexican ancestry that are available to other public school children regardless of their ancestry. A paramount requisite in the American system of public education is social equality. It must be open to all children by unified school association regardless of lineage (*Méndez v. Westminster* 1946).

Despite the ruling, there were school districts and even some courts that continued to abet segregation practices, and by some counts the practice of separating Hispanic children from non-Hispanic whites actually increased in the wake of *Méndez* (Galicia 2007). Still, the ruling had established a precedent for other court decisions that would gradually tilt state laws toward desegregation (Diaz 2007; Meier and Stewart 1991),[4] and by reinterpreting the Fourteenth Amendment it had laid the ground for the U.S. Supreme Court's unanimous *Brown v. Board of Education* ruling in 1954 (Gonzalez 1990).

Brown v. Board of Education (1954)

While the *Méndez* decision established, de jure, the illegality of segregating youth of Mexican origin from their peers, a lack of will to implement the ruling posed serious barriers to desegregation efforts not only in California but throughout the nation. It took another eight years for the U.S. Supreme Court to disavow the practice of segregation at the national level and thereby challenge the conventional dual system of public education in American society. Working with empirical data and integrationist arguments much like those employed in *Méndez*, the plaintiffs in *Brown v. Board of Education* also argued that segregation of any identified minority group was contradictory to the protections of the Fourteenth Amendment and therefore unconstitutional. In the final ruling, Chief Justice Earl Warren and the other justices of the court gave legal expression to a changing America as they unanimously rejected the "separate but equal" doctrine that had been established in the 1896 *Plessy* verdict, and thereby created at long last a national standard of equality in educational opportunity (Greenburg 2004; Valencia 2008).

Of course, the consequences of even the most promising court rulings and legislative initiatives depend on the capacity and will of individuals to enact reform in real-life contexts at the local level. In the wake of *Brown*, the limited reach of even the highest court in the land was made apparent, as the call for school integration with "all deliberate speed" moved forward often haltingly and sometimes stalled altogether. Many communities continued segregationist practices in the name of integration by grouping, or integrating, Hispanics and blacks together while leaving well-off whites to themselves (Valencia 2008;

---

4   Two years following *Méndez*, a federal district court also denied the language deficiency argument for separate Mexican American schools by ruling in *Delgado v. Bastrop Independent School District* (1948) that the segregation practices of that Texas district were in violation of the Fourteenth Amendment (Salinas 1971).

Valencia, Menchaca, and Donato 2002). In still other cases Anglo school officials cynically used Hispanic children deemed "white" to offer the appearance of cooperating with federal racial integration orders;[5] and, in response to tactics of this sort, African Americans and Hispanics often collaborated in resistance (MacDonald 2004). Moreover, the *Brown* ruling had not addressed de facto segregation practices rationalized on the premise of language deficiency (Diaz 2007). Not until the civil rights movement would legislators, this time in advance of the courts, develop bilingual education programs to address the literacy needs of English learners without the punishing effects of segregation.

Bilingual Education Act (1968)

It was in Florida in response to the influx of refugees of the Cuban Revolution that the first modern-day dual-language and biethnic education program was implemented in 1963 (Garcia and Wiese 2002; Valencia 2008). Three years later, in the widely read report *The Invisible Minority . . . Pero No Vencibles*, the National Education Association (NEA) proclaimed bilingual education a key strategy for improving the educational experiences of Hispanic children in the Southwest (National Education Association 1966). Shortly thereafter, Democratic U.S. Senator Ralph Yarborough of Texas went on to sponsor an amendment to the 1965 Elementary and Secondary Education Act (the original version of the No Child Left Behind Act of 2001), which provided federal funding for bilingual programs in schools with Spanish-speaking students. Subsequent legislation by Democratic Congressman James Scheuer of New York was designed to meet the "special needs" of all non-English-speaking children by providing federal financial assistance to local school districts, so that they might develop and implement bilingual education programs. Signed into law in 1968, the Bilingual Education Act did not require school agencies to participate, and many districts failed to take advantage of the newly available resources. In fact, less than 3 percent of the Mexican American student population in the Southwest was enrolled in bilingual education a full year after the act had been signed into law (Valencia 2008). Even among those districts and schools that attempted to capitalize on this new opportunity, implementation of the law was impinged by vagaries of purpose (no particular program of instruction had been

---

5   As a glaring example, the *Ross v. Eckles* (1970) ruling stands out for granting authority to school districts to treat Mexican Americans as whites so as to facilitate segregation by other means (Meier and Stewart 1991; San Miguel 2001).

recommended) as well as by lack of capacity among educators and by funding irregularities (García and Wiese 2002). This compelled further litigation and subsequent policy activity.

Lau v. Nichols (1974)

In 1974 the U.S. Supreme Court was once again called upon to adjudicate a major class-action lawsuit pertaining to educational quality and equality. When Chinese Americans in San Francisco filed the case soon to be known as *Lau v. Nichols*, English remained the only required language of instruction in U.S. public schools and most English learners (ELs)[6] were still precluded from a meaningful educational experience (Roos 1978; Valencia, Menchaca, and Donato 2002). Though it is commonly thought of as a language rights ruling, the Supreme Court's decision in *Lau* did not require school districts to implement bilingual education as the means to provide language minority students with an equitable educational opportunity. It did rule, however, that public schools must provide a curriculum comprehensible to students who did not speak English, and recognized bilingual education as one such avenue for addressing the special needs of minority students. Furthermore, since the ruling obligated the Office for Civil Rights of the U.S. Department of Education to ensure compliance, policymakers and educators began to search in earnest for better ways to instruct ELs (Gonzalez and Lam 2007). In 1976 California became the third state, after Massachusetts and Texas, to pass legislation that exceeded the prescriptions of either the 1968 Bilingual Education Act or the 1974 *Lau* ruling by requiring schools with specific numbers of English learners to offer bilingual education. Other states followed suit: 31 states had bilingual education provisions in place by 1979 (Crawford 1989; Gary et al. 1981). A decade later, however, bilingual education had become a contentious and highly politicized topic of debate, and by the late 1990s the reaction against bilingual education sentiment reached a tipping point with the 1998 passage of California's Proposition 227, which was designed to limit the practice of native-language instruction in public schools (Guerrero 2002). Shortly thereafter Arizona voters passed a similar measure, Proposition 203, which effectively dismantled bilingual education in Arizona public schools in favor of single-year English-immersion programming.

---

6   We use "English learner" to describe students who initially learn a language other than English in their home. The term includes students who are just beginning to learn English and students who are approaching proficiency in English but may need additional assistance in schooling situations.

The Williams Case (2000)

Although our brief historical review has focused mainly on cases of collective resistance to school segregation pursued through legal channels, it is important also to recall the perpetual debate over school finance and resource distribution pertaining to segregation issues. Indeed, school segregation and school finance are historically and fundamentally intertwined in ways that bear heavily on children from Spanish-speaking households. English learners, the vast majority of whom are Hispanics, are especially set apart in schools where facilities and conditions are poor. Furthermore, they are more likely than any other group of children to be taught by emergency-credentialed teachers who receive little professional support and development aimed at bolstering their capacity to teach children whose home language is Spanish. If the numbers of children were declining the situation might not be critically important, but the situation is entirely the opposite: approximately 14.5 million children are English learners nationwide, and the numbers are on the rise. In many California schools more than one quarter of the student body is not fluent in English (Rumberger and Gándara 2004). Due in no small part to concerns of this nature, Eliezer Williams and nearly one hundred other students filed a class-action suit in San Francisco County Superior Court against the state of California in May 2000. The advocates for *Williams* charged the state with failure to provide safe and decent school facilities, qualified teachers, and equal access to instructional materials (Oakes 2004). The students most affected by these problems were Latinos and other underrepresented minorities. The case was resolved out of court in 2003 when Governor Arnold Schwarzenegger took office and asked the state's attorney general to negotiate a settlement. As a result, California schools are required to report the overall condition of their facilities, the number of teachers assigned to instruct classes for which they lack credentials, and the availability of textbooks or instructional materials. Moreover, millions of dollars in additional funding have been allocated to California public schools deemed to be performing below average levels (see: http://www.cde.ca.gov/eo/ce/wc/wmslawsuit.asp).[7]

---

7   Critics of the ruling assert, however, that it fails to guarantee a high-quality education to all the state's children and "merely seeks a minimum threshold for educational provisions, below which no child must be made to suffer" (Oakes 2004, 1891).

BRIEF SUMMARY

Although at least some empirical data suggest the American Dream remains an important narrative for explaining Hispanic intergenerational mobility (Smith 2003), we have emphasized in this chapter that a critical reading of the history of Latinos in education requires us to see the Hispanic "achievement gap" as a historically unreconciled "educational debt." To avoid placing the onus for attaining the American Dream solely in the hands of individuals, we have attempted here to shift the narrative for American self-understanding to another well-recognized story that extols the idea of the national community—a story of neighbor helping neighbor as part of the ongoing process of becoming a better nation (Reich 2005). The 1931 Lemon Grove Incident exemplifies this second version of American narrative, in which a community (within the larger national community) pried back open the doors to educational opportunity on behalf of young Roberto Alvarez and his classmates. So, too, in 1946 the Méndez family and their friends made a similar push to advance educational opportunity through the courts; and only eight years later the plaintiffs in *Brown* successfully argued against the longstanding practice of segregated education in which schools were imagined "as separate as the fingers,"[8] thereby debunking the notion that schools might be segregated but no less equal. More recently, the Bilingual Education Act (1968), *Lau* (1974), and *Williams* (2000) show how collective action and empirical research can effectively destabilize rationalities built upon individualistic cultural narratives, which when left unchallenged perpetuate the status quo.

By communal acts such as those we have considered, the possibility of individual liberty and upward mobility through quality education has been at least partly restored not only for Hispanic youth but for all children thanks to educational reforms spurred by historically underrepresented groups. Although our focus here has by necessity been limited and even selective, in effect accounting for only a small portion of the history of Latinos in public education, there is a significant pattern here. On the strength of that pattern of collective advocacy we want to turn by way of conclusion to what might be

---

8   Once the most famous African American in the United States, nothing brought Booker T. Washington more notoriety than his 1895 speech at the Cotton States and International Exposition in Atlanta, where only one year prior to the U.S. Supreme Court ruling legalizing segregation in *Plessy* (1896) he proclaimed that "in all things purely social we can be as separate as the fingers" (Hahn 2009).

thought of as a prologue of educational events to come, specifically, by attending to acts of "critical witnessing" in new and emergent literature written for Hispanic youth. Such work seems especially important insofar as it challenges the detrimental effects of communal trauma even as it expands our sense of how such trauma works in groups, as a consequence of a shared history of injustice. One area in which the effects of such trauma can be witnessed is in the intergenerational transfer of inequality, which arises from the efforts of minority groups to confront—often with only limited success—the exclusions practiced against them by well-resourced institutions such as those to which we have called attention above. In short, the cumulative effects of being denied equal access to good schools and effective curricula are lasting, intergenerational, and (by the modern connotation of the term) even traumatic. A certain strain of children's literature written by prominent Latino authors for Latino youth is designed, as we read it, to inoculate readers from the transmitted ill effects of historical injustices. By making Latino children cognizant of (without being merely determined by) injustice, this work inspires a praxis that would instigate change in our understanding of the education experience of minority youth in this country.

MOVING FORWARD: THE ACT OF CRITICAL WITNESSING

According to Tiffany Ana Lopez, the list of scholars and writers who draw from the past as a means to inspire through children's literature the possibility of corrective action is rapidly expanding (Lopez 2009). Lopez works within the parameters of modern trauma studies, but we suspect that the value of her notion of "critical witnessing" has a broader potential: (1) to stimulate resistance among Hispanic youth to the strains of trauma that perpetuate their sense of "otherness," and (2) to translate the offenses of the past into present possibilities (Spargo 2002). Insofar as a lack of knowledge perpetuates the traumatic effect, then "the ability of Latina/o children to navigate an openly hostile and debilitating world depends," Lopez insists, "on their being taught active modes of engagement such as those offered through literatures of critical witnessing" (Lopez 2009, p. 206).

Until fairly recently there had been little in the way of a Latino children's literature working to make young readers aware of and better able to resist social injustice, and in effect also helping to transform subtractive schooling practices into its opposite, additive institutional praxis. Of late, however, examples of liberatory children's literature abound. For instance, Luis Rodriguez (author of the memoir *Always Running—La Vida Loca: Gang Days in L.A.*) challenges "the crazy life" in gangs and sees the phenomena of gang warfare, racism, and poverty as interrelated. Ultimately, he exposes the gang lifestyle as a self-defeating response to the historically perpetuated stereotypes and stigmas that bear down on Hispanic youth. In her critical account of Rodriguez's illustrated children's books (such as *It Doesn't Have to Be This Way* and *America Is Her Name*), Lopez highlights the role of mentors in helping children to *imagine* beyond the limits of the violence they face on a day-to-day basis and the debilitating alienation that so often follows from it. So, also, the late Gloria Anzaldúa (award-winning author of *Borderlands/La Frontera*) taps the power of imagination in her children's book *Friends from the Other Side* in order to create a new horizon arising from the reader's empathy for the characters. In *Friends* the young protagonist Prietita sees much more clearly than her peers the humanity in Joaquin, an immigrant child from Mexico whose language and comportment make it hard for him to fit into his new American community. Anzaldúa creates a narrative space "driven by empathy and understanding, rather than presumptions born from stereotypes, fear, or ignorance" (Lopez 2009, p. 218). Through the act of imagining made possible by literature, she extends the engagement with injustice evident in her writing for adult audiences into children's literature, and thereby creates fertile ground both for acts of self-help for "at-risk" youth and for collective efforts to transforming children's lives from the state of being at-risk to the state of being of-promise. Much as Lopez observes the critical and liberatory potential of Rodriquez, Anzaldúa, and a number of other authors, we are persuaded that acts of critical witnessing serve as gifts to the imaginative identity development of Hispanic youth while also potentially transforming the practices of the school personnel charged with their education. For if students are to be protected from the injustices they inherit and face daily—and if we as educators are to be moved to intervene in their traumatic experience—we must first be able to imagine the reality and nature of those injustices and to conceive of ways in which they can be resisted.

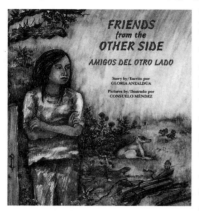

Cover image from Friends From the Other Side / Amigos del otro lado. *Story © 1993 by Gloria Andadúa. Illustrations © 1993 by Consuelo Mendez. Reprinted with permission of the publisher, Children's Book Press, San Francisco, CA, www.childrensbookpress.org.*

REFERENCES

Alvarez, Robert, Jr. "The Lemon Grove Incident: The Nation's First Successful Desegregation Court Case." *Journal of San Diego History* 32, no. 2 (1986): 116–135.

Bean, Frank D., and Marta Tienda. *The Hispanic Population of the United States.* New York: Russell Sage Foundation, 1987.

California Department of Education. "The *Williams* Case: An Explanation." http://www.cde.ca.gov/eo/ce/wc/wmslawsuit.asp (accessed November 13, 2009).

Chapa, Jorge. "The Question of Mexican American Assimilation: Socioeconomic Parity or Underclass Formation?" *Public Affairs Comment* 35 (1988): 1–14.

Coleman, James S., Earnest Campbell, Carol Hobson, James McPartland, Alexander Mood, Frederic Weinfield, and Robert York. *Equality of Educational Opportunity.* Washington, DC: U.S. Government Printing Office, 1966.

Crawford, James. *Bilingual Education: History, Politics, Theory and Practice.* Trenton, NJ: Crane, 1989.

Diaz, Gerardo. "Court Struggles and Latino Education." In *Latino Education in the U.S.*, ed. by Lourdes Diaz Soto, 88–92. New York: Rowman & Littlefield, 2007.

Galicia, Laura. "Americanization." In *Latino Education in the U.S.*, ed. by Lourdes Diaz Soto, 31–35. New York: Rowman & Littlefield, 2007.

Gans, Herbert J. "Second-Generation Decline: Scenarios for the Economic and Ethnic Futures of the Post-1965 American Immigrants." *Ethnic and Racial Studies* 15, no. 2 (1992): 173–192.

García, Eugene E., and Ann-Marie Wiese. "Language, Public Policy, and Schooling: A Focus on Chicano English Language Learners." In *Chicano School Failure and Success: Past, Present and Future*, 2nd ed., ed. by Richard Valencia, 149–169. London: Routledge Falmer, 2002.

Gibson, Margaret, Patricia Gándara, and Jill Koyama, eds. *School Connections: U.S. Mexican Youth, Peers and School Achievement.* New York: Teachers College Press, 2004.

Gonzalez, Gilbert G. *Chicano Education in the Era of Segregation.* Philadelphia: Balch Institute Press, 1990.

Gonzalez, Josue, and Ha Lam. "The Lau v. Nichols Supreme Court Decision." In *Latino Education in the U.S.*, ed. by Lourdes Diaz Soto, 283–295. New York: Rowman & Littlefield, 2007.

Greenberg, Jack. *Brown v. Board of Education: Witness to a Landmark Decision.* New York: Twelve Tables Press, 2004.

Guerrero, Michael D. "Research in Bilingual Education: Moving Beyond the Effectiveness Debate." In *Chicano School Failure and Success: Past, Present and Future*, 2nd ed., ed. by Richard Valencia, 170–191. London: Routledge Falmer, 2002.

Hahn, Steven. "The Race Man." *New Republic* 240 (2009): 50–55.

Ladson-Billings, Gloria. "From the Achievement Gap to the Education Debt: Understanding Achievement in U.S. Schools." *Educational Researcher* 35, no. 7 (2006): 3–12.

Lopez, Tiffany Ana. "Reading Trauma and Violence in U.S. Latina/o Children's Literature." In *Ethnic Literary Traditions in American Children's Literature,* ed. by Michelle Pagni Stewart and Yvonne Atkinson, 205–239. New York: Palgrave Macmillan, 2009.

MacDonald, Victoria-María, ed. *Latino Education in the United States: A Narrated History, 1513–2000.* New York: Palgrave Macmillan, 2004.

McMurrer, Daniel P., and Isabel Sawhill. *Getting Ahead: Economic and Social Mobility in America.* Washington, DC: The Urban Institute, 1998.

Meier, Kenneth J., and Joseph Stewart, Jr. *The Politics of Hispanic Education: Un paso pa'lante y dos pa'tras.* Albany: State University of New York Press, 1991.

Mendez et al. v. Westminster School District, 64 F. Supp. 544 (S.D. Cal. 1946).

Miller, L. Scott. *An American Imperative: Accelerating Minority Educational Advancement.* New Haven, CT: Yale University Press, 1997.

Moll, Luis C. "The Diversity of Schooling: A Cultural-Historical Approach." In *The Best for Our Children: Critical Perspectives on Literacy for Latino Students*, ed. by M. de la Luz Reyes and J. J. Halcón, 13–28. New York: Teachers College Press, 2001.

National Center for Education Statistics (NCES). *Dropout Rates in the United States: 2005.* Washington, DC: U.S. Government Printing Office, 2005.

National Education Association. *The Invisible Minority . . . Pero No Vencibles.* Report of the NEA-Tucson Survey on the Teaching of Spanish to the Spanish-Speaking. Washington, DC: Department of Rural Education, 1966.

National Research Council. *Multiple Origins, Uncertain Destinies: Hispanics and the American Future: Panel on Hispanics in the United States.* Ed. by Marta Tienda and Faith Mitchell. Committee on Population, Division of Behavioral and Social Sciences and Education. Washington, DC: National Academies Press, 2006.

Oakes, Jeannie. "Investigating the Claims in *Williams v. State of California*: An Unconstitutional Denial of Education's Basic Tools?" *Teachers College Record* 106, no. 10 (2004): 1889–1906.

Pew Hispanic Center. "Between Two Worlds: How Young Latinos Come of Age in America." http://pewhispanic.org/files/reports/117.pdf (accessed January 20, 2010).

Portes, Alejandro, and Ruben Rumbaut. *Legacies: The Story of the Immigrant Second Generation.* Berkeley, Calif.: University of California Press, 2001.

Ream, Robert. *Uprooting Children: Mobility, Social Capital and Mexican American Underachievement.* New York: LFB Scholarly Publishing, 2005.

Ream, Robert, Jose Espinoza, and Sarah Ryan. "The Opportunity/Achievement Gap." In *Psychology of Classroom Learning: An Encyclopedia*, ed. by Eric M. Anderman and Lynley H. Anderman, 657–664. Detroit, MI: Macmillan Reference, 2009.

Reich, Robert. "Story Time: The Lost Art of Democratic Narrative." *New Republic* 232 (2005): 16–19.

Roos, Peter D. "Bilingual Education: The Hispanic Response to Unequal Educational Opportunity." *Law and Contemporary Problems* 42, no. 4 (1978): 111–140.

Rothstein, Richard. *Class and Schools: Using Social, Economic, and Educational Reform to Close the Black-White Achievement Gap.* New York: Teachers College Press, 2004.

Rumberger, Russell, and Patricia Gándara. "Seeking Equity in the Education of California's English Learners." *Teachers College Record* 106 (2004): 2031–2055.

Salinas, Guadalupe. "Mexican-Americans and the Desegregation of Schools in the Southwest." *Houston Law Review* 8 (1971): 929–970.

San Miguel, Guadalupe, Jr. *Brown, Not White: School Integration and the Chicano Movement in Houston.* Houston: Texas A&M University Press, 2001.

Smith, James. "Assimilation Across the Latino Generations." *AEA Papers and Proceedings* 93, no. 2 (2003): 315–319.

Soto, Lourdes Diaz, ed. *Latino Education in the U.S.* New York: Rowman & Littlefield, 2007.

Spargo, R. Clifton. "Trauma and the Specters of Enslavement in Morrison's *Beloved.*" *Mosaic: A Journal for the Interdisciplinary Study of Literature* 35, no. 1 (2002): 113–132.

Valencia, Richard. *Chicano Students and the Courts.* New York: New York University Press, 2008.

Valencia, Richard, Martha Menchaca, and Rubén Donato. "Segregation, Desegregation, and Integration of Chicano Students: Old and New Realities." In *Chicano School Failure and Success: Past, Present and Future*, 2nd ed., ed. by Richard Valencia. London: Routledge Falmer, 2002.

Valenzuela, Angela. *Subtractive Schooling: U.S.-Mexican Youth and the Politics of Caring.* Albany: State University of New York Press, 1999.

Wollenberg, Charles. "*Mendez v. Westminster*: Race, Nationality and Segregation in California Schools." *California Historical Quarterly* 53, no. 4 (1974): 317–332.

CHAPTER 2

Embracing the Face at the Window: Latino Representation in Children's Literature and the Ethnic Identity Development of Latino Children

Jamie Campbell Naidoo

> I was a child who could not find myself in the literature [I read]. There was no one telling my story. I don't want that to ever happen to any child. . . . To really see yourself as nonexistent is the worst kind of insult that a person can have (Santiago 2000, p. 133).

Books are windows into the soul of society, illuminating the social, political, and cultural mores that underlie our world. It is through the illustrations and narratives of books that Latino children encounter these messages and discern the dominant culture's view toward their cultural group. The potency of the visual image and its effects on a child's construction of reality can assist or prevent a child's ethnic identity development. Roethler (1998) warns that "children, especially young children, are sensitive to illustrations. . . . The images these children soak up remain with them for the rest of their lives" (p. 96). Repeated exposure to negative images about their cultural groups in children's books can have negative influences on the ethnic identity of Latino children. York (2002) also notes that children's books are replacing storytellers as "purveyors of cultural history and pride" (p. 1), and it is through these cultural moderators that children learn to value and respect parallel and cross cultures.

Considering the power that books hold for children of all cultures, authors and illustrators of Latino children's literature have the responsibility to construct high-quality works with positive and authentic messages that will facilitate positive ethnic identity development and improve the self-esteem of Latino children, while promoting acceptance and understanding in non-Latino children and educators. However, as mentioned in other chapters, very few of the books published each year authentically represent Latino cultures. This problem seems quite extraordinary considering the strong presence of Latinos in the U.S. population. According to the U.S. Census Bureau (2003), Latinos became the largest ethnic minority in the United States on July 1, 2002, with 38.8 million residents identifying as Latino. The most recent estimate indicates that 48.4 million U.S. residents identify as Latino, with an expected increase to 132.8 million by 2050 (U.S. Census Bureau 2010). This estimate does not include the additional 4 million residents of Puerto Rico (U.S. Census Bureau 2010).

Latino/Hispanic Cultural Group	Population Size	Percent of Latino/Hispanic Population
All Latinos/Hispanics	45, 427	100.0
Cuban	1,611	3.5
Dominican	1,208	2.7
Puerto Rican	4,120	9.1
Costa Rican	118	0.3
Guatemalan	872	1.9
Honduran	533	1.2
Mexican	29,167	64.2
Nicaraguan	302	0.7
Panamanian	135	0.3
Salvadoran	1,474	3.2
Other Central American	106	0.2
Argentinean	194	0.4
Bolivian	83	0.2
Chilean	107	0.2
Colombian	799	1.8
Ecuadorian	533	1.2
Peruvian	462	1.0
Uruguayan	50	0.1
Venezuelan	178	0.4
Other South American	93	0.2
Other Hispanic (includes people who did not select a specific country of origin or who identified as Spaniard)	3,283	7.2

FIGURE 2.1. *Latino/Hispanic population of any race by country of origin in 2007. Numbers in thousands. Source: U.S. Census 2010.*
Available at http://www.census.gov/prod/2010pubs/acs-11.pdf.

In addition to being the largest and fastest-growing ethnic minority in the United States, Latinos are also the youngest. Approximately 22 percent of the children enrolled in U.S. nursery schools, kindergartens, or elementary schools identify as Latino (Fry and Passel 2009). These children represent a heterogeneous group of people celebrating diverse perspectives, heritages, and cultures. Similarly, they embody various races, appearances, and immigration and socioeconomic statuses. Kevane (2003) remarks that to be Latino is to be "a hybrid, bilingual, bicultural individual who is sharing two worlds, straddling the fence, belonging neither here nor there, belonging both here and there, being from two worlds, living in the borderlands, living on the hyphen" (p. 9). The Latino experience has also been described as a social and cultural mosaic (Carrasquillo 1991; Day 2003; Koss-Chioino and Vargas 1999) encompassing people from Mexico, Central America, South America, Puerto Rico, Cuba, and the Caribbean with their own distinct cultures, traditions, and, for some, languages. According to Ada (2003), "There are twenty Hispanic countries . . . [and] the mixed heritage of these people makes the Latino child of today the inheritor of an extraordinarily diverse culture with Spanish, indigenous, and African roots that has contributed achievements in all areas of human endeavor" (p. 53). See Figure 2.1 for examples of the various cultural groups represented in the United States by people labeled as Hispanic or Latino.

Unfortunately, this diversity in Latino culture can become a hindrance for children of Latino heritage enrolled in U.S. schools. The following sections synthesize research from several disciplines in an attempt to describe some of the cultural challenges faced by Latino children enrolled in U.S. schools; the ways in which Latinos are depicted in U.S. media, including children's books; and the negative and positive effects of these representations on learning for both Latino and non-Latino children.

LATINO CHILDREN, ETHNIC IDENTITY, AND EDUCATIONAL ACHIEVEMENT

Latino children live in two disparate realities created by their home and school lives. The values of their home culture do not always coincide with the values they are taught at school. This disconnect can cause undue stress for Latino children and can negatively influence their school performance and ethnic identity development.

Sheets (2005) describes how Latino children experience cognitive dissonance—"discord between behavior and belief"—when they encounter psychological discomfort and stress because they are required to participate in social habits that conflict with their personal beliefs. This discord surfaces in educational settings when Latino children must act and behave according to the social customs and culture at school, often contradicting the Latino social customs and culture of their homes. The theory of cultural discontinuity mirrors the premise of cognitive dissonance, suggesting that minority children fail in U.S. schools because their home and school cultures clash (Au 1993; Thomas 2004). Additionally, Eggers-Piérola (2005) indicates, "Disconnection between the home and the educational setting's language and culture can adversely affect Latino children's progress through school" (p. 21), causing their academic performance to be below that of non-Latino children.

Noting additional stressful experiences that many Latino children encounter, Shelley-Robinson (2005) cites disorientation, severe emotional trauma, and often poor self-esteem as phases of the immigrant experience and subsequent acculturation into an unknown environment. For the estimated 1.7 million Latino children who are new immigrants to the United States (Fry and Passel 2009), several adjustments will need to occur:

> reacquainting themselves with parents and siblings from whom they might have been separated for a long time and to whom they are almost strangers; . . . getting acclimated to extremely cold temperatures in contrast to the tropical heat of their homeland; entering and successfully mastering the school system, which often includes dealing with hostile authority figures and peers; linguistic barriers; [and] encountering and learning to handle overt racism (Shelley-Robinson 2005, p. 16).

Bernal and Knight (1997) also note that Latino children share several cultural characteristics that distinguish them from other ethnic minorities. These characteristics include respecting their elders, having a strong sense of family, being cooperative, and a strong ethnic identity. Strongly linked to their self-conceptions, the ethnic identity of Latino children comprises their beliefs and appreciation for the unique traits that encompass their cultural heritage.

The major influence on the development of Latino children's ethnic identities is their social and contextual surroundings, or their everyday worlds. Many factors influence their social and contextual environment, including the desires of their family, unique Latino cultural traditions, peer influences, teacher perceptions, and educational and learning atmospheres (Koss-Chioino and Vargas 1999; Vera and Quintana 2004). Social identity theory also indicates that self-esteem is largely influenced by the way the Latino child and overall society view the social or ethnic group in which the child belongs (Bernal,

Saenz, and Knight 1995; Koss-Chioino and Vargas 1999; Vera and Quintana 2004). Henderson (1991) comments, "Our perceptions of who we are have grown out of our understanding of how we are perceived and treated by others. Other people may see the same reality that we do, but perceive it differently" (p. 15). Likewise, research indicates that educators' views about Latino culture can influence how non-Latino children view Latino culture and relate to Latino children (Eggers-Piérola 2005). Thus, if Latino culture is not valued by society or by non-Latino children and educators, then Latino children will develop a low self-esteem and a negative ethnic identity, and fail to appreciate their rich cultural heritage.

As a result of the cognitive dissonance, cultural discontinuity, and poor ethnic identity stemming from their social, contextual experiences in U.S. schools, many Latino children do not graduate from high school. Beginning in the 1990s, the high school dropout rate for Latinos in the United States has been the largest of any race/ethnic group, with almost 30 percent of Latino students leaving high school before graduation (Collins and Ribeiro 2004; Wainer 2004). Recent estimates suggest a growth in the dropout rates, with 38 percent of all Latino children failing to graduate from high school (National Center for Education Statistics 2008). Yet the U.S. educational system can take immediate action toward correcting this problem by providing Latino students with positive reflections of Latino cultures from the moment they enter school. According to the National Education Association (2002), "Exposing Latino children to books that reflect their culture as well as their language is one of the most effective ways of motivating them to stay in school" (par. 2).

NEGATIVE IMAGES OF LATINO CULTURES IN U.S. MEDIA

Too often, however, the U.S. media do not represent the diversity of Latino cultures; instead the media make generalizations. For instance, it is a common misperception that all Latinos speak Spanish when, in actuality, some Latinos are only English speakers, some are bilingual, and some are Spanish-speakers in the process of learning English. Similarly, all Latinos are presumed to have the same or a similar physical appearance; however, a true "Latin look" does not exist. Indeed, Ada (2003) notes, "The look and coloring of Latinos are as diverse as their class, education, language repertoire, or degree of assimilation into the majority culture, reflecting the richness of their heritage. Even within the same family, people can look and think very differently" (p. 36). Similarly,

Ada (2005) asserts that Latinos vary according to their level of bilingualism, country of origin, length of time in the United States, reasons for immigrating to the United States, educational and social background, degree of assimilation into the U.S. society, mix of heritages, and religious practices (pp. 47–48).

Stereotypes and misunderstandings of Latino culture often emerge in educational curricula and teaching materials as well as in children's literature. According to several studies, preconceptions are that all Latinos:

- ❀ are from Mexico and/or are part of a monolithic culture (Barrera, Liguori, and Salas 1993; J. Naidoo 2007; Rasmussen and Rasmussen 1995)

- ❀ look the same (Ada 2003; J. Naidoo 2007; Nieto 1993; Pérez and Torres-Guzmán 1992)

- ❀ are dirty and poor (Carrasquillo 1994; Council on Interracial Books for Children 1982; Mestre and Nieto 1996; Nieto 1983; Rasmussen and Rasmussen 1995)

- ❀ are violent and involved in gangs (Mora 1998; Nieto 1993)

- ❀ are non-assertive and easily overpowered (Barrera and de Cortes 1997; Carrasquillo 1994)

- ❀ are illegal immigrants (Barrera and de Cortes 1997; Council on Interracial Books for Children 1982)

- ❀ are shiftless (Council on Interracial Books for Children 1982; Moore and MacCann 1987a)

- ❀ spend their time relaxing, putting things off until mañana, and having fiestas (Council on Interracial Books for Children 1975; J. Naidoo 2007)

As a result, these stereotypes ignore the unique contributions and beauty of the people within each Latino culture—Puerto Ricans, Cubans, Dominicans, Mexicans, Costa Ricans, Guatemalans, Ecuadorians, Peruvians, and others whose roots are in Central and South America and the Caribbean.

EFFECTS OF NEGATIVE REPRESENTATIONS OF LATINOS IN CHILDREN'S LITERATURE

Negative images, omissions, and misconstructions of Latino identity are harmful not only to Latino children but to non-Latino children and educators as well. Mora (1998) stresses, "How the media depicts a group affects how a group sees itself—such is the power of images, the power of words" (p. 281). Similarly, Bishop (1997) indicates that children's literature can serve as a mirror reflecting a child's own life and culture, or as a window providing an opportunity to peer into someone else's life. Vygotsky also emphasizes the importance of language and culture in a child's construction of meaning, explaining that children use expressive media, such as books, to relate to their social and contextual surroundings (Koss-Chioino and Vargas 1999; Sheets 2005).

The negative images of their culture that Latino children encounter in instructional material and children's literature serve as broken mirrors, causing these children to feel worthless, embarrassed, or alienated, and undervaluing their cultural heritage and identity. Additionally, stereotypes confuse Latino children with misinformation about their cultural heritage (Nieto 1997), resulting in the development of low self-esteem and a negative ethnic identity. Ada (2003) remarks:

> Latino children in the United States have suffered a great deal from the ways in which their culture, particularly in its most creative and representative aspects, has been rendered invisible by the mass media and within the school curriculum. . . . Latino children seldom have an opportunity to see . . . representations of their culture. This silence . . . erodes their self-esteem (p. xiv).

Similarly, omission of a child's unique Latino culture (Cuban, Mexican, Puerto Rican, and so forth) in instructional material and children's literature has the potential to reduce the importance of significant contributions of the child's culture (Barrera et al. 1993); to overlook and erase the existence of the child's culture (Council on Interracial Books for Children 1982; Day 2003); and to cause a child to lose his/her ethnic identity (Day 2003). "Invisibility," warn Lo and Lee (1993), "is dangerous to one's self-esteem. If the world is described and you are not in it, you feel lessened" (p. 15).

For non-Latino children and educators interacting with the literature that they encounter, stereotypes and omissions of the Latino culture in instructional material and children's literature are equally powerful. These images serve as distorted windows that promote and exacerbate cultural bias (Barrera, Liguori, and Salas 1993; Carrasquillo 1994; Mendoza and Reese 2001), create the illusion of a homogeneous Latino culture (Barrera, Liguori, and Salas 1993; J. Naidoo 2007; Nieto 1997), elevate Anglo (white) culture over Latino culture (Carrasquillo 1994; Council on Interracial Books for Children 1972; Moore and MacCann 1987b), and construct social barriers (Carrasquillo 1994). As a result, negative representations and generalizations of Latino culture in instructional material and children's literature can construct hostile learning environments or contexts that isolate Latino children and destroy their cultural pride and ethnic identity.

In a study of Latinos' attitudes toward the U.S. educational system, the Kaiser Family Foundation and the Pew Hispanic Center (2004) found that 47 percent of Latinos believe that Latino children achieve poorly in school because non-Latino educators are not knowledgeable about Latino cultural differences. Research supports these findings, suggesting that non-Latino educators have a difficult time relating to Latino children because they are not familiar with the diverse culture and traditions of the unique Latino cultures (Collins and Ribeiro 2004; Nathenson-Mejia and Escamilla 2003; Wainer 2004). In addition, 75 percent of Latinos, 54 percent of Anglo (white) Americans, and 55 percent of African Americans perceive discrimination against Latino children as a problem in U.S. schools, while 38 percent of Latinos indicate that discrimination toward Latino children is a *major* problem in U.S. schools (Kaiser Family Foundation and Pew Hispanic Center 2002). Further, a report from the Tomás Rivera Policy Institute establishes that Latino children educated in U.S. southern schools encounter discrimination as a direct result of non-Latino children's and educators' misperceptions and ignorance of Latino culture (Wainer 2004).

All of these studies highlight the immediate need for accurate representations of Latino cultures in educational materials and children's literature. The next section describes some of the positive benefits of including high-quality, authentic materials and literature about Latinos in classrooms and libraries.

EFFECTS OF POSITIVE REPRESENTATIONS OF LATINOS IN CHILDREN'S LITERATURE

Literature that provides positive and accurate representations of Latino culture can be influential in developing and changing attitudes of both Latino children and non-Latino children and educators. Numerous researchers advocate educator training (Rasmussen and Rasmussen 1995; Sheets 2005; Wainer 2004), as well as the incorporation of authentic multicultural teaching materials and Latino children's literature into the curriculum, thus providing non-Latino children and educators with accurate information about the diverse Latino population and cultures (Barrera, Liguori, and Salas 1993; Beaty 1997; Isom and Casteel 1997; Kibler 1996; Marantz and Marantz 2005; Nathenson-Mejia and Escamilla 2003; Smolen and Ortiz-Castro 2000).

Children's literature that accurately reflects the Latino people and culture has the potential to do the following:

❀ provide positive role models for Latino children (Day 2003; Mora 1998; Nilsson 2005)

❀ offer Latino characters with similar experiences and emotions (Ada 2003; Marantz and Marantz 2005; Watson 2000)

❀ convey the richness and beauty of Latino cultures, thus infusing ethnic pride and increasing the self-esteem of Latino children (Day 2003; Isom and Casteel 1997; Smolen and Ortiz-Castro 2000)

❀ reinforce a distinct cultural identity (Kibler 1996; Smolen and Ortiz-Castro 2000)

❀ promote love of reading as well as language and literacy development in Latino children (Schon 1995; Smolen and Ortiz-Castro 2000)

❀ inspire learning of other Latino cultures and general cultural knowledge (Medina and Enciso 2002; Smolen and Ortiz-Castro 2000)

❀ sponsor learning and acceptance of other cultures different from that of the Latino child (Carrasquillo 1994; Freiband and Figueras 2002; Isom and Casteel 1997)

❀ motivate Latino children to stay in school (National Education Association 2002)

Dame (1993) asserts, "Ethnic minority students want to see and read images and stories in their native languages and in the context of their own cultures. Through these materials, they can meet people like themselves and learn to appreciate the beauty of their ethnicity and of all people" (p. 70).

Likewise, children's literature that accurately and positively represents the Latino people and culture assists non-Latino children and educators in developing an appreciation and accurate understanding of their Latino classmates/students and their culture (Ada 2003; Medina and Enciso 2002), an awareness of cultural diversity within their immediate environment and pluralistic world (Ada and Campoy 2001; Day 2003; Medina and Enciso 2002; Smolen and Ortiz-Castro 2000), a desire to learn about Latino cultures (Medina and Enciso 2002; Smolen and Ortiz-Castro 2000), and "an aesthetic appreciation of different beliefs and value systems" (Isom and Casteel 1997, p. 83).

The following section describes a few examples of authentic representations of Latinos in children's books, and details what these books offer to both Latino and non-Latino children.

EMBRACING THE WORLD'S REFLECTIONS: THE CREATIVE EXPRESSIONS OF MAYA CHRISTINA GONZALEZ

By Dr. Jamie Campbell Naidoo

Listen! Do you hear it? It's in the rustle of the gentle breeze that tickles your cheek and in the cool water that laughs as it caresses your ankles. A clear, small voice sings "come, come follow me and I will show you Mother Earth's beauty." As I stop to inhale the fresh mountain air and tickle the fish playing at my feet, I am suddenly overwhelmed by the peaceful warmth radiating from a beautiful creature in the river, floating and laughing as the water's tender fingers stroke her long hair.

From the first moment you meet her, you realize that award-winning artist and author Maya Christina Gonzalez is very connected to the environment, embracing its peaceful beauty that has provided her a sense of belonging since she was very young. The artist's work reflects this creative connection; her three most recent books *My Colors, My World/Mis colores, mi mundo* (2007), *Animal Poems of the Iguazú/Animalario del Iguazú* (2008, written by Francisco X Alarcón), and *I Know the River Loves Me/Yo sé que el río me ama* (2009) all celebrate the gifts that our environment bestow upon us.

Photo used with permission of Maya Christina Gonzalez.

I beckon to Maya as she glides towards the shore and ask her to rest for un momento to share with us the latest gifts that Mother Earth has given her. As she gently dries her hair, Maya begins by briefly explaining the journey that led her to become an accomplished artist, advocate for social equality, and author/illustrator for San Francisco based Children's Book Press.

Making a Serendipitous Start

Like many acclaimed artists, Maya had no intention of becoming a children's book illustrator. She considers herself to be an artist that happens to create illustrations. Initially, she designed and sold jewelry to support herself as she moonlighted as an artist. Realizing that she was spending too much time on the jewelry and not enough on her true passion, Maya moved from Oregon to San Francisco where she began painting and exhibiting her artwork full time. It was at one of her exhibits at Galería de la Raza that she met Harriet Rohmer, the founder of Children's Book Press, and was invited to illustrate Gloria Anzaldúa's *Prietita and the Ghost Woman/Prietita y la Llorona* (1995). Since that time, the artist has used a variety of art techniques such as acrylics, collage, cut paper, photography, pastels, and charcoal to create the stunning visual imagery for over twenty picture books, mostly published by Children's Book Press.

Maya's books have been well received by the literary and library community, garnering her a Pura Belpré Honor Award, Américas Award, Américas Honor Award, Américas Commended, and Tomás Rivera Mexican American Children's Book Award, to name a few. Much to her astonishment, she has won many of these awards multiple times. "I am surprised this has worked out so well and is such a great fit for me," Maya comments. "I'm honored by the awards but they are not my impetus. I'm just a dorky artist doing what I need to do. I was not educated as an illustrator and have a different relationship with my books because of that. They are very personal to me, like my children. When I create my artwork, I am guided by the creative process and not the end product. Creativity is so important to me and when art came up as a career option I trusted and went with it."

The artist's process of creating illustrations is very organic with many inspirations originating from Mother Earth's soft whispers. One only needs to take a look at her blog (http://www.reflectionpress.com/blog/) to get a sense of how Maya relinquishes herself to her art. In her post "Gathering Ghosts," she describes how she was "hit on the head" with a book idea and how the art and the tale kept pushing and growing inside her until she was forced to let it flow from her fingertips. "I watched drawings of children start pouring out of my hands," Maya remarks. "I could not have stopped them if I had wanted to, which of course I didn't . . . Everything that had been pushing up and up now fell down, down onto the page. It was just a matter of continuing to let go."

Like children, all of Maya's books are unique and embody different types of creative artwork and expression. Her bright, cheery illustrations for the first book in Francisco X. Alarcón's poetry series, which began in 1997 with *Laughing Tomatoes and Other Spring Poems/Jitomates risueños y otros poemas de primavera*, were rendered with watercolors and exhibited the magical realism present in all of Maya's artwork. The next two books in the series *From the Bellybutton of the Moon and Other Summer Poems/Del ombligo de la luna y otros poemas de verano and Iguanas in the Snow and Other Winter Poems/ Iguanas en la nieve y otros poemas de invierno*, along with later titles—such as Amada Irma Pérez's *My Diary from Here to There/Mi diario de aquí*, Mary-Joan Gerson's *Fiesta Femenina: Celebrating Women in Mexican Folktale*, and her own *My Colors, My World/Mis colores, mi mundo*—contained bold, vibrant illustrations fashioned with acrylics. For the final book in the poetry series, *Angels Ride Bikes and Other Fall Poems/Los Ángeles andan en bicicleta y otros poemas de otoño*, Maya introduced photo collage to her acrylic paintings to imbue additional elements of magical realism into the energetic illustrations. After this title, her artwork became even more organic for Amada Irma Pérez's *Nana's Big Surprise/Nana, ¡Qué Sorpresa!*, including bursting, energetic collage imagery comprised of acrylics, photos, beads, fabric, and textured paper. In her latest book with Alarcón, *Animal Poems of the Iguazú/Animalario del Iguazú*, multi-talented Maya continued to use mixed-media illustrations, embodying a collage of cut paper and acrylics.

Yet, it is her most recent "child" that reflects a huge shift in Maya's creative expression. Up until the publication of *I Know the River Loves Me/Yo sé que el río me ama*, her artwork has been characterized by heavily saturated paintings pulsating with a mosaic of colores. The illustrations in *River* are notably devoid of this thick, heavy color; instead, Maya has chosen to use inks and charcoal to craft soft, flowing earthtone lines on a brilliant white background. The effect is a peaceful, almost washed out landscape representing the fragility of the environment.

This shift in artistic technique is the direct consequence of Maya's previous paint drenched artwork. In a print-making accident where she was not provided with the proper protection, she received a massive toxic overload as the result of a poor ventilation system. The toxins permeated her body and left her incapacitated for three years and extremely sick for a total of ten. During this time, she was awfully weak and washed out. Although she wanted to return to her previous stylized art, Maya found that being ill had changed her artistic vision, providing her with a different kind of softness and drawing her even closer to her nature friends.

Channeling Creativity

It is at the mention of these nature friends that Maya's face lights up as she begins to explain how *River* was a special gift from her friend, the Yuba River in eastern California—the very river she was communing with when I found her. Two summers ago as the artist was sitting beside Yuba during one of her yearly visits, the river began to tell her a story and Maya patiently listened, not quite sure if the story was for children or if it should even be written down. Out of respect for her long-time friend, Maya tucked the story away in the back of her mind only to have it resurface later. After she returned home to San Francisco, the artist received a phone call from Dana Goldberg at Children's Book Press, asking Maya if she could create a book for them. "I said 'Yes, I just got back from visiting the Yuba River and she told me a story. So boy have I got a book for you. She must have known I was going to need one,'" recalls Maya; "the book was very organic, rising from my relationship with the river."

Cover image from I Know the River Loves Me / Yo sé que el río me ama. *Story and illustrations © 2009 by Maya Christina Gonzalez. Reprinted with permission of the publisher, Children's Book Press, San Francisco, CA, www. childrensbookpress.org.*

As a continuation of the author-illustrator's family upbringing to be one with nature, *River* follows a young Maya as she visits her river friend and recalls the many ways that she and the river express their affection for one another. With a nod towards social and environmental responsibility, the artist's latest "child", truly reflects her gentle spirit and relationship with Mother Earth while also conveying a universal message. In fact, Maya notes, "The girl just happens to be Chicana, she could represent any child, but the relationship with nature is a very Chicano experience."

Seeking a Face Like Her Own

Growing up in a world where she never saw herself reflected within the pages and illustrations of her books, Maya is empowered by her fortuitous opportunity to create children's books representing the experiences of real Chicanas. She remarks, "I like Children's Book Press because they connected me with people's stories that are my stories—moving and personal stories that I never had as a child."

When she was younger, Maya loved the library, the smell, lighting, etc., and would go out of her way to get there. It was a type of haven for her that made her feel as if she belonged. Yet, she was always searching the aisles and books in the library, looking for something that she could not find. Something was always missing, but she did not know what it was. "It wasn't until I started working with kids that I remembered this experience. As a child, I couldn't express this feeling. I would just draw my pictures," asserts Maya. "As an adult I can reflect back and see that I was really looking for my face in my coloring and storybooks but I never found my round, Chicana face, my long dark hair. So I would go to that blank page in the back or the front of these books and draw my own big face right in where it belonged. When we see ourselves, something fundamental happens inside of us."

Through her collaborations with other authors at Children's Book Press and Barefoot Books, Maya has created powerful images of Latinas and Latinos that were missing during her childhood reading adventures. And, while she is quick to point out that she enjoys playing with these other fabulous authors, Maya also recounts her excitement when she had the remarkable opportunity to both illustrate and write *My Colors, My World/Mis colores, mi mundo*. "Colors was an amazing experience for me," she notes. "I got to be boss of the world which felt super good." Having been afforded the chance to be Mz. Maya Queen of el mundo, the artist applied her skill for creating vivid imagery of strong females and constructed a dazzling gem featuring a child Maya as she opens her eyes extra wide to experience the amazing colors that the environment has created for her. At long last, the author-illustrator literally created the book she never had as a child. Instead of drawing her round Chicana face on the end papers, Maya's likeness was the pulsating and flowing lifeline of an entire book!

The artist has taken this experience and shared it with children during art programs that she teaches in elementary and high schools. Instead of making these children of color wait until they are adults to create reflections of themselves, Maya teaches them how to channel their creative energy to create imagery that depicts their life experiences. Many of these children represent underserved populations that are stressed out, trying to find their place in a world that does not value them. Maya asserts, "I relate to these children because I didn't see myself when I was younger and I was always stressed out too. I relate to them on a gut level. I want to share my books, my art with them. I say to them, 'Do you see yourself in the books in your hands and in your literature? When I was a kid there was nada.'"

Maya concurs that even now it is laughable how few books there are depicting Latinos. Yet, children need to see themselves reflected in their literature. No book can represent every child but collectively they should represent the Latino experience. "If Latino children don't see themselves, then we as educators need to provide tools to allow them to see their reflections," Maya affirms. "I want to share creativity with children and say, 'We can create our own reality and reflection when we don't see it.'"

Reflecting the World

Speaking of seeing reflections of reality, Maya begins to describe how she and her partner Matthew recently created Reflection Press (http://reflectionpress. org) as a way to showcase her artwork and her educational programs that help children use creativity and art to express and reflect themselves. Essentially,

Matthew uses the Web site to formalize the artist's work, making it more accessible to educators. Maya comments, "He translates me. Our fantasy is to change the world by dismantling the education system from the inside."

The duo wants to empower educators, teachers and librarians, so they can serve as models for positive change in the classroom. Using creativity as a foundation, Maya has developed a curriculum entitled Claiming Face, which is rooted in providing children with internal perspectives that allow them to see reflections of themselves in the environment and empower them to self-explore and express themselves in such a way to better support themselves, their families, and ultimately their planet for generations to come. The key to the program's success revolves around educators knowing how to effectively use creativity in the classroom to not only meet mandated standards but also to help children better understand themselves and the world. Maya comments, "So many educators are on to the fact that creativity needs to be in the classroom. Educators are hungry for a creative, fluid, and less judgmental style in the classroom. I wanted to create a place where people can go, get support, and be inspired as educators to serve children. Last year, I had an opportunity at the 2nd Annual Celebration of Latino Children's Literature Conference in South Carolina to see how educators really need and want to know how to reach Latino children. My curriculum allows a reflection of all of us to come through, reaching out to children of color."

Cover image from My Colors, My World / Mis colores, mi mundo. *Story and illustrations © 2007 by Maya Christina Gonzalez. Reprinted with permission of the publisher, Children's Book Press, San Francisco, CA, www.childrensbookpress.org.*

The artist's curriculum also utilizes her *My Colors, My World / Mis colores, mi mundo* and *I Know the River Loves Me / Yo sé que el río me ama* to help children understand how to create art that is a true reflection of themselves; art where the children are in control, fully expressive, valuing themselves, and making the changes that they want to see in the world. This gives children an opportunity to fully embrace Mahatma Gandhi's charge to "be the change you want to see in the world." Maya emphasizes, "If children paid attention to the majority of books available, the world would be straight, white, and male. My books and my curriculum allow children to go to a place where they know themselves, see themselves in their environment. By drawing themselves, children must have a sense of who they are and possess a knowing that allows them to want to care for their culture, environment, and world. I look like I'm teaching creativity, but I'm actually trying to change the world. I trust the children; they get what I'm doing. They are full of wisdom and allow the creative force to move through them."

Translating Gender—Now

The whole concept of natural reflections is the impetus for all of Maya's creative endeavors. While her art has exclusively focused on children of color as a way of reflecting her own biracial heritage (Caucasian mother, Mexican father), the artist is also very interested in the reflections that transgender children see in their books. She has friends that are trans and her daughter had a trans friend when she was in preschool. When Maya went searching for trans resources to share with her daughter, she couldn't find any. "The reflections were nil," the author-artist laments. "I know how important it was to see images of trans people from my work with children of color; but, trans children are severely underrepresented in this area."

This dearth of resources is not surprising to Maya who has been a member of the lesbian, gay, bisexual, trans, and queer/questioning (LGBTQ) community for upward of 25 years. Even in this community which is often perceived as encompassing members on the outskirts of society, trans is taboo. Trans children, people, and families have a difficult time finding their place in the world. Maya notes, "Our society likes to put people in neat little boxes. You just can't do that. Research suggests that 1 in 100 children have sexual organs that are non gender specific—intersex children. These children are a huge community that we deny. I don't understand how in nature there can be such gender variance and, for humans, we try to force only two genders. There are more gender variant children born in this country than there are Jews. What are we afraid of? I believe the fear of trans is rooted in a cultural misogyny. If we take down the social constructs of gender, we will really change a lot of things."

Tackling these and other social constructs are the next steps in Maya's quest to make the world a better place. Her research has shown her that trans children are at the highest risk of any children for drug abuse, suicide, etc. because of all the judgment directed towards them. In an effort to reach out to these children and to educate other children about trans people, the artist has created a coloring book, *Gender Now*, which discusses transgender children and history. "When I thought of a book for trans kids," Maya recalls, "I thought of a coloring book; a space that is interactive, engaging, creative, playful, and more informal than a traditional book. *Gender Now* is intended for children ages three and up. I have six different images of gender-variant children—of all stages. I have created imagery that dismantles what girls and boys do. I have a boy-boy who is sewing and a girly-girl raising goats."

The children in the coloring book are naked which might raise both the eyebrows and ire of parents. But, the author iterates that young children are very curious about their bodies and want to know everything. Maya's innocently, natural book explores multiple genders of children beyond the traditional male and female, providing the long-absent reflections of trans children. "I wanted to demystify things but I had to wait until I was more established as an author before creating this very radical work. I waited until I looked good on paper," comments Maya. "This book is one that parents will definitely have to review first and decide how to share with their children. Parents will have to negotiate their own judgment and fear around gender. I will get in trouble but there are more and more parents that don't want to see their children commit suicide at thirteen or fourteen. Books like this are important to help children accept themselves and others at a young age. Other authors and illustrators don't want to question gender. Because of the life that I have led with close trans friends, I understand the vulnerability and nuances that trans people express. I know how trans people were as children and this makes me want to bring about a better awareness."

Queering Her Stories

At this point, Maya explains how her experiences as an openly queer Chicana have influenced her work which is seamlessly infused with imagery from her Latino heritage. Although she was disowned by her biracial, semi-Mexican family, the artist still feels deeply rooted ancestrally in the Latino culture and notes that it is with queers of color that she best identifies. "I've always been on the outside as a person of color, Chicana, biracial child, fem lesbian, etc.," affirms Maya, "but I tell people that Latinos are taking the U.S. back and we aren't afraid to use art to do it. If we are queer on top of being Latino, it is like an extra bonus—the frosting."

Certainly, it is this feeling of being on the "outside" that has helped Maya create emotionally-charged artwork that speaks loudly to people of color, queers, and other societal outsiders. However, the author-illustrator relates that she does not see herself creating a book for queer children. Instead, she believes that her books which challenge gender will dismantle social scripts, including homophobia. In the mean time, she "rewrites" books for her young daughter Zai as she reads to her, adding mothers and fathers that reflect the girl's own queer family of three moms and a dad.

With this last comment, the remarkable artist gently slides back into the river and begins to glide away. I wish her and Matthew luck on their exciting journey to reshape the world one book at a time. After Maya has disappeared, I examine my own reflection in the river, wondering where Mother Earth will lead me and if I will be as brave as Maya once I reach my destination. I think I will, for I know the river loves me too. Splash!

Reprinted with permission from Naidoo, J. C. (2009). "Embracing the World's Reflections: The Creative Expressions of Maya Christina Gonzalez." REFORMA Newsletter, *27 (3/4), 16–19.*

EXAMPLES OF AUTHENTIC REPRESENTATIONS OF LATINOS IN CHILDREN'S LITERATURE

In a recent interview, award-winning Latina author and illustrator Maya Christina Gonzalez noted that "When she was younger, [she] loved the library—the smell, lighting, etc.—and would go out of her way to get there. It was a type of haven for her that made her feel as if she belonged. Yet, she was always searching the aisles and books in the library, looking for something that she could not find" (J. Naidoo 2009, p. 17). The "something" that she was unable to find was a representation of her culture. Historically, positive images of Latinos have been scarce in children's literature; but, through current works of Latino artists like Gonzalez, young Latino children are finally able to see themselves reflected in their books. In her picture book *My Colors, My World/Mis colores, Mi mundo*, Gonzalez creates the face absent from her childhood books, noting "The little girl in this book is me . . . with [my] big round face" (p. 32).

Gonzalez's story is a prime example of the influence that Latino children's literature can have on young Latinos. Positive and accurate representations of Latino cultures—particularly award-winning biographies such as Carmen T. Bernier-Grand and David Diaz's *Cesar: Si, Se Puede!/Yes, We Can!* or Francisco Jiménez's *Breaking Through*—provide strong role models for Latino and non-Latino children. Authentic representations of Latinos in children's books also contain characters with similar experiences, emotions, and heritages as contemporary Latino children found in Alma Flor Ada's *My Name Is Maria Isabel* or Amada Irma Pérez and Maya Christina Gonzalez's *My Diary from Here to There/Mi diario de aquí hasta allá*. Medina confirms:

> Latino/a authors explore diverse ideological constructions of gender, race and class in the literature as it relates to [their] previous reality before coming to the United States. Furthermore, they also explore how those constructions acquire new ideological meanings and are among the factors that situate the [Latino] characters in different contexts once they arrive in the United States. Rather than a homogenous perception of Latinos as one race and one social class the reader encounters a range of representations (2006, p. 73).

Authentic Latino children's books can also convey the richness and beauty of Latino cultures, infusing ethnic pride and increasing the self-esteem of Latino children while educating non-Latino children about the accomplishment of Latinos. Latino artists such as Yuyi Morales, Rafael López, Raúl Colón, Joe Cepeda, Lulu Delacre, David Diaz, and Carmen Lomas Garza provide children with authentic illustrations suffused with the cultural fibers that celebrate the multicolored tapestry of Latino cultures. Similarly, Latino authors including Pat Mora, Lucía González, Julia Alvarez, Francisco X. Alarcón, Juan Felipe Herrera, Gary Soto, Carmen Agra Deedy, Marisa Montes, and Pam Muñoz Ryan create engaging narratives that mirror the families, lives, and experiences of many Latino children in the United States, while also representing many of the common childhood emotions shared across cultures.

High-quality, accurate books about Latinos further reinforce a distinct cultural identity and encourage Latino (as well as non-Latino) children to learn about other Latino cultures beyond their own. Books such as Amelia

Lau Carling's *Mama and Papa Have a Store,* Margarita Engle and Sean Qualls's *The Poet Slave of Cuba: A Biography of Juan Francisco Manzano,* and Antonio Skármeta and Alfonso Ruano's *The Composition* provide windows into the lives of Latino cultures outside the traditional Mexican and Mexican American cultures depicted in children's literature. Positive children's books representing Latino cultures help Latino children enjoy reading, enhance their language and literacy development, and motivate them to stay in school. Latino children, like all children, want to see reflections of themselves (their experiences, languages, and cultures) in the books they encounter, thus affirming their self-worth and presence in society.

CONCLUDING REMARKS

It is crucial for Latino and non-Latino educators and children to realize that the United States is a social and cultural mosaic representing many cultures with unique compositions rather than a melting pot of assimilated cultures. Children's literature should represent this mosaic, providing mirrors of our own cultures and windows into those cross-cultures of the *other.* Educators, embracing the metaphorical face of the other, will need to include in their classrooms and libraries all types of books that portray our culturally pluralistic society authentically and accurately. Providing such literature allows non-Latino students the opportunity to "reach beyond the bounds of race, ethnicity, sex, sexual orientation, and class" (Rochmann 1993, p. 22) and better understand their classmates and friends. At the same time, sharing these books with both Latino and non-Latino children advocates for a common, neutral platform for discussing issues of culture and race that are raised through interactions with multicultural literature (B. Naidoo 1992). Children's books with their positive and negative representations of Latino cultures should be shared on such a platform to facilitate discussion of the social and cultural mosaic of the Latino experience.

REFERENCES

Ada, Alma Flor. *Alma Flor Ada and You.* Ed. by Sharron L. McElmeel. Westport, CT: Libraries Unlimited, 2005.

———. *A Magical Encounter: Latino Children's Literature in the Classroom.* 2nd ed. Boston: Allyn and Bacon, 2003.

Ada, Alma Flor, and F. Isabel Campoy. "Latina/o Literature." In *The Continuum Encyclopedia of Children's Literature*, ed. by Bernice E. Cullinan and Diane G. Person, pp. 462–464. New York: Continuum, 2001.

Au, Katherine H. *Literacy Instruction in Multicultural Settings*. Fort Worth, TX: Harcourt Brace College, 1993.

Barrera, Rosalinda B., and Oralia Garza de Cortes. "Mexican American Children's Literature in the 1990s: Toward Authenticity." In *Using Multiethnic Literature in the K–8 Classroom*, ed. by Violet J. Harris, pp. 129–154. Norwood, MA: Christopher-Gordon, 1997.

Barrera, Rosalinda B., Olga Liguori, and Loretta Salas. "Ideas a Literature Can Grow On: Key Insights for Enriching and Expanding Children's Literature About the Mexican-American Experience." In *Teaching Multicultural Literature in Grades K–8*, ed. by Violet J. Harris, 203–241. Norwood, MA: Christopher-Gordon, 1993.

Beaty, Janice J. *Building Bridges with Multicultural Picture Books: For Children 3–5*. Upper Saddle River, NJ: Merrill, 1997.

Bernal, Martha E., and George P. Knight. "Ethnic Identity of Latino Children." In *Psychological Interventions and Research with Latino Populations*, ed. by Jorge G. Garcia and Maria Cecilia Zea, pp. 15–38. Boston: Allyn and Bacon, 1997.

Bernal, Martha E., D. S. Saenz, and George P. Knight. "Ethnic Identity and Adaptation of Mexican American Youth in School Settings." In *Hispanic Psychology: Critical Issues in Theory and Research*, ed. by A. M. Padilla, pp. 71–88. Thousand Oaks, CA: Sage, 1995.

Bishop, Rudine Sims. "Selecting Literature for a Multicultural Curriculum." In *Using Multiethnic Literature in the K–8 Classroom*, ed. by V. J. Harris, pp. 1–20. Norwood, MA: Christopher-Gordon Publishers, 1997.

Carrasquillo, Angela L. *Hispanic Children and Youth in the United States: A Resource Guide*. New York: Garland, 1991.

———. "A Rationale for Hispanic Representation in Instructional Materials." *The Journal of Educational Issues of Language Minority Students* 14, no. 4 (1994): 115–126.

Collins, Ray, and Rose Ribeiro. "Toward an Early Care and Education Agenda for Hispanic Children 2, 2004." http://ecrp.uiuc.edu/v6n2/collins.html (accessed August 28, 2010).

Council on Interracial Books for Children. "Chicano Culture in Children's Literature: Stereotypes, Distortions, and Omissions." *Interracial Books for Children Bulletin* 5, no. 7/8 (1975): 7–14.

———. "100 Children's Books About Puerto Ricans: A Study in Racism, Sexism, and Colonialism." *Interracial Books for Children Bulletin* 4, no. 1/2 (1972): 1, 14–15.

———. "School Books Get Poor Marks: An Analysis of Children's Materials About Central America." *Interracial Books for Children Bulletin* 13, no. 2/3 (1982): 3–12.

Dame, Melvina Azar. *Serving Linguistically and Culturally Diverse Students: Strategies for the School Library Media Specialist.* New York: Neal-Schuman, 1993.

Day, Frances Ann. *Latina and Latino Voices in Literature: Lives and Works.* 2nd ed. Westport, CT: Greenwood Press, 2003.

Eggers-Piérola, Costanza. *Connections and Commitments: Reflecting Latino Values in Early Childhood Programs.* Portsmouth, NH: Heinemann, 2005.

Freiband, Susan, and Consuelo Figueras. "Understanding Puerto Rican Culture: Using Puerto Rican Children's Literature." *Multicultural Review* 11, no. 2 (2002): 30–34.

Fry, Richard, and Jeffrey S. Passel. *Latino Children: A Majority Are U.S.-Born Offspring of Immigrants.* Washington, DC: Pew Hispanic Center (May 2009).

Gonzalez, Maya Christina. *My Colors, My World/Mis colores, mi mundo.* San Francisco: Children's Book Press, 2007.

Henderson, Virginia M. "The Development of Self-Esteem in Children of Color." In *The Multicolored Mirror: Cultural Substance in Literature for Children and Young Adults*, ed. by Merri V. Lindgren, pp. 15–30. Fort Atkinson, WI: Highsmith Press, 1991.

Isom, Bess A., and Carolyn P. Casteel. "Hispanic Literature: A Fiesta for Literacy Instruction." *Childhood Education* 74, no. 4 (1997): 83–89.

Kaiser Family Foundation, and Pew Hispanic Center. *2002 National Survey of Latinos.* Washington, DC: Henry J. Kaiser Family Foundation and Pew Hispanic Center, 2002.

———. "Latinos Are Optimistic About Schools and Education: Attitudes Differ from Whites and African Americans on a Range of Education Issues, 2004." http://www.kff.org/kaiserpolls/pomr012604nr.cfm (accessed August 21, 2005).

Kevane, Bridget. *Latino Literature in America, Literature as Windows to World Cultures.* Westport, CT: Greenwood Press, 2003.

Kibler, John M. "Latino Voices in Children's Literature: Instructional Approaches for Developing Cultural Understanding in the Classroom." In *Children of La Frontera: Binational Efforts to Serve Mexican Migrant and Immigrant Students*, ed. by Judith LeBlanc Flores, pp. 239–268. Charleston, WV: ERIC, 1996.

Koss-Chioino, Joan D., and Luís A. Vargas. *Working with Latino Youth: Culture, Development, and Context.* San Francisco: Jossey-Bass, 1999.

Lo, Suzanne, and Ginny Lee. "Asian Images in Children's Books: What Stories Do We Tell Our Children?" *Emergency Librarian* 20, no. 5 (1993): 14–18.

Marantz, Sylvia S., and Kenneth A. Marantz. *Multicultural Picturebooks: Art for Illuminating Our World.* 2nd ed. Lanham, MD: Scarecrow Press, 2005.

Medina, Carmen. "Interpreting Latino/a Literature as Critical Fictions." *The ALAN Review* 33, no. 2 (Winter 2006): 71–77.

Medina, Carmen, and Patricia Enciso. "'Some Words Are Messengers / Hay Palabras Mensajeras': Interpreting Sociopolitical Themes in Latino/a Children's Literature." *New Advocate* 15, no. 1 (2002): 35–47.

Mendoza, Jean, and Debbie Reese. "Examining Multicultural Picture Books for the Early Childhood Classroom: Possibilities and Pitfalls 2, 2001." http://ecrp.uiuc.edu/v3n2/mendoza.html (accessed August 28, 2010).

Mestre, Lori S., and Sonia Nieto. "Puerto Rican Children's Literature and Culture in the Public Library." *Multicultural Review* 5, no. 2 (1996): 26–38.

Moore, Opal, and Donnarae MacCann. "Paternalism and Assimilation in Books About Hispanics: Part One of a Two-Part Essay." *Children's Literature Association Quarterly* 12, no. 2 (1987a): 99–102, 10.

———. "Paternalism and Assimilation in Books About Hispanics: Part Two of a Two-Part Essay." *Children's Literature Association Quarterly* 12, no. 3 (1987b): 154–157.

Mora, Pat. "Confessions of a Latina Author." *New Advocate* 11, no. 4 (1998): 279–290.

Naidoo, Beverley. *Through Whose Eyes?: Exploring Racism: Reader, Text and Context.* Stoke-on-Trent, England: Trentham Books, 1992.

Naidoo, Jamie Campbell. "Embracing the World's Reflections: The Creative Expressions of Maya Christina Gonzalez." *REFORMA Newsletter* 27, no. 3/4 (2009): 16–19.

———. "Forgotten Faces: Examining the Representations of Latino Subcultures in Américas and Pura Belpré Picturebooks." *The New Review of Children's Literature and Librarianship* 13, no. 3 (2007): 117–138.

Nathenson-Mejia, Sally, and Kathy Escamilla. "Connecting with Latino Children: Bridging Cultural Gaps with Children's Literature." *Bilingual Research Journal* 27, no. 1 (2003): 101–116.

National Center for Education Statistics. "Student Effort and Educational Progress, 2008." http://nces.ed.gov/programs/coe/2010/section3/table-sde-2.asp (accessed August 22, 2010).

National Education Association. "NEA's Read Across America Releases Hispanic Book List: K–12 Recommended Reading List Honors Hispanic Heritage Month, 2002." http://www.nea.org/nr/nr021004.html (cited August 21, 2005).

Nieto, Sonia. "Children's Literature on Puerto Rican Themes—Part I: The Messages of Fiction." *Interracial Books for Children Bulletin* 14, no. 1/2 (1983): 6–9.

————. "We Have Stories to Tell: A Case Study of Puerto Ricans in Children's Books." In *Teaching Multicultural Literature in Grades K–8*, ed. by Violet J. Harris, pp. 171–201. Norwood, MA: Christopher-Gordon, 1993.

————. "We Have Stories to Tell: Puerto Ricans in Children's Books." In *Using Multiethnic Literature in the K–8 Classroom*, ed. by Violet J. Harris, pp. 59–94. Norwood, MA: Christopher-Gordon, 1997.

Nilsson, Nina L. "How Does Hispanic Portrayal in Children's Books Measure Up After 40 Years?: The Answer Is 'It Depends.'" *Reading Teacher* 58, no. 6 (2005): 534–548.

Pérez, Bertha, and María Torres-Guzmán. *Learning in Two Worlds: An Integrated Spanish/English Biliteracy Approach.* New York: Longman, 1992.

Rasmussen, Jay B., and Roberta Hernandez Rasmussen. "Welcome to Mexican American Culture and Authentic Children's Literature." Paper presented at the National Council of Teachers of English Spring Conference 1995.

Rochman, Hazel. *Against Borders: Promoting Books for a Multicultural World.* Chicago: American Library Association, 1993.

Roethler, Jacque. "Reading in Color: Children's Book Illustrations and Identity Formation for Black Children in the United States." *African American Review* 32, no. 1 (1998): 95–105.

Santiago, Esmeralda. "A Puerto Rican Existentialist in Brooklyn: An Interview with Esmeralda Santiago." In *Latina Self-Portraits: Interviews with Contemporary Women Writers*, ed. by Bridget Kevane and Juanita Heredia, pp. 130–140. New Mexico University Press, 2000.

Schon, Isabel. "Latinos/as and Families: Books to Enhance Reading Togetherness." *Reading Teacher* 48, no. 7 (1995): 636–638.

Sheets, Rosa Hernandez. *Diversity Pedagogy: Examining the Role of Culture in the Teaching-Learning Process.* Boston: Pearson Education, 2005.

Shelley-Robinson, Cherrell. "Finding a Place in the Sun: The Immigrant Experience in Caribbean Youth Literature." *Children and Libraries* 3, no. 1 (2005): 14–20, 62.

Smolen, Lynn Atkinson, and Victoria Ortiz-Castro. "Dissolving Borders and Broadening Perspectives Through Latino Traditional Literature." *Reading Teacher* 53, no. 7 (2000): 566–578.

Thomas, Sandra C. "African American Children's Reconstruction of Existing Ideas About Mexican American Children Through Children's Literature (Doctoral Dissertation, University of Alabama, 2004)." *Dissertation Abstracts International* 66, no. 02 (2004): 498.

U.S. Census Bureau. "Hispanic Heritage Month 2009: September 15–October 15." http://www.census.gov/Press-Release/www/releases/archives/facts_for_features_ special_editions/013984.html (accessed December 27, 2009).

———. "Race and Hispanic Origin of the Foreign-Born Population in the United States: 2007." http://www.census.gov/prod/2010pubs/acs-11.pdf (accessed February 10, 2010).

———. "Young, Diverse, Urban: Hispanic Population Reaches All-Time High of 38.8 Million, New Census Bureau Estimates Show, 2003." http://www.census. gov/Press-Release/www/releases/archives/hispanic_origin_population/001130. html (cited August 23, 2005).

Vera, Elizabeth M., and Stephen M. Quintana. "Ethnic Identity Development in Chicana/o Youth." In *The Handbook of Chicana/o Psychology and Mental Health*, ed. by Robert Velásquez, Leticia Arellano, and Brian McNeill, pp. 43–59. Mahwah, NJ: Lawrence Erlbaum Associates, 2004.

Wainer, Andrew. *The New Latino South and the Challenge to Public Education: Strategies for Educators and Policymakers in Emerging Immigrant Communities*, p. 48. Los Angeles, CA: Tomás Rivera Policy Institute, 2004.

Watson, Dana. "Connecting Readers' Advisors and Youth." In *Library Services to Youth of Hispanic Heritage*, ed. by Barbara Immroth and Kathleen McCook, pp. 31–39. Jefferson, NC: McFarland & Co., 2000.

York, Sherry. *Picture Books by Latino Writers: A Guide for Librarians, Teachers, Parents, and Students*. Worthington, OH: Linworth, 2002.

PART 2

LATINO CHILDREN'S LITERATURE: THEN AND NOW

❀ CHAPTER 3

A Brief Historical Overview of Latino Children's Literature in the United States

Jamie Campbell Naidoo

According to the National Education Association (2002), "Exposing Latino children to books that reflect their culture as well as their language is one of the most effective ways of motivating them to stay in school" (par. 2). Providing such books also improves the ethnic identity and self-esteem of Latino children, and provides positive and accurate representations of the Latino cultures that can be embraced by non-Latino children and educators (Naidoo 2008). Mora (1998) affirms, "Latino children, like all children, are hungry to see themselves in books, and all families deserve to see Latino reality and folklore and imagination" (p. 283).

Unfortunately, for the 16 million Latino children living in the United States (Fry and Passel 2009), a large portion of the literature in their classrooms and school and public libraries either ignores the Latino cultures, presents stereotyped views of the Latino cultures, or contains textual and visual representations of Latinos as a homogenous group (Carrasquillo 1994; Medina and Enciso 2002; Nilsson 2005). In fact, compared with their strong presence in U.S. society, Latino children are tremendously underrepresented in their books. Each year the Cooperative Children's Book Center (CCBC) compiles annual statistics of children's books published in the United States. According to the CCBC (2009), of the approximately 5,000 books published in the United States in 2008, an estimated 79 books contained Latino themes/topics and roughly 48 books were created specifically by Latino authors/illustrators. These statistics have remained consistent for more than a decade, reinforcing researchers' concern that while the number of Latinos in the United States increases each year, the number of children's books published about and by them does not grow (Ada 2003; Barry 1998; Mathis 2002).

This lack of representation of a cultural group is not a new trend in U.S. children's book publishing. In her seminal article "The All-White World of Children's Books," Larrick (1965) described the paucity and mediocrity of the representation of African Americans in children's books. Surveying 5,206 children's books published during a three-year period by 63 publishers, the author found only 6.7 percent had African American characters, most of them perpetuating stereotypes. Thus, Larrick surmised, "Integration may be the law of the land, but most of the books children see are all white" (p. 63). The same can be said about the representation of Latinos in U.S. children's books today. Few represent the Latino cultures and even fewer portray the population's diversity and many subcultures. In addition, positive images of Latinos in children's literature are often fleeting as most Latino children's literature quickly goes out of print. What follows is a brief chronological overview of some of the trends in Latino children's literature.

TRENDS IN U.S. CHILDREN'S BOOKS ABOUT LATINOS

The 1920s and 1930s

From the 1920s to the late 1930s, few positive representations of Latinos in children's books existed. The depictions that were prevalent highlighted "exotic" people and lifestyles from South America or showed Mexicans taking siestas, celebrating fiestas, or swinging sticks at piñatas. Cimino (1940) notes that "In addition to their [folk] tales, the South American Indians furnish amazingly good material for adventure stories and picture books" (p. 672). This notion is quite evident from the sheer number of children's picture books and novels published during this period that highlight quirky traditions and unusual tales as well as lighthearted antics of the various Indian tribes throughout South America. An example is the 1925 Newbery winner, *Tales from Silver Lands* (Finger 1924), a collection of unsettling and sometimes macabre folktales featuring indigenous people from South America. These and other books were written by tourists who spent anywhere from a few days to a few months living with their "exotic" southern neighbors in order to collect amazing stories that could be recast as children's books.

Similarly, books representing Mexican cultures also suffered from the outsider problem. One of the first U.S. children's picture books to portray Mexican culture was *The Painted Pig*, written by Elizabeth Morrow and illustrated by René d'Harnoncourt, and published in 1930. That same year, deemed the

"Mexican year" by *Publishers Weekly* (Bader 1976, p. 47), two other U.S. picture books portraying the Mexican culture were published: *Pancho and His Burro* and *Tranquilina's Paradise*. All three books, written by non-Latino authors who were not very familiar with the Mexican people and culture, took a tourist approach to the culture, highlighting those elements that might seem odd, unusual, or intriguing to non-Mexican children in the United States. Another example of stereotyped images of Latinos could be found in Leo Politi's first picture book, *Little Pancho*, which was published in 1938. Although some of his later illustrations of Latinos would be celebrated, Politi's book contained grossly exaggerated caricatures of Mexicans that did little to improve the depiction of Latinos in children's literature.

During this period the majority of the authors writing about Latinos at this time were non-Latinos with little affiliation with Latino cultures.[1] One exception to this restricted view of Latino cultures was the work of Puerto Rican storyteller and librarian Pura Belpré. While working at the New York Public Library, Belpré interacted daily with Latino children, many of whom were Puerto Rican immigrants. This astute librarian wanted to share stories with the children about their cultural heritage, and as few books existed she began telling the children stories that she remembered from her childhood in Puerto Rico. Eventually, Belpré began publishing these stories. Her most notable work was *Perez and Martina: A Portorican Folk Tale*, published in 1932. See Figure 3.1 for a brief biographical sketch of this important figure in Latino children's literature and librarianship.

The 1940s

While there were still few high-quality books about Latinos during the 1940s and while most of these books were perpetuations of stereotypes, several picture books representing Latinos in southern California received the Caldecott or Caldecott Honor for their distinguished illustrations: *Pedro, the Angel of Olvera Street* was awarded a Caldecott Honor in 1947, *Juanita* received a Caldecott Honor in 1949, and *Song of the Swallows* won the Caldecott Medal in 1950. All of these books were created by muralist and author/illustrator Leo Politi and modeled upon children in neighborhoods throughout the Los Angeles area. According to Fuentes (2008), Politi's books "foretold the deeper story of a city's

---

1   For additional information on children's titles published during this decade, consult Wilgus (1938).

PURA BELPRÉ: STORYTELLER, LIBRARIAN, AUTHOR, AND CULTURAL ADVOCATE

Pura Teresa Belpré was a dedicated, passionate advocate and pioneer for library services to Latinos, particularly the Puerto Rican communities in New York City. Born in Cidra, Puerto Rico on February 2, 1903, Belpré spent her formative years surrounded by a family of storytellers who instilled in her a love for the rich, oral traditions of family and folktales that had been handed down from generation to generation. In August 1920, she migrated to New York City amid the flood of Puerto Ricans entering the city throughout this decade. Less than a year later in May 1921, Belpré began her library career at the 135th Street Branch of the New York Public Library system as the Hispanic assistant, establishing herself as the first Puerto Rican librarian in the system. She would work with libraries throughout New York, particularly those serving large Puerto Rican populations, until 1945 and then later from 1960–1978. During this time period, she initiated cultural programming for the Puerto Rican communities, developed a lasting reputation as a skilled storyteller, and performed life-like puppet shows celebrating Puerto Rican culture and *cuentos*.

In 1925, as part of her course work for a storytelling course at the Library School of the New York Public Library, Belpré wrote the first draft of her career-defining book *Pérez and Martina: A Portorican Folk Tale*. This folktale, which had been passed down to Belpré by her *abuela*, had been shared with the hundreds of Puerto Rican children attending the librarian's puppet shows and storytime programs, and has always been a favorite, particularly when it was accompanied by Belpré's handmade cockroach and mouse puppets. When *Pérez and Martina* was published in 1932, it was the first Puerto Rican folktale to be published in the United States (Hernández-Delgado 1992). Fourteen years later, the talented storyteller would publish *The Tiger and the Rabbit and Other Tales*, which became the first collection of Puerto Rican folktales to be published in the United States.

In the years that followed, Belpré would spend her time storytelling, writing, and traveling with her husband, Clarence Cameron White—the renowned African American conductor and violinist—until his death in June 1960 when she would return to the New York Public Library system. In 1962, she published *Juan Bobo and the Queen's Necklace: A Puerto Rican Folk Tale* and, just four years later, she published the first Spanish translation about Pérez and Martina, *Pérez y Martina: Un cuento folklórico puertorriqueño*. Belpré went on to publish nine other books including a professional book for librarians and teachers, *Libros en espanol: An Annotated List of Children's Books in Spanish* (1971). One of the final gifts to the library community from the author, storyteller, and librarian would be her active involvement in the South Bronx Library Project, where she created a mobile puppet theatre and traveled to branch libraries, community organizations, and youth centers, sharing Puerto Rican folktales and igniting a love of reading in both Spanish- and English-speaking children from various cultural backgrounds.

Belpré joined the hosts of celestial storytellers on July 1, 1982, just one day after she was honored by the Coordinator's Council of the New York Public Library for her tenure as a dynamic outreach services librarian. "Pura

Belpré once commented that she wished to be remembered as the Puerto Rican 'Johnny Appleseed' in the United States" (Hernández-Delgado 1992), sowing a beloved history for Puerto Rican folklore. Certainly, she will be remembered as a visionary who believed in the power of celebrating and connecting cultures with rich *cuentos* steeped in the oral traditions of Puerto Rico.

Sources for Additional Biographical Information on Belpré

❀ Centro de Estudios Puertorriqueños. "Puerto Rican Writers and Migration: Folklore, Autobiography, and History: Pura Belpré: Biographical Essay," (cited February 9, 2010). Hunter College/City University of New York. Available from http://www.centropr.org/prwriters/belpre.html.

❀ Garza de Cortés, Oralia. "Who Was Pura Belpré?" In *The Pura Belpré Awards: Celebrating Latino Authors and Illustrators*, ed. by Rose Z. Treviño. Chicago: American Library Association, 2006.

❀ González, Lucía, and Lulu Delacre. *The Storyteller's Candle / La velita de los cuentos*. San Francisco: Children's Book Press, 2008.

❀ Hernández-Delgado, Julio. "Pura Teresa Belpré, Storyteller and Pioneer Puerto Rican Librarian." *Library Quarterly* 62, no. 4 (October 1992): 425–440.

Books Written by Pura Belpré

❀ *Pérez and Martina: A Portorican Folk Tale*. New York: Frederick Warne, 1932.

❀ *The Tiger and the Rabbit and Other Tales*. Boston: Houghton Mifflin, 1946.

❀ *Juan Bobo and the Queen's Necklace: A Puerto Rican Folk Tale*. New York: Frederick Warne, 1962.

❀ *"The Tiger and the Rabbit" and Other Tales*. 2nd ed. Philadelphia: Lippincott, 1965.

❀ *Pérez y Martina: Un cuento folklórico puertorriqueño*. New York: Frederick Warne, 1966.

❀ *Oté: A Puerto Rican Folk Tale*. New York: Pantheon, 1969.

❀ *Oté: Un cuento folklórico puertorriqueño*. New York: Pantheon, 1969.

❀ *Santiago*. New York: Frederick Warne, 1969.

❀ With Conwell, Mary K. *Libros en Español: An Annotated List of Children's Books in Spanish*. New York: New York Public Library, 1971.

❀ *Santiago*. Translated by Pura Belpré. New York: Frederick Warne, 1971.

❀ *Dance of the Animals: A Puerto Rican Folk Tale*. New York: Frederick Warne, 1972.

❀ *Once in Puerto Rico*. New York: Frederick Warne, 1973.

❀ *The Rainbow Colored Horse*. New York: Frederick Warne, 1978.

❀ *Firefly Summer*. Houston: Piñata Books, 1996. (Published posthumously, this is Belpré's only novel for older children).

FIGURE 3.1. *Spotlight on Pura Belpré*

ethnicity . . . without stepping away from religious and cultural traditions . . . [and gave] historical Olvera Street an identity beyond the 1930s commercial recreation of a Mexican village" (par. 1). Critics of Politi's work provide mixed reviews of his representations of Latinos in the United States. Some, like Fuentes, applaud the artist for his realistic depiction of Mexicans in Los Angeles while others complain that his works did little to extend the perceptions of U.S. Latinos.

One noteworthy book of this time period, however, is Anita Brenner's *The Boy Who Could Do Anything and Other Mexican Folk Tales* (1942). Brenner, a native of Mexico and a historian of Mexican culture, shares 26 Mexican folktales in her book while depicting various social classes, cultural groups, and viewpoints present in Mexico at the time. Children who read these stories encounter indigenous cultures and peoples along with smart-witted Mexican children who provide for their families. Unfortunately, while the stories in the book exhibit quality and authenticity, the sparse pencil illustrations, consistent with other Mexican-themed picture books illustrated by Jean Charlot throughout the 1940s, 1950s, and 1960s, do little more than perpetuate stereotypes about the Mexican culture.

Throughout the mid-1940s and into the 1950s, various picture books, novels, and nonfiction titles featuring people from Mexico, Central America, and South America were published to give children a better understanding of their "neighbors" and to represent the rich resources that could be unearthed in these countries. As with almost all the other books published about Latinos in the United States, these books were written by non-Latinos who had visited these countries a few times and wanted to highlight the "costumes" of the people and their unusual customs. However, these titles, particularly the nonfiction, had a very distinct purpose: to highlight what these countries had to offer the United States. During this time period, the Good Neighbor Policy was in full effect and being taught as part of the public school curriculum. Children's books about South America, particularly, were in abundance at this time, including a few titles by Walt Disney.[2]

---

2   For additional information on the role of Walt Disney in the Good Neighbor
     Policy and its influence on his films and the media-related books featuring
     Disney characters such as Donald Duck touring South America, consult *South of
     the Border with Disney: Walt Disney and the Good Neighbor Program, 1941–1948*
     (Kaufman 2009).

The 1950s

In the 1950s there were still few representations of Latinos in U.S. children's books and, like books in the decades before and after, those published during this period were primarily continuing perpetuations of misconceptions about Latinos in the United States and about Latin Americans in general. A few exceptions can be noted. *Secret of the Andes* (1952), by Ann Nolan Clark, received the 1953 Newbery Medal and has been both lauded and criticized for its portrayal of indigenous Peruvian cultures. While the overall premise of the book accurately depicts the strain between various cultural groups in South America, loaded words and some stereotyped imagery place the book on the boundary of acceptability for cultural representation.

The very next year, Joseph Krumgold and Jean Charlot published the novel . . . *And Now Miguel* (1953), which received the 1954 Newbery Medal. This book has been described by many critics as an authentic portrait of a boy coming of age in northern New Mexico in a village near Taos. The picture book *Nine Days to Christmas: A Story of Mexico,* by Mary Hall Ets and Aurora Labastida, received the 1960 Caldecott. The book has been lauded for its accurate portrait of Mexican children during the time period, but the illustrations, typical of book illustrations at the time, do not fully capture the richness of the culture.

The 1960s

Garza de Cortés (2009) describes U.S. Latino children's books in the 1960s as problematic. She details two books as examples: *What's Wrong with Julio?* by Virginia H. Ormsby (1965), and *Bad Boy, Good Boy*, by Marie Hall Ets (1967). In both books, she notes, "Julio and Roberto are problem children who misbehave and act out in the classroom because they lack English skills and cannot communicate with their fellow students. They come from families laden with problems. Solutions are resolved only when the two boys of Mexican origin learn English" (par. 3).

Ethnocentrism was also prominent in U.S. children's books representing Latinos in the 1960s. Whereas the books mentioned by Garza de Cortés featured Latinos learning English to solve their problems, other books published during the 1960s intimated that Latinos were incapable of meeting their basic needs without the assistance of whites. Moore and MacCann (1987) provide examples of two books published during this decade that exemplify this problem: *Benito*, by Clyde Bulla (1961), and *The Street of the Flower Boxes*, by Peggy Mann (1966).

The 1970s and Early 1980s

During the 1970s more U.S. children's books about Latinos were published, but these books were still loaded with stereotypes in both the narrative and the illustrations. Cruz Martel's *Yagua Days* (1976), a Reading Rainbow book and a Council on Interracial Books for Children honor award winner, was one of the few books published during this time period that described Puerto Ricans accurately. The majority of the books depicted Puerto Ricans and other Latinos as a poor, dirty people relying on Anglos for help with their problems.

Throughout the late 1970s and early 1980s the Council on Interracial Books for Children conducted several studies of Latino children's literature (Council on Interracial Books for Children 1972, 1975, 1982; Nieto 1983a, 1983b). These studies reported a record of historical inaccuracies, cultural misunderstandings, gender stereotypes, omissions, and Anglo ethnocentrism in U.S. children's books about Puerto Ricans, Chicanos, and Central Americans. (See Chapter 4 for more information on these and other studies of Latino children's books.)

The Late 1980s and 1990s

By the late 1980s and throughout the 1990s, the landscape of Latino children's literature began to change to include higher-quality books written by Latinos. Adult Latino authors such as Gloria Anzaldúa, Francisco Jiménez, Pat Mora, Juan Felipe Herrera, Sandra Cisneros, Rudolfo Anaya, Julia Alvarez, Judith Ortiz-Cofer, and Gary Soto began publishing books for children. At the same time, multiculturalism became the trend in the children's publishing industry, resulting in a surge in multicultural picture books about various cultures. More Latino children's books began to appear on publishers' lists, with an increase in titles by Latino authors.

At the same time, small press publishers specializing in children's books about Latinos began to appear, including Children's Book Press, Lee & Low Books, Cinco Puntos Press, Piñata Books, and the University of New Mexico Press. Yet, despite these many advancements, the number of books about and by Latinos, while increasing in quality, did not increase in quantity. In an effort to correct this problem, three major awards for U.S. Latino children's literature were created in the early to mid-1990s. The Américas Award for Children's and Young Adult Literature was created in1993, the Tomás Rivera Mexican American Children's Book Award in 1995, and the Pura Belpré Award in 1996. These awards established guidelines for high-quality Latino children's literature, opened the door for Latino authors and illustrators to create children's books, and led to an increase in the publication of children's books about the Latino cultures. (See Chapter 5 for more information on each of these awards.)

2000 to the Present

During recent years, a greater emphasis has been placed in the children's publishing industry on creating Spanish/English bilingual books and high-quality Latino children's books. Numerous small press and specialty publishers make high-quality Latino children's literature accessible in the United States. In addition to the publishers mentioned in the previous section, these publishers include Luna Rising, Lectorum, Santillana USA, and Groundwood Books, to name a few. Many of these publishers go to great lengths to ensure the cultural authenticity of their Latino children's book titles as well as accurate translation of their Spanish and bilingual titles. Naidoo and López-Robertson (2007) expound on the efforts of these bilingual publishers, providing specific examples of high-quality bilingual children's books, such as Herrera and Simmons's *Calling the Doves / El canto de las palomas*, Sáenz and García's *A Gift from Papá Diego / Un regalo de Papá Diego*, Delacre's *Arrorró, mi niño: Latino Lullabies and Gentle Games,* and Pérez and Gonzalez's *My Diary from Here to There / Mi diario de aquí hasta allá.*

Another trend is the attention to current issues such as immigration reform and same-sex families. Two recent children's books, Julia Alvarez's *Return to Sender* (2009) and René Colato Laínez and Joe Cepeda's *From North to South / Del norte al sur* (2010), address the topic of undocumented Latino immigrants and the influence that immigration laws can have on families whose members include both documented and undocumented immigrants. The picture book *Antonio's Card / La tarjeta de Antonio* by Rigoberto Gonzalez and Cecilia Alvarez (2005) features a Latino boy who is initially embarrassed by his two mothers but learns to celebrate the uniqueness of his family. Similarly, Gonzalez's *Gender Now* (2010) celebrates gender variant and transgender Latino children.

SUMMARY

Despite the increase in the publication of Latino children's titles, these books still have not found their way into mainstream children's literature and they rarely receive the major U.S. children's book awards (such as the Caldecott or Newbery awards) that launch specific children's book titles into the mainstream library and education markets. The end result is that books about

Latino children do not always reach the hands of those who need to learn more about their cultural heritage—children who are seeking a face like their own within the pages of their books. Similarly, children from non-Latino cultures may not have ready access to books describing the cultures of their classmates, neighbors, and peers.

U.S. Latino children's literature suffers from the same problems that plague the field of multicultural children's literature. Publishers and distributors see the market for these books as specialized and limited market. Consequently, books about Latinos go out of print quickly, even if they have received one of the major Latino children's literature awards. Some children's books about Latinos still take the tourism approach, highlighting only the foods, celebrations, customs, and clothes of a particular Latino culture. This approach results in a narrow view of Latinos in U.S. society.

In recent years, representations of Latinos in U.S. children's literature have progressed, albeit minimally, to present vibrant images of a diverse people with roots in countries throughout Latin America. Little by little, *poca a poca*, the quality of books representing Latino cultures is improving, thus allowing non-Latino children to connect with cultures different from their own and providing an opportunity for Latino children to celebrate their cultural heritage.

REFERENCES

Ada, Alma Flor. *A Magical Encounter: Latino Children's Literature in the Classroom.* 2nd ed. Boston: Allyn and Bacon, 2003.

Alvarez, Julia. *Return to Sender.* New York: Knopf, 2009.

Bader, Barbara. *American Picturebooks from Noah's Ark to the Beast Within.* New York: Macmillan, 1976.

Barry, Arlene L. "Hispanic Representation in Literature for Children and Young Adults." *Journal of Adolescent and Adult Literacy* 41, no. 8 (1998): 630–637.

Belpré, Pura, and Carlos Sánchez. *Perez and Martina: A Portorican Folk Tale.* New York: Frederick Warne, 1932.

Brenner, Anita, and Jean Charlot. *The Boy Who Could Do Anything and Other Mexican Folk Tales.* New York: William R. Scott, 1942.

Bulla, Clyde Robert, and Valenti Angelo. *Benito.* New York: Thomas Y. Crowell, 1961.

Carrasquillo, Angela L. "A Rationale for Hispanic Representation in Instructional Materials." *The Journal of Educational Issues of Language Minority Students* 14, no. 4 (1994): 115–126.

Cimino, Maria. "South America in Children's Books." *Publishers Weekly* 138 (August 31 1940): 671–676.

Clark, Ann Nolan, and Jean Charlot. *Secret of the Andes*. New York: Viking Press, 1952.

Cooperative Children's Book Center. *Children's Books by and About People of Color Published in the United States*, 2009 (cited December 28, 2009). Available from http://www.education.wisc.edu/ccbc/books/pcstats.asp.

Council on Interracial Books for Children. "Chicano Culture in Children's Literature: Stereotypes, Distortions, and Omissions." *Interracial Books for Children Bulletin* 5, no. 7/8 (1975): 7–14.

———. "100 Children's Books About Puerto Ricans: A Study in Racism, Sexism, and Colonialism." *Interracial Books for Children Bulletin* 4, no. 1/2 (1972): 1, 14–15.

———. "School Books Get Poor Marks: An Analysis of Children's Materials About Central America." *Interracial Books for Children Bulletin* 13, no. 2/3 (1982): 3–12.

Delacre, Lulu. *Arroró, mi niño: Latino Lullabies and Gentle Games*. New York: Lee & Low Books, 2004.

Ets, Mary Hall. *Bad Boy, Good Boy*. New York: Ty Crowell, 1967.

Ets, Mary Hall, and Aurora Labastida. *Nine Days to Christmas: A Story of Mexico*. New York: Viking, 1959.

Finger, Charles, and Paul Honoré. *Tales from Silver Lands*. New York: Doubleday, 1924.

Fry, Richard, and Jeffrey S. Passel. "Latino Children: A Majority Are U.S.-Born Offspring of Immigrants." Washington, DC: Pew Hispanic Center (May 2009).

Fuentes, Ed. "Capturing the Heart of Los Angeles," 2008 (cited December 28, 2009). Available from http://blogdowntown.com/2008/01/3087-capturing-the-heart-of-los-angeles.

Garza de Cortés, Oralia. "La Bloga: Latino Children's Literature at the 2009 Los Angeles Latino Family and Book Festival: Presente!" 2009 (cited December 28, 2009). Available from http://labloga.blogspot.com/2009/10/latino-childrens-literature-at-2009-los.html.

Gay, Zhenya, and Jan Gay. *Pancho and His Burro*. New York: Morrow, 1930.

Gonzalez, Maya Christina. *Gender Now*. San Francisco: Reflection Press, 2010.

Herrera, Juan Felipe, and Elly Simmons. *Calling the Doves / El canto de las palomas*. San Francisco: Children's Book Press, 1995.

Kaufman, J. B. *South of the Border with Disney: Walt Disney and the Good Neighbor Program, 1941–1948*. New York: Disney Editions, 2009.

Krumgold, Joseph, and Jean Charlot. . . . *And Now Miguel.* New York: HarperCollins, 1953.

Larrick, Nancy. "The All-White World of Children's Books." *Saturday Review,* September 11, 1965, 63–85.

Laínez, René Colato, and Joe Cepeda. *From North to South/Del Norte al Sur.* San Francisco: Children's Book Press, 2010.

Mann, Peggy, and Peter Burchard. *The Street of the Flower Boxes.* New York: Coward-McCann, 1966.

Martel, Cruz, and Jerry Pinkney. *Yagua Days.* New York: Dial, 1976.

Mathis, Janelle B. "Literacy Possibilities and Concerns for Mexican-American Children's Literature: Readers, Writers, and Publishers Respond." In *Celebrating the Faces of Literacy,* ed. by Patricia E. Linder and Mary Sampson, 189–204. Readyville, TN: College Reading Association, 2002.

Medina, Carmen L., and Patricia Enciso. "'Some Words Are Messengers/Hay Palabras Mensajeras': Interpreting Sociopolitical Themes in Latino/a Children's Literature." *New Advocate* 15, no. 1 (2002): 35–47.

Moore, Opal, and Donnarae MacCann. "Paternalism and Assimilation in Books About Hispanics: Part One of a Two-part Essay." *Children's Literature Association Quarterly* 12, no. 2 (1987): 99–102, 110.

Mora, Pat. "Confessions of a Latina Author." *New Advocate* 11, no. 4 (1998): 279–90.

Morrow, Elizabeth, and René d'Harnoncourt. *The Painted Pig: A Mexican Picture Book.* New York: Knopf, 1930.

Naidoo, Jamie Campbell. "Opening Doors: Visual and Textual Analyses of Diverse Latino Subcultures in Américas Picture Books." *Children and Libraries* 6, no. 2 (2008): 27–35.

Naidoo, Jamie Campbell, and Julia López-Robertson. "Descubriendo el sabor: Spanish Bilingual Book Publishing and Cultural Authenticity." *Multicultural Review,* 16 no. 4 (2007): 24–37.

National Education Association. *NEA's Read Across America Releases Hispanic Book List: K–12 Recommended Reading List Honors Hispanic Heritage Month,* 2002 (cited August 21 2005). Available from http://www.nea.org/nr/nr021004.html.

Nieto, Sonia. "Children's Literature on Puerto Rican Themes—Part I: The Messages of Fiction." *Interracial Books for Children Bulletin* 14, no. 1/2 (1983a): 6–9.

———. "Children's Literature on Puerto Rican Themes—Part II: Non-fiction." *Interracial Books for Children Bulletin* 14, no. 1/2 (1983b): 10–16.

Nilsson, Nina L. "How Does Hispanic Portrayal in Children's Books Measure Up After 40 Years? The Answer Is 'It Depends'." *Reading Teacher* 58, no. 6 (2005): 534–548.

Ormsby, Virginia. *What's Wrong with Julio?* New York: Lippincott, 1965.

Pérez, Amada Irma, and Maya Christina Gonzalez. *My Diary from Here to There/Mi diario de aquí hasta allá.* San Francisco: Children's Book Press, 2002.

Politi, Leo. *Juanita.* New York: Charles Scribner's Sons, 1948.

———. *Little Pancho.* New York: Viking, 1938.

———. *Pedro, the Angel of Olvera Street.* New York: Scribner, 1946.

———. *Song of the Swallows.* New York: Scribner, 1949.

Sáenz, Benjamin Alire, and Geronimo García. *A Gift from Papá Diego/Un regalo de Papá Diego.* El Paso, TX: Cinco Puntos Press, 1998.

Smith, Susan, and Thomas Handforth. *Tranquilina's Paradise.* New York: Minton, Balch, 1930.

Wilgus, A. Curtis. "Some Recent Children's Stories Dealing with Spain and Spanish America Published in the United States." *Revista de Historia de América* 4 (December 1938): 97–105.

CHAPTER 4

Reviewing the Representation of Latino Cultures in U.S. Children's Literature

Jamie Campbell Naidoo

"Much like a quilt woven intricately with many beautiful fibers, Latinos are a proud and diverse people interwoven with indigenous, Spanish/European, African, and Asian roots. . . . [They] are citizens not only of the United States of America, but also of all the Americas and of the Latin American countries around the world" (Olmos 1999, p. 9). Too often, the U.S. media do not represent "the multicolored fibers of the Latino cultures." Instead, a "Latin look" of brown skin and dark hair and eyes, and a predilection for the Mexican culture reigns through the pages and images created by the media that purport to represent the diversity of the Latino people and cultures. These distorted and limited recreations of the Latino experience are also present in children's books.

It is important for Latino children, as well as their non-Latino classmates and teachers, to encounter accurate and positive representations of the Latino people and cultures in the books they read. Vandergrift and Agosto (1995) assert that "Strong images of . . . [their] many cultures can make Hispanic and Latin American audiences feel admired and respected, while teaching non-Hispanic and non-Latin American audiences to appreciate these communities. Most importantly, these positive images can serve to remind us all of the universality of human life" (par. 1).

Unfortunately, research studies looking at images of Latinos in children's literature indicate a history of perpetuated cultural inaccuracies and stereotypes. These studies span a broad range of Latino cultures and describe children's literature from the 1930s through 2005. The following review of the studies describes how the general Latino cultures and the Mexican, Puerto Rican, Caribbean, and Central and South American cultures are represented in the visual and textual imagery of U.S. children's literature. Research that fails to specify a particular Latino culture or with findings generalized for the entire Latino culture is described under "General Latino Culture." Some children's books about Latinos describe characters from cultures in both America and their native country of origin. When a designation is made in the body of research that the characters are, for instance, Mexican American instead of Mexican, that designation is made in this review.

GENERAL LATINO CULTURE

O verall, Latino culture is "rich and vibrant, full of traditions, celebrations, and strong relationships. Our culture includes lively songs, delicious foods, strong religious beliefs, and the Spanish language. . . . Our culture [plays] an important role in keeping the family together and keeping it strong through traditions and rituals" (Rodriguez 1999, pp. 20–21). Sadly, children's literature that embodies this abundant cultural heritage is lacking in the United States. Mora (1998) recalls that the history of children's books about Latinos is plagued by stereotypes, as well as by the underlying belief that Latinos were incapable of writing about themselves. Similarly, Wadam (1999) ascertains that the representation of Latinos in U.S. children's literature prior to the 1970s was defined by non-Latinos attempting to reflect the Latino cultures. Thus, the literature during this time period is overflowing with stereotypes of poor, helpless Latinos needing an Anglo savior to rescue them from their squalor (Wadham 1999).

In her review of Latino portrayal in children's books, Nilsson (2005) examines 21 content analysis studies from 1966 to 2003, and notes the disparity among researchers in defining the term Hispanic, selecting book samples, and applying methodology. Particularly applicable to the current overview of the literature is Nilsson's observation, "While Hispanic [children's] literature was not always explicitly defined or identified by relevant subgroups, researchers across studies used the term differentially" when describing the Latino cultures (p. 536). As a result, many of Nilsson's findings can only be applied to the representation of the general Latino population in children's literature. She reports an improvement in the volume of children's books published with Latino themes, a disproportionate lack of children's books about Latinos compared with the relative population of Latinos in the United States, progress in the positive portrayal of Latinos' societal roles, and a demand for more children's books about Latinos "with exceptionalities, in more varied socioeconomic levels, in upper class neighborhoods, and in leadership roles in homes and professions" (p. 546). Regarding future research, Nilsson stresses the following:

> Researchers who undertake analyses of multicultural literature in the future should be careful to clearly define which Hispanic subgroups(s)

they are investigating, as well as to identify the language (e.g., Spanish, English) and specific linguistic features of the texts (e.g., bilingual, interlingual) in their book samples. More studies of the language-use and the linguistic components (e.g., code switching, glossaries, dual-language text) of culturally diverse text[s] are also needed in order to discover ways in which these features can serve as resources to the reader (p. 546).

Examining ten award-winning children's books published from 1932 to 2000, Gomez (2003) discerns that the books contain numerous stereotyped images and symbols contrary to the Latino culture they purport to depict. However, the author indicates that visual and textual imagery did gradually change over time, resulting in greater representation and authenticity in picture books about Latinos published in the 1990s. Ada (2003), Kanellos (2003), and Wadham (1999) confirm this sentiment, noting that the 1990s saw an influx of authentic children's literature created by Latino authors and illustrators.

Analyzing the depiction of Latino cultures in educational texts, Elissondo (2001) finds that more than 90 percent of their illustrations have carefully selected images of light-skinned, middle-class Latinos of European ancestry and overlook the dark-skinned Latinos who "constitute the majority of Spanish speakers . . . in the world" (p. 96). The few dark-skinned Latinos in the illustrations of the books are depicted either in sports or folk images. Likewise, Nieto (1997) laments that traditionally children's literature about Latinos has mainly focused on folktales, food, and customs rather than the daily experiences of Latino children in the United States. Those books that do focus on the everyday lives of Latinos stereotype the Latino family structure, portraying Latino adults as abusive, negligent, and unable to care for their children (Moore and MacCann 1987a, 1987b). In a study of eight Latino-themed children's books, Moore and MacCann cite gender stereotyping of Latinas, white supremacy, stereotypical settings, and inaccurate presentation of cultural information as common elements of books published during the 1960s, 1970s, and early 1980s.

Studying teacher-identified stereotypes persisting in children's literature about Latinos, Carrasquillo (1994) finds numerous derogatory images of Latinos in the literature. These representations include oversimplification of time, doing things mañana; female gender stereotyping; depiction of Latinos as passive, as well as holding a low self-image; portrayal of poor, uneducated children with negligent parents; stereotyping of male machismo; and depiction of all Latinos as speaking only Spanish or limited English. The catalyst for these omissions, cultural stereotypes, and inaccuracies is non-Latino authors' and illustrators' lack of cultural insight and general misunderstanding of the Latino population (Hecker and Jerrolds 1995; Kibler 1996). "The further removed the author is from the cultural or ethnic experience of the material," assert Mestre and Nieto (1996), "the more difficult it is to write convincing and accurate literature" (p. 28).

Negative Images of Latinos in Award-Winning Books

Omission of Latinos and their cultures from award-winning books is also a problem in U.S. children's literature. Barry (1998) observes an absence of Latinos in the Newbery Medal books from 1986 to 1996, while another study indicates that only 10 percent of the characters in Newbery Medal books from 1922 to 1994 are Latino (Gillespie et al. 1994). Similarly, in an analysis of 80 Américas and Pura Belpré award winners published between 1991 and 2004, Naidoo (2007) indicates that the award-winning picture books do not represent the complete social and cultural mosaic of the Latino people. While some cultures, such as the Mexican and Mexican American cultures, are overrepresented in terms of diversity, other cultures, such as the Cuban or South American cultures, receive little or no recognition. Likewise, the Américas and Pura Belpré picture books continue to present the "Latin look" as the dominant physical appearance of Latino characters, ignoring Latinos who appear black, Asian, or white. Latino characters with physical or mental disabilities and Latino children of mixed race or multiple origins are tremendously underrepresented, while gay and lesbian characters are simply nonexistent in these award-winning books. Finally, Naidoo asserts that the socioeconomic status of Latinos depicted in the award-winning picture books has slightly increased, with more Latino characters representing the middle class; however, more than half of these award-winning books still portray Latinos in low socioeconomic conditions. This figure is significantly higher than the 21.9 percent of Latinos living in poverty in 2004 according to the U.S. Census Bureau (2005).

Spanish Language Use in Children's Books

The use of Spanish in U.S. children's books about Latinos can influence perceptions of the Latino cultures. Barrera and Quiroa (2003) analyze 13 picture books about Latinos, published in the United States between 1995 and 2001, to discern the use of the Spanish language within their narratives. Initially, the authors discuss the power of proper Spanish use in children's books about Latinos, stating, "Spanish words and phrases hold considerable potential for enhancing the realism and cultural authenticity of English-based text, specifically by creating powerful bilingual images of characters, settings, and themes" (p. 247). However, the researchers comment that many books misspell Spanish words or use them in unnatural and inauthentic ways. In addition, they cite literal translations of Spanish into English and English into Spanish as recurring problems that result in "disjointed text with inauthentic speech or narration" (p. 258). The study concludes with the summation that bilingual and interlingual picture books, purporting to authentically represent the Spanish language of portions of the Latino population, often choose formulaic themes and simple uses of the Spanish language that will not be too difficult for readers who know only the English language (Barrera and Quiroa 2003).

Latina author Campoy (2004) also discusses the effectiveness of the Spanish language in bilingual children's books about the Latino cultures, noting that properly used Spanish preserves the Latino heritage and passes along Latino traditions. Yet, Schon (2004) acknowledges, while there is a large demand for bilingual books:

> Many bilingual books show a complete disrespect for the Spanish language. Readers must spend an inordinate amount of time deciphering inept, graceless Spanish: vague, unintelligible, ambiguous syntax; mixed metaphors; mangled grammar; typographical errors; inappropriate expressions; and literal interpretations that make no sense (p. 136).

Additionally, Nathenson-Mejía and Escamilla (2003) describe how the placement of Spanish in a dual-language bilingual book and the physical characteristics of the font can influence the reading accessibility of the book. "In most dual-language books, the Spanish is underneath the English, in a font (such as italics) that is more difficult for children to read and sometimes in a color (such as blue) that is more difficult to see. These differences [reinforce] the lower status that Spanish occupies in the dominant U.S. culture" (Nathenson-Mejía and Escamilla 2003, p. 107).

Nieto (1997) also discusses the use of Spanish language as a prop in children's literature about Latinos. Often, the language is used by non-Spanish-speaking authors to make the narrative appear more authentic. But the result is misspellings, misusage, nonsensical literal translations, and misplaced accent marks. Nonetheless, Nieto (1997) maintains that the proper use of Spanish language in a narrative is useful, considering that code-switching is highly common in the daily speech of Latinos. Naidoo and López-Robertson (2007) comment:

> Not every Spanish bilingual book is equal in the quality of translation or representation of the Latino culture. Few high-quality bilingual books exist, and trouble arises when publishers try to fill the huge void. In an effort to exploit the market, publishers sometimes allow quantity to replace quality, resulting in stereotypical images, poor translations, and cultural inaccuracies. Books that were originally created with the best intentions have often paved a rutty road, misrepresenting the very people they were intended to carry forward (p. 24).

The authors also mention that the Spanish used in some children's books does not represent the regionalisms of the country depicted. For instance, a book about Puerto Rico might use Mexican Spanish regionalisms. Schon (2004) provides criteria for selecting bilingual books that accurately represent the Spanish language of many Latinos. She suggests that only bilingual books "faithful to the spirit, rhythm, and symmetry of both languages, and books that reflect all the linguistic differences, colloquialisms, and popular expressions that add charm to the work" (p. 136) should be used for educational purposes.

Positive Representations

Despite the overwhelming persistence of negative depictions and cultural stereotypes of Latinos in U.S. children's books, positive representations do exist. Medina and Enciso (2002) study Américas Award winners and other selected children's books written and illustrated by Latinos, noting that many of the books "express pride and engagement in Latino/a customs and family relations . . . [and] specifically address the experience of living fully, with difficulty and with joy, in relation to a larger community and society that is neither homogenous or equitable" (p. 36). Additionally, Medina and Enciso assert that the books "embrace the breadth and complexities of shaping a Latino/a identity in a society that highly values assimilation to European, English, middle class, and masculinist [sic] norms" (p. 36).

Similarly, Dresang (2000) describes positive representations in children's books about the general Latino culture. In her study of selected Américas Award winners published from 1993 to 1997 and Pura Belpré Award winners published from 1990 to 1997, she identifies changing formats, perspectives, and boundaries throughout the books. Particularly, she describes the following changes in format: improved appearance of graphics, increased synergy levels created by words and pictures, utilization of nonlinear text with multiple layers of meaning, and the occurrence of "magical realism, a literary/life concept familiar to Latino and Latina children" (Dresang 2000, p. 3). Further, Dresang observes changes in perspectives throughout these selected award-winning books, embracing the presence of unheard cultural voices and the ability of young people to speak for themselves. Finally, the changes in boundaries that Dresang discusses include "previously omitted and overlooked subjects and settings," "characters portrayed in new, complex ways," "new types of communities," and "unresolved endings leaving interactive readers making more decisions for themselves" (p. 75).

Consistent with Medina's and Enciso's (2002) and Dresang's (2000) studies, Naidoo's (2007) analysis of the picture books receiving the Américas and Pura Belpré awards indicates an increase of Latino characters in the roles of community leaders and a greater presence of active, elderly Latinos. Also, Naidoo ascertains that these award-winning books include fewer stereotypical images and cultural props than books published during the 1970s and 1980s.

MEXICAN AND MEXICAN AMERICAN CULTURES

The history of stereotypes and distorted images of Mexican and Mexican American cultures in U.S. children's literature began in 1930 with the publication of *The Painted Pig* (Morrow and d'Harnoncourt 1930), acclaimed at the time as "the first Mexican picture book" published in the United States (Bader 1976, p. 46). Two other picture books about Mexico were published that year (called the "Mexican year" by *Publishers Weekly*) (Bader, p. 46): *Pancho and His Burro* (Gay and Gay 1930) and *Tranquilina's Paradise* (Smith and Handforth 1930). All three books were created by Anglos and riddled with cultural stereotypes (Bader 1976).

In its landmark evaluation of depictions of Mexican Americans in children's literature, the Council on Interracial Books for Children (1975) confirmed that fewer than 200 children's books published in the United States from 1940 to 1973 were about Mexican Americans. Moreover, those scant few books that purported to represent the Mexican American experience were written mostly by Anglo-Americans, and were loaded with cultural stereotypes, historical inaccuracies, and gross misrepresentations. Often, Mexican American characters were portrayed as dirty, passive, poor, unhappy, self-sacrificing migrant workers who needed to assimilate to the U.S. culture. The Council on Interracial Books for Children (CIBC) also noted that numerous children's books claiming to represent Mexican Americans were actually about the culture and people of Mexico. As a result of its findings, the CIBC concluded that these books had a negative effect on a Latino child's self-image and that they "undermine self-confidence, encourage dependency and feelings of helplessness, sap pride in culture and language and encourage the self-deprecating aspects of a sense of 'otherness'" (Council on Interracial Books for Children 1975, p. 7).

Schon (1978) analyzes more than 70 children's picture books and novels about Mexicans and Mexican Americans published between 1930 and 1976. Her study finds only a meager offering of books that accurately and positively celebrate the Mexican and Mexican American cultures. Often, Mexicans and Mexican Americans are portrayed in the children's books as poor, lazy, and dirty people who can only afford to eat tortillas. Similarly, stereotypical images such as sombreros, serapes, fiestas, and piñatas pervade Mexican villages, bullfighting is portrayed as the favorite pastime, everyone takes siestas and puts things off until mañana, the only form of transportation is the donkey, and the Spanish language is often misspelled or misused (Schon, 1978).

Barrera, Liguori, and Salas (1993) examine 28 children's books published in the United States between 1980 and 1991 about Mexican Americans. The authors surmise that children's books written by non-Latino writers display several problems, which include cultural inaccuracies or cultural bias resulting from ignorance of the Mexican American culture, culturally sterile narratives that provide little cultural information about Mexican Americans, and acultural story lines that create the illusion of a monolithic, homogenous Latino culture. However, Barrera, Liguori, and Salas (1993) proclaim that a few of the books published during this time period *do* accurately represent the Mexican American culture. Specifically, children's books written by Mexican American authors create traditional and contemporary representations of Mexican American life by providing authentic and rich narratives, weaving both bilingual and bicultural elements into the images and text, and constructing detailed visual imagery of everyday experiences and special occasions (Barrera, Liguori, and Salas 1993).

In a follow-up to that study, Barrera reports similar findings concerning the representation of Mexican Americans in children's literature (Barrera and Garza de Cortes 1997). In a study of 67 U.S. children's books about Mexican Americans published between 1992 and mid-1995, the authors report that the number of children's books written by Mexican American authors increased throughout the 1990s and of these, 48 percent were written by Gary Soto; the use and variety of Spanish in children's books has grown; four themes are observable in the literature: holidays, migrants, immigrants, and food; Mexican Americans are portrayed as exotic; and some Mexican American characters are living in cities, although most Mexican American characters are still depicted as immigrants or migrants. Additionally, while "some stereotypic symbols may be fading (e.g., serapes, burros, and huaraches), new ones are taking their place (e.g., mariachis, Santa Fe furniture, religious icons), and others are just enduring (e.g., piñatas, fiestas, tacos)" (Barrera and de Cortes 1997, p. 136). Finally, the study indicates four prominent elements in this area of children's literature: an underlying theme of ethnocentrism or white supremacy, an overabundance of stereotypical images, a romanticism that overlooks real problems faced by Mexican Americans, and the typecasting of characters in such roles as migrant farm worker, domestic maid, and newly landed immigrant (Barrera and Garza de Cortes 1997).

Barrera and her research assistants continue their research into the depictions of Mexican Americans in children's literature by examining 92 books (58 percent of which are fiction, 22 percent biography, 12 percent informational, and 7 percent poetry) published in the United States from late 1995 to late 1998 (Barrera, Quiroa, and West-Williams 1999). The authors acknowledge several themes in these children's books: the importance of family, intergenerational connections, childhood memories, growing up, cultural transition into school, and family celebrations. In addition, male Mexican American characters outnumber female characters in biographies, and the majority of all the books studied have a contemporary rather than historical setting. Gary Soto is the primary author of the books, as noted in the 1997 study, followed by Pat Mora. Also, the majority of the fiction books in this study were written for older readers and feature "gripping content, cultural authenticity, and skilled writing" (Barrera, Quiroa, and West-Williams 1999, p. 322). On the other hand, the fiction books for younger children are a mixture of both laudable and repressive books, the latter containing "contrived plots, shallow characters, didactic text, and . . . stereotypical art" (p. 324). The study also indicates that numerous richly illustrated, bilingual, and culturally appropriate poetry collections about Mexican Americans were published during this time period. In addition, informational books about Mexican Americans comprised fewer "'clone-like' editions of holiday and celebration books that were so prominent a finding in early analyses" (p. 325). Finally, the study mentions that the relative number of books about Mexican Americans does not parallel the growing U.S. population, and the authors note that future researchers should "conduct comparative analyses, quantitative as well as qualitative, of the different ethnic literatures under the Latino umbrella, and . . . establish a longitudinal, critical focus on a particular strand" or culture of the Latino population in the United States (p. 327).

Reséndez (1985) criticizes the work of researchers who conclude that stereotypes and omissions do not exist in children's literature about the Mexican culture, emphasizing that these researchers "apply inadequate criteria in their studies and come to incomplete conclusions" (p. 108). Further, Reséndez laments the absence of Mexican children's authors and lists numerous stereotypes of Mexicans and Mexican Americans in children's literature. These stereotypes include judging the culture by Anglo standards, refusing to represent daily experiences of children, failing to provide historical accuracy, disregarding the Spanish language, and showing a "lack of concern for the causes of social, political, psychological, educational, and economic problems that have burdened the Chicano" (p. 108).

PUERTO RICAN CULTURE

In reporting on its examination of 100 children's books published in the United States between 1932 and early 1972, the first analysis of Puerto Ricans in children's books, the Council on Interracial Books for Children (1972) laments that "extraordinary distortions and misconceptions ranging all the way from simple misusages of Spanish to the grossest insensitivities and outright blunders" are prevalent in the children's books (p. 1). Specifically, these children's books about Puerto Ricans perpetuate white ethnocentrism over the Puerto Rican culture, and are overloaded with historical inaccuracies and blatantly sexist stereotyping that places women in subordinate roles.

Ada (2003) cites the work of Pura Belpré as the exception to the prevailing stereotypes and inaccuracies about the Puerto Rican culture depicted in children's literature during this time period. Ada states that from the publication of Belpré's first book, *Perez and Martina: A Portorican Folk Tale* (Belpré and Sánchez 1932), her work reflected the rich heritage and folklore of the Puerto Rican culture. In the late 1960s Belpré transitioned to realistic fiction for children with the publication of *Santiago* (Belpré and Shimin 1969). This change, according to Ada, is greatly significant as it "exemplifies what would become a trend among Latino writers: the need first to rescue the roots, recording and celebrating them, as is the case in the folktales . . . of Belpré . . . , before beginning to look at and re-create the existing present-day reality" (Ada 2003, p. 42). Moreover, Ada asserts that Belpré's work reconstructs the difficulties of living in two conflicting cultural worlds, allowing Latino children to see themselves mirrored in books and extending to non-Latino children "an awareness of who these brown children with sparkling eyes and funny accents are, whose inner richness they may otherwise perhaps never suspect and who, for all their external differences, are children no more no less than themselves" (p. 43).

Studying the textual and visual representation of Puerto Ricans in 56 children's fiction and 29 nonfiction books published from 1972 to 1982, Nieto (1983a; 1983b) discerns major bias in the majority of the books. In the children's fiction books about Puerto Ricans, white supremacy is rampant, assimilation into the U.S. culture is a major goal for Puerto Ricans, ghetto communities thrive, racial and physical diversity in the culture is ignored, Puerto Ricans have a plethora of social problems, and gender stereotypes of women abound (Nieto 1983a). Likewise, the children's nonfiction books depicting Puerto Ricans are laden with historical inaccuracies, white ethnocentrism, cultural and gender stereotypes, and Spanish language misspellings (Nieto 1983b).

Continuing her 1983 study, Nieto (1993) examines 19 U.S. children's books published between 1983 and 1991 about Puerto Ricans, to determine the representation of the Puerto Rican culture. From this analysis, she concludes:

> Puerto Rican children's literature is woefully underrepresented in mainstream children's literature. Rather than simply negative images, there are almost *no* images of Puerto Ricans in children's books. Of those few books that are published, some are still full of stereotypical and unconvincing story lines, characters, and situations (Nieto 1993, p. 195).

Completing a follow-up study of the images of Puerto Ricans in children's literature published in the United States from 1983 to 1995, Nieto (1997) finds only marginal changes, and observes the persistent lack of Puerto Rican characters, the demeaning or exclusion of the family unit, and the presence of the wealthy Anglo savior who rescues the poor, dirty Puerto Rican child. Nieto further notes the misuse and misspelling of Spanish, the sprinkling of Spanish throughout the text to make the story more "authentic," and the incorporation of illustrations reflecting the Mexican rather than Puerto Rican culture. At the same time, she notes the emergence of a small, noteworthy body of literature by Latino authors whose work realistically reflects the Puerto Rican culture and community.

CARIBBEAN CULTURES

Generally, the majority of children's books about the Caribbean culture are set in the country of origin (Higgins 2002). Indeed, Lazú (2004) posits that the islands of the Caribbean serve as a metaphor identifying the "wider issues of (post)colonialism particularly in relation to representation" (p. 189). Specifically, children's literature about the Caribbean culture challenges the "aggressive agenda of popular culture and both contemporary and classical representations of the islands" (p. 189). Lazú examines four children's books and stresses the powerfulness of children's literature about the Caribbean in creating images of distinct, rich characters who embody the history and culture of the islands rather than popular culture's exotic imagery of the Caribbean. These children's books depict "the individual's search for the self, and strength and potential for achievement. Like an island, the characters additionally search for their position in relation to their world . . . who they are in relation to two societies, the island colony and the mainland nation state" (p. 193). Overall, according to Lazú, children's literature positively and authentically portraying Caribbean cultures deconstructs the mass media's interpretation of a monolithic, homogenized Latino culture.

Many of these same themes are recognized in Shelley-Robinson's (2005) examination of 14 picture books and novels depicting the Caribbean immigrant experience. Shelley-Robinson asserts, "The pervasiveness and impact of the immigrant experience on the lives of Caribbean people have motivated many authors to write picture books and full-length novels about the nature of this experience from a variety of perspectives" (p. 16). Particularly, the researcher focuses on representation of the Caribbean immigrant experience in two ways: the struggle and turmoil felt by those children left behind, and the social displacement and confusion faced by those children embarking on the immigrant journey. Further, Shelley-Robinson explains that some picture books "have been written with a strong nostalgic tone aimed at helping Caribbean children living abroad recall the way of life in their [birth] country" (p. 17). Many of the novels that the study describes reflect themes noted by Lazú (2004), including the search for self, ethnic identity development, and acculturation to a new environment. The study concludes that the current body of children's literature about the Caribbean culture provides "valuable insights into the nature of the search for identity among Caribbean youths belonging to the African diaspora" (Shelley-Robinson 2005, p. 62).

Bello (1993) describes the various genres of children's books about the Caribbean culture, detailing the positive aspects of each. "Of all the characters in Caribbean children's literature," states Bello, "Anansi [the Spiderman] is the one that most clearly embodies the struggle of the masses of the common people first against the ravages of slavery and later against the oppression wrought by colonialism" (p. 248). The trickster Anansi uses his wit and skill to overcome the oppressions of various animals and situations, thus symbolizing the Caribbean child's struggle for identity and belonging. Equally, myths, legends, and folktales of the Caribbean cultures are grounded in the rich heritage of the Caribbean people and serve to "instill in the children basic lessons in resistance, survival and identity" (p. 251). Moreover, while picture books about the Caribbean supply rich, vivid, and colorful images that enliven the narrative and personify the heritage of the Caribbean culture, realistic fiction written about the Caribbean exemplifies the vast diversity in language, ethnicity, color, religion, and culture of the Caribbean people (Bello 1993). Finally, a theme underlying all of the children's books about the Caribbean is "the struggle of the region's people to define and develop for themselves their culture and language now freed from the restraints imposed by colonialism" (p. 259).

In describing and recommending the children's books available about the Caribbean, Greenblatt (2001) comments that the cultures on the various Caribbean Islands are quite diverse; yet children's literature about the Caribbean culture has the propensity to group these island nations together. For instance, many picture books about the Caribbean countries will include lush "palm trees, beautiful beaches, and sparkling blue waters, producing books that are set in the Caribbean but give the reader no specific cultural detail" (p. 13). As a result, Greenblatt contends, "Although similarities exist due to language, religious influences, historical forces, geographic proximity, and climate, children . . . should be introduced to the diversity of Caribbean countries and cultures through many different resources [representative of this unique mixture of people and heritages]" (p. 13).

According to Mahurt (2005), "The foundation of the picture book genre in the Caribbean is built on the oral tradition from Africa. . . . These stories were handed down through generations, typically through storytelling sessions in an island village" (p. 277). During the 1950s Caribbean children's literature focused on the morals and traditions of the Afro-Caribbean people. While the various islands in the Caribbean published their own children's books, most of these titles were poorly bound and not available to other Caribbean islands or the United States. Today, more books about the Caribbean cultures are available in the United States, yet many of these books are created by authors and/or illustrators who are not from the Caribbean culture. As a result, visual or textual inaccuracies abound because the creators are not completely familiar with the culture they purport to represent. Similarly, Mahurt notes that some U.S. children's picture books about the Caribbean culture are inconsistent in visual format and lack the vibrant illustrations present in picture books about other cultures. She laments, "Until there is an abundance of picture books created by Caribbean artists and authors that can be [made] available for Caribbean children, we must look for those that are the best of those available" (Mahurt 2005, p. 280).

CENTRAL AND SOUTH AMERICAN CULTURES

Central American Cultures

O nly one study that focused on the representation of Central American cultures in children's literature could be found. Completed by the Council on Interracial Books for Children (1982), this study of 71 U.S. children's books published prior to 1982 suggests a widespread ignorance about Central America's people and cultures. Results of this study reveal that these children's books about Central America: (1) "suggest that Central America is not important"; (2) "contain racial and ethnic stereotypes," depicting the people as indigent and lazy, low-class citizens who love music; (3) "lead students to conclude that the major cause of underdevelopment and poverty are climate, physical terrain and the shortcomings of Central Americans"; (4) "communicate that Central American countries are important only insofar as they directly affect U.S. economic or strategic interests"; (5) "distort the role of the U.S. in Central America, portraying it only as the perennial 'helper'"; (6) "emphasize 'exotic' differences, creating an obstacle to the fullest understanding of Central America"; and (7) "convey one of two distorted images: Central America is either a lush, tranquil backwater with rural peasants and no problems, or it is a violent politically unstable, trouble-torn area where governments topple swiftly at the hands of machine-gun toting guerrillas" (1982, pp. 3–7).

South American Cultures

Few studies have discussed the representation of South Americans in U.S. children's literature. Cimino (1940) examines the representation of various South American cultures in U.S. children's books published from 1916 to 1939 and describes the overall high quality of the offerings. She notes that South America "offers rich material to the writer: an extremely varied and exotic scene, a romantic and adventurous history, many diverse and fascinating ways of life—all sorts of intermingling of Latin and Negro and Indian customs" (pp. 671–672). Indeed, the majority of the books that she recommends highlight the "exotic" customs and "amusing" lives of South Americans. For example, she recommends *Mario and the Chuna* by Esther Greenacre Hall as a "very realistic and quite amusing story of the lazy life of a family on an Argentine rancho" (p. 675). Almost all of her suggested titles were written by English-speaking tourists who happened upon the untapped goldmine of their colorful southern neighbors. Cimino ends her report with the encouraging remarks that "The very old and interesting coastal cities of Brazil with their fascinating Negro population have received little notice. There is splendid photographic material here, a mine for travel and adventure stories and picture books" (p. 676).

U.S. authors heeded Cimino's suggestions, as evidenced in a brief article by White (1954) that recommends more than 81 children's titles about South America published after 1940. She notes that an impetus for this dramatic rise in literature about South America was the increasing emphasis of the "Good Neighbor Policy" in schools. As textbooks did not provide enough information on the United States' southern neighbors, children's literature on the topic became a hot commodity. However, with titles such as *Donald Duck Sees South America* (Disney and Palmer 1945) and *I Lived With Latin Americans* (Strohm 1943), one does have to consider the lens casting these cultures: visitors to South America looking for the exciting and exotic.

CONCLUDING REMARKS

"Latino children's literature is as diverse in character and theme as Latino children themselves" (Wadham 1999, p. 25). This review of the literature strongly validates Wadham's assertion and reiterates the plea for additional culturally authentic literature about the Latino people and their cultures.

Updates to the analyses of the children's literature available about the various Latino cultures are long overdue. In addition, further research that documents Latino and non-Latino children's responses to culturally appropriate children's literature about the diverse Latino cultures is necessary, as well as evidence-based practice that links self-esteem, ethnic identity, and cultural pride to multicultural children's literature. The multicolored fibers of Latino representation in children's literature needs to be brightened to include the diversity of the individual Latino cultures. Based on the studies available about this representation, this tapestry is looking quite tattered. Who is ready with the thread?

IMPORTANT NOTE

The literature examined by the majority of the studies discussed above comprises works published in the United States about Latinos. There is a wealth of excellent stories published outside the United States representing Latin American countries and their respective cultures. For information on some of these books, the works of Figueras (2000), Malvido and Cerda (2000), Penteado

(2000), Zaidman (2000), Diaz (2000), Doppert (2000), Beuchat (2000), Weinschelbaum (2000), and Arizpe (2007a; 2007b) are good places to start.

REFERENCES

Ada, Alma Flor. *A Magical Encounter: Latino Children's Literature in the Classroom.* 2nd ed. Boston: Allyn and Bacon, 2003.

Arizpe, Evelyn. "Finding a Voice: The Development of Mexican Children's Literature, Part I." *Bookbird: A Journal of International Children's Literature* 45 (2007a): 5–13.

———. "Finding a Voice: The Development of Mexican Children's Literature, Part II." *Bookbird: A Journal of International Children's Literature* 45 (2007b): 29–37.

Bader, Barbara. *American Picturebooks from Noah's Ark to the Beast Within.* New York: Macmillan, 1976.

Barrera, Rosalinda B., and Oralia Garza de Cortes. "Mexican American Children's Literature in the 1990s: Toward Authenticity." In *Using Multiethnic Literature in the K–8 Classroom*, ed. by Violet J. Harris, 129–154. Norwood, MA: Christopher-Gordon, 1997.

Barrera, Rosalinda B., Olga Liguori, and Loretta Salas. "Ideas a Literature Can Grow On: Key Insights for Enriching and Expanding Children's Literature About the Mexican-American Experience." In *Teaching Multicultural Literature in Grades K–8*, ed. by Violet J. Harris, 203–241. Norwood, MA: Christopher-Gordon, 1993.

Barrera, Rosalinda B., and Ruth E. Quiroa. "The Use of Spanish in Latino Children's Literature in English: What Makes for Cultural Authenticity?" In *Stories Matter: The Complexity of Cultural Authenticity in Children's Literature*, ed. by Dana L. Fox and Kathy Gnagey Short, 247–265. Urbana, IL: National Council of Teachers of English, 2003.

Barrera, Rosalinda B., Ruth E. Quiroa, and Cassiette West-Williams. "Poco a Poco: The Continuing Development of Mexican American Children's Literature in the 1990s." *New Advocate* 12, no. 4 (1999): 315–330.

Barry, Arlene L. "Hispanic Representation in Literature for Children and Young Adults." *Journal of Adolescent and Adult Literacy* 41, no. 8 (1998): 630–637.

Bello, Yahaya. "Caribbean Children's Literature." In *Teaching Multicultural Literature in Grades K–8*, ed. by Violet J. Harris, 243–265. Norwood, MA: Christopher-Gordon, 1993.

Belpré, Pura, and Carlos Sánchez. *Perez and Martina: A Portorican Folk Tale.* New York: Frederick Warne, 1932.

Belpré, Pura, and Symeon Shimin. *Santiago*. New York: Frederick Warne, 1969.

Beuchat, Cecilia. "Chile, A Country with Poetry for Children." *Bookbird: A Journal of International Children's Literature* 38, no. 2 (2000): 36–39.

Campoy, F. Isabel. "Latino Authors on the Publishing Industry for Kids." *Críticas*, July/August 2004, 18.

Carrasquillo, Angela L. "A Rationale for Hispanic Representation in Instructional Materials." *The Journal of Educational Issues of Language Minority Students* 14, no. 4 (1994): 115–126.

Cimino, Maria. "South America in Children's Books." *Publishers Weekly* 138 (August 31, 1940): 671–676.

Council on Interracial Books for Children. "Chicano Culture in Children's Literature: Stereotypes, Distortions, and Omissions." *Interracial Books for Children Bulletin* 5, no. 7/8 (1975): 7–14.

———. "100 Children's Books About Puerto Ricans: A Study in Racism, Sexism, and Colonialism." *Interracial Books for Children Bulletin* 4, no. 1/2 (1972): 1, 14–15.

———. "School Books Get Poor Marks: An Analysis of Children's Materials About Central America." *Interracial Books for Children Bulletin* 13, no. 2/3 (1982): 3–12.

Diaz, Enrique Perez. "In Search of the Lost Footprint: Detective Stories for Children in Cuba." *Bookbird: A Journal of International Children's Literature* 38, no. 2 (2000): 32–34.

Disney, Walt, and H. M. Palmer. *Donald Duck Sees South America*. New York: Heath, 1945.

Doppert, Monika. "How Does a Venezuelan King Dress?" *Bookbird: A Journal of International Children's Literature* 38, no. 2 (2000): 6–11.

Dresang, Eliza T. "Outstanding Literature: Pura Belpré and Américas Selections with Special Appeal in the Digital Age." In *Library Services to Youth of Hispanic Heritage*, ed. by Barbara Immroth and Kathleen McCook, 69–87. Jefferson, NC: McFarland, 2000.

Duarte, Margarida, and P. Werneck. *The Legend of the Palm Tree*. New York: Grosset, 1940.

Elissondo, Guillermina. "Representing Latino/a Culture in Introductory Spanish Textbooks." Ed. by Lemuel Berry, Jr., 72–99. Houston: National Association of African American Studies, National Association of Hispanic & Latino Studies, National Association of Native American Studies, and International Association of Asian Studies, 2001.

Figueras, Consuelo. "Puerto Rican Children's Literature: On Establishing an Identity." *Bookbird: A Journal of International Children's Literature* 38, no. 2 (2000): 23–27.

Gay, Jan, and Zhenya Gay. *Pancho and His Burro*. New York: Morrow, 1930.

Gillespie, C. S., J. L. Powell, N. E. Clements, and R. A. Swearingen. "A Look at the Newbery Medal Books from a Multicultural Perspective." *Reading Teacher* 48, no. 1 (1994): 40–50.

Gomez, Nancy. "Perceptions of Stereotypes in Hispanic Children's Literature." *Dissertation Abstracts International* 64, no. 03 (2003): 776.

Greenblatt, Melinda. "Caribbean." In *Venture into Cultures: A Resource Book of Multicultural Materials and Programs*, ed. by Olga R. Kuharets, 12–27. Chicago: American Library Association, 2001.

Hecker, Nelly, and Bob W. Jerrolds. "Cultural Values as Depicted in Hispanic Contemporary Fiction Books Written for Children." In *Linking Literacy: Past, Present, and Future*, ed. by K. Camperell, 115–124. Logan: Utah State University, 1995.

Higgins, Jennifer Johnson. "Multicultural Children's Literature: Creating and Applying an Evaluation Tool in Response to the Needs of Urban Educators, 2002." http://www.newhorizons.org/strategies/multicultural/higgins.htm (cited August 14, 2005).

Kanellos, Nicolás. *Hispanic Literature of the United States: A Comprehensive Reference*. Westport, CT: Greenwood Press, 2003.

Kelsey, Vera, and Candido Portinari. *Maria Rosa: Everyday Fun and Carnival Frolic with Children in Brazil*. New York: Doubleday Doran, 1942.

Kibler, John M. "Latino Voices in Children's Literature: Instructional Approaches for Developing Cultural Understanding in the Classroom." In *Children of La Frontera: Binational Efforts to Serve Mexican Migrant and Immigrant Students*, ed. by Judith LeBlanc Flores, 239–268. Charleston, WV: ERIC, 1996.

Lazú, Jacqueline. "National Identity. Where the Wild, Strange and Exotic Things Are: In Search of the Caribbean in Contemporary Children's Literature." In *Children's Literature: New Approaches*, ed. by K. Lesnik-Oberstein, 189–205. New York: Palgrave Macmillan, 2004.

Mahurt, Sarah F. "The Aesthetics of Caribbean Children's Literature." In *Exploring Culturally Diverse Literature for Children and Adolescents: Learning to Listen in New Ways*, ed. by Darwin L. Henderson and Jill P. May, 277–285. Boston: Allyn and Bacon, 2005.

Malvido, Adriana, and Rebeca Cerda. "The Flower of the Word in the Song of Indigenous Literature." *Bookbird: A Journal of International Children's Literature* 38, no. 2 (2000): 12–17.

Medina, Carmen L., and Patricia Enciso. "'Some Words Are Messengers / Hay Palabras Mensajeras': Interpreting Sociopolitical Themes in Latino/a Children's Literature." *New Advocate* 15, no. 1 (2002): 35–47.

Mestre, Lori S., and Sonia Nieto. "Puerto Rican Children's Literature and Culture in the Public Library." *Multicultural Review* 5, no. 2 (1996): 26–38.

Moore, Opal, and Donnarae MacCann. "Paternalism and Assimilation in Books About Hispanics: Part One of a Two-Part Essay." *Children's Literature Association Quarterly* 12, no. 2 (1987a): 99–102, 110.

———. "Paternalism and Assimilation in Books About Hispanics: Part Two of a Two-Part Essay." *Children's Literature Association Quarterly* 12, no. 3 (1987b): 154–157.

Mora, Pat. "Confessions of a Latina Author." *New Advocate* 11, no. 4 (1998): 279–290.

Morrow, Elizabeth, and René d'Harnoncourt. *The Painted Pig.* New York: Knopf, 1930.

Naidoo, Jamie Campbell. "Forgotten Faces: Examining the Representations of Latino Subcultures in Américas and Pura Belpré Picturebooks." *The New Review of Children's Literature and Librarianship* 13, no. 3 (2007): 117–138.

Naidoo, Jamie Campbell, and Julia López-Robertson. "Descubriendo el sabor: Spanish Bilingual Book Publishing and Cultural Authenticity." *Multicultural Review*, 16 no. 4 (2007): 24–37.

Nathenson-Mejía, Sally, and Kathy Escamilla. "Connecting with Latino Children: Bridging Cultural Gaps with Children's Literature." *Bilingual Research Journal* 27, no. 1 (2003): 101–116.

Nieto, Sonia. "Children's Literature on Puerto Rican Themes — Part I: The Messages of Fiction." *Interracial Books for Children Bulletin* 14, no. 1/2 (1983a): 6–9.

———. "Children's Literature on Puerto Rican Themes — Part II: Non-Fiction." *Interracial Books for Children Bulletin* 14, no. 1/2 (1983b): 10–16.

———. "We Have Stories to Tell: A Case Study of Puerto Ricans in Children's Books." In *Teaching Multicultural Literature in Grades K–8*, ed. by Violet J. Harris, 171–201. Norwood, MA: Christopher-Gordon, 1993.

———. "We Have Stories to Tell: Puerto Ricans in Children's Books. In *Using Multiethnic Literature in the K–8 Classroom,* ed. by Violet J. Harris, 59–94. Norwood, MA: Christopher-Gordon, 1997.

Nilsson, Nina L. "How Does Hispanic Portrayal in Children's Books Measure Up after 40 Years? The Answer Is 'It Depends.'" *Reading Teacher* 58, no. 6 (2005): 534–548.

Olmos, Edward James. "Prefacio / Preface." In *Americanos: Latino Life in the United States*, ed. by Edward James Olmos, Lea Ybarra, and Manuel Monterrey, 9–10. Boston: Little, Brown, 1999.

Penteado, J. Roberto Whitaker. "The Children of Lobato: The Imaginary World in Adult Ideology." *Bookbird: A Journal of International Children's Literature* 38, no. 2 (2000): 18–22.

Reséndez, Gerald A. "Chicano Children's Literature." In *Chicano Literature: A Reference Guide*, ed. by Julio A. Martínez and Francisco A. Lomelí, 107–121. Westport, CT: Greenwood Press, 1985.

Rodriguez, Gloria. *Raising Nuestros Niños: Bringing Up Latino Children in a Bicultural World*. New York: Fireside, 1999.

Schon, Isabel. *A Bicultural Heritage: Themes for the Exploration of Mexican and Mexican-American Culture in Books for Children and Adolescents*. Metuchen, NJ: Scarecrow Press, 1978.

———. "Bilingual Books: Celebration vs. Confusion." *Booklist*, September 1, 2004, 136–137.

Shelley-Robinson, Cherrell. "Finding a Place in the Sun: The Immigrant Experience in Caribbean Youth Literature." *Children and Libraries* 3, no. 1 (2005): 14–20, 62.

Smith, Susan, and Thomas Handforth. *Tranquilina's Paradise*. New York: Minton, Balch, 1930.

Strohm, John L. *I Lived With Latin Americans*. New York: Interstate, 1943.

U.S. Census Bureau. "Income Stable, Poverty Rate Increases, Percentage of Americans Without Health Insurance Unchanged, 2005." http://www.census.gov/Press-Release/www/releases/archives/income_wealth/005647.html (accessed December 5, 2009).

Vandergrift, Kay, and Denise Agosto. "Powerful Hispanic and Latin-American Images Revealed in Picture Books, 1995." http://www.scils.rutgers.edu/~kvander/ChildrenLit/hispanic.html (cited September 9, 2005).

Wadham, Tim. *Programming with Latino Children's Materials: A How-to-Do-It Manual for Librarians*. New York: Neal-Schuman, 1999.

Weinschelbaum, Lila. "Beyond the 'Torquemadas,' or the Freedom to Write for Children." *Bookbird: A Journal of International Children's Literature* 38, no. 2 (2000): 39–41.

White, Evelyn C. "Down South America Way." *Illinois Libraries* 36 (April 1954): 145–154.

Zaidman, Laura M. "Latin America: A Fertile Ground for Reading Promotion Programs." *Bookbird: A Journal of International Children's Literature* 38, no. 2 (2000): 50–52.

CHAPTER 5

Celebrating Cultures and Cuentos: Highlighting Three Awards for Latino Children's Literature

Jamie Campbell Naidoo, Jennifer Battle, and Oralia Garza de Cortés

Although the number of books about Latinos began to increase during the 1990s, many beginning Latino authors and illustrators continued to experience difficulty publishing their work. Often Latino children's books created by established Anglo authors and illustrators were selected for publication over the works of their Latino counterparts. As Anglo authors generally published in other genres of children's literature, they had more cross-over appeal and were a "safe" option for publishing houses compared with Latino authors who had more name recognition within the small field of Latino literature. To remedy this situation and end the cultural stereotypes perpetuated about Latinos throughout the history of U.S. children's literature, three major Latino children's book awards were created in the early to mid-1990s: the Américas Award for Children's and Young Adult Literature, the Tomás Rivera Mexican American Children's Book Award, and the Pura Belpré Award. These awards established guidelines for quality Latino children's literature, opened the door for Latino authors and illustrators to create children's books, and attempted to increase the number of U.S. children's books published about the Latino cultures.

Although each of these awards has its distinct mission, goals, and objectives, collectively they connect both Latino and non-Latino cultures by celebrating the best cuentos that highlight the authenticity, richness, and beauty of the Latino cultures. In the following sections, we highlight the origins, criteria, importance, and selected winners of each award, detailing how the awards seek to help Latino children find a reflection of themselves in the literature they encounter.

THE AMÉRICAS AWARD FOR CHILDREN'S AND YOUNG ADULT LITERATURE

The first award for Latino children's literature in the United States was the Américas Award, created in 1993 and sponsored by the national Consortium of Latin American Studies Programs (CLASP), an organization of post-secondary Latin American studies programs throughout the United States devoted to teaching, program development, and outreach about Latin America and the Caribbean. Coordinated by Dr. Julie Kline at the University of Wisconsin–Milwaukee's Center for Latin American and Caribbean Studies, the award is given annually to U.S. picture books, novels, poetry collections, folktales, and nonfiction books published the previous year, in English or Spanish, that authentically and accurately depict the lives and experiences of people in Latin America and the Caribbean, or of Latinos living in the United States. The award's criteria for winners, honors, and commended titles include distinct literary quality in design and illustration, authentic cultural representation of Latino cultures, and applicability for use in classrooms.

The idea for the Américas Award was proposed to the CLASP Teaching and Outreach Committee by Kline in early 1992. The award was modeled partly after the Outreach Council of the African Studies Association's Children's Africana Book Awards. The need for the award was made clear by the lack of high-quality children's and young adult books available in the United States that accurately represented the Latino experience. The creators of the award also wanted to highlight the unity of cultures throughout all of the Americas—North, Central, and South—representing the rich contributions of all peoples with Caribbean and Latin American origins. Dr. Graciela Italiano-Thomas, then at California State Polytechnic University in Pomona, played an integral role in shaping and establishing the Américas Award. Members of the CLASP Teaching and Outreach Committee and early members of the award's review committees also assisted in refining the idea of the award to include books not only published but also distributed in the United States by high-quality publishers such as Canada's Groundwood Books. Initially, the Américas Award was given as a single award accompanied by a list of other noteworthy commendable titles. Later, in 1995, Américas Award honor books were also named, in addition to the winning and commended titles. After decades of stereotyped images and omissions in children's literature, Latino children were finally given the opportunity to meet children just like themselves between the pages of a book.

In 2008 the Américas Award celebrated 15 years of recognizing positive and accurate portrayals of Latin Americans, U.S. Latinos, and Caribbeans in children's and young adult literature. Numerous Latin American and Caribbean cultures (including those of Brazil, Colombia, Costa Rica, Cuba, the Dominican Republic, Guatemala, Haiti, Jamaica, Mexico, Panama, Puerto Rico, Trinidad, and Venezuela) have been represented by recipients of the award. Since the award's inception, 291 titles have been recognized as Américas Award winners, honor books, or commended titles. The award has significantly impacted the quality of U.S. juvenile books written about and by these diverse populations (Naidoo 2008). More artists, both Latino and non-Latino, have begun to realize the importance of creating literary works for young people that celebrate the traditions of Latin American and Caribbean cultures throughout the Americas. Cultures long silenced have finally been given a voice. Américas Award-winning author Amelia Lau Carling emphasizes the importance of the award stating:

> The Américas Award matters because it opens doors to views about American life and life in Latin America to people—especially children—who have not been exposed to them, and reinforces in those who already know about them, the importance of our stories in terms of family and culture. These books are very personal, and the young reader will discover how rich the connections can be between the young and the old, between community and self, and will be encouraged to find creativity in his/her own home environment (Kline 2003, p. 48).

The complex themes covered by books winning the Américas Award include finding a sense of place, celebrating indigenous past and present, the African diaspora, contemporary issues facing Latinos, maintaining and celebrating cultural traditions, immigration and migrant life within the United States, and political repression and social justice throughout Latin America and the United States. In stories such as Victor Martínez's *Parrot in the Oven* (1996) or Benjamin Alire Sáenz's *Sammy and Juliana in Hollywood* (2004), readers see reflections of the daily experiences of Mexicans within the United States, while cuentos such as Amelia Lau Carling's *Mama and Papa Have a Store* (1998) and Lulu Delacre's *Vejigante Masquerader* (1993) celebrate daily life in Guatemala and Puerto Rico. Through books such as Antonio Skármeta's *The Composition* (2000) and Julia Alvarez's *Before We Were Free* (2002) children gain firsthand experience of how it feels to be a Latin American child living under a dictatorship. The bond of familia can be experienced in books such as Amy Costales's *Abuelita Full of Life/Abuelita llena de vida* (2007), Laura Resau's *Red Glass* (2007), and Carmen Lomas Garza's *In My Family/En mi familia* (1996). The lives and accomplishments of notable Latinos and Latinas can be highlighted and celebrated in titles like Lucía González and Lulu Delacre's *The Storyteller's Candle/La velita de los cuentos* (2008), Robin Doak's *Dolores Huerta: Labor Leader and Civil Rights Activist* (2008), and Monica Brown and Rafael López's *My Name Is Celia: The Life of Celia Cruz/Me llamo Celia: La vida de Celia Cruz* (2004). Moreover, celebrating cuentos such as Pat Mora and Rafael López's *Yum! ¡Mmmm! ¡Que Rico!: America's Sproutings* (2007) and Maya Christina Gonzalez's *I Know the River Loves Me/Yo sé que el río me ama* (2009) open the doors to the universality of Latino experiences and cultures, while books such as George Ancona's *Mayeros: A Yucatec Maya Family* (1997), Yuyi Morales's *Little Night* (2007), and Julia Alvarez's *El mejor regalo del mundo: La leyenda de la Vieja Belén/The Best Gift of All: The Legend of la Vieja Belén* (2008) provide distinct cultural flavor.

From the beginning, the Américas Award has been well received by researchers in the library and children's literature fields. Dresang (2000) suggests that titles winning the Américas Award have particular appeal to youth in the digital age, helping them "gain the necessary experiences for 21st-century literacy" (p. 69). She posits that a significant portion of the Américas books embody *radical change*—a shift in formats and perspectives that coincides with advances in technology and multimodal texts. These changes create "books that provide the type of reading experience that, because of their interactivity, connectivity, and access, may appeal particularly to net-generation youth" (Dresang 2000, p. 72). Similarly, Bloem (2006) notes that the Américas winners authentically highlight the various facets of Latino cultures and remarks "as the world gets more complicated and complex because of immigration, language diversity and mobility, how good and important it is to have a major award such as the Americas [sic] that focuses on cultural rather than national boundaries!" (p. 44).

Like most award-winning books, titles receiving the Américas Award have been incorporated into the educational curricula by teachers and librarians. Numerous Latino early-literacy programs recommend the Américas books to parents and educators of Latino children. Curriculum guides for these award-winning books are also available on the award's Web site, and numerous library programming ideas are available in print and electronic resources. Additional information about the award, including a list of award-winning titles, is available on the Américas Award Web site: http://www4.uwm.edu/clacs/aa/index.cfm.

JUST A MINUTE WITH YUYI MORALES: REFLECTIONS ON LIBRARIES, LIBROS, Y FAMILIA

By Dr. Jamie Campbell Naidoo

As I was about to enjoy a steamy mug of *café con leche*, I heard a knock, knock, knockety, knock, knock at my door. I looked out the window and, oh my, waiting outside was none other than Señor Calavera! I opened the door to let in the skinny gentleman who I had come to know as a dear friend over the past few years. Indeed, Señor Calavera was here this very afternoon to tell me it was almost time to go some place very special. He had just finished his 25th reading of Gabriel García Márquez's book *Cien Años de Soledad* and was on his way to Grandma Beetle's birthday party. Unfortunately, Señor Calavera was having a little trouble selecting a gift for Grandma Beetle. While we were making lists of possible gifts, Yuyi Morales (Señor Calavera's beautiful mamá) dropped by for *just a minute* to chat about the importance of libraries, her award-winning books, and family connections across borders.

Since Señor Calavera was not familiar with all of the accomplishments of his mamá, I asked Yuyi to tell us what inspired her to become an amazing artist and creator of dazzling books for children. She laughed and said that it was a long story that began with her immigration into the United States from Veracruz, Mexico.

A Vacation to Last a Lifetime

At the age of 24, Yuyi wanted to come to the U.S. with her fiancé Tim to visit his family. She was pregnant, his family wanted to meet her, and he also needed to renew his visa. Unfortunately, Yuyi could not obtain a tourist visa because the government believed she did not have enough ties to Mexico to encourage her to return after

Author/illustrator Yuyi Morales. Photograph by Ryan Darcy. Used with permission.

visiting the U.S. A little while later, her son Kelly was born, and Tim's grandfather became really sick and they thought he was going to die. Tim's mother investigated how she could bring her two-month-old grandson to the U.S. before Tim's grandfather died. Eventually, she learned about a fiancé visa that would allow Yuyi to come across the border as long as she was willing to marry Tim. She called to tell Tim, who translated to Yuyi, that if they came to the El Paso border in two days, then Yuyi would be allowed in with the fiancé visa. This was the day before Mother's Day and Yuyi went to visit her mother for a couple of hours to tell her that she was coming to the U.S. and, if they let her across the border, she would marry Tim and be back in 2 to 3 weeks.

Yuyi received the fiancé visa, came into the U.S., was married, and planned to go back to Mexico to their lives, jobs, and her family at the end of two weeks. Then at the San Francisco immigration office they discovered that Yuyi could not go back because she did not have a visitor's visa; she would have to stay in the U.S. because her fiancé visa was actually a resident visa (something that was completely unexpected to Yuyi). At first, she thought it was a joke and that it was only a matter of talking to someone and everything would be sorted out. She soon learned that immigration is a very serious process with consequences. Yuyi laments, "We were a family and wanted to be together. If I had decided that I wanted to go back to Mexico no matter what, I would have been prevented from applying for a visa again for many years, seven I think. Our fear was that while Tim and our son would be free to come into the U.S. at any time, I would not have that same freedom. So, I stayed. Now everything was becoming personal with immigration. We weren't on vacation anymore. We had to find a house, jobs, etc. and begin a new life here." Yuyi knew that when they returned to Mexico they would not have their old lives there. She would have to begin the long process of accepting the U.S. as her new home and learning that immigration laws and structure are very strict. Eventually, her mother, father, and brother were able to visit the United States but, to this day, her sister has not been granted a tourist visa to visit Yuyi and her new family. The author/artist relates,

> "Unless I go back to Mexico, I can't share my world and life with my family and people that I love. I know this is silly but it makes me sad. My situation isn't as bad as others' when they are caught in the immigration process and worse. The people I know that come here from Mexico (my people) come here to work really, really, hard. The only hope many of them have is to come to the U.S. to make a life for their family. I don't have an answer on how to change things. For the most part, I think we forget how human these processes should be. As we go from one country to another, we leave so many things behind. This process of living and working here requires you to adopt ways that are so harsh; but if you don't do it, you suffer even more. It is so painful. I wish more people were aware of how emotional the process is and how some people have to come here out of integrity to provide for their family. It really hurts me. I only see what I feel and how others feel. I get carried by my emotions and forget the practicality of the immigration process, which is often easier for me to deny. You should not have to decide: do I stay with the people I love or do I go somewhere else and try to make a better life for them ."

Out of Sorrow Blooms Joy

After all of this happened, Yuyi, Tim, and Kelly initially lived with Tim's family. Without a job and separated from her husband while he worked, Yuyi felt empty, lacking purpose and direction in life. She spoke little English and could not look for a job. During this time period, her mother-in-law took her to the public library. Yuyi recalls, "I had never seen anything like the public libraries here in the U.S. We have them in Mexico but they aren't like the ones here. The quality of the books here is wonderful. Previously, I had never seen the children's section in a public library. When I saw the books for the first time, I fell in love with them. The picture books were so beautiful and the art had such a high quality. I couldn't take my eyes off them."

It was after a trip to the library that Yuyi decided she would make her own books, not to publish, but to share with Kelly. She started writing stories in Spanish about the experience she and her son were enduring. Then she began making drawings for the books, although she had never painted before. Initially, her work was created in a fashion similar to coloring books. She would make drawings and then fill them in with colored pencils. Yuyi would put the pages together and create rudimentary books. Eventually, the stories that she wrote were stories about her Mexican heritage and stories that she remembered from being a child. "I was inspired by stories. I felt isolated at first and felt I had lost my voice, but the stories I wrote were familiar to me and helped me feel better," remarks Yuyi. At the time, the only person she was really able to communicate with was Kelly. Her husband Tim spoke Spanish but was working away from home for the first time, and his family did not know Spanish very well. Yuyi developed a strong bond with her son, talking to him in Spanish, communicating with him the things that were important to her and telling him stories of her heritage. Yuyi reminisces, "My stories and drawings were all for him. I wanted to share a bond that I couldn't give him anymore since we weren't in Mexico. Whatever I had here didn't belong to me. What I could give him were the things I love and that were familiar to me."

At first, she created all of these stories in Spanish but then she decided she must learn English in order to share the stories with other people besides Kelly. Yuyi started taking writing classes and continued to develop the stories that provided emotional stability and boosted her confidence during this tumultuous time when she was living in a country completely foreign to her. The more that she wrote, the more she became interested in writing, practicing at home and reading lots of books. Yuyi notes, "This period of uncertainty and emptiness had to happen for me to start all over in a new career in a new country. I had nothing to lose because I felt I had already left everything behind in Mexico. I could take on the art and storytelling without fear."

Awards, Honors, and More Awards!

Certainly, it was this fearless attitude and commitment to reach out to her son and preserve her cultural heritage that led to Yuyi's success. She has written and/or illustrated six published books for children—almost all of which have won major literary awards—and currently has other titles forthcoming this year. In 2003, she illustrated her first book *Harvesting Hope: The Story of Cesár Chavez* which was written by Kathleen Krull. Yuyi's illustrations for this picture book biography won a 2004 Pura Belpré Honor Award and a 2003 Américas Honor Award.

Also in 2003, she wrote *and* illustrated her first book *Just a Minute: A Trickster Tale and Counting Book*, which won the 2004 Pura Belpré Illustrator Award, 2003 Américas Award, and the 2004 Tomás Rivera Award. In 2006, Yuyi illustrated Marisa Montes' *Los Gatos Black on Halloween* which won the 2008 Pura Belpré Illustrator Award and the 2008 Tomás Rivera Award. The next year, the talented Ms. Morales wrote and illustrated *Little Night* and *Nochecita* which won a 2008 Américas Honor Award. Her most recently published book, *Just in Case: A Trickster Tale and Spanish Alphabet Book*, received the 2009 Pura Belpré Illustrator Award, the 2009 Pura Belpré Author Honor Award, and the 2009 Américas Award.

"I never thought I'd be this successful," admits Yuyi. When she started creating her books, she had never painted before and, although she put considerable time and

Just a Minute: A Trickster Tale and Counting Book *© 2003 by Yuyi Morales. Used with permission from Chronicle Books. All rights reserved.*

energy into the books and knew she could make something really good, she did not think people would like her work. She created the books for Kelly and the initial positive responses from her teachers were an added bonus. Yuyi attended the Every World (Reading the World) Conference in San Francisco where she met Latina author and children's literature professor Alma Flor Ada who invited Yuyi to observe one of her classes to decide if she really wanted to write stories as a profession. Although Yuyi could not afford the tuition to attend the course, Ada allowed her to visit and write her own stories. Eventually, when Ada saw Yuyi's work, she helped connect Yuyi with a publisher. It was not long afterwards that Yuyi began creating illustrations for her first books.

The first time Yuyi won the Belpré award she was completely amazed. She knew that her work was being considered but never dreamed that she'd actually win! On the morning of the call from Belpré Awards chair, Yuyi initially thought she had won for the illustrations in *Harvesting Hope* since it was written by an established author (Kathleen Krull) and because it has already received several awards and honors that year. The author remembers, "When they told me it was for *Just a Minute*, my very own little story that I had created from scratch, I couldn't believe it! Previously, *Just a Minute* had not received much attention other than a few reviews that were okay. Most people didn't know the book existed. It felt like a triumph to win the Belpré. I had succeeded in something that was completely mine!"

Just in Case: A Trickster Tale and Spanish Alphabet Book © *2008 by Yuyi Morales. Used with permission from Roaring Brook Press. All rights reserved.*

Currently, the author/illustrator just finished the illustrations for the book *My Abuelita* written by Tony Johnston and published by Harcourt. For these illustrations, Yuyi set aside her paint brush and pulled out her magical needle and thread which allowed her to create the tiny dolls, clothes, and intricate scenes unlike any of her previous works. Yuyi exclaims, "I really liked making this book. It was like being a child again—having your dolls, making all their little clothes, putting things together to make the homes of my dolls. I had an opportunity to make the beautiful things that I could only dream of as a child. I so enjoyed playing make-believe again!"

Kudos to Public Libraries

Yuyi goes on to say that she credits the public library as playing a major role in her success as an author/illustrator and in her education here in the United States. She notes, "The library was super important in opening my eyes to a new possibility, opening my eyes to a new world. I was in love with the books I found in the children's department of the library and I never imagined that I could make my own books like them." Yuyi would take Kelly to the library and together they would look at beautiful illustrations, read amazing stories, and learn English.

Once they moved to San Francisco, Yuyi and Kelly would go every day to the public library, which was less than 4 blocks from their house, and often stay until closing time. If they left before closing time, Kelly would want to know why they were leaving so early. For Yuyi, the library was an island oasis where she did not have to interact with others if she did not want to; she could simply interact with the books. The librarians came to know Yuyi by name and were always pulling books for her and allowing her to take home special "in-house only" books such as pop-up or reference items. Yuyi fondly comments, "The library was this place that was giving me so much. Kelly and I were learning our English and children's books were the places where my learning was taking place. I learned words by looking at the pictures in books, just as children do." Yuyi found the library to be an amazing place where you could find books on anything that you would ever want to learn: sewing, papermaking, art, etc.

Who is Señor Calavera?

It is about this time in our conversation that Señor Calavera begins tugging on his mamá's arm and begs her to tell his story—the story about who he really is. His mamá laughs, rubs his bald head, and begins to reminisce, "You know in a way I never wanted to tell children myself who Señor Calavera really was. When I wrote *Just a Minute*, I knew who he was—he was death; in fact, I initially called him Señor Death but my editors did not like his name. They couldn't believe I was making a children's book about a death skeleton." Once the book was sold to a publisher, they asked Yuyi to change his name eventually to Señor Calavera. In the beginning, she was not happy with this change because she felt that children needed to know who he was. But, this decision turned out to be good as it allows children to give him the personality or create the idea of who they want him to be.

Although children always ask *Who is Señor Calavera?* Yuyi allows them to decide for themselves. She crafted her little fellow out of papier-mâché and painted decorations on him with the intent that his skull would represent the candy sugar skulls created for *El día de los muertos* celebrations. Some children understand who he is and others do not. To assist in answering the questions about Señor Calavera's origin, Yuyi created a video (http://www.srcalavera.com/jarana.html) that explains his role as a companion to the afterlife. Of course, Señor Calavera gets lonely from time to time and he decided to create his own Myspace page (http://www.myspace.com/senorcalavera) to social network with others and help them better understand his mysterious existence. To date he has 23 friends (Of course, his mamá rarely allows him online by himself and he is very busy being a friend to those in the afterlife who don't have MySpace). "There is one thing that is always important to remember about Señor Calavera," Yuyi remarks, "He's always on time—never before, never after, just at the right time."

It is with this remark that she sends Señor Calavera off to Grandma Beetle's birthday party with the best gift of all—hope. Hope for a brighter tomorrow when people are allowed to celebrate with their families—to live, love, and laugh without borders and immigration laws separating familial bonds that should never have been broken. Feliz cumpleaños Grandma Beetle! I hope your birthday party was a scream and that you had fun like never before!

FIGURE 5.1. *Interview with Latina author/illustrator Yuyi Morales who has received all three Latino children's literature awards. Reprinted with permission from J. C. Naidoo (2009). "Just a Minute with Yuyi Morales: Reflections on Libraries, Libros, y Familia."* REFORMA Newsletter, *27 (1/2), 12–14.*

THE TOMÁS RIVERA MEXICAN AMERICAN CHILDREN'S BOOK AWARD

Bartolo pasaba por el pueblo por aquello de diciembre cuando tanteaba que la mayor parte de la gente había regresado de los trabajos. Siempre venía vendiendo sus poemas. Se le acababan casi para el primer día porque en los poemas se encontraban los nombres de la gente del pueblo. Y cuando los leía en voz alta era algo emocionante y serio. Recuerdo que una vez le dijo a la raza que leyeran los poemas en voz alta porque la voz era la semilla del amor en la obscuridad (Rivera 1987, p. 71).

Bartolo passed through town every December when he knew that most of the people had returned from work up north. He always came by selling his poems. By the end of the first day, they were almost sold out because the names of the people of the town appeared in the poems. And when he read them aloud it was something emotional and serious. I recall that one time he told the people to read the poems out loud because the spoken word was the seed of love in the darkness (Rivera 1987, p. 147).

In 1995 the faculty in the Department of Curriculum and Instruction at the College of Education at Texas State University–San Marcos established the Tomás Rivera Mexican American Children's Book Award to honor and encourage authors, illustrators, and publishers of books that authentically reflect the lives of Mexican American children and young adults in the United States. It was the hope of the faculty that this award would increase the number of children's books about the Mexican American. The award was named in honor of Dr. Tomás Rivera, the first Mexican American to be selected a Distinguished Alumnus of Texas State University–San Marcos. Tomás Rivera was a native of Crystal City, Texas, and the son of migrant workers. Graduating with a bachelor of science degree in English (1958) and a master of arts in educational administration (1964) from Texas State University–San Marcos, he went on to earn his doctorate in Romance languages and literature at the University of Oklahoma (1969). He rose to become chancellor of the University of California, Riverside.

Dr. Rivera is known for his landmark novel . . . *y no se lo tragó la tierra*/. . . . *And the Earth Did Not Devour Him* (1987). His writings, in both English and Spanish, focus on the lives of Mexican American migrant farm workers and their children. Rivera emphasizes their enduring, highly resilient human spirit. His foremost concerns were for their education and liberation from oppressive living conditions. Rivera's writings have provided tremendous hope for generations of migrant workers who had previously not seen their lives appear in literature. Rivera's presence through his literature provides inspiration for others to tell their stories and honor their communities. Particularly focused on education for Hispanics, Rivera's motto was "A high quality education provided at all levels for the Hispanic communities will insure stronger individuals, and in turn, a stronger community" (McGraw Hill Companies, Inc. 2010, par. 3).

The creation of the Tomás Rivera Mexican American Children's Book Award in Dr. Rivera's honor keeps his literary legacy alive and sustains his vision for the education of Mexican Americans in the United States. It is the hope of educators at Texas State University–San Marcos that parents and children, as well as teachers and librarians, will become aware of the distinguished books chosen as award recipients, so that these books will take their place in libraries, classrooms, and school curricula (Leavell, Hatcher, Battle, and Ramos-Michail 2002), and also in homes to educate, inspire, and entertain all children.

The books chosen for this award go through a specific evaluation process. Submissions for consideration are accepted from authors, illustrators, and publishers, as well as from the public at large. Specific criteria are established to determine the qualification of books submitted for consideration for this award. To qualify, a book should be an authentic reflection of the Mexican American culture and experience. It can be fiction or nonfiction and represent one of a variety of genres. It was recently decided to separate the books under consideration into two categories: works for younger children (ages 0 to 11 years) and works for older children (ages 12 to 16 years). Works published within the previous two years are considered, and awards are conferred in each category in alternate years.

A regional committee, comprising Texas State University (Education, English, Anthropology) and other university faculty, community librarians, and Central Texas bilingual teachers, conducts an initial screening of all submissions. After narrowing the submissions to an outstanding subset, the regional committee forwards review copies to the six members of the national committee. Both committees use an evaluation instrument that emphasizes five characteristics: high-quality text and illustration, memorable use of language authentic to Mexican American cultures (Spanish, English, or Caló), positive representations of Mexican American characters, an avoidance of stereotypes, and an insider perspective.

National committee members are located in different parts of the country, represent a variety of strengths and areas of expertise, and sustain the credibility of this award because of their celebrity. The Tomás Rivera Award endowment annually brings the standing national committee members to

Texas State University–San Marcos for discussion and final selection of the recipient(s). Recipients of this prestigious award receive a commemorative plaque at an award ceremony (which is often hosted by the president of Texas State University–San Marcos), along with a cash prize totaling $3,000. The Tomás Rivera Award project provides opportunities for the award-winning authors and illustrators to do presentations, readings, and book signings for pre-service teachers, children at schools, and sessions at the Texas Book Festival. In 2010 the Tomás Rivera Award celebrated recipients for the 14th year. In the first year of the prize, 1996, the regional and national committees had only six books from which to choose, but in recent years the number has increased, sometimes to more than 50 books. This award was created to be an instrument for social justice, to promote reading and education, and to promote pride in the cultural roots of the Mexican American community, which has historically been neglected by the publishing industry.

Books that have won this award, when considered collectively, represent a distinctly diverse group of authors, reflecting regional influences ranging from Texas to California, from New Mexico to New York. Winners also come from various genres. Some are biographical stories that feature cultural heritage icons, such as *A Library for Juana* (2002) by Pat Mora and Beatriz Vidal and *José! Born to Dance* (2005) by Susanna Reich and Raúl Colón. *Tomás and the Library Lady* (1997), by Pat Mora and Raúl Colón, recounts a young Tomás Rivera's experience with a public librarian in Iowa when he was a migrant child. Some recipients, like Francisco Jiménez's *Breaking Through* (2001), are autobiographical, and others are realistic fiction, such as *My Very Own Room / Mi propio cuartito* (2000) by Amada Irma Pérez and Maya Christina Gonzalez, or stories from the ancient oral tradition, such as *My Land Sings: Stories from the Río Grande* (1999) by Rudolfo Anaya and Amy Córdova. These cautionary tales remind us about what happens to children who forget the warnings of their parents, like Dulcinea who dances with the Devil in a short story in Anaya and Cordova's collection *My Land Sings*. Juan Felipe Herrera, in *Downtown Boy* (2005), adds to the range of genres with his unique novel in verse that examines urban life in San Francisco.

The protagonists of the Rivera books are Mexican American children and youth facing life's challenges, solving their own problems, realizing their dreams. The books are rich resources, presenting languages in a bilingual format, in separate Spanish and English versions, or by way of the code-switching characteristic of the Mexican American communities in particular settings (as in Gary Soto and Susan Guevara's *Chato's Kitchen* (1995) set in East Los Angeles). Animal tales, often containing humor and wonderful artistic imagery, are represented among the recipients. Bobbi Salinas's *The Three Pigs / Los tres cerdos: Nacho, Tito, and Miguel* (1999) features pictures of three pigs who are a pianist, a painter, and a computer-toting writer. Thematically, many of the books emphasize the importance of reading and the support of the family in encouraging children. Characters' lives are full of generosity, hard work, affection, and family loyalty. Decorated like the *calaveras* of *Día de los muertos*, Señor Calavera in Yuyi Morales's trickster tale *Just a Minute: A Trickster Tale and Counting Book* (2003) joins to help Grandma Beetle's preparations for her birthday celebration and has enough fun to postpone his errand for another year.

These are just a few examples of the rich cultural heritage found within the pages of books winning the Tomás Rivera Award. To further explore winners of the award, visit its Web site (http://www.education.txstate.edu/departments/Tomas-Rivera-Book-Award-Project-Link.html) to view streaming video of award recipients and a list of past and current winners. It is hoped that this award inspires the Mexican American community to share their stories, to create their self-defined identities, validate their experiences, and inspire a future of hope to honor their traditions.

THE PURA BELPRÉ AWARD

The Pura Belpré Award honors Latino authors and illustrators whose work authentically "portrays, affirms, and celebrates the Latino cultural experience in an outstanding work of literature for children and youth" (American Library Association 2008, par. 1). Although the award was not officially established until 1996, discussion about the award began in earnest between two passionate children's librarians, Oralia Garza de Cortés and Sandra Rios Balderrama, in 1986. The Pura Belpré Award was the last of the three Latino awards to roll out within a four-year period. It was established through a collaborative effort between REFORMA (the National Association to Promote Library and Information Services to Latinos and the Spanish Speaking, an affiliate of the American Library Association) and ALSC (the Association for Library Service to Children, a division of the American Library Association). All three awards, while differing in their respective criteria, were developed because of a glaring gap in publishing that underrepresented, but mostly overlooked, yet another shade of the face of America's children.

In the decades preceding the establishment of the Pura Belpré Award, published Latino authors and illustrators were few and far between. Interestingly enough, the first books written by any Latina during the first half of the 20th century were those that Pura Belpré herself authored. They were the beloved folktales from Puerto Rico that Belpré first heard as a child. She wrote a total of eight children's stories, all published by major New York-based children's publishing houses. Her last children's book, *Once in Puerto Rico*, was published in 1973.

In the decades that followed, those of us in the library field who felt it important to build our collections with significant, meaningful titles approached publishers at the annual and midwinter meetings of the American Library Association (ALA). Year after year the response was always the same: "There are no Latino authors and illustrators," but we knew this was wrong. Those authors and illustrators were in our communities and in our *barrios*. We knew they existed because we had heard their voices, listened to their stories, viewed their magnificent artwork. They were the voices of our *abuelitas* and *abuelos*, *tías* and *tíos*, parents, and maestros—the adults in our lives who imparted a strong sense of story, character, and drama, as well as pride in who we were and where we came from. Whether because they lacked proximity to the publishing houses, the right connections, or agents willing to represent them, these everyday authors and illustrators failed to gain entrée into the children's publishing world. Nevertheless they framed our literary world for us.

Although the 20th-century Latino population was not as large as it is today, the presence of Latinos in the United States was not small enough to be overlooked. The Latino population in the United States, based on the 1990 U.S. Census, stood at 20 million people, or 8 percent of the total U.S. population. Rather, it was more the case that publishers were not as familiar with Hispanic/Latino cultures, in spite of the fact that antecedents of this group settled on American soil in present-day St. Augustine, Florida, in 1565, predating the arrival of the colonists at Jamestown by 42 years.

It has been reiterated several times throughout this book but it stands to be said again: as the Latino population continues to grow at a rapid rate, the books representing the daily experiences, hopes, dreams, and lives of the Latino people are not being published. According to the latest estimate from the Cooperative Children's Book Center (CCBC), of the 5,000 or so children's books published in 2009 only around 1 percent were about and/or by Latinos (CCBC 2009). This percentage has changed very little since the CCBC began keeping track of the publishing trends of Latino books. The statistics are staggering and reveal much about lack of access to and the narrow perspective of the publishing industry. Without major changes in the industry (such as an increase in the number of Latino editors and editorial directors who know and understand Latino cultures, who have a voice in editorial direction, acquire manuscripts, and decide what contracts are awarded and what stories get published), book publishing is destined to remain static although by 2023 the minority children in America will comprise more than half of all children in the United States (U.S. Census Bureau 2008). In a highly competitive industry that relies on the bottom line for its existence, the disparities and inequities in children's book publishing will only serve to widen the gap between those who have access and those outside the realm of the publishing world. We can only hope that awards such as the Pura Belpré Award will serve to influence and strengthen the quality and quantity of Latino works in the field of children's book publishing.

Awards Criteria

The Pura Belpré Award defines Latinos as "people whose heritage emanates from any of the Spanish-speaking cultures of the Western Hemisphere" (Association of Library Service to Children 2005, p. 8). The original Belpré Committee charged with creating the criteria felt it would be difficult enough to find competent ALSC or REFORMA librarians with strong Spanish language reading skills; adding additional language criteria would be impractical. For this reason, titles from Portuguese-speaking Brazil are not presently included. While the literature of the Latino population derives primarily from the United States, the committee also recognizes works rooted in any of the cultures found in the countries that compose Spanish-speaking Latin America, including the Spanish-speaking Caribbean. However, these works must be published in the United States or Puerto Rico, and the authors and/or illustrators, while they need not be American citizens, must reside in the United States. At its inception, the award was established as a biennial award. This was changed in 2008, and the award is given each year.

High Expectations

The creators of the Pura Belpré Award hoped to achieve many things: to establish the Pura Belpré Award winners as a body of work that best represents the wealth and diversity of books and stories about the Latino cultural experience for all children, to develop high standards for high-quality writing and illustration of the Latino cultural experience in books for children, to increase the number of published Latino authors and illustrators relative to the size of the Latino population, to honor and recognize the authors and illustrators of the Latino cultural experience as cultural literary heroes and role models for children, to recognize the breadth and depth of cultural authenticity that surfaces when stories from within the culture are allowed to flourish, and to acknowledge that

CRITICAL THOUGHTS ON LATINO CHILDREN'S LITERATURE

AUTHENTIC STORIES, AUTHENTIC VOICES

In considering significant works of historical consequence, it is important to analyze and evaluate the accuracy of the history, including the author's point of view. Who is telling the story and what story is being told are two important questions to ask, regardless of whether the story is fiction or nonfiction. Stories such as Margarita Engle and Sean Qualls's *The Poet Slave of Cuba* (2006) are significant because they expand upon children's understanding of slavery. By reading Engle's piercing narrative, children will learn the selective, cruel application of slavery as practiced by a selfish Marquessa. Reading Pam Muñoz Ryan's *Esperanza Rising* (2000), children will learn that the story is based on the author's grandmother's actual experiences. It also represents the experiences of thousands of Mexican Americans, citizens of this country who were deported during yet another dark period of American immigration history. Readers unfamiliar with Mexican American history will learn about the thousands of Americans of Mexican descent who were repatriated, based mostly on faulty evidence of stereotyped images and erroneous assumptions about nationality and citizenship. Children will read for the first time about a young girl's riches-to-rags story, a unique theme in historical fiction seldom associated with the Mexican American experience. While well-received in the year that it was published, *Esperanza Rising* received its much-deserved accolade only after it was awarded the Pura Belpré Award the following year.

Biographical stories such as Alma Flor Ada's *Under the Royal Palms* (1998) provide insight into family relationships and dynamics. In Ada's case, her biography serves as a window into the life of a young female child prodigy. If we study this biography carefully, we can learn about the significance of adults in the lives of Cuban children, transmitting values and beliefs that children carry forth as they begin to shape their own social identities. *Breaking Through* (2001), Francisco Jiménez's poignant biography, is one that only a person who has experienced such harsh realities could tell. That Jiménez can recall these vivid memories with such a steady calm in the midst of such abject poverty is a tribute to the strength of his own character, shaped by life's harshness yet shielded by the steady love of and for his *familia*.

readers respond best to literature when they recognize that the story is authored and/or illustrated by someone just like them.

Time, statistics, and research will determine whether these goals were practical and realistic or lofty. What the creators of the Pura Belpré Award did not foresee was another layer of unintended yet welcome consequences. Over the 14-year period that the award has been in existence, the Pura Belpré Award has given REFORMA children's librarians greater opportunities to use their professional evaluative book skills. Serving on the award committee, REFORMA librarians have begun to attend both the midwinter and annual meetings of the American Library Association. Through their work as award committee members, they are better able to evaluate and select books for children. They have been able to

CRITICAL THOUGHTS ON LATINO CHILDREN'S LITERATURE

WHAT'S WRONG WITH *WHAT'S WRONG WITH JULIO?*

Contrast these wonderfully written stories with other stories written about Mexican children in the late 1960s. A classic example is Virginia Ormsby's *What's Wrong with Julio?* (1965). In this realistic picture book story, Julio is a young Mexican child attending school for the first time. He is a problem child, refusing to communicate with his teacher or his classmates. As it turns out, Julio is not living with his parents. Julio, of course, misses his mother terribly and, as any normal child would, acts out his anger in the classroom. Julio is a little pariah among his classmates, who try to communicate with him to no avail. It is only after Julio begins to speak in English that he becomes well liked by his classmates. What is wrong with books like *What's Wrong with Julio?* In addition to using illustrations that dress Julio in outdated, traditional peasant, white clothing, the author glaringly lacks an understanding of the basics of child development—much less an understanding of the more complex issues of a child's confusion and alienation when placed in a sterile learning environment that does little to honor his culture, traditions, or way of speaking. Marie Hall Ets's *Bad Boy, Good Boy* (1967) is yet another book about a Mexican American child riddled with emotional and social problems.

Both *What's Wrong with Julio?* and *Bad Boy, Good Boy* were to be found on the shelves of several Texas libraries in the early 1980s when Oralia Garza de Cortés first began to seek out stories about Mexican Americans to share with her young children. The sight of these demeaning works, which served to perpetuate stereotypes about Mexican American children and families, infuriated teachers and mothers like Oralia. They deplored the fact that these titles were still on library shelves. Such titles only fueled Oralia's fire, motivating her to seek quality, authentic stories that she could be proud to share with her own children. This type of stereotypical literature also led Oralia and other organizing agents to insist that affirmation and celebration of Latino cultural experiences be major criteria for evaluating authenticity in books for children.

contribute both their professional and their cultural expertise when discussing high-quality Latino-based books for children. The Pura Belpré Award offers prestige and recognition to all professionals who serve. At the same time, ALSC appointees to the Belpré award committee can expand their understanding of Latino cultures and acquire cultural competencies regarding Latino cultures that they may not have previously had. They also bring a wealth of expertise about children's book selection that they can share with the entire committee, especially if they have served on other prestigious book award committees. The win-win situation established through joint appointment and joint selection has provided further professional opportunities for REFORMA children's librarians who have served on the Belpré award committee. Many have subsequently served on other children's panels. One such librarian, Rose Treviño, has since chaired the prestigious Newbery Medal committee, becoming the first Latina to serve as chair in the history of that award. Another REFORMA member, Jamie Campbell Naidoo, went on to serve on the noted Caldecott award committee after serving as a member of the Belpré award committee.

Several other factors have also served to diversify and change the public face of ALA. The inclusion of the Belpré award-winning titles in ALSC's Notable Books for Children has also helped to diversify that list; the list now includes winners of both the Pura Belpré and Coretta Scott King awards, a practice begun shortly after the Pura Belpré Award was initiated. Moreover, the inclusion of the Belpré Award winners in the yearly ALA Youth Media Awards press conference has allowed for the simultaneous announcement of the Pura Belpré Award in both English and Spanish, with ALA's Public Information Office working to ensure that the Belpré announcements are distributed to the Spanish-language media.

Over the years, the Pura Belpré Award has brought much-deserved attention and recognition to authors and books that might have otherwise gone unnoticed. Nonetheless, REFORMA, through the Children's and Young Adult Services Committee, celebrates the accomplishments of these distinguished authors and illustrators. In the ceremonial ritual known as the *Celebración*, librarians, publishers, family members, and children all come together to honor and celebrate the accomplishments of these deserving authors and illustrators. In the course of these gatherings, we listen to their stories of struggle as artists and human beings. In each and every case, the authors and illustrators are grateful for the recognition, because it emphasizes the importance of their work and inspires them to continue. The Pura Belpré Award Celebración also gives non-Latino librarians a rare opportunity to learn about Latino cultures, to hear firsthand the thought processes that the authors and illustrators experienced in the course of creating their works. Finally, the Pura Belpré Award serves a greater purpose for the American Library Association in that it meets four of ALA's seven Key Action Areas: Diversity, Equity of Access, Education and Continuous Learning, and 21st Century Literacy (American Library Association 1998). While no doubt the winners of the Pura Belpré Award provide children from Latino cultures with an opportunity to see themselves reflected in literature through the best possible light, clearly *all* children can experience joy and delight as they celebrate Grandma Beetle's birthday in Yuyi Morales's *Just a Minute* (2003) or *Just in Case* (2008). In the current climate of anti-immigration sentiment and at a time when many of America's schoolchildren have come to equate "illegal" with "Mexican," the Pura Belpré Award clearly serves a vital role in showcasing America's pluralism through exceptional literature. A list of the current and past winners of the Pura Belpré Award can be found on the award's Web site: http://ala.org/ala/mgrps/divs/alsc/awardsgrants/bookmedia/belpremedal/index.cfm.

CONCLUDING REMARKS

Historically, positive images of Latinos have been scarce in children's literature; but, through the works of the Américas, Tomás Rivera, and Pura Belpré award-winning authors and illustrators, Latino children are finally able to see their families, *barrios,* cultures, experiences, and lives reflected within the words and illustrations of their books. At the same time, these award-winning books allow non-Latino children a glimpse into the rich cultural experiences, languages, and traditions of their fellow Latino classmates. It is through these culturally authentic, accurate collections of children's literature that librarians and educators can celebrate diverse cultures and Latino cuentos!

REFERENCES

American Library Association. "ALA Governing and Strategic Documents, 1998." http://www.ala.org/ala/aboutala/governance/alagoverning.cfm (accessed December 13, 2009).

———. "Belpré Medal, 2008." http://ala.org/ala/mgrps/divs/alsc/awardsgrants/bookmedia/belpremedal/index.cfm (accessed December 4, 2009).

Association of Library Service to Children. "The Belpré Award Committee Manual, 2005." http://www.ala.org/ala/mgrps/divs/alsc/awardsgrants/bookmedia/belpremedal/Belpre_Manual_Aug05.pdf (accessed December 15, 2009).

Battle, Jennifer. "Bobbi Salinas Weaves a New Tale of Three Pigs." *The State of Reading* 6, no. 1 (2001a): 9–14.

———. "A Conversation with Rudolfo Anaya." *The New Advocate* 14, no. 2 (2001b): 103–109.

Bloem, Patricia. "The Americas Award." *Bookbird: A Journal of International Children's Literature* 44, no. 1 (2006): 41–44.

Cooperative Children's Book Center. "Children's Books by and About People of Color Published in the United States, 2009." http://www.education.wisc.edu/ccbc/books/pcstats.asp (accessed December 28, 2009).

Dresang, Eliza T. "Outstanding Literature: Pura Belpré and Américas Selections with Special Appeal in the Digital Age." In *Library Services to Youth of Hispanic*

Heritage, ed. by Barbara Immroth and Kathleen McCook, 69–87. Jefferson, NC: McFarland, 2000.

Kline, Julie. "Weaving Stories: Celebrating the Tenth Anniversary of the Américas Award for Children's and Young Adult Literature." *Children and Libraries* 1, no. 2 (2003): 45–48.

Lasky, Katherine. "To Stingo with Love: An Author's Perspective on Writing Outside One's Culture." In *Stories Matter: The Complexity of Cultural Authenticity in Children's Literature*, ed. by Dana L. Fox and K. G. Short, 84–92. Urbana, IL: National Council of Teachers of English, 2003.

Leavell, J. A., B. Hatcher, Jennifer Battle, and N. Ramos-Michail. "Exploring Hispanic Culture Through Trade Books." *Social Education* 66, no. 4 (2002): 210–215.

McGraw Hill Companies, Inc. "Study Guide for . . . And The Earth Did Not Devour Him." http://www.glencoe.com/sec/literature/litlibrary/pdf/earth_did_not_devour.pdf (accessed January 21, 2010).

Naidoo, Jamie Campbell. "Opening Doors: Visual and Textual Analyses of Diverse Latino Subcultures in Américas Picture Books." *Children and Libraries* 6, no. 2 (2008): 27–35.

Rivera, Tomás. *. . . y no se lo tragó la tierra / . . . And the Earth Did Not Devour Him*. Trans. by Evangelina Vigil-Piñón. Houston, TX: Arte Público Press, 1987.

Rochman, Hazel. *Against Borders: Promoting Books for a Multicultural World*. Chicago: American Library Association, 1993.

U.S. Census Bureau. "An Older and More Diverse Nation by Mid Century." http://www.census.gov/newsroom/releases/archives/population/cb08-123.html (accessed January 29, 2010).

PART 3

DEVELOPING COLLECTIONS OF LATINO CHILDREN'S MATERIALS

The Story of the Américas Collection: Gathering PreK–12 Spanish-Language Books and Resources

Ruth E. Quiroa

Newly published picture books of short stories and poems by Argentinean author María Elena Walsh captivated the imagination of three sisters, Lilianna (age 11), Carolina (age 8), and Emmalucía (age 4), who were visiting Argentina for the first time during the summer of 2005. The girls grew up in a highly biliterate family, with easy access to high-quality multicultural children's literature, in both English and Spanish. They were particularly familiar with literature that presented Mexican American and Guatemalan American themes. However, they had no background knowledge about Argentinean culture or literature and the discovery of Walsh's books at the Feria del Libro Infantil y Juvenil in Buenos Aires resulted in repeated requests to hear her stories read aloud. Emmalucía even memorized all the songs from one of Walsh's CDs, especially the song from her favorite picture book, *Manuelita* (2005).

The story of Manuelita, together with Walsh's large body of children's poetry and songs, is familiar to parents, children, and grandparents in Argentina. The major newspaper in Buenos Aires, *La Nación*, recently described Walsh as "la más prestigiosa autora de libros para niños" (Guerriero 2005). In 1992 she was nominated the Argentinean author candidate for the prestigious Hans Christian Andersen Award. This award is given biannually by the International Board on Books for Young People (IBBY) to a living author and illustrator whose complete works have made a lasting contribution to children's literature. Walsh's ability to transcend Latino cultures and Spanish language variations for the three sisters caused me to seek out her texts upon my return to the United States. These experiences spurred an inquiry project involving the American Library Association—FIL Free Pass Program and attendance at other book fairs

Note: This chapter was supported in part by the Shaw Fund for Literacy.

in Central and South America. This in turn resulted in the development of new partnerships, and eventually blossomed into the creation of the National-Louis University (NLU) Américas Collection of more than 800 books, including works originally written in Spanish, as well as bilingual Spanish and English books and texts in English with Latino themes.

This chapter describes the development of the Américas Collection, highlighting the processes and resources helpful in its creation and continued growth, and its goal to be a resource for teachers and librarians across the United States. A brief discussion of the need for K–12 Spanish-language texts in the United States is first provided, in order to place in context the description of the initial search for Spanish-language texts and materials within the United States. Then follows a description of the continued search for texts available outside the country, at the Feria Internacional del Libro (FIL) in Guadalajara, Mexico, and in Argentina and Bolivia. Future goals of dissemination and growth are also discussed, followed by an extensive resource list.

SCHOOLS, LIBRARIES, AND LANGUAGES IN THE UNITED STATES

Many Latino children growing up across the United States, particularly those in suburban and rural communities, find meager offerings in school and public libraries of children's literature that is originally written in Spanish. Yet curricular issues relating to languages of instruction are becoming increasingly important in schools (Hill and Flynn 2006). Latinos currently represent the largest minority community in the United States, estimated at 15.1 percent of the population (U.S. Census Bureau 2009) with projections that this population will triple over the next half century. These statistics are particularly important given that 22 percent of all U.S. children under the age of 18 are of Latino descent and speak Spanish as their primary language (Fry and Passel 2009).

Despite the importance of the Spanish language for instruction in bilingual education programs, and as a resource in general education and English language learner classrooms, many of the texts available or included in commercial school curricula are translated stories and books. Yet even highly qualified monolingual and bilingual literacy teachers who work with Latino children can do little without access to books of stellar literary quality and cultural accurateness (Cai 2002), inclusive of native language texts. Unfortunately, the body of Latino-themed children's trade books published in the United States in bilingual and Spanish-language editions has often presented problematic translations from English into Spanish (Barrera and de Cortes 1997; Barrera and Quiroa 2003). Thus, the need is great for high-quality, original works in Spanish published both within the United States and in other countries, particularly in Latin America.

INITIATING THE COLLECTION

Following the joyous discovery of Walsh's books in Argentina, the three girls mentioned above wanted to read more of her texts upon returning to the United States. A quick perusal of the closest public libraries in the western Chicago suburbs was disappointing, which led me on an electronic search of public and university libraries' holdings. This 2006 inquiry identified only 37 titles in libraries connected to electronic databases across the state of Illinois, for a total of 81 books (multiple copies of some titles were available). Unfortunately, only three of Chicago's western suburban city libraries held eight texts among them, a surprising discovery given the large and growing Latino populations in the area (Ready and Brown-Goert 2005).

The Walsh book search coincided with one of my regular visits to National-Louis University Library, where I spoke with colleague and university library instructor Barbara Evans about my recent trip to South America, my purchase of Spanish-language children's literature at the Feria Internacional del Libro Infantil y Juvenil in Buenos Aires, and the difficulty of locating other such texts in the Chicago area. She encouraged me to bring my books to her office so that purchase requests could be made to add these titles to the university library. This casual conversation started a partnership between our university's College of Education/Department of Reading and Language and the university library. My role was to search for new Spanish-language preK–12 book titles, while Barb and other library staff members began identifying vendors and purchasing as many of these texts as possible. During this first year, approximately 300 books focusing on Latinos and published in Spanish, English, or in bilingual editions were purchased, catalogued, and made available at NLU and any Illinois universities or colleges that were members of CARLI, a consortium of more than 75 academic libraries across the state. In addition, the Mexican Consulate in Chicago donated a set of national curriculum K–12 content area texts, that added greatly to this growing collection. We also brainstormed potential names for the collection in order to assist with cataloging purposes, and finally decided that the term "Américas" best fit the nature of these books. Of course, this entire process was only successful due to the many library staff members with Spanish language skills and/or an interest in literature for children and adolescents at all levels.

About a year later, while in the midst of a regular shopping trip to a local Mexican grocery store, I received a phone call from Barb. Gazing at the colorful *papel picado* hanging from the ceiling, I listened as she described an American Library Association (ALA) grant opportunity to attend the Feria Internacional del Libro in Guadalajara, Mexico.

ALA AND FIL

In that brief phone conversation, I learned that the ALA-FIL Free Pass Program is provided through a partnership between ALA and FIL (the large book fair held in Guadalajara) to provide support for ALA members wishing to attend FIL. The Free Pass Program includes three nights at a hotel (six if shared with a colleague also part of the program), three continental breakfasts, FIL registration, and a stipend toward the costs of airfare. In 2010 the program was available for 150 school, public, and academic librarians working in the area of Spanish-language acquisitions and/or to build Spanish-language collections to better serve their communities. Notably, FIL also provides free registration to all American librarians interested in attending FIL even if not selected for the Free Pass Program.

The idea of attending FIL was exciting, because it is considered the most important exhibition of Spanish-language books in the world. Created in 1987 by the University of Guadalajara, this nine-day fair offers firsthand access to more than 300,000 titles and to the complete catalogs of more than 1,600 editorial houses from 40 countries. It also provides a festive site for networking opportunities with 15,000 book professionals as well as 600 hours of programming. Each year FIL is visited by more than half a million people including authors, academics, artists, intellectuals, local residents, and 100,000 children and adolescents. Events include lectures on Mexican culture, music, and presentations by Latin American authors, all of which draw large crowds and set the stage for an interchange of ideas around contemporary Hispanic culture(s). Additionally, FIL features a different invited Guest of Honor country or region each year.

We decided that the ALA-FIL Free Pass would provide the perfect opportunity to advance our small collection of Spanish-language books and quickly scrambled to complete the application process. This resulted in a significant budgetary commitment from the university library to purchase books, as well as great support from the university's Center for Teaching Through Children's Books and its co-director, Junko Yokota. Armed with the strength of this new and growing partnership, we were extremely pleased when we were each awarded the Free Pass.

THE FIL EXPERIENCE

In preparation for the FIL trip, Barb conducted another statewide library search, this time to better determine the numbers of preK-12 Spanish-language texts available in university and public libraries. She discovered that most collections were very small, primarily comprising translations of English-language books or U.S.-published bilingual and Spanish-language editions/translations. Very few Latin American authors were represented in these collections, although some public libraries held small numbers of such books. This finding added to our excitement as the November date of FIL approached, and we began identifying potential titles for purchase.

Working with the Center for Teaching Through Children's Books, we started our search for Spanish-language book titles. We compiled a list from titles recommended by A Leer/IBBY Mexico and from reviews in professional journals (Arizpe 2007a, 2007b; Beuchat 2000). We also gathered titles of works by familiar Argentinean, Chilean, and Costa Rican authors identified in my own professional experiences. In addition we consulted two important Web sites, the first being the database available through the Barahona Center for the Study of Books in Spanish for Children and Adolescents/Centro para el Estudio de Libros Infantiles y Juveniles en Español. The Barahona Center's Web site provides invaluable information based on the work of the center's recently retired director, Isabel Schon—a compilation of Spanish-language book recommendations in journal articles and books spanning more than 30 years. The Barahona Center's Web database provides information in both English and Spanish about more than 10,000 Latino-themed texts, as well as books in Spanish. Books reviewed on this site are published both in the United States and internationally, and they are notable for their quality of art, writing, presentation of material, and appeal to the intended audience. The second online resource consulted was *Críticas*, which provides English-language reviews by *Library Journal* and *School Library Journal* of children's titles from the national and international Spanish-language publishing world.

In the weeks leading up to FIL, the volume of information from publishers and advice from ALA and seasoned librarians left me amazed and a little apprehensive as I was apparently the only non-librarian in the grant-sponsored group. Barb sifted through vendor offers of assistance, and selected Latin American Book Source, Inc., because of its mission to serve as a bridge to the Spanish-speaking world and its commitment to provide any print title published in Latin America or Spain. The feelings of apprehension quickly dissipated when we connected with librarians from other states on our journey to Mexico. Upon arrival we decided to visit the fair during general public hours, before the professional time slots started. I experienced a sense of awe at the initial sight of the vast exposition building, which extended as far as the eye could see and was filled with books and people. A personal meeting with our book vendor, together with ALA informational sessions and numerous tips on how to get the most out of FIL, prepared us for finding texts of interest among the many publishers on the floor.

The next day we woke early and made our way back to the exposition center where we worked as a team. I communicated in Spanish to request books, sought advice from publishers' representatives, reviewed the piles of books stacked before me at each stand, and made purchase decisions. Barb diligently recorded titles and other information to provide to our vendor for purchase, and kept us highly organized. We did make a point to visit the Salón del Libro (now called the Salón de Novedades), which housed what were considered the "best picks" of books sold at the fair. This area was a great resource and granted a brief respite from our routine, which slowly resulted in a mounting exhaustion as the day lengthened. With so many books to scan, it was difficult to keep all our purchase criteria in mind. We sought materials that represented as many Latin American countries as possible, were suitable for preK–12, represented different genres and formats (including graphic novels, board books, and "big books"), and would be useful for varying instructional purposes (such as books for read-alouds, leveled books for guided reading, books for literature circles, and texts appropriate for Descubriendo la Lectura). We ended the day at a table in the Uruguayan stand where I read the following title, which prompted laughter: *Una pulga interplanetaria* (Velando 2007). To date, so few Latino-themed fantasy or science fiction books have been published in the United States that this title was a welcome sight at the end of a long day! We spent the next two days scrambling to spend our entire budget, a task difficult to accomplish one book at a time.

PLANS FOR CONTINUED COLLECTION DEVELOPMENT

We were surprised to receive our new books only a few months after the fair. The librarians and staff delighted in opening the boxes and reviewing the brightly colored texts from so many different countries. Cataloging decisions were made and the books were interfiled with the regular collection to make sure that students would run across them when browsing. At the same time, the books were highlighted in a specialized Web-based LibGuide, which then allowed for limited searches of this collection.

These purchases raised the Américas Collection to more than 700 books, and we began making presentations at national conferences, such as the United States Board on Books for Young People biannual convention, as well as at local conferences, faculty meetings, and classes.

Today, the Américas Collection provides teachers and librarians across the Chicago metropolitan region with model texts for classroom instruction, library programs, and collection development. The National-Louis University Library continues to commit funds each year to expand the collection, and professional trips I make to Latin American countries generally coincide with a book fair, such as FIL in La Paz, Bolivia, in August 2009. I comb these fairs, speak with authors, collect publishers' catalogs, and bring these materials back to our library for consideration for purchase. We also scrutinize the Salon del Novidades selections posted electronically by FIL Guadalajara, the titles recommended annually by IBBY, and the winners of other Spanish-language book awards.

According to an African proverb, "it takes a village to raise a child." In our case, it took a turtle to build an extensive Spanish-language collection. A little green turtle named Manuelita, a well-loved character in Argentinean children's literature, helped spur a university partnership and led to a new collection of books rich in Spanish-language materials. The development process resulted in the compilation of important online resources for Spanish-language books and materials. Some of these resources are highlighted below, together with our favorite books from the Américas Collection (see also http://libguides. nl.edu/americascollection). It is my hope in sharing the story of the Américas Collection that librarians and teachers will understand the steps involved in developing a collection of high-quality, Spanish-language texts for children and adolescents, and become aware of the many resources available for locating these materials.

REFERENCES

Arizpe, Evelyn. "Finding a Voice: The Development of Mexican Children's Literature, Part I." *Bookbird: A Journal of International Children's Literature* 45 (2007a): 5–13.

———. "Finding a Voice: The Development of Mexican Children's Literature, Part II." *Bookbird: A Journal of International Children's Literature* 45 (2007b): 29–37.

Barrera, Rosalinda B., and Oralia Garza de Cortes. "Mexican American Children's Literature in the 1990s: Toward Authenticity." In *Using Multiethnic Children's Literature in Grades K–8,* ed. by Violet J. Harris, 129–154. Norwood, MA: Christopher Gordon Publishers, 1997.

Barrera, Rosalinda B., and Ruth E. Quiroa. "The Use of Spanish in Latino Children's Literature in English: What Makes for Cultural Authenticity?" In *Stories Matter: The Complexity of Cultural Authenticity in Children's Literature,* ed. by Diane L. Fox and Kathy G. Short, 247–265. Urbana, IL: National Council of Teachers of English, 2003.

Beuchat, Cecilia. "Chile, a Country with Poetry for Children." *Bookbird: A Journal of International Children's Literature 38* (2000): 36–39.

Cai, Mingshui. *Multicultural Literature for Children and Young Adults: Reflections on Critical Issues.* Westport, CT: Greenwood Press, 2002.

Fry, Richard and Jeffrey S. Passel. "Report: Latino Children: A Majority Are U.S.-Born Offspring of Immigrants." Washington, DC: Pew Hispanic Center, 2009. http://pewhispanic.org/files/reports/110.pdf (accessed December 22, 2009).

Guerriero, Leila. "En el país de María Elena." *La Nación,* July 31, 2005. Revista section.

Hill, Jane D., and Kathleen M. Flynn, *Classroom Instruction that Works with English Language Learners.* Alexandria, VA: Association for Supervision and Curriculum Development, 2006.

Ready, Timothy, and Allert Brown-Goert. *The State of Latino Chicago: This Is Home Now.* Notre Dame: Institute for Latino Studies, Notre Dame, 2005. http://www.nd.edu/~latino/pubs/pubs/StateofLatino-final.pdf (accessed December 16, 2009). Also available in print form.

U.S. Census Bureau. "Fact for Features: Hispanic Heritage Month 2009, Sept. 15–Oct. 15." http://www.census.gov/Press-Release/www/releases/archives/facts_for_features_special_editions/013984.html (accessed December 10, 2009).

———. "Hispanic and Asian Americans Increasing Faster than Overall Population." Press release. 30 December 2005. http://www.census.gov/Press-Release/www/releases/archives/race/001839.html

Velando, Helen. *Una pulga interplanetaria.* Montevideo, Uruguay: Editorial Sudamericana Uruguaya, 2007.

Walsh, María. *Manuelita.* Buenos Aires: Editorial Alfaguara, Colección AlfaWalsh (Pequeños Lectores), 2005.

ONLINE RESOURCES

A Leer/IBBY México. "A Leer"
http://www.ibbymexico.org.mx/ (accessed December 19, 2009).
This is the Web site of the Mexican national section of the International Board on Books for Young People (IBBY). It provides important links to upcoming local and international events relating to Spanish-language books for children and adolescents, as well as to their publications relating to literature for children.

American Library Association. "Celebrate the Guadalajara International Book Fair with ALA FIL FREE PASS Program"
http://www.ala.org/ala/aboutala/offices/iro/awardsactivities/guadalajarabook.cfm (accessed December 19, 2009).
The American Library Association and the Feria Internacional del Libro (FIL) in Guadalajara, Mexico, partner to provide support for ALA members to attend FIL in late November through early December each year. Applications are generally due the last week in August, and this award covers hotel, breakfast, FIL registration, and a stipend to offset airfare costs.

Biblioteca Virtual Miguel de Cervantes. "La biblioteca de literatura infantil y juvenil."
http://www.cervantesvirtual.com/seccion/bibinfantil/ (accessed December 20, 2009).
This Web site is a virtual catalog of Spanish and Spanish American authors for children and adolescents, as well as magazines, stories, author libraries, classic books on tape, workshops, and links to related research and educational sites.

California State University of California, San Marcos. "Barahona Center for the Study of Books in Spanish for Children and Adolescents/Centro para el Estudio de Libros Infantiles y Juveniles en Español."
http://www2.csusm.edu/csb (accessed December 17, 2009).
This site provides a searchable database of recommended books published in Spanish, both in the United States and in other countries, as well as Latino-themed literature.

Cuatrogatos. "Cuatrogatos: Libros para Niños y Jovenes."
http://www.cuatrogatos.org/index.shtml (accessed December 17, 2009).
This portal is dedicated to books in Spanish for children and adolescents. It is based in Miami, Florida.

EdeLIJ. "EdeLIJ: Espacio de Literatura Infantil y Juvenil."
http://www.espaciodelij.blogspot.com/ (accessed August 26, 2010).
The EdeLIJ site is home to a free virtual bulletin produced monthly in Argentina
and dedicated to the discussion of themes relating to literature for children and
adolescents. Regular sections focus on national and international topics, and the site
provides extensive links to the sites of authors, journals, and important organizations
relating to Spanish-language literature.

Fundación para el Fomento de la Lectura. "Fundalectura."
http://www.fundalectura.org/# (accessed December 19, 2009).
Fundalectura is a Colombian site that promotes reading and literature for children
and adolescents and includes lists of recently published, recommended books.

Fundación para el Fomento de la Lectura. "Fundalectura: Premio latinoamericano
de literatura infantil y juvenil Norma."
http://www.fundalectura.org/sccs/seccion.php?id_seccion=11 (accessed December 20,
2009).
An award initiated in 1996 by Fundalectura and the Grupo Editorial Norma
publishing company is described here. The award seeks to stimulate the creation
of literary Latin American works for children and adolescents. Unpublished works
written in Spanish and Portuguese (from Brazilian writers) may be considered for the
award.

Fundación SM. "Literatura infantil y juvenil."
http://www.fundacion-sm.com/ver_seccion.aspx?id=4772 (accessed December 20,
2009).
Links to several important Spanish-language literature and illustrator awards are
available here.

Guadalajara International Book Fair. "Guadalajara International Book Fair."
http://www.fil.com.mx/ingles/i_index.asp (accessed December 18, 2009).
This site provides multiple links with information about Feria Internacional del Libro
(FIL), including a searchable database for the Salón de Novedades (formerly called the
salón de libros). This database comprises books published during the year prior to FIL
(including books for children and adolescents), as selected by experts in the field of
literature.

Imaginaria. "Imaginaria: Revista quincenal sobre literatura infantil y juvenil."
http://www.imaginaria.com.ar/ (accessed December 20, 2009).
This bimonthly online journal originated in Buenos Aires, Argentina, in 1999. It
focuses on literature for children and adolescents and is directed by teachers, parents,
librarians, authors, illustrators, and specialists in the field.

International Board on Books for Young People. "IBBY."
http://www.ibby.org/ (accessed December 20, 2009).
The site provides extensive information relating to international literature. Honor lists of high-quality literature from around the world appear, including titles of books originally published in Spanish. Additionally, links provide information about the prestigious Hans Christian Andersen Award given to a living author for his or her body of works. The list of winners includes authors whose works were originally published in Spanish.

La casa del árbol. "La casa del árbol: Un lugar para fomentar la lectura y niñez peruana."
http://i-elanor.typepad.com/casadelarbol/ (accessed December 18, 2009).
This Peruvian Web site provides book reviews and information relating to Peruvian authors and illustrators, as well as links to digital libraries of literature for children.

Latin American Book Source, Inc. "Latin American Book Source, Inc."
http://www.latambooks.com/ (accessed December 18, 2009).
Latin American Book Source's site provides one of the largest and most up-to-date selections of books and audiobooks from Latin America and Spain. The mission is to be a bridge to the Spanish-speaking world, and the company has a commitment to provide any in-print title published in Latin America or Spain.

Latino Book and Family Festival.
http://lbff.us/latino-book-awards (accessed December 16, 2009).
The Latino Book and Family Festival is sponsored by Latino Literacy Now, a nonprofit organization that supports and promotes literacy and literary excellence within the Latino community. The festival honors literary excellence in a variety of categories, including several for children and adolescents.

Miguel D. Cervantes. "Babar: Revista de literature infantile y juvenile."
http://www.cervantesvirtual.com/hemeroteca/babar/ (accessed December 18, 2009).
This site holds the archives of *Babar*, a journal of literature for children and adolescents, from March 1989 through October 2000.

Multicultural Books and Videos. "Multicultural Books and Videos."
http://multiculturalbooksandvideos.com/mcbv/Main (accessed December 19, 2009).
This company specializes in providing material in more than 40 languages to North America, including an extensive collection of materials from around the world. Materials include books, dictionaries, CDs, DVDs, and audiobooks.

National-Louis University. "Américas Collection."
http://libguides.nl.edu/content.php?pid=20562&sid=261985&search_terms=Americas (accessed August 26, 2010).

This resource guide for the Américas Collection provides a direct link to its focus catalog, which allows specific searches of the collection materials.

Reed Business Information. "Críticas: An English Speaker's Guide to the Latest in Spanish Language Titles." http://www.libraryjournal.com/csp/cms/sites/LJ/Reviews/Spanish/index.csp (accessed August 21, 2010).
This online journal, sponsored by *Library Journal* and *School Library Journal*, provides English-language book reviews of literature published in Spanish.

RevistaBabar.com. "Revistababar.com: Revista de literatura infantil y juvenil." http://revistababar.com/wp/ (accessed December 18, 2009).
This is an online journal of literature for children and adolescents. It provides articles, author interviews, an encyclopedia of important authors, news relating to literature, book reviews, awards books, and information relating to newly published texts.

Santillana USA. "Santillana USA." http://www.santillanausa.com/ (accessed December 19, 2009).
Santillana USA is a subsidiary of Grupo Santillana and one of the largest educational publishers in the Spanish-speaking world. The company provides second-language instructional materials and children's literature for K–12 education, with some books and DVDs available as kits for recommended age levels. This site provides information relating to the texts available through Santillana.

Scholastic. "Lectorum." http://www.lectorum.com/ (accessed December 19, 2009).
Lectorum is a division of Scholastic, and its site provides information about the more than 25,000 Spanish-language titles the company provides. This company is the U.S. distributor of children's books for Anaya, Bruño, Corimbo, Edebé, Edilupa, Ekaré, Entrelibros, Everest, Fondo de Cultura Económica, Global, La Galera, Juventud, Kalandraka, Kókinos, Litexsa, Lóguez, Melhoramentos, Molino, Noguer, Serres, and Tandem.

CHAPTER 7

Latino Children's Literature and Literacy in School Library Media Centers

Jamie Campbell Naidoo and Hope Crandall

Latino children's literature has the potential to make a rich and varied contribution to the academic and social lives of children in U.S. schools. It is essential for Latino children to find their heritage reflected in library and curricular materials, as well as in school activities. Access to positive materials authentically and accurately reflecting Latino cultures also helps children of other ethnicities gain appreciation for and knowledge of this significant part of the U.S. population. Even if school staff and students are not predominantly Latino, the school library media center (SLMC) can and should provide materials and activities that represent the wide diversity of the peoples of many countries in Latin America. In schools that support the learning and use of Spanish and English, the SLMC can serve as the heart of this endeavor, assisting English as a Second Language (ESL) educators and English Language Learners (ELLs). The SLMC is therefore in a unique position to impact the lives of many children, especially those who sometimes feel "other" because of their culture or linguistic skills.

Collaboration and leadership roles are inherent in the responsibilities of SLMC staff. Promoting appropriate and culturally diverse materials and finding ways to incorporate them into the curricular and social life of the school are part of these responsibilities. When teachers request library resources on a topic, the SLMC staff can think widely to add resources that reflect the Latino cultures. This chapter provides suggestions for library media specialists that will help broaden their understanding of how to select, organize, and utilize Spanish-language and Latino cultural materials in the SLMC. Many of the suggestions for materials and collections development are also applicable to classroom teachers, ESL teachers, public librarians, and other educators serving Latino and Spanish-speaking children.

MATERIALS IN THE SLMC

Traditionally an SLMC collection serves the educational and recreational reading needs of the school population, which includes educators, students, and parents. An updated collection includes print and electronic materials as well as realia and visual and audio materials. In addition to building a collection in English, a bilingual school needs to build a strong collection of Spanish and Spanish/English bilingual materials for everyone. Equity in materials dictates locating, purchasing, promoting, and using the fullest array of materials that the school can afford. This section highlights various types of materials for the SLMC collection, including books, magazines, Web sites, audiobooks, music, videos, cultural dolls, and realia.

Books

Books form the backbone of the collection. Many books portray multicultural themes and characters, some are authored or illustrated by Latinos, and some are available in Spanish or bilingual editions. Decisions about where to shelve the bilingual and Spanish books should be made on the basis of what best serves the needs of the users. In some bilingual schools all materials are shelved together regardless of language, with some highly visible designation on the book spines indicating the language. In other schools materials are shelved separately by language. The spine label call numbers may have S or Sp at the top. Bilingual books are often housed with Spanish books, perhaps with a bilingual label. Separating books by language assists the youngest browsers and their parents in finding books in the language they want. Care should be taken that the shelving does not give preferential treatment to either language. Recommended books on a variety of topics of interest to Latino children will be discussed later in this chapter.

Magazines and Web Sites

Magazines and Web sites offer informational and recreational materials in an appealing format, often providing more current information than is available in book format. While it can be difficult to locate high-quality, age-appropriate Web sites for children in Spanish, particularly if a school library media specialist does not speak the language, it is important to ensure that Spanish-speaking Latino children have access to high-interest, high-quality Web sites. Fortunately, REFORMA (an affiliate of the American Library Association dedicated to serving Latinos and Spanish-speaking patrons) and the Broward County (FL)

Library have provided a helpful Web site, entitled Great Web Sites in Spanish para Niños, which lists recommended Web sites of interest to a wide age-range of children. The site is available at http://libraries.tds.lib.mn.us/smile/ Great%20Sites%20for%20Kids%20in%20Spanish%20compiled%20by%20 YSADM.htm.

English-language periodicals can be augmented with Spanish-language magazines to ensure that all children have access to exciting, recreational reading regardless of their linguistic abilities. The following recommended Spanish-language periodicals present topics that relate to curricular areas commonly covered in schools and are not heavy with pop culture.

Iguana is a Spanish-language magazine published in Arizona for children ages 7 to 12. Highly regarded by teachers, students, and parents, the magazine contains kid-friendly articles, short stories, interviews with notable Latino figures, and a variety of activities that span the curriculum. More information on the magazine can be found at http://www.nicagal.com/iguana/ eng/index.html.

Covering a range of age levels, several Spanish-language children's magazines are published in Spain by Bayard Revistas. *Caracola*, intended for children ages 4 to 6, contains games, activities, short stories, comic strips, book suggestions, and other information of interest to this age group. More information on *Caracola* can be found at http://www.conmishijos.com/ rincones2/rinconCARACOLA/. Created for children ages 7 to 9, *Leo Leo* provides levelized fiction stories (by leading Latin American children's authors and illustrators), games, informational bytes, comic strips, recipes, and activities that are appropriate for boys and girls in this age group. Additional information on *Leo Leo* can be found at http://www.conmishijos.com/rincones2/ rinconLEOLEO/. Intended for children ages 9 and up, *Reportero Doc* is a visually appealing, nonfiction magazine covering a wide range of topics that support the curriculum. It contains eye-catching photographs, projects, hands-on activities, comic strips, informational bytes, and stories with high appeal to all children, particularly boys. Additional information on the magazine, including an online preview, can be found at http://www.conmishijos.com/ rincones2/rinconREPORTERO/. For tweens and adolescents, *Okapi* is a high-interest, visually appealing magazine covering a wide range of topics of interest to the junior high and older crowd. It includes comic strips, news bytes, unusual and interesting facts, and interviews with celebrities. An online preview of the magazine and further information can be found at http://www.conmishijos. com/rincones2/rinconOKAPI/.

For children in grades 1 to 3, Scholastic produces a bilingual, leveled-reading magazine called *Scholastic News English/Español*, which contains flashy pictures, informational bytes, stories, activities, and other topics of interest to both English-speaking and ELL children. Additional information on this magazine is available at http://teacher.scholastic.com/products/classmags/sn_esp.htm. Scholastic also publishes Spanish-language magazines of interest to upper elementary children, tweens, and adolescents. *Ahora* (grades 6 to 8), *¿Qué tal?* (grades 4 to 6), and *El sol* (grades 8 to 12) all provide high-interest, age-appropriate, educational, recreational, and informational articles, news bytes, and activities covering topics in Latin American countries and around the world. More information on these magazines can be found at http://teacher.scholastic.com/products/classmags/mgm_spanish.htm.

Skipping Stones is a nonprofit, international, multicultural magazine for elementary-age children. Published in Oregon, the periodical includes submissions of poetry, short stories, and letters written by children around the world, describing their daily lives and culture, global understanding, and intercultural connections. The magazine includes writings in many languages, with the original language plus an English translation. More information on the magazine is available from http://www.skippingstones.org/.

Read-Alongs/Audiobooks

Books with recordings are a very popular, important purchase for the SLMC. Often labeled by vendors as "read-alongs," audiobooks have a unique educational role to fill in schools. Audiobooks can improve both the reading and linguistic abilities of children trying to learn the English language, making it important to include audiobooks in library collections serving Latino youth who do not speak English. Those read-alongs that offer the recording, as well as the book, in both English and Spanish are especially valuable to both young Latino children and their families. Parents and students who wish to boost their first or second language often clamor for them. The Educational Record Center (http://www.erckids.com) makes many of these read-alongs available. Cinco Puntos Press, a publisher of Latino-themed Spanish and English stories, has various audiobook versions of its books as well (http://www.cincopuntos.com/). Similarly, Live Oak Media has bilingual and Latino picture-book read-alongs (http://www.liveoakmedia.com/) as do Scholastic (http://www.scholastic.com/librarians/) and its Spanish-language imprint, Lectorum (http://www.lectorum.com/eng/) .

Special audiobooks can also be purchased that specifically aid non-English-speaking Latinos with their English-language acquisition. These audiobooks are read at a slower pace and without the use of any distracting music. Examples of these special audiobooks are Carbo Recorded Books, produced in the United States by the National Reading Styles Institute (http:// www.nrsi.com/), and Smartreaders/Steadyreaders, produced in the United States by Recorded Books (http://www.recordedbooks.com/). Recorded Books also offers three additional products for assisting ELL students with language skills: English for You, Begin in English, and The Oxford Picture Dictionary.

Spanish-language audiobooks can be considered for the library collection, too. Recorded Books, Live Oak Media, and Listening Library (http:// www.randomhouse.com/audio/listeninglibrary/) all carry Spanish-language audiobooks appropriate for Latino and ELL children and their families. Also, school library media specialists can encourage Latino parents and family members to record themselves reading children's books in their native language. While duplicates of the recorded readings cannot be made available for circulation because of copyright issues, parents could share them with each other.

If an SLMC cannot afford to purchase audiobooks or read-alongs, there are numerous free online e-books featuring Latino topics and themes. These can be found on Web sites such as Reading Is Fundamental (http://www.rif.org/), Between the Lions (http://pbskids.org/lions/stories/), and the International Children's Digital Library (http://en.childrenslibrary.org/). Incidentally, this last resource includes books published in Latin American countries and written in the country's native language. A listing of some additional e-books and Latino children's literature resources can be found on the Imaginense Libros Blog (http://imaginenselibros.blogspot.com/).

Music

Another surefire way to incorporate Latino cultures and heritage into the SLMC collection and program is through Spanish and Latin American music. Latino music provides both Latino and non-Latino children with a rich resource that reinforces and celebrates the Latino cultures. In addition, Latino children's music and Spanish-language children's music can provide non-Spanish-speaking librarians with examples of how particular rhymes, songs, and words should be sung and pronounced. Numerous Latino songbooks and music CDs are available for youth. Popular artists include José-Luis Orozco, Suni Paz, Maria Elena Walsh, and Tish Hinojosa.

José-Luis Orozco, a native of Mexico City now living in California, has created 13 collections of children's songs, games, and rhymes, available in songbook, cassette, or CD formats. Three of his collections (*De colores, Diez deditos,* and *Fiestas*) have been illustrated by Elisa Kleven. In a lively and energetic bilingual DVD, he sings and shares his songs. Orozco's music collections are available at http://www.joseluisorozco.com/.

Suni Paz, a musical artist from Argentina now living in the United States, has worked with Latina authors Alma Flor Ada and F. Isabel Campoy to create *Música amiga*, a collection of ten books and ten musical cassettes/CDs that combine poetry and song to teach Spanish. In addition to this collection, Paz has created numerous other musical collections and videos highlighting Latin American music and cultures. Her music melds a global social consciousness with her Latino roots, making it sonorous and appropriate for school use. More information on her work is available at http://www.folkways.si.edu/explore_folkways/suni_paz.aspx and http://www.delsolbooks.com/sunipaz.htm.

Also from Argentina, internationally acclaimed Maria Elena Walsh has created a large body of children's books, songs, and poetry collections in Spanish. Her music for young children is widely available in Latin America and is beginning to find popularity in the United States. For additional information on Walsh, consult http://www.literatura.org/MEWalsh/MEWalsh.html and the *Críticas* article, "Doing the Alfawalsh: Argentina's Spirited Grand Dame of Children's Books Debuts in the United States" (Doss 2002).

Tish Hinojosa is a Mexican American Tejana who sings and composes wonderful children's music in English and Spanish. Her best-known songbook and music CD/cassette for children is *Cada niño/Every Child*, which received wide praise and several awards. The bilingual CD and songbook is available from Cinco Puntos Press. More information on the artist is available at http://www.mundotish.com/Tish_Hinojosa_Bio_2008.pdf.

From Mexico come the timeless Cri-Crí recordings of Francisco Gabilondo Soler, who created well-loved music for children in Mexico during the early part of the last century. Librarians can play his recordings during family activities in the library, and Latino parents will light up with smiles of recognition. Many of his songs are available for free download from the unofficial Web site Cri-Crí (http://www.cri-cri.net/), which also contains lyrics, biographical information on Cri-Crí, and a discography.

Films/Videos/DVDs

Many children's books, folktales, and stories have been reproduced in animated or movie format. Various Latino children's books, such as Gary Soto's *Chato's Kitchen* and *Too Many Tamales* and Nancy Andrew-Goebel's *The Pot that Juan Built*, have been animated by Weston Woods/Scholastic (www.scholastic.com). *Maya and Miguel*, an animated cartoon about Latino twins, is also created by

Scholastic. The series, airing on PBS, follows the adventures and misadventures of ten-year-olds Maya and Miguel Santos, and features their family, relatives, and diverse neighborhood of friends. For more information about the series, go to http://www.scholastic.com/mayaandmiguel/.

Spoken Arts, like Weston Woods, has iconographic videos (slightly modified, animated versions of book illustrations) of Latino children's books. Titles include *A Birthday Basket for Tía* by Pat Mora, *Alejandro's Gift* by Richard E. Albert, *No Dogs Allowed* by Sonia Manzano, and *The Umbrella* by Jan Brett. Information on Spoken Arts is available from http://www.spokenartsmedia. com/home.htm.

The literature-based, classic children's television program *Reading Rainbow* highlighted Latino children's books from time to time. Featured books include *Alejandro's Gift, Hill of Fire* by Thomas P. Lewis, *Saturday Sancocho* by Leyla Torres, *Bread Is for Eating* by David and Phillis Gershator, *My Little Island* by Frané Lessac, *A Chair for My Mother* by Vera B. Williams, and *Borreguita and the Coyote* by Verna Aardema. The videos/DVDs are available at http://gpn.unl. edu/rainbow/.

Cuentos y Más (Stories and More) is a bilingual (Spanish and English), Latino literacy television program that promotes reading, literacy, and cultural appreciation among both English- and Spanish-speaking children. Produced by the Arlington Virginia Network (AVN) and Arlington Public Library, the children's early literacy program shares stories, songs, and games relating to the Latino cultures. It also promotes the importance of books and libraries in the daily lives of children and their families. Think of a bilingual Reading Rainbow and you have Cuentos y Más. Free Webstreams of programs are available from http://www.arlingtonva.us/cuentos.

Disney Educational Video has a series much like *Reading Rainbow*, entitled *Beyond the Page*. Two videos in this series are based on the Latino children's books *Under the Lemon Moon*, by Edith Hope Fine, and *I Love Saturdays y domingos*, by Alma Flor Ada. Disney Educational Video is available at http://dep.disney.go.com/educational/store/.

Informational films on Latino cultures are also available. Schlessinger Media has produced several videos/DVDs about Latino cultures, including *Central American Heritage, Cesar Chavez, Cinco de Mayo*, the Mexico for Children series, *Mexican-American Heritage, My Family from Brazil, My Family from Chile, My Family from Cuba*, and *Puerto Rican Heritage*. More information is available from http://www.libraryvideo.com/. Master Communications also has three Latin American films in its Families of the World series (http://www. familiesoftheworld.com/products.html). They are filmed in the highlighted country and include *Families of Brazil, Families of Mexico, and Families of Puerto Rico*.

Puppets and Cultural Dolls

Puppets offer a great way for Latino children to explore their cultural heritage. Puppets provide a hands-on extension to Latino folktales and stories, allowing children to use their imagination to act out other plots or versions of the folktales that they know from their specific subculture. Puppetry can also be used as a nonthreatening way to help ELL Latino children master verbal English or to help children deal with social problems.

Although some Latino children are hesitant to participate in large group discussions with the librarian, our experience indicates that often they will not hesitate to interact with a puppet. Similarly, puppets can be used to explain confusing concepts encountered within informational text and to introduce cultural aspects found in folklore. Bilingual storytimes that include puppets help non-Spanish-speaking Latino and non-Latino children appreciate the Spanish language. Frey (2005) notes, "Puppet shows, like many good children's books, provide a mirror for children to see themselves in, often using animal characters to depict real human dilemmas—the types of situations and problems in which the children in the audience may find themselves. Somehow, it feels safe, less threatening, for the child to watch a puppet character deal with these problems. The child can vicariously 'test the waters.'" (p. 3).

There are several wonderful suppliers of puppets. Folkmanis creates detailed and affordable animal puppets that can accompany almost any story or Latino folktale. Sunny Puppets has a cheap assortment of human puppets of most ethnicities. Puppet Universe (www.puppetuniverse.com) has an extensive listing of various puppets and supplies, including the Sunny and Folkmanis brands. Lakeshore Learning (http://www.lakeshorelearning.com/) offers a number of puppet sets that include Latino characters—Let's Talk! Family, Let's Talk! Kid, Let's Talk! Community Helpers, and Let's Talk! Multicultural. Puppet Revelation (http://www.puppetrevelation.com/) has numerous character, animal, and human puppets in various styles: full body, hand, marionette, and finger puppets. Their human puppets are available in a variety of skin tones. Puppetville (http://www.puppetville.com/) has an extraordinary collection of marionettes in addition to free storytime scripts and instructions for operating the different puppet types.

Like puppets, cultural dolls also offer something unique to both Latino and non-Latino children in the SLMC. These dolls can be checked out as companions to read-along books and can be displayed along with posters to make the environment reflective of Latino cultures. They can be used as accessories during programs to make the stories come alive, and shared with children on a daily basis in song and rhyme programs. An example of a cultural doll is the ragdoll Rosalba, modeled after the girl in Arthur Dorros's *Abuela*. A more interactive cultural doll is Baby Abuelita, designed to look like a grandmother. This soft, plush doll sings traditional Latin American lullabies and is accompanied by an oversized board book that includes lyrics to the songs in Spanish and English as well as recordings of the actual rhyme. Librarians can play the songs from the book and sing with the children. The doll can be passed around at storytime or used as a storytelling prop. The accompanying Web site contains educator information, coloring pages, and Webstreams of cartoons featuring Baby Abuelita. Additional information can be found at http://babyabuelita.org/.

Realia and Decorations

It is well worth the effort to locate and display realia, decorations, and examples of arts and crafts from Latino cultures and Latin American countries. Including realia around the SLMC will help make the environment more reflective of the student population's culture and encourage non-Latino students to learn more about the Latino cultures. Children enjoy using all their senses to learn, and such objects add an invaluable, extra dimension to cultural studies. However, it is important to distinguish between the authentic and symbolic use of these objects in Latino and indigenous heritage rather than using them as mere decorations.

Student-made *ojos de dios* echo the Huichol culture of Sonora, Mexico. They are easily made of brightly colored yarn and dowels (or even pencils). Yarn and glue can also be used to replicate Huichol paintings. School library media specialists can share Endredy's *The Journey of Tunuri and the Blue Deer: A Huichol Indian Story* or Love's *Watákame's Journey: The Story of the Great Flood and the New World*, both of which include yarn-art illustrations created by Huichol Indians.

Piñatas also add a festive touch as they hang from the ceiling. These brightly decorated paper or clay figures containing candy, fruit, and small toys are hung and then broken during birthdays and other celebrations such as Christmas and *Día de los muertos*. It is important to explain that piñatas are not used on a daily basis in the Latino culture. Too often there is a misconception that Latino children spend much of their time swinging sticks at piñatas. A wonderful book to share with children about how piñatas are created is Ancona's *The Piñata Maker: El piñatero.*

Banners of *papel picado* can be hung across the library or classroom and used in conjunction with family and community celebrations, as is done in Mexico. Crepe-paper or tissue-paper flowers can also brighten up any space and accompany the cut-paper art. *Papel picado* banners can be purchased cheaply from party stores and Mexican groceries, or they can be created by the children themselves. Two wonderful books to share with children about the art of papel picado are Garza's *Magic Windows: Ventanas mágicas* and *Making Magic Windows: Creating Papel Picado/Cut-Paper Art with Carmen Lomas Garza.*

Media specialists can locate and display examples of famous Mexican arts and crafts such as *alebrijes* (fantastical wooden creatures with marvelous, painted details) and Talavera tiles and pottery. Colorful and whimsical figures, toys, and masks of clay, wood, metal, plant materials, and papier-mâché are popular with all ages. Many of these originate in Mexico. School librarians can also share books highlighting Mexican arts and crafts and invite artists or family members of Latino children to share the significance of various items. Picture books highlighting *alebrijes* and various Mexican pottery include Weill's *ABeCedarios: Mexican Folk Art ABCs in English and Spanish* and *Opuestos: Mexican Folk Art Opposites in English and Spanish,* Cohn's *Dream Carver,* and Andrews-Goebel's *The Pot that Juan Built.*

Molinillos, tortilleros, and *molcajetes* are several of the cooking utensils used everywhere in Mexico. Librarians should consider inviting family members of their Latino students to bring some of these utensils and demonstrate how they are used. Extending the demonstration with a cooking lesson will be a hit—most librarians know that food will draw just about anyone to the library!

Lotería is a favorite game commonly played throughout Mexico by both children and adults. It is a form of bingo that depicts many objects of Mexican culture. Having children create their own *lotería* cards to display and use in the school library could be a very exciting activity for both Latino and non-Latino children. Public libraries have even created library-themed *lotería* cards to help children learn the Spanish words for various library-related terms. Children's books related to the game include Laínez's *Playing Lotería/El juego de la lotería,* Contreras's *Trencitas/Braids,* and Morales's *Just in Case: A Trickster Tale and Spanish Alphabet Book.*

Media specialists will score a big hit with children, particularly boys, if they can find someone to drive to school in a lowrider. These hot-rod classic vehicles are the result of an artistic cultural practice that hydraulically alters the cars' suspension so they will ride as low as possible to the ground. The vehicles are given customized paint jobs and are frequently redecorated to make their interiors highly luxurious. Most owners are proud and pleased to show off their precious cars. Books to share with children about lowriders include Doeden's *Autos lowriders/Lowriders* and Soto's *My Little Car.*

Another crowd-pleaser for children, particularly girls, would be to invite someone (perhaps a students' relative) who recently celebrated her quinceañera. She could bring the flowing, frilly dress and her last doll to show, and explain what this fifteenth-year, coming-of-age ceremony signifies, and how grand it is. Three books for elementary children that could be shared are Hoyt-Goldsmith's *Celebrating a Quinceañera: A Latina's 15th Birthday Celebration*, McCormack's *The Fiesta Dress: A Quinceañera Tale*, and Bertrand's *The Last Doll/La última muñeca.*

The following books tie in with the use of realia to highlight Latino cultures:

Ancona, George. *The Piñata Maker: El piñatero.*

Andrews-Goebel, Nancy, and David Diaz. *The Pot That Juan Built.*

Bertrand, Diane Gonzales, and Anthony Accardo. *The Last Doll/La última muñeca.*

Cohn, Diana. *El tallador de sueños.*

Cohn, Diana, and Amy Córdova. *Dream Carver.*

Contreras, Kathleen, and Margaret Lindmark. *Trencitas/Braids.*

Doeden, Matt. *Autos lowriders/Lowriders.*

Endredy, James, María Hernández de la Cruz, and Casimiro de la Cruz López. *The Journey of Tunuri and the Blue Deer: A Huichol Indian Story.*

Garza, Carmen Lomas. *Magic Windows: Ventanas mágicas.*

———. *Making Magic Windows: Creating Papel Picado/Cut-Paper Art with Carmen Lomas Garza.*

Hoyt-Goldsmith, Diane. *Celebrating a Quinceañera: A Latina's 15th Birthday Celebration.*

Laínez, René Colato. *Playing Lotería/El juego de la lotería.*

Love, Hallie, and Bonnie Larson. *Love's Watákame's Journey: The Story of the Great Flood and the New World.*

McCormack, Caren McNelly, and Martha Avilés. *The Fiesta Dress: A Quinceañera Tale.*

Morales, Yuyi. *Just in Case: A Trickster Tale and Spanish Alphabet Book.*

Olmos, Gabriela. *Cómo bailan los monstruos.*

Soto, Gary. *My Little Car.*

Weill, Cynthia, K. B. Basseches, Moisés Jiménez, and Armando Jiménez. *ABeCedarios: Mexican Folk Art ABCs in English and Spanish.*

Weill, Cynthia, Quirino Santiago, and Martín Santiago. *Opuestos: Mexican Folk Art Opposites in English and Spanish.*

HOLIDAY PROGRAMS CELEBRATING LATINO CULTURES IN THE SLMC

A commonly employed and useful way to incorporate Latino heritage into library programming is to follow a calendar. However, cultural programming should not center solely on Latino holidays and celebrations. Highlighting these celebrations is only one avenue. It is important to showcase the contributions of Latinos throughout the year. Latino staff and parents can provide librarians with other ideas of how to incorporate Latino culture into their regular programs.

The recordings of José-Luis Orozco and adult books on Indo-Hispanic folk art traditions by Bobbi Salinas offer excellent music and activities for many Latino celebration days. Additionally Latino heritage can be highlighted throughout Hispanic Heritage Month, beginning on September 15 and ending October 15. Following are many of the most widely celebrated holidays:

September 16	El día de la independencia de México
November 1, 2	El día de los muertos
December 12	El día de la virgen de Guadalupe
December 19–24	Las Posadas
December 25	La Navidad
January 5, 6	El día de los tres magos
April 30	El día de los niños/El día de los libros
May 5	El cinco de Mayo

El día de la independencia de México (Mexican Independence Day)

With an impassioned shout by the Catholic priest Miguel Hidalgo y Costilla on September 16, 1810, the struggle for independence from Spain was launched. It is important for all children to know about this monumental event in Mexican history. The following books are useful for students and teachers wanting to expand their knowledge of this celebration:

Burr, Claudia, Krystyna Libura, and Ma C. Urrutia. *Doña Josefa y sus conspiraciones.*

Bustos, Eduardo. *El panteón de la patria: Calaveras de la Independencia.*

De Varona, Frank. *Miguel Hidalgo y Costilla: Father of Mexican Independence.*

Gerson, Sara. *Una nueva nación: México independiente.*

MacMillan, Dianne M. *Mexican Independence Day and Cinco de Mayo.*

El día de los muertos (All Souls' Day)

For several days at the beginning of November, loved ones who have died are remembered in Latin American cultures in *El día de los muertos* ceremonies. This tradition marries indigenous and Catholic religious beliefs throughout Latin America in both family and communal activities. Librarians can invite family and community members to speak about the holiday from their own experiences. Students can make comparisons with Halloween, build an altar of remembrance, prepare sugar skulls, construct a kite, make *pan de muertos* (bread), cut out *calaveras* (skeletons), and write remembrance poems. The following resources provide additional information on the Day of the Dead:

Amado, Elisa. *Un barrilete para el Día de los muertos.*

Ancona, George. *Pablo recuerda: La fiesta del Día de los muertos.*

―――. *Pablo Remembers: The Fiesta of the Day of the Dead.*

Celebrating History—Texas Style.

Gnojewski, Carol. *El Día de los muertos: Una celebración de la familia y la vida.*

Hiriart, Berta. *En días de muertos.*

Hoyt-Goldsmith, Diane. *Day of the Dead: A Mexican-American Celebration.*

Lasky, Kathryn. *Days of the Dead.*

Montes, Marisa, and Yuyi Morales. *Los Gatos Black on Halloween.*

San Vicente, Luis. *The Festival of the Bones/El festival de las calaveras.*

Winter, Jeanette. *Calavera abecedario: A Day of the Dead Alphabet Book.*

El día de la virgen de Guadalupe (Our Lady of Guadalupe Day)

On December 12, 1531, Mary the mother of Jesus appeared miraculously to a poor Indian. Her appearance was taken as a sign to build a shrine where Mexico City now stands. Mary, or Our Lady of Guadalupe, is the patron saint of Mexico and much of the Americas. Many Mexicans who do not adhere to the predominant Roman Catholic Church nonetheless consider themselves Guadalupanos. Mary represents the essence of Mexico, the fusion of two cultures, Catholic Spain and indigenous Mexico. Included in the list below are English and Spanish editions of a book by Serrano; the pop-up format makes these items popular with all ages. The book by de Avalle-Arce includes many of the most revered madonnas of Mexico. It features clear, attractive drawings that students like to copy in their artwork.

> de Avalle-Arce, Diane. *Madonas de Mexico.*
> dePaola, Tomie. *The Lady of Guadalupe.*
> ———. *Nuestra señora de Guadalupe.*
> Serrano, Francisco. *La virgen de Guadalupe.*
> Serrano, Francisco, and Eugenia Guzmán. *Our Lady of Guadalupe.*
> Stuart, Kelly. *Canción de cuna de la virgen de Guadalupe.*

Las Posadas

The Christmas season lasts for many weeks, and for Latinos several celebrations are woven throughout the festivities. One of the most widely enjoyed is *Las Posadas*, from December 16 to Christmas Eve. In commemoration of Mary and Joseph's search for shelter in Bethlehem, people journey from house to house in their neighborhoods singing and praying. On the 24th they finish with a celebration, which typically includes a piñata for the children. Mary Hall Ets's book *Nine Days to Christmas*, one of many books that tell of *Las Posadas*, won the Caldecott Medal in 1960.

> Ancona, George. *Fiesta U.S.A.*
> dePaola, Tomie. *The Night of Las Posadas.*
> Ets, Marie H., and Aurora Labastida. *Nine Days to Christmas.*
> Hoyt-Goldsmith, Diane. *Las Posadas: A Hispanic Christmas Celebration.*
> Kroll, Virginia L. *Uno, dos, tres, posada!/Let's Celebrate Christmas.*

Mora, Pat, and Charles R. Berg. *The Gift of the Poinsettia / El regalo de la flor de nochebuena.*

La Navidad (Christmas Day)

On *La Navidad* families and friends join together for mass at church and family dinners. Presents are not exchanged as the focus of this *celebración* is the birth of Christ. Many homes and central city parks display elaborate nativities. The following picture books are recommended:

Ada, Alma Flor. *The Christmas Tree / El árbol de Navidad: A Christmas Rhyme in English and Spanish.*

Ada, Alma Flor, and F. Isabel Campoy. *Merry Navidad! Christmas Carols in English and Spanish / Merry Navidad: Villancicos en español e inglés.*

Anaya, Rudolfo A. *Farolitos for Abuelo.*

———. *The Farolitos of Christmas.*

———. *The Santero's Miracle: A Bilingual Story.*

dePaola, Tomie. *The Legend of the Poinsettia.*

———. *La leyenda de la flor de nochebuena.*

Elya, Susan Middleton, Merry Banks, and Joe Cepeda. *N Is for Navidad.*

Jiménez, Francisco. *The Christmas Gift / El regalo de Navidad.*

Oppenheim, Joanne. *El milagro de la primera flor de Nochebuena.*

Soto, Gary. *Qué montón de tamales!*

———. *Too Many Tamales!*

Thaae, Soren. *Navidad de papel.*

El día de los tres magos (Three Kings Day)

On Three Kings Day (January 5 or 6) the wise men gave gifts to baby Jesus, so that is when children receive their presents for the Christmas season. Special foods at this time include an egg bread, hot chocolate, and often tamales. Below are books that are about or include elements of Three Kings Day:

Alvarez, Julia, and Ruddy Núñez. *El mejor regalo del mundo: La leyenda de la Vieja Belén / The Best Gift of All: The Legend of La Vieja Belén.*

Carlson, Lori Marie, and Ed Martinez. *Hurray for Three Kings' Day!*

González, Lucía, and Lulu Delacre. *The Storyteller's Candle / La velita de los cuentos.*

Hoyt-Goldsmith, Diane. *Three Kings Day: A Celebration at Christmastime.*

Lázaro León, Georgina, and Morella Fuenmayor. *¡Ya llegan los reyes magos!*

Mora, Pat, and Magaly Morales. *A Piñata in a Pine Tree: A Latino Twelve Days of Christmas.*

Slate, Joseph. *The Secret Stars.*

Vidal, Beatriz. *Federico and the Magi's Gift: A Latin American Christmas Story.*

El día de los niños/El día de los libros

Many nations designate a date for Children's Day. In Mexico it is April 30. American author Pat Mora chose this date in 1996 to found *Día de los niños/Día de los libros*. Día, as the holiday is commonly called, celebrates children and books. It advances multicultural and multilingual literacy for all children. While the holiday is associated with April 30, the activities can be incorporated into year-round programming. Many libraries also plan a month of Día activities in April with a finale on April 30. Libraries, schools, and other agencies and organizations that serve families across the country collaborate to strengthen family literacy through Día celebrations. The Association for Library Service to Children (ALSC), a division of the American Library Association, is now a national clearinghouse for Día celebrations. REFORMA, the National Association to Promote Library and Information Services to Latinos and the Spanish Speaking, is also a major supporter of and collaborator in Día activities. Additional ideas and planning information for Día celebrations can be found in other chapters in this book. Mora recently wrote this book, to spread what she calls "book joy":

Mora, Pat, and Rafael López. *Book Fiesta! Celebrate Children's Day/Book Day/Book Fiesta: Celebremos El día de los niños/El día de los libros.*

Cinco de Mayo (May 5th)

El cinco de Mayo commemorates another important juncture in Mexican history. It often is more broadly observed in the United States than Mexican Independence Day. On May 5, 1862, Mexican peasants defeated occupying French soldiers. This historic victory is a symbol of freedom, patriotism, and success against greater forces. Speeches, parades, dances, dramas, and manifestations of cultural pride entertain and remind Latinos of their grand heritage.

Campoy, F. Isabel, and Alma Flor Ada. *Celebra el Cinco de mayo con un jarabe tapatío.*

———. *Celebrate Cinco de Mayo with the Mexican Hat Dance.*

Flanagan, Alice K. *Cinco de mayo.*

Gnojewski, Carol. *Cinco de mayo: Se celebra el orgullo.*

Hoyt-Goldsmith, Diane, and Lawrence Migdale. *Cinco de Mayo: Celebrating the Traditions of Mexico.*

Levy, Janice. *Celebrate! It's Cinco de Mayo!/¡Celebremos! ¡Es el Cinco de mayo!*

MacMillan, Dianne M. *Mexican Independence Day and Cinco de Mayo.*

Palacios, Argentina, and Alex Haley. *¡Viva México! The Story of Benito Juárez and Cinco de Mayo.*

Urrutia, Ma C. *La batalla del Cinco de mayo: Ayer y hoy.*

Saying Gracias and Giving Thanks

Although Thanksgiving is not a specific holiday observed in Latin America, it is important to remind children to give thanks every day for the many things that they have. Often school library media specialists celebrate Thanksgiving by reading books about the holiday. Below are a few books relating to Latino cultures that incorporate ideas of giving thanks:

Ada, Alma Flor, and Vivi Escrivá. *¿Pavo para la cena de gracias? ¡No gracias!*

Ada, Alma Flor, and Simón Silva. *Gathering the Sun: An Alphabet in Spanish and English.*

Alvarez, Julia, and Beatriz Vidal. *A Gift of Gracias: The Legend of Altagracia.*

Campoy, F. Isabel, and Alma Flor Ada. *Celebra el Día de acción de gracias con Beto y Gaby.*

Cowley, Joy, and Joe Cepeda. *Gracias the Thanksgiving Turkey.*

Mora, Pat, and John Parra. *Gracias/Thanks.*

TRADITIONAL LITERATURE

Latino cultural heritage is found richly represented in the traditional literature of the Americas. Librarians serve their patrons well by regularly incorporating into programming examples of folktales, myths, legends, rhymes, riddles, proverbs, and the like. Traditional literature helps to build strong bonds of knowledge and appreciation among Latino family members. It also makes the library setting and resources more familiar and accessible to the Latino populace, while bringing to life Latino cultures among non-Latinos. The following are examples of traditional characters from Latino cultures.

La Llorona and El Cucuy

Two well-known Mexican characters are La Llorona and El Cucuy. Latino adults sometimes warn youngsters that La Llorona or El Cucuy will spirit them away if they don't obey their elders. The former is a woman who wanders through the night, wailing for the children whom she threw to their deaths in a fit of rage by the river. Her story and image often appear in Latino songs and art as well. El Cucuy is a shadowy bogeyman who may snatch away naughty children. The following list includes several traditional and modern variants of Llorona and Cucuy tales. (Note: Other Latino cultures also have stories filled with characters like Llorona and Cucuy. For instance, Jorge Argueta's *Zipitio* (2003) describes a small man called Zipitio who has backwards legs and tries to lure young Pipil/Nahua girls into the rivers of El Salvador.)

> Anaya, Rudolfo A. *Maya's Children: The Story of La Llorona.*
>
> Anzaldúa, Gloria, and (Maya) Christina Gonzalez. *Prietita and the Ghost Woman/Prietita y la Llorona.*
>
> Galindo, Claudia, and Jonathan Coombs. *Do You Know the Cucuy?/ ¿Conoces al Cucuy?*
>
> ———. *It's Bedtime, Cucuy!/¡A la cama, Cucuy!*
>
> Garza, Xavier. *Creepy Creatures and Other Cucuys.*
>
> Hayes, Joe. *La Llorona/The Weeping Woman: A Hispanic Legend Told in Spanish and English.*
>
> Hayes, Joe, and Honorio Robledo. *El Cucuy!: A Bogeyman Cuento in English and Spanish.*

Juan Bobo

Juan Bobo is a simple, foolish boy who gets himself into humorous, often difficult, situations. He appears in tales found throughout Latin America. Generally, after making a series of funny errors, the young fellow has good luck without seemingly doing anything to deserve it. His stories, sometimes referred to as noodlehead tales, are found in many anthologies for children and can be compared with the Anansi spider stories brought to the Americas by African slaves. The following are a few suggested Juan Bobo stories for children:

Belpré, Pura, and Christine Price. *Juan Bobo and the Queen's Necklace: A Puerto Rican Folk Tale.*

Bernier-Grand, Carmen T., and Ernesto Ramos Nieves. *Juan Bobo: Four Folktales from Puerto Rico.*

Mike, Jan M. *Juan Bobo y el caballo de siete colores: Una leyenda Puertorriqueña.*

Montes, Marisa, and Joe Cepeda. *Juan Bobo busca trabajo: Un cuento tradicional puertorriqueño.*

———. *Juan Bobo Goes to Work: A Puerto Rican Folk Tale.*

Montes, Marisa, and Maurie J. Manning. *Juan Bobo Goes Up and Down the Hill: A Puerto Rican Folk Tale.*

Pitre, Felix, and Christy Hale. *Juan Bobo and the Pig: A Puerto Rican Folktale.*

Martina la Cucaracha

The lovely young cockroach Martina is featured in folktales throughout Latin America. In most Martina stories, she is met by a long line of suitors vying for her leg in marriage. She finds something wrong with each of these suitors until she meets her one true love: Perez the mouse. The versions of the story differ in terms of ending and outcome of the Martina and Perez relationship. Below are several well-received picture-book renderings of this folktale. Other versions of the tale can be found in collections such as *Tales Our Abuelitas Told: A Hispanic Folktale Collection* (Campoy and Ada) and *Señor Cat's Romance and Other Favorite Stories from Latin America* (González and Delacre).

Ada, Alma Flor, and Ana López Escrivá. *The Great-Great-Granddaughter of la Cucarachita Martina.*

Belpré, Pura, and Carlos Sanchez. *Perez and Martina: A Portorican Folktale.*

La cucarachita Martina: Adaptación de un cuento popular. Illus. by Héctor Cuenca.

Deedy, Carmen Agra, and Michael Austin. *Martina the Beautiful Cockroach: A Cuban Folktale.*

———. *Martina una cucarachita muy linda: Un cuento cubano.*

Moreton, Daniel. *La Cucaracha Martina: A Caribbean Folktale.*

Other Latino Folklore

Myriad other examples of Latino folklore could fill many library shelves. The following are but a few of those titles that are engaging for children of all cultural heritages:

> Ada, Alma Flor. *El gallo que fue a la boda de su tío: Cuento popular hispanoamericano.*
>
> ———. *The Lizard and the Sun / La lagartija y el sol.*
>
> ———. *Mediopollito / Half Chicken.*
>
> Campoy, F. Isabel, and Alma Flor Ada. *Cuentos que contaban nuestras abuela: Cuentos populares hispánicos.*
>
> ———. *Tales Our Abuelitas Told: A Hispanic Folktale Collection.*
>
> Delacre, Lulu. *Golden Tales: Myths, Legends, and Folktales from Latin America.*
>
> Gabán, Jesús. *El libro de los cuentos y leyendas de América Latina y España.*
>
> Garralón, Ana. *Cuentos y leyendas hispanoamericanos.*
>
> Gerson, Mary-Joan, and Maya Christina Gonzalez. *Fiesta femenina: Celebrating Women in Mexican Folktale.*
>
> González, Lucía, and Lulu Delacre. *The Bossy Gallito / El gallo de bodas: A Traditional Cuban Folktale.*
>
> ———. *Señor Cat's Romance and Other Favorite Stories from Latin America.*
>
> Kohen, Clarita. *El conejo y el coyote.*
>
> Loya, Olga. *Momentos mágicos / Magic Moments.*
>
> Philip, Neil. *Horse Hooves and Chicken Feet: Mexican Folktales.*

TRADITIONAL CULTURAL LITERACY: WELL-LOVED BITS AND PIECES

Throughout the ages, short bits and pieces of traditional humor, wisdom, and solace have enriched, enlightened, and soothed the lives of all peoples. From oral heritage to printed books these sayings live on, to promote traditional cultural literacy for our students. For example, in a school with a large Spanish-speaking Latino student population you might see a teacher or parent leaning over a bumped or scraped child, saying *"Sana, sana, colita de rana, si no sanas hoy sanarás mañana."* Roughly translated this means "Heal, heal, little frog's tail, if you don't heal today you will heal tomorrow." These are soothing, familiar words for Spanish-speaking Latino children. Another example of a traditional saying follows the conclusion of a story when the teller closes with *"Colorín colorado, este cuento se ha acabado."* In English the teller may say the comparable "Snip, snap, snout, this tale's told out."

An especially bonding activity to promote cultural literacy involves compiling and illustrating booklets of proverbs that are familiar to family members. This activity works well as an intergenerational program where children write down and illustrate the *dichos* of their grandparents. The language development involved in studying these traditional stories and sayings cannot be overestimated as they introduce children to literary devices such as metaphors and similes.

The most common types of traditional sayings are *adivinanzas* (riddles), *dichos* (proverbs/sayings), *trabalenguas* (tongue twisters), and *rimas infantiles* (nursery rhymes). Some of the oldest examples feature vocabulary that is unfamiliar to children living in the United States today. Carefully choosing age-appropriate examples, with a touch of stretch, guarantees both fun and comprehension. Many books compile these bits and pieces into rich treasuries of traditional folklore. The following titles are some of the best for children:

Ada, Alma Flor, and F. Isabel Campoy. *Mamá Goose: A Latino Nursery Treasury/Mamá Goose: Un tesoro de rimas infantiles.*

Ada, Alma Flor, F. Isabel Campoy, and Alice Schertle. *¡Pío Peep! Traditional Spanish Nursery Rhymes.*

Aranda, Charles. *Dichos y frases hechas.*

Calles Vales, José. *Adivinanzas y trabalenguas.*

Delacre, Lulu. *Arrorró, mi niño: Latino Lullabies and Gentle Games.*

———. *Arroz con leche: Popular Songs and Rhymes from Latin America.*

Gonzalez, Ralfka, and Ana Ruiz. *My First Book of Proverbs/Mi primer libro de dichos.*

Griego, Margot, Betsy Bucks, Sharon Gilbert, Laurel Kimball, and Barbara Cooney. *Tortillitas para mamá and Other Nursery Rhymes: Spanish and English.*

Hall, Nancy A., Jill Syverson-Stork, and Kay Chorao. *Los pollitos dicen/The Baby Chicks Sing: Juegos, rimas y canciones infantiles de países de habla hispana/Traditional Games, Nursery Rhymes, and Songs from Spanish-Speaking Countries.*

Jaramillo, Nelly P., and Elivia. *Las nanas de abuelita: Canciones de cuna, trabalenguas y adivinanzas de suramérica/Grandmother's Nursery Rhymes: Lullabies, Tongue Twisters, and Riddles from South America.*

Longo, Alejandra. *Trabalenguas.*

Longo, Alejandra, and Daniel Chaskielberg. *Refranes.*

Lopéz, Diana. *Confetti Girl.*

Robleda Moguel, Margarita. *Trabalenguas, colmos, tantanes, refranes, y un pilón.*

POETRY

Books of poetry include traditional children's poetry from Spanish-speaking countries and modern poetry grounded in Latino life in the United States. The latter may be bilingual or monolingual, either English or Spanish. All types of poetry celebrating the rich diversity of the Latino cultures should be represented in the SLMC. The following are recommended poetry collections. (Note that the works by Alarcón, Argueta, Luján, Herrera, Medina, Mora, and Soto contain modern poetry.)

Alarcón, Francisco X., and Maya Christina Gonzalez. *Angels Ride Bikes and Other Fall Poems / Los ángeles andan en bicicleta y otros poemas de otoño.*

———. *From the Bellybutton of the Moon and Other Summer Poems / Del ombligo de la luna y otros poemas de verano.*

———. *Iguanas in the Snow and Other Winter Poems / Iguanas en la nieve y otros poemas de invierno.*

———. *Laughing Tomatoes and Other Spring Poems / Jitomates risueños y otros poemas de primavera.*

Andricaín, Sergio, and Olga Cuéllar Serrano. *Arco iris de poesía.*

Argueta, Jorge, and Elizabeth Gómez. *A Movie in My Pillow / Una película en mi almohada.*

Argueta, Jorge, and Rafael Yockteng. *Sopa de frijoles / Bean Soup.*

Bernier-Grand, Carmen T., and David Diaz. *Diego: Bigger than Life.*

Darío, Rubén, and Olga Lucía García. *Margarita.*

Herrera, Juan F., and Elly Simmons. *Calling the Doves / El canto de las palomas.*

Lee, Claudia M., and Rafael Yockteng. *A la orilla del agua y otros poemas de América Latina.*

Luján, Jorge, and Manuel Monroy. *Rooster / Gallo.*

Martí, José, and Lulu Delacre. *Los zapaticos de rosa.*

Medina, Jane, and Robert Castilla. *The Dream on Blanca's Wall / El sueño pegado en la pared de Blanca.*

Mora, Pat, and Paula Barragán. *Love to Mamá: A Tribute to Mothers.*

Mora, Pat, and Rafael López. *Yum! ¡MmMm! ¡Qué Rico!: Americas Sproutings.*

Mora, Pat, and Enrique O. Sanchez. *Confetti: Poems for Children.*

Morvillo, Mabel, Susana Garcia, Cecilla Pisos, and Vicky Ramos. *Poemas con sol y son.*

Soto, Gary. *Canto familiar.*

———. *Neighborhood Odes.*

HEROES AND ROLE MODELS

Whether they are shelved with biographies or in other areas of the collection, it is important to have many books in the school library about the lives and contributions of Spanish-speaking and Latino role models. There are numerous children's books on famous artists such as Juan Quezada, José Limón, Frida Kahlo, Diego Rivera, and Celia Cruz; well-known authors such as Gabriela Mistral, José Martí, Sor Juana Inez, and Gabriel Márquez; and prominent historical figures including Miguel Hidalgo, Juan Coronado, Benito Juárez, and César Chávez. Lectorum Publishing has a Spanish children's picture-book biography series called Cuando los Grandes Eran Pequeños. It is written by Georgina Lázaro and includes books about important figures in Latin America, such as Julia de Burgos, Federico Garcia Lorca, and Jorge Luis Borges. Below are a few other biographies covering notable Spanish-speaking and Latino role models:

Alegre, Cesar. *Extraordinary Hispanic Americans.*

Bernier-Grand, Carmen T. *Frida: ¡Viva la vida! Long live life!*

Bernier-Grand, Carmen T., and David Diaz. *César: ¡Sí, se puede! Yes, We Can!*

Brown, Monica, and Joe Cepeda. *Side by Side: The Story of Dolores Huerta and Cesar Chavez / Lado a lado: La historia de Dolores Huerta y César Chávez.*

Brown, Monica, and Rafael López. *My Name Is Celia: The Life of Celia Cruz / Me llamo Celia: La vida de Celia Cruz.*

Engle, Margarita, and Sean Qualls. *The Poet Slave of Cuba: A Biography of Juan Francisco Manzano.*

Krull, Kathleen, and Yuyi Morales. *Harvesting Hope: The Story of Cesar Chavez.*

Mora, Pat, and Beatriz Vidal. *A Library for Juana: The World of Sor Juana Inés.*

Ray, Deborah Kogan. *To Go Singing Through the World: The Childhood of Pablo Neruda.*

Reich, Susanna, and Raúl Colón. *José! Born to Dance: The Story of José Limón.*

Sciurba, Katie, and Edel Rodriguez. *Oye, Celia! A Song for Celia Cruz.*

Serrano, Francisco, and Pablo Serrano. *The Poet King of Tezcoco: A Great Leader of Ancient Mexico.*

SPORTS

Soccer (*fútbol*) is the most popular sport in Latin America. Pelé of Brazil is the international father of soccer aficionados. In the Caribbean, baseball also has many supporters. Roberto Clemente, a revered baseball giant from Puerto Rico, sought to play great ball and support humanitarian efforts. Latino children are also interested to learn of lesser-known sports, such as the ancient ball game of the indigenous Mixtec people in Mexico and the game/dance/ martial art of *capoeira* from Brazil. *Lucha libre*, a theatrical form of professional wrestling, also has a following. Whether traditional or modern, sports remains a perennial favorite that children can explore in the following titles:

Ancona, George. *Capoeira: Game! Dance! Martial Art!*

Brown, Monica. *Pelé, King of Soccer/Pelé, el rey del fútbol.*

Contró, Arturo. *Rafael Márquez.*

Garza, Xavier. *Lucha libre: The Man in the Silver Mask: A Bilingual Cuento.*

Mansour, Vivian. *El enmascarado de Lata.*

Page, Jason. *El fútbol.*

Stewart, Mark, and Mike Kennedy. *Latino Baseball's Hottest Hitters/Los mejores bateadores del béisbol Latino.*

Variana del Ángel, Gabriela L. *El juego de pelota mixteca.*

Winter, Jonah. *Roberto Clemente: Pride of the Pittsburgh Pirates.*

IMMIGRANTS AND FARMWORKERS

The immigrant experience touches the lives of many Latinos living in the United States. Regardless of whether they left their homes for financial, educational, political, or other reasons, they or their ancestors migrated to start a new life. Agricultural work was often the only employment available to those newly arrived, so they toiled, and still do, in the fields. Some immigrants follow the harvest of crops across the country from one area to another in search of work. Others with education and years of perseverance reach the highest levels of achievement in their chosen vocations. The following titles present the farmworker and immigrant experience from different perspectives. (Note: For titles that include information about the late César Chávez, the notable Mexican American leader who strove to improve the lives of farmworkers, see the list above in "Heroes and Role Models.")

Ada, Alma Flor, and Judith Jacobson. *El vuelo de los colibríes.*

Ancona, George. *Harvest.*

Anza, Ana L. C. *Amigos del otro lado.*

de Ruiz, Dana C., and Richard Larios. *La Causa: The Migrant Farmworkers' Story.*

Pérez, Amada I., and Maya Christina Gonzalez. *My Diary from Here to There/Mi diario de aquí hasta allá.*

Robleda, Margarita. *Paco: Un niño latino en Estados Unidos.*

Ryan, Pam Muñoz. *Esperanza renace.*

———. *Esperanza Rising.*

MONARCH BUTTERFLIES

The monarch butterfly presents another link between the United States and Mexico. Monarchs migrate between the two environments, spending winters in the south and summers in the north. Students with families from Michoacan, Mexico, may be able to relate personal experiences with the monarchs in their state.

Brown, Monica, and Gabriela B. Ventura. *Butterflies on Carmen Street/Mariposas en la calle Carmen.* Houston: Piñata Books, 2007.

Jiménez, Francisco, and Simón Silva. *La Mariposa*.

Johnston, Tony, and Susan Guevara. *Isabel's House of Butterflies*.

O'Connor, Crystal B. *Jake y la migración de la monarca*.

Ó Flatharta, Antoine. *Hurry and the Monarch*.

Secretaría de Educación Pública. *Lo mejor de México desconocido*.

LATINO AUTHORS AND ILLUSTRATORS

It is critical to include in the school library, and in classroom libraries, books written and illustrated by Latinos. These works present cultural content from an insider's perspective, whether it is in English, Spanish, or both. The authors and illustrators also serve as role models for future authors and artists. Works published outside the United States often have a very different style from those published here. Exposing our students to such international diversity is enriching.

The following is a short list of Latino authors and illustrators who should be well represented in library collections. Some of their works are cited earlier in this chapter. See the Bibliography at the end of the book for links to Latino author and illustrator Web sites. (Note that two important names are missing from these lists. Joe Hayes, a famed bilingual storyteller of Arizona, is not Latino but he writes authentic Latino folklore. Ana María Machado of Brazil writes in Portuguese. Her works are highly acclaimed in Latin America, and are translated well into Spanish.)

Latino Authors and Illustrators in the United States

Alma Flor Ada	Margarita Engle
Francisco Alarcón	Lucía González
Julia Álvarez	Maya Christina Gonzalez
Rudolfo Anaya	Juan Felipe Herrera
George Ancona	Francisco Jiménez
Jorge Argueta	Carmen Lomas Garza
Carmen Bernier-Grand	Victor Martínez
Monica Brown	Marisa Montes
Sandra Cisneros	Pat Mora
Carmen Agra Deedy	Yuyi Morales
Lulu Delacre	José-Luis Orozco

Amada Irma Pérez   Gary Soto

Pam Muñoz Ryan   Carmen Tafolla

Isabel Schon

Latino Authors and Illustrators Outside the United States

Ana Anza   Guillermo Murray Prisant

Ivar Da Coll   Hilda Perera

Silvia Dubovoy   Luis María Pescetti

Francisco Hinojosa   Carmen Posadas

Alejandra Longo   María Puncel

Jorge Elias Luján   Margarita Robleda

Vivian Mansour Manzur   Lawrence Schimel

Magaly Morales

LATINO LITERACY-RELATED ACTIVITIES

Throughout this chapter and book there are numerous suggestions for celebrating Latino children's literature in classroom activities and library programs. For school library media specialists who are unfamiliar with the Latino cultures or Spanish language or who have little time to plan activities and programs for Latino children and their families, many online and print resources are available.

As mentioned earlier in this chapter, Día is a wonderful way to celebrate Latino literacy. Numerous free Web resources detail activities and programs for celebrating this holiday and Latino cultures. Any of these activities could be used throughout the school year. Resources include Texas State Library and Archives Commission's Dígame un cuento / Tell Me a Story: Bilingual Library Programs for Children and Families (http://www.tsl.state.tx.us/ld/pubs/bilingual/), the American Library Association's official Día Web site (http://www.ala.org/dia), and the Texas Library Association's El día de los niños/El día de los libros Tool Kit (http://www.texasdia.org/toolkit.html).

Reading Is Fundamental, a nonprofit literacy agency, provides links on its Web site (http://www.rif.org/) to literacy activities in English and Spanish, online Spanish music resources, interactive games and books in English and Spanish, and the free guide Let's Read as a Family: Bilingual Activities and

Games for Kids at Home and on the Go (http://www.rif.org/kids/pdf/leer/en/ English_activities.pdf).

In addition, ¡Colorín Colorado! (http://www.colorincolorado.org/), created by Reading Rockets, is a free reading literacy program providing information on the importance of reading in the lives of English Language Learner (ELL), Spanish-speaking, and Latino children. The site includes downloadable and interactive activities, interviews with Latino authors and illustrators, and lists of recommended resources and ideas for working with ELL and Latino children. Librarians and educators can use the free 92-page planning booklet to launch services and programs to Latino children and their families.

Another Latino literacy program, Lee y serás (http://www.leeyseras. net/), is sponsored by Scholastic, Verizon, and the National Council of La Raza. The program provides support for Latino parents with training about early literacy, offers resources for educators and librarians to create print-rich learning environments for Latino children, and supplies information to public agencies on how to support Latino literacy in the community. Online activities, games, and e-stories along with downloadable program and activity booklets help both librarians and educators to foster the literacy development of Latino children and their families.

There are also numerous printed professional resources that help librarians make appropriate decisions about services to Latino youth. Wadham's *Programming with Latino Children's Materials* (1999) provides a plethora of information for children's and school library media specialists serving Latino populations. The author describes the various cultures, provides sample programs, offers suggestions for working with various groups, and discusses how to locate Latino children's materials. Dame's *Serving Linguistically and Culturally Diverse Students: Strategies for the School Library Media Specialist* (1993) details the various social needs of culturally diverse and ESL children, explaining special services and program ideas for these students. This resource can be adapted to meet the needs of Latino children. "Kids Are Kids: Preschool to Early Elementary," "Reading to Learn: The Middle Years," and "The Teenage Years," all chapters in Moller's *Library Service to Spanish Speaking Patrons* (2001), provide sample library programs, discuss program marketing, and suggest strategies for implementing successful library programs for Latino children and young adults. Another book focused on librarians, Immroth and McCook's *Library Services to Youth of Hispanic Heritage* (2000), explains how to plan, implement, and evaluate programs for Latino children as well as how to determine the needs of Latino youth.

Ada's *A Magical Encounter: Latino Children's Literature in the Classroom* (2003, 2nd ed.) defines various activities that use Latino children's literature to promote cognitive and social development. While geared toward classrooms, the activities can be modified for library programs. Also aimed at classroom teachers, Eggers-Piérola's *Connections and Commitments: Reflecting Latino Values in Early Childhood Programs* (2005) describes how to make preschool and elementary programs welcoming to Latino youth and details several literature-related activities using Latino children's literature. The suggestions in the book could be incorporated into programs, services, and activities that are welcoming to Latino children and their families. Hadaway, Vardell, and Young's *Literature-Based Instruction with English Language Learners: K–12* (2002) is another great resource for librarians serving Latino children who are learning English. The text explains the usefulness of the various literary genres and suggests activities for using literature with these students.

Very specialized holiday and family-focused programs could be planned and implemented using the following resources. Menard's *The Latino Holiday Book: From Cinco de Mayo to Día de los Muertos—The Celebrations and Traditions of Hispanic-Americans* (2004, 2nd ed.) lists many of the holidays celebrated in the various Latino subcultures and provides recipes and/or crafts for each holiday. This is an excellent resource for background information about the various Latino holidays. A great book to pair with *The Latino Holiday Book* is Pavon and Borrego's *25 Latino Craft Projects* (2003). This highly useful resource supplies program and craft ideas for holiday, family, and everyday Latino library programs. A brief description of the holiday or event is given, followed by detailed instructions for implementing the program with both children and families. Turck's *Mexico and Central America: A Fiesta of Cultures, Crafts, and Activities for Ages 8–12* (2004) is a combined craft guide and fact book about Mexico and the countries of Central America. Recipes, activities, and crafts are themed around the arts, foods, school life, history, and daily life of people living in Mexico, Guatemala, Belize, El Salvador, Honduras, Nicaragua, Costa Rica, and Panama. A very practical resource for planning a hands-on, intergenerational program is Garza's *Making Magic Windows: Creating Papel Picado/Cut-Paper Art with Carmen Lomas Garza* (1999). The book perfectly complements the author's picture book *Magic Windows: Ventanas mágicas* (1999), providing instructions for creating ten *papel picado* designs.

FAMILY LITERACY

The SLMC can support family outreach services in many meaningful ways. Some Latino families may not have transportation to the public library and they will benefit immensely if the SLMC opens its doors to them in addition to their children. Indeed, family literacy can be an integral part of the library's mission. One example of a powerful and transformative program is an adaption of the work begun with migrant parents in California in the 1980s by Alma Flor Ada. Del Sol Books has published a manual for the program, *Transformative Family Literacy: Engaging in Meaningful Dialogue with Spanish Speaking Parents*, by Rosa Zubizarreta (2006).

If such a program is not currently feasible, there are other successful ways to reach the families. School librarians can open the library during back-to-school night and invite students to bring their families to meet the staff and check out books. Also at the start of the year, school library media specialists can go to the first meeting of the parent advisory council and promote the library resources for family use. Many Latino parents will be pleasantly surprised to learn that they can check out materials and that the SLMC has materials of special interest to Latinos. When teachers meet with Latino parents and students during parent conference time, the teachers can suggest that they visit the SLMC to check out books specific to their academic needs.

School library media specialists can also host family reading or storytelling nights, perhaps during Read Across America week at the beginning of March or for *Noche de cuentos* on March 20. They can create a lively bilingual student and parent book club that meets monthly. Each month the librarian would choose a different title, available in both English and Spanish, and build a variety of entertaining activities centered on the book. If possible, the club should meet in the early evening, providing snacks and child care. School library media specialists should consider working in partnership with the public library and others to promote multicultural, multilingual family literacy during *Día de los niños/Día de los libros* as described earlier in this chapter. Partnering with the public library or other local organizations on a variety of reading initiatives strengthens families and children in the community.

The bottom line to remember is that the SLMC serves all our children and their families. We are in the education business, and we can do well to keep in mind two of César Chávez's famous quotes: "The end of all education should surely be service to others," and *"Sí, se puede."*

REFERENCES

Argueta, Jorge, and Gloria Calderón. *Zipitio*. Toronto: Groundwood Books, 2003.

Campoy, F. Isabel, and Alma Flor Ada. *Tales Our Abuelitas Told: A Hispanic Folktale Collection*. New York: Atheneum, 2006.

Doss, Yvette. "Doing the Alfawalsh: Argentina's Spirited Grand Dame of Children's Books Debuts in the United States." *Críticas Online* (April 1, 2002). http://www.criticasmagazine.com/article/CA201305.html (accessed December 29, 2009).

Frey, Yvonne Amar. *One Person Puppetry: Streamlined and Simplified with 38 Folktale Scripts*. Chicago: American Library Association, 2005.

González, Lucía, and Lulu Delacre. *Señor Cat's Romance and Other Favorite Stories from Latin America*. New York: Scholastic, 1997.

Zubizarreta, Rosa. *Transformative Family Literacy: Engaging in Meaningful Dialogue with Spanish Speaking Parents*. San Diego, CA: Del Sol Books, 1996.

PART 4

LATINO CHILDREN'S LITERATURE AND LITERACY PROGRAMS IN CLASSROOMS AND LIBRARIES

CHAPTER 8

Have Books, Will Travel: Bebés, Libros y Early Literacy

María E. Arroyo and Guillermina "Gigi" Towers

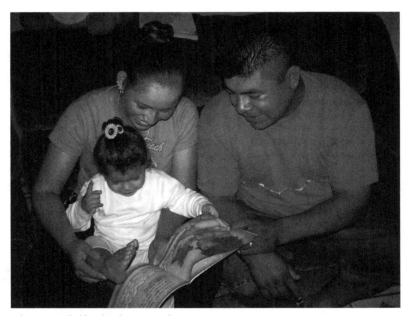

Photo provided by the chapter authors.

I've seen children touch, fondle books, smell books, and it's all the reason in the world why books should be beautifully produced.
— Maurice Sendak (Marcovitz 2006, p. 24)

I remember my first home visit, how nervous I felt inside of myself. Although my mother tongue is Spanish, I was afraid that mothers would not welcome me. I am from Ecuador and the mother I was visiting was from Mexico. Immediately after we introduced ourselves, we communicated very well. The session was eloquent and amiable, and just at that moment I knew that our early literacy program was going to be a success among Spanish-speaking families.

—María Arroyo, parent educator

The Bilingual Parenting Program of Lexington (SC) School District One began about ten years ago, with the purpose of strengthening the bond between Spanish-speaking families and preparing their children to succeed academically. Three Latina mothers were enrolled, and the journey began—a journey of enthusiasm and incredible participation on the part of young families in an effort to introduce children to a love of reading at the earliest age possible. Since 1998 the program has been fully enrolled solely by word of mouth; mothers refer their neighbors and other mothers to the program, informing them of the many benefits of early literacy. We proudly say that our program is parent approved!

During daily home visits, the Bilingual Parenting Program uses the curriculum from both Parents as Teachers (www.parentsasteachers.org) and the Parent-Child Home Program (http://www.parent-child.org/). Our core value is that parents are their children's first and most influential teachers. The goal of the Parents as Teachers (PAT) program is "to empower parents to give their child the best possible start in life, laying the foundation for school and life success" (Parents as Teachers 1985, p. 5). The Parent-Child Home Program is "a research-based early literacy, school readiness, parenting education program that prepares young children for school success by increasing language and literacy skills, enhancing social-emotional development, and strengthening the parent-child relationship" (Parent-Child Home Program).

Latino families with children younger than 12 months participate in the Parents as Teachers program. Children who are 12 months old participate in the Parent-Child Home Program in addition to Parents as Teachers. At three years of age, children and their families graduate from our Bilingual Parenting Program and can be enrolled in the four-year-old program at school.

The program's parent educators are bilingual parents who share many of the same experiences that enrolled parents may have with their children every day. This helps parents feel comfortable and relaxed when they are struggling with a parenting issue, especially when it relates to the hardships of life in a different culture and adjusting to a new language.

The home visitation component of our program solves Latino families' lack of transportation—a big obstacle facing first-generation Spanish-speaking families in our county—by taking the program to their homes. We use newsletters, calendars, magazines, and booklets to encourage parent involvement, produce flyers about library events, and supply information about workshops and activities. After the sessions, we help parents with any problems they have, assisting with school information or doctor's appointments, for example.

We are a link between the families and the community, and this relationship helps families overcome homesickness and isolation, tough issues during their first years living in the United States. Through this interaction, our program has become one of the best options for new immigrants to preserve their own culture and to learn the second culture in a gentle manner. The following sections describe various components and activities of our program that have led to its success in promoting early literacy among Latino children and their families. Here we describe the success of our home visits, Books on Wheels component, newsletter/blog, and bilingual library programming partnerships that engage parents in the literacy education of their children.

HOME VISITS

Home visits are one of the major components of our program and allow us to connect with our Latino families on a personal level. During these visits, we often provide the families with bilingual books to share with their children. Unfortunately, although there are many bilingual books available in the United States, a large percentage of them contain Spanish misspellings or grammatical errors. In addition, many of the children's literature classics common to English-language early literacy programs are not available in Spanish or bilingual editions. If we want specific titles available to use with our families, we have to translate them ourselves.

As bilingual educators we want to ensure that the books have the best translation possible and strongly believe that this meticulous work is essential to our program's success. At the beginning of each school year, we spend many hours on these translations in order to provide the parents with bilingual books that will facilitate verbal interaction with their young children. Some words and sentences are very easy to translate while others we have to interpret according to the cultural and linguistic context of the story. Unfortunately, some words and sentences are impossible to translate. A typical example is the nursery rhyme "Humpty Dumpty;" no equivalent in the Spanish language exists for "Humpty Dumpty." We explain this situation to the parents and provide an approximation of the rhyme in Spanish, maintaining the original English text so they can become intuitively acquainted with the song's structure and eventually learn the English version too.

We believe these books serve a twofold purpose: to assist the parents and their children in learning English and to help maintain the home language of the families. One of the mothers explained that her daughter came home from school one day, went straight to her room, and found her *Goodnight Moon* book. She then told her mother that the teacher read the book at school, and both parent and child were thrilled to read it again at home in a language familiar to them! Another child told her teacher that they have *Snowy Day* at home and her mom reads to her in Spanish. Later the teacher invited the mother to read the book in Spanish to the entire class. Mother and child could not have been happier or prouder! These are just two of the many examples of the potential our program has to connect Spanish-speaking Latino parents and their children with the English-speaking classroom.

In addition to translating books for our home visits, the Bilingual Parenting Program teaches Latino parents how to verbally interact with their children. By the age of five every child should have a minimum of 5,000 words in his or her vocabulary. Parents must talk and interact with their children all the time, using verbal fluency. Often Latino parents will give commands to their children and barely engage in conversation, especially when children are

The bilingual book is an important tool for the Spanish-speaking parent as it provides both English and Spanish versions of the text that can one day be read by both child and parent. Photo provided by the chapter authors.

in the "why" stage. This stage can be frustrating for parents when they run out of answers.

To assist parents, we prepare Verbal Interaction Guide Sheets that accompany the bilingual books shared with the family. These guides provide parents with ideas and a script on how to engage in a conversation with their children about the book and set the stage for literacy development. See Figure 8.1 for an example of the guide sheet in Spanish and Figure 8.2 for an example of the guide sheet in English.

Soaring to Success Through Books and Play...
The Parent-Child Home Program
SINCE 1965

PARENT-CHILD-HOME PROGRAM
LEXINGTON SCHOOL DISTRICT ONE

Verbal Interaction Stimulus Materials
GUIDE SHEET
Materiales de Estimulación para la Interacción Verbal
GUÍA DE ACTIVIDADES
BOOK OUTLINE / PERFIL DEL LIBRO

VISM TITLE (LIBRO): **BUENAS NOCHES LUNA** Por: Margaret Wise Brown

PROGRAMA I   VISM # 13

Nombre y estimule a su niño/a a que diga:

Colores: Globo rojo, pantalla amarilla, pared verde, cielo azul, luna blanca
Formas y tamaños: Ratón pequeño, globo grande y redondo, cuadrante del reloj pequeño y redondo, cuerda larga y fina
Números: 1 ratón, 2 gatitos, 3 osos
Relacionarlo: Encima del armario, dentro de la chimenea, el peine está al lado del cepillo, debajo de la cama.
Clasificar: Animales, muebles, vestimenta, juguetes
Provocar cosas que sucedan: ¿Cuántos gatitos jugaban con la madeja de lana, qué pasó?
¿Cuándo el conejito cerró los ojos, se quedó dormido?

Invite al niño/a a que diga sus experiencias:
¿Qué te pones cuando te vas a acostar? ¿Puedes encontrar el reloj, el teléfono, la lámpara en la sala o en el dormitorio de tu casa?

Hágale preguntas sobre los dibujos para que le ayuden a razonar:
¿Por qué está obscureciendo? Veamos si podemos encontrar al ratón en cada una de las páginas de colores. ¿Qué está haciendo el ratón? Vamos a imaginarnos que estamos calentándonos las manos al frente de la chimenea. Vamos a despedirnos de todas las cosas que hacen ruido.

FIGURE 8.1.

¡DIVIÉRTASE CON EL LIBRO BUENAS NOCHES LUNA!

¡Qué hermoso libro para leer a la hora de acostarse! Nos habla sobre el *anochecer* y cada página se obscurece más mientras avanza la noche. Los niños disfrutan cuando se baja la voz y se susurra "shhh" y ellos harán lo mismo.

Deténgase en cada página de color, porque hay un ratoncito travieso que no está quieto. Pídale a su niño que trate de encontrar al ratoncito. Dígale: "Frío, frío, frío... ¡caliente!", para hacer más divertida la búsqueda.

Mirar la luna y las estrellas desde la ventana es una actividad que les gusta a los niños. Cuando es noche de luna llena no se pierdan de verla. Para los niños es una experiencia inolvidable y no se diga para los padres.

No se olvide que siempre es bueno tener cerca un papel y crayones para que los niños puedan expresarse libremente a través del dibujo y esperamos que con este libro, ¡los pequeñines tengan un buen motivo para dibujar sobre el *anochecer*!

FIGURE 8.1. *(cont.)*

Libros sobre Ruedas (Books on Wheels)

A young child exploring her new basket of books provided by the Libros sobre Ruedas program. Photo provided by the chapter authors.

Many of our Latino families do not have books in their homes and our program may be their first or only introduction to children's books. We strongly believe that every child should have access to high-quality books, and our rolling

Soaring to Success Through Books and Play...

The Parent-Child Home Program

SINCE 1965

PARENT-CHILD-HOME PROGRAM
LEXINGTON SCHOOL DISTRICT ONE

Verbal Interaction Stimulus Materials
GUIDE SHEET
Materiales de Estimulación para la Interacción Verbal
BOOK OUTLINE

VISM TITLE (BOOK): <u>**GOODNIGHT MOON**</u> by Margaret Wise Brown

PROGRAM: 1   VISM: 13

<u>**Name and encourage to your child to say:**</u>
Colors: green wall, red balloon, yellow lampshade, blue sky, white moon
Shapes and sizes: tiny mouse, large, round balloon, small, round clock face, long thin string
Numbers: 1 mouse, 2 kittens, 3 bears
Relationships: on top of bookcase, in the fireplace, comb next to brush, under the bed
Categories: animals, furniture, clothes, toys
Causing things to happen: "When the kittens played with the ball of yarn, it unraveled."
Textures: smooth pages

<u>**Invite him or her to tell about his experiences:**</u>
"What do you wear when you go to bed?"
"Can you find a (clock, telephone, lamp, etc.) in this room that's like the one in the picture?"
<u>**Ask questions about the illustrations to help him or her to reason things out:**</u>
"Why is the room getting darker?"
"Let's see if we can find the mouse in each of the colored pictures."
"What do you think the mouse is doing?"

HAVE A GOOD TIME WITH GOODNIGHT MOON!

© The Parent-Child Home Program 2009

FIGURE 8.2.

library—*Libros sobre Ruedas*—presents this opportunity to the families by providing developmentally appropriate books that facilitate children's language development through literacy.

Our *Libros sobre Ruedas* is housed in our Parenting Center, which is the home-base for our family activities that take place outside the home. The rolling library has about 4,000 bilingual books, which include many of the classics in European and Latin American children's literature as well as contemporary books with Latino themes. For each home visit, we gather a basket of books to deliver to the homes of our families. The parents and their children then select books to check out for a week.

From the moment we place the basket in front of the children and parents, it is a joy to watch the mother and child bonding over books. They select titles together, touch and feel various books, and laugh over old "favorites." The work that is initially put into the library might be hard; however, once that is over and we embark on the adventure of bringing the library into a home where we know this is the family's first interaction with books, the end result is magical.

EL RECADO

Our program serves first-generation immigrant families from various Latin American countries and regions. Each family has its own traditions specific to its country or region, and family members feel the need to share these to achieve a sense of belonging. In response to this need, we created *El Recado*, a newsletter and blog (http://elrecadodemaria.blogspot.com/) that allows families to contribute and share lullabies, nursery rhymes, riddles, artwork, recipes, book reviews, and holiday traditions. The first issue of the newsletter was published in December 2000. By January 2010, we had published more than 80 issues and the newsletter has become a repository of cultural memories brought to this country by first-generation Spanish-speaking families.

Below is an example of a lullaby contributed by the first mother enrolled in the program. It was published in the February 2001 edition of *El Recado*.

CAMPANITA DE ORO (CANCIÓN DE CUNA)	GOLDEN LITTLE BELL
Campanita de oro	*Golden little bell*
cántale a mi niña	*sing it to my little girl*
que se va a dormir	*she is going to sleep*
y esta niña linda	*and this pretty little girl*

que nació de día	*who was born during the day*
quiere que le lleven	*wants to go*
a ver su tía	*to see her aunt*
y esta niña linda	*and this pretty little girl*
que nació de noche	*who was born during the night*
quiere que le lleven	*wants to go*
a pasear en coche.	*for a ride in the car.*

Parents enjoy using *El Recado* to share their feelings and point of view about the books they share with their children. Because parent recommendations are powerful, suggested books are often requested by parents again and again. Below are a few examples of parent book reviews that have been published. Note that we do not edit the book reviews for grammar. We allow the parents' true words to shine through in their reviews.

Me llamo Celia/My Name Is Celia by Mónica Brown
> This book is colorful and tells us about Celia Cruz's life the unforgettable singer from Cuba that serenade like a nightingale to the world. Perla. *El Recado*, May 2009.

¿Dónde está el gatito?/Where's the Kitten? by Cheryl Cristian
> We love this book and read about fifteen times! The book had little doors, I said: Where's the kitten? I opened the door and my little boy yells out. . . there! Reading it was like playing hide-and-seek with the kitten. Leticia. *El Recado*, November 2005.

Mi ropa/My Clothes by Rebecca Emberly
> I liked this book because you learn about everyday activities by playing. The author has other books that help children to learn about colors, toys, etc. Since are bilingual not only are good for children also for the parents. Laura. *El Recado*, October 2004.

Los colores de Élmer by David McKee
> This book was the highlight of the week. My children asked me to read it like twenty times. The enjoyed at the end when I ask questions like: Where is Elmer's tail? Leticia. *El Recado*, April 2006.

Chiquero (Pigsty) by Mark Teague

My daughter enjoyed this book, she remembers, that the little pigs are herself that does not want to clean up the room, because they are busy playing and having fun. My daughter asked me to buy little pigs so they can help her clean her room and be nice and tidy at bedtime. Perla. *El Recado*, November 2004.

BILINGUAL EVENTS AT THE LIBRARY

For seven years the Bilingual Parenting Program and our county library have sponsored bicultural, bilingual activities with the mission of making it possible for new immigrant families to adjust to the culture in South Carolina. During the school year the entire community—both Latino and non-Latino families—enjoys three events: *Día de los muertos* in October, *Feliz Navidad* in December, and *Pascua* in March. At every event, families enjoy making crafts, watching puppet shows, singing rhymes and songs, listening to bilingual storytimes, participating in folkloric dances, and eating traditional foods brought by the participants. See Figure 8.3 for an example of the *Día de los muertos* program at the public library.

Forming a partnership with the public library was a logical outreach component of our program with several benefits. First, it allowed us to extend our financial resources, which are tight at times due to budgetary restrictions.

Mothers set up and decorate an altar outside the library. This activity was an initiative to connect reading with a traditional celebration. The first altar was made in 2007 to pay tribute to Francisco "Cri-Cri" Gabilondo Soler whose children's songs "The Road to School," "Letters Parade," and many more will be forever in our memory, and to Margaret Wise Brown, author of Goodnight Moon, Run Away Bunny, *and* The Big Red Barn. *Photo provided by the chapter authors.*

**THE PARENT INFORMATION AND RESOURCE CENTER,
LEXINGTON SCHOOL DISTRICT ONE
AND THE LEXINGTON MAIN LIBRARY
INVITE YOU TO:**

Día de los muertos
Saturday, October 28th, 2006

Activities

2:00–3:00 Craft Tables and Game: Children and parents will make:

    Table 1: *la Llorona* puppet

    Table 2: a pumpkin and ghost hangers

    Table 3: decorate a candy paper bag with fall motives

    Game: Witch ring toss

3:00–3:30 Bilingual Storytime

    The legend of *La Llorona*

    The Little Old Lady Who Was Not Afraid of Anything by Linda Williams

    Brujitas by María Antonia Peralta

3:30–4:00 Entertainment

    Music

    Food

    Door Prize

    Knock the door. . .

    Surprise

FIGURE 8.3. *Example of a Bilingual Event at the Public Library.*

While the public library may not have unlimited financial resources, combining what we have allows us to make a little go a long way! Another benefit of our partnership was to introduce our families to the wealth of rich children's literature and other materials offered at the public library. Many of our families never used libraries in their home countries. Bilingual programs draw them into the library where they can see firsthand all that the library has for Spanish-speaking families. A final benefit of our partnership was to showcase to the community and other Latino families the success of the Bilingual Parenting Program. When people outside our program interact with our families at the library events, they hear about the exciting opportunities that we offer. Often, it is at the bilingual library events that word of mouth leads new families to our doorstep.

CONCLUDING REMARKS

B udgetary restrictions are one of the biggest challenges that teachers, librarians, and other educators may confront in starting programs similar to ours. In our experience, financial difficulties and limited staffing threaten the program but do not compromise the ultimate goal: to promote a love of reading as a foundation for succeeding in school. We recommend forming partnerships with other organizations (as we have with the public library) and inviting volunteers to help with translating books, preparing the rolling library, printing the newsletter, and assisting at the bilingual library programs.

In November 2009, with great excitement, one of our parent educators visited the first mother who enrolled in the Bilingual Parenting Program. It was a special visit: to help her firstborn daughter enroll in college. This is truly what early literacy and family literacy programs are about. When parents are empowered, children graduate from high school and begin their journey toward a college degree and a wide array of opportunities.

REFERENCES

Marcovitz, Hal. *Maurice Sendak.* New York: Chelsea House, 2006.

Parent-Child Home Program. *Who We Are.* http://parent-child.org/aboutus/index. html (accessed December 27, 2009).

Parents as Teachers. *PAT Parent Educator Manual.* St. Louis, MO: Parents as Teachers National Center, 1985.

CHAPTER 9

Bilingual Storytimes

Katie Cunningham

I t's Wednesday night at the Village Branch library in Lexington, Kentucky, and the building is packed. Local elementary and middle school students are receiving homework help from high school and college volunteers. Teachers from the local middle school are distributing report cards to parents and students. All of the computers are in use, and people are browsing for materials to take home. The energy is high, and a *mezcla* of English and Español can be heard in every corner. Contributing to the bustle of the evening is Bilingual Family Storytime / Cuentos bilingües para toda la familia, which attracts families who come to storytime each week and new families curious about the program. The crowd is as diverse, with local families born and raised in Kentucky and immigrant families from countries far away all interacting through bilingual music, books, stories, and activities. Babies babble, toddlers waddle, and preschoolers excitedly call out the names of colors in both languages as we sort various props. When it's time to go, we sing *adiós* to all of our *amigos* as we do each week, and the families spill out into the already busy building. As families browse books to take home and prepare to leave, they are exposed to the variety of resources the library has freely available to support them in their learning and development across their lifespan.

Bilingual storytimes can mean different things to different people, based on their library, their community, and their own skill sets and experiences. Before discussing the benefits, challenges, and techniques that are part of bilingual storytimes, it is useful to clarify what we mean by bilingual storytimes. For the purposes of this chapter, a bilingual storytime is a standing storytime program that uses traditional elements such as books, music, and fingerplays, as well as flannelboards and other storytelling techniques, to equally promote and encourage the development of early literacy skills in both English and Spanish. Most often, bilingual storytime programs will be planned and implemented by children's librarians who are themselves bilingual.

If you see a need for bilingual storytimes at your library but are not bilingual yourself, this chapter is still for you. All librarians, regardless of their ability to speak Spanish, can and should be incorporating into their storytimes books and stories that positively feature Latino children and families. This is especially important for the Latino children in your community; it is important that they see themselves and their culture represented at the library and in books. Talented Latino authors and illustrators are creating beautiful picture books that can be included in programs on nearly any theme. The publishing industry is beginning to understand that there is a real demand for bilingual books, and there are many good titles available to choose from. If you are not bilingual, you still have many options. Bilingual music is easy to incorporate into storytimes, regardless of your own language (or for that matter, singing) ability. Many fingerplays are available in both languages and could be shared with families to do themselves at home. The list of resources at the end of this chapter and at the end of the book offer many suggestions.

There are many benefits and challenges to establishing a bilingual story-time program. Bilingual storytimes cast a wide net. They provide an opportunity for diverse groups of children who may not live in the same neighborhoods to interact socially before attending school. They are a way for libraries to welcome their Spanish-speaking communities into their buildings, and to expose them to the wealth of free resources that are available. As with any storytime, there is the opportunity to model for parents ways in which they can help their child develop the early literacy skills that will help them be successful in school; an extra benefit with bilingual storytimes is the opportunity to stress to parents the importance of reading and talking with their children in their native language. However, not everyone will be thrilled by the idea of a bilingual storytime. Staff may feel stressed by the idea of having to serve increased numbers of customers with whom it may be difficult to communicate. Supervisors and administrators feeling budget pressures may be unsure of the benefit of investing funds in staff and resources to implement such a program. As controversial issues such as immigration reform become hot topics in media and politics, some vocal ele-ments in the community may resist the idea of a storytime program in English and Spanish.

Essential for maximizing benefits and minimizing challenges is having a clear understanding at the outset of why you are developing a bilingual storytime at your particular library. Who is the program designed to reach? What are the goals? How will you know if you are being successful? A library wanting to establish a bilingual storytime as part of an outreach initiative to increase its numbers of Latino customers will have different considerations from a library that is already well-established within the Latino community. A library with a new immigrant community may find its intended audience facing challenges such as poverty and low levels of literacy. It is essential to know your community. This will impact such decisions as the materials you choose to use and the approach you take in incorporating early literacy messages for parents; it may also impact when and where you offer the program. Understanding your community will also impact the way you advocate for the program, which is an essential—though not often discussed—part of the process for implementing a successful bilingual storytime. Financial resources and support are scarce for everyone, and your program will need resources ranging from bilingual staff to materials and time to design and market your program. Your program and its goals need to be strategically aligned with the goals of your organization. It is important that you as a librarian are aware of the expectations that your administration has for the program as this will provide the language and framework in which to present success and advocate for the needs of your Spanish-speaking Latino community. Support for the program from your administration, supervisors, and co-workers are all critical for success.

This chapter will also provide information, resources, and ideas useful for practitioners who are already offering bilingual storytimes in their libraries or those who are interested in introducing a bilingual storytime at their library. Librarians interested in making their English storytime programs more inclusive of the Latino community will benefit as well. Readers will gain a greater understanding of the literacy needs of children growing up in a bilingual environment and how the bilingual storytime can help libraries address those needs. Readers will also find ideas for designing and implementing bilingual storytimes, including sample storytime plans and resources to consult for further information.

LITERACY NEEDS OF THE BILINGUAL CHILD

Recently, a very well-meaning early literacy advocate in my community wanted my opinion. She said she had heard that many Latino children were behind other students in terms of reading development because Latino families do not have books in the home, and reading with children is not a part of Latino culture. I am sharing this, because it illustrates the kind of stereotypes that need to be assessed. In my community, literacy needs are vast and varied. Many of our families face extreme adversity and find themselves in survival mode. Poverty, a language barrier, illiteracy, low skill levels, split families, and a general uncertainty about the future are real elements of their lives. For these families, yes, books are an extra luxury and reading for pleasure may not be a part of daily life. However, within the same community, I see families that bring their children to the library every day to foster a love of reading and to build a foundation for further education. It is important to be mindful of the challenges faced by the community you are trying to reach.

There seems to be an urge to paint the Latino community with a very broad brush, to be able to make generalizations about who Latinos are. The reality is not that simple. There is no one poster child of the Latino or bilingual child in America. Not all Latinos are bilingual, not all Latinos speak Spanish, not all bilingual people are immigrants, and not all immigrants are living in poverty or are Spanish-speaking. It is essential that you know the needs of your specific community and ensure that the program you design is relevant to those needs.

One of the best ways to understand the literacy needs of preschool children, including those growing up bilingually, is through the framework of Every Child Ready to Read (ECRR). Storytime is a natural opportunity to communicate ECRR messages to parents, and with bilingual storytimes this can be done in two languages. For those unfamiliar with ECRR, it is a joint initiative of the Association for Library Services to Children and the Public Library Association (both divisions of the American Library Association) that outlines the six preliteracy skills that children need to develop in order to be ready to read and able to achieve school success when they enter kindergarten. These skills are vocabulary, letter knowledge, phonological awareness—the ability to recognize the small sounds in words, print awareness—knowing how to use books, narrative skills—the ability to tell and comprehend stories, and print motivation—loving books and reading. There is a wealth of research available at the ECRR Web site (http://www.ala.org/ala/mgrps/divs/alsc/ecrr/index.cfm) that supports the importance of achieving these skills and the learning differences between children who have these skills before kindergarten and those who do not.

In my community, poverty and low literacy levels (in Spanish as well as English) make children very much at risk for low literacy and low educational success themselves. Bilingual storytimes provide an opportunity to educate parents on the importance of these skills, providing exposure and access to materials they can take home to use, and modeling ways in which they can use them effectively. I intentionally include these messages for parents in my programs, along with a variety of suggestions beyond reading. It is important that parents who may not be able to read with their children are empowered as their children's first teachers to help them develop early literacy skills in other ways, such as singing, rhyming, and talking with their child in their native language.

This need to make explicitly clear to immigrant parents the importance of reading and talking with their children in their native language became apparent to me when I first began working in libraries. I was working at a branch with a growing community of new Spanish-speaking immigrants and a young bilingual girl asked me for a copy of *Click, Clack, Moo: Cows That Type* by Doreen Cronin to read to her little sister. We didn't have any copies available, but we did have the Spanish version. I offered to read it to the two of them. Crestfallen, the little girl rejected my offer, saying that her father did not want her and her sister reading in Spanish, because he wanted them to learn English. Unfortunately, it has not been my experience that this is a rare situation.

One generalization that I will make about the Latino community, particularly Latino immigrants, is that they highly value the education of their children. They want very much for their children to learn English in order to integrate successfully with the broader society. Many are fearful that reading or talking too much with their children in Spanish will confuse the children or impede their ability to learn English, when in fact the opposite is true. Children who have a solid foundation of words and concepts in their native language have a much easier time learning a second language (Tabors 1997). Parents are able to use more words and richer descriptions in their native language, factors that are important in the early literacy development of their children. Additionally, language retention can be an important tie to cultural heritage. Bilingual storytime is an opportunity to calm parents' fears about using their native language with their children. It is an opportunity to celebrate the many advantages of being bilingual.

HOW TO PLAN AND CONDUCT A BILINGUAL STORYTIME

Whenever I talk with someone interested in a bilingual storytime, the questions are most often about practical details: What books should I select? Should I read everything exactly in English and Spanish? Is my Spanish good enough for bilingual storytime? Is it okay to tell stories in English using some Spanish words? There is a lot of variation, and even controversy, in how to approach a bilingual storytime. The objective for this section is not to answer definitively how one *should* plan and present a bilingual storytime, but rather to provide a variety of options on how one *could* approach it. I will also present my own techniques as an example of one way to proceed.

There are many factors that can influence how one may choose to present bilingual storytime programs; two that are very important are the needs of your specific community and the skill set of the librarian or programmer. A colleague of mine can speak some Spanish, enough to greet and welcome people and to get through basic customer service transactions. There are often Latino children who attend her storytime programs, and so she likes to incorporate some Spanish words and phrases. She will choose bilingual books, and though she reads just the English, she will point out to families that such bilingual formats are available and perhaps pick a few key Spanish vocabulary words to reinforce throughout the reading. She may also take a traditional song that the kids already know and sing it in Spanish—changing "Head, Shoulders, Knees, and Toes" to *"Cabeza, hombros, rodillas, y pies,"* for example. For her, this is an opportunity to validate the bilingual experience of the Latino children in her storytime group by introducing elements of their language. It is also an opportunity to share songs and books with Spanish-speaking caregivers that they can then take home. Though not a truly bilingual storytime, this is a way in which non-bilingual librarians can celebrate the linguistic and cultural experiences of Latino children in their libraries.

Another approach non-bilingual librarians can take to implementing bilingual programs in their libraries is to invite Spanish-speaking community members to volunteer. Librarians can select books and stories that are available in both languages and present a tandem storytime, with the librarian presenting the English and the community volunteer communicating the Spanish. Because it may be difficult to find a volunteer who can commit to a regular weekly storytime, this approach may work best for occasional programs, such as those celebrating Hispanic Heritage Month, *El día de los niños/El día de los libros,* and other cultural celebrations.

CASE STUDY OF A BILINGUAL (NON-NATIVE) LIBRARIAN

I approach a bilingual storytime within the framework of Every Child Ready to Read, and everything I do is selected to reinforce the development of one or more of the six preliteracy skills and to model ways in which parents can continue that development at home. An additional component I strive to incorporate into each program is cultural relevance—being sure to include

Latino authors, illustrators, songs, characters, and/or traditional stories into each program. I generally select books and other storytelling techniques appropriate for a preschool audience. However, I use a family storytime format in order to include siblings, cousins, and neighbors who may come along. Therefore I am always prepared with bilingual board books, bilingual fingerplays, and soft toys for toddlers and babies who may not be able to sit still and follow a story in the same way a preschooler can. It may be a little harder to prepare for a program that has a wide range of age, but I have found that the inclusiveness of this approach is a great benefit to gaining and maintaining an audience.

When I first began doing bilingual storytimes, I was unsure what types of books I should use. I wanted to use Spanish children's books written by Latino authors, but my library did not own many. I wanted bilingual books, but most of what I found was much too wordy to use in storytime. I wanted to use books with Latino characters, but was surprised at how many times those characters fell into stereotypes. Thankfully, the publishing industry has taken notice that there is a demand for high-quality bilingual books and books that present a positive picture of Latino children by Latino authors and illustrators.

When I select books for bilingual storytime now, my ideal choices are bilingual titles that present simple text appropriate for a preschool audience in both English and Spanish. Excellent examples are the books in the My Family = Mi familia series by Pat Mora, such as *Let's Eat = A comer,* in which a Latino family gathers to enjoy a healthy meal of *ensalada, tortillas y frijoles.* The first time I used this book, I was thrilled to see the way the Latino children in the group responded to seeing the foods they know, calling out "We eat *frijoles* at my house!" The key to selecting books for bilingual storytime is choosing titles that are developmentally appropriate and that will resonate with the children. In addition to bilingual books, I will read books in Spanish (including translations of English titles), followed by a synopsis of the page in English if necessary. This is a matter of my personal preference—I want a bilingual storytime to feature materials my library has available that are either bilingual or in Spanish. Sometimes I also select books that are mostly in English that incorporate Spanish words, such as those by Susan Middleton Elya and Ann Whitford Paul.

Learning to recognize rhyme is an important part of developing phonological awareness. *Hello Night/Hola noche* by Amy Costales is a rare example of a bilingual rhyming book. However, most titles that rhyme in one language do not maintain the rhyme when translated. Every once in a while I will come across some exceptions, such as *¿Como dan las buenas noches los dinosaurios?* by Jane Yolen (Spanish translation of *How Do Dinosaurs Say Goodnight?*) and

Abuelita fue al mercado by Stella Blackstone (Spanish translation of *My Granny Went to Market*). With such books, the words are often slightly changed in order to work in the rhyme. When I incorporate such books, I present them in Spanish, reading the text either from memory or from a typed copy as written in English. The words may not be exactly the same in both languages, but the integrity of the rhyme is maintained.

The most important criterion in selecting books for a bilingual storytime is to choose books that you as the presenter love to read, because your enthusiasm will captivate the attention of the children and reinforce print motivation. If you are reading something that you think you "should" include but don't really enjoy, the children will pick up on this and lose attention. My personal programming style involves high energy with a lot of movement, so I like to use stories with motions we can act out together, such as *De la cabeza a los pies* by Eric Carle (Spanish translation of *From Head to Toe*) and *La oca boba* by Petr Horáček (Spanish translation of *Silly Goose*). The books you select should ignite your enthusiasm, which will in turn ignite the enthusiasm of your audience.

In addition to books, I use music, fingerplays, and other storytelling techniques, such as drawing stories and creative dynamics. I have found many great resources by looking at the materials my colleagues use and by making translations, either to tell the entire story in both languages or to tell it in English with specific words or phrases repeated in Spanish. Rather than reinventing the wheel for every program, look for what can be modified to meet the needs of your audience.

I am especially fond of using Spanish or bilingual movement songs and flannelboard storytelling. Movement songs, in addition to promoting phonological awareness, can provide a much-needed break from sitting still. This is especially important if you choose a family storytime format where you may have children of various ages and attention spans. Spanish versions of traditional songs most American children recognize, such as "Head, Shoulders, Knees and Toes," and "The Itsy Bitsy Spider" are easy to learn and work well, as do traditional Spanish songs such as "La granja" and "Juanito." I like reinforcing songs with puppets, props, and musical instruments when appropriate. Be sure to make lyrics available to parents and have copies of the CDs available to check out.

Like picture books, which can expose readers to words they do not use in everyday conversation, flannelboard storytelling can be an excellent way to reinforce the development of vocabulary. Cumulative tales that repeat specific words are especially useful. Flannels pair the introduction of words with visual images, and can be interactive. For example, I use flannel pieces to tell the story *Brown Bear, Brown Bear, What Do You See?* by Bill Martin, Jr. This introduces color and animal vocabulary in both languages with each piece. After telling, you can use the flannel pieces to review the vocabulary and interact with the children by asking them questions: *"¿Cual es lo azul? ¿Como se dice azul en ingles? ¿Ves algo azul en el cuarto?"* Having the children help you retell a story using flannelboard pieces after you have read the book also helps develop narrative skills.

PASSION + PATIENCE = SUCCESS

Developing a successful bilingual storytime program takes passion and patience. It may take time for your community to begin attending regularly, and you may need to make an effort to promote the program through channels outside the library. It will take more time to plan and design than an English-only storytime, because you will need translations for some of the materials and stories you want to use. You may feel increased pressure or stress, particularly if there are few bilingual staff members. However, the benefits are worth the challenges. The bilingual storytime is a way to welcome Latino families into the library, to promote diversity and inclusiveness at your location, and to help the children in your community develop the early literacy skills they need to be ready to read. Good luck in your planning and have fun!

RESOURCE LISTS

Recommended Bilingual Storytime Books by Early Literacy Skill

VOCABULARY

Cumpiano, Ina, and José Ramírez. *Quinito's Neighborhood/El vecindario de Quinito.*

Ehlert, Lois. *A sembrar sopa de verduras.* Translated by Alma Flor Ada and F. Isabel Campoy.

Grejniec, Michael. *Buenos días, buenas noches.* Translated by Alis Alejandro.

Guy, Ginger Foglesong. *¡Perros! ¡Perros! = Dogs! Dogs!*

Wellington, Monica. *Ana cultiva manzana/Apple Farmer Annie.* Translated by Eida del Risco.

PHONOLOGICAL AWARENESS

Beaton, Clare. *Cerdota grandota.* Translated by Yanitzia Canetti.

Costales, Amy. *Hola noche / Hello Night.*

Fox, Christyan, and Diane Fox. *¡Ratón, que te pilla el gato!*

Montes, Marisa. *Los Gatos Black on Halloween.*

Serrano, Esteban. *Leonidas y su perro Luis.*

PRINT AWARENESS

Blackstone, Stella. *Una isla bajo el sol.* Translated by Yanitzia Canetti.

Cronin, Doreen. *Clic, clac, muu: Vacas escritoras.* Translated by Alberto Jimenez Rioja.

Gonzalez, Maya Christina. *Mis colores, mi mundo / My Colors, My World.*

Horáček, Petr. *La oca boba.*

Masurel, Claire. *Un gato y un perro / A Cat and a Dog.*

LETTER KNOWLEDGE

Campoy, F. Isabel. *Mi dia de la A a la Z.*

Mora, Pat. *Marimba! Animales from A to Z.*

Morales, Yuyi. *Just in Case.*

Reed, Lynn Rowe. *Pedro, His Perro, and the Alphabet Sombrero.*

Weill, Cynthia. *ABeCedarios: Mexican Folk Art ABCs in English and Spanish.*

NARRATIVE SKILLS

Chaundler, Rachel. *Mariluz avestruz.*

Deedy, Carmen Agra. *Martina, the Beautiful Cockroach: A Cuban Folktale.*

De la Hoya, Oscar. *Super Oscar.*

Henkes, Kevin. *La primera luna llena de gatita.* Translated by Osvaldo Blanco.

MacDonald, Margaret Read. *Conejito: A Folktale from Panama.*

PRINT MOTIVATION

Browne, Anthony. *La feria de los animales.*

Carle, Eric. *De la cabeza a los pies.*

Ferri, Francesca. *Cucú—¡te veo!*

Mora, Pat. *Book Fiesta! Celebrate Children's Day/Book Day / Book Fiesta! Celebremos El día de los niños/El día de los libros.*

Sendak, Maurice. *Donde viven los monstruos.*

Recommended Music

Anaya, Jorge. *¡A bailar! Let's dance! Spanish Learning Songs.*

Barchas, Sarah. *¡Piñata! and More! Bilingual Songs for Children.*

————. *¡Todos, listos, canten! Canciones para niños y para aprender el español.*

Del Rey, Maria. *Universe of Song.*

Feldman, Jean R. *Ole! Ole! Ole! Dr. Jean en Español.*

Jordan, Sara. *Bilingual Preschool: English-Spanish.*

Orozco, José-Luis. *Canto y cuento: Lírica infantil.*

————. *De Colores and Other Latin-American Folk Songs.*

————. *Diez Deditos: Ten Little Fingers and Other Play Rhymes and Action Songs from Latin America.*

Sol y Canto. *El doble de amigos / Twice as Many Friends.*

SAMPLE STORYTIME PLANS

Following are several bilingual storytime plans that I have used many times, as well as a general outline of how I typically design a bilingual storytime program. Programs generally last about 30 minutes. Plans are designed by theme, with multiple titles appropriate for a preschool audience. The outline can be modified as necessary to fit the needs of the audience and the presenter's personal style. Rather than presenting many themes with a few suggestions each, I have chosen to present a few themes with a wealth of possible ideas. Each of the presented plans could be used to generate multiple storytimes.

General Bilingual Storytime Outline

- ❀ Opening Song or Rhyme
  - ❀ Suggested options: "Hola amigo" from *Ole! Ole! Ole! Dr. Jean en Español* by Jean Feldman, "Buenos días" from *De Colores and Other Latin-American Folk Songs* by José-Luis Orozco, or "Open Them, Shut Them = Abranlas, ciérrenlas" from *Ring a Ring O'Roses: Fingerplays for Preschool Children* by the Flint Public Library.
- ❀ Book One

❀ Storytelling: Flannel, Drawing Story, Creative Dramatic or other technique

❀ Book Two

❀ Movement Song

   ❀ Suggested options for any theme: "Si juntamos las manitas" from *Canto y cuento: Lírica infantil* by José-Luis Orozco, "Groovin' and Movin' = Ritmo y movimiento" from *Bilingual Preschool: English-Spanish* by Sara Jordan, and "Mi cuerpo hace musica" from *El doble de amigos = Twice as Many Friends* by Sol y Canto.

❀ Book Three

❀ Closing Song

   ❀ Suggested options: "Adios amigos" *Ole! Ole! Ole! Dr. Jean en Español* by Jean Feldman or "Adios amigos" from *Diez Deditos: Ten Little Fingers and Other Play Rhymes and Action Songs from Latin America* by José-Luis Orozco.

❀ Free play activity or craft: This is optional, and will depend on your style, as well as the standards of your location. Some libraries may like to include a theme-based craft to do at the library or to take home. Others may have free play time with early-literacy- or science-based manipulatives. Whatever you do, this is your time to talk with families, answer their questions, thank them for coming, and invite them back next week.

Suggested Themes

BODY/MOVEMENT

With this theme I would use more music than normal and select stories that have a lot of movement that the children can act out.

Books

Carle, Eric. *De la cabeza a los pies.*

Cronin, Doreen. *¡A tu ritmo!* Translated by Yanitzia Canetti.

Davis, Katie. *Who Hops? = ¿Quién salta?*

Fancy, Colin. *Los cocodrilos no se cepillan los dientes.*

Tafolla, Carmen. *What Can You Do with a Rebozo?/¿Que puedes hacer con un rebozo?*

Walsh, Ellen Stoll. *Salta y brinca.* Translated by Alma Flor Ada and F. Isabel Campoy.

Songs/Fingerplays

❀ "Juanito" from *Diez Deditos: Ten Little Fingers and Other Play Rhymes and Action Songs from Latin America* by José-Luis Orozco or "Los niños cuando bailan" from *¡A bailar! Let's dance! Spanish Learning Songs* by Jorge Anaya.

❀ "Pulgarcito, ¿dónde estás? / Where Is Thumbkin?"

Pulgarcito, ¿dónde estás?	*Where is Thumbkin? Where is Thumbkin?*
¡Aquí estoy! ¡Aquí estoy!	*Here I am! Here I am!*
¿Cómo está usted?	*How are you today sir?*
¡Muy bien, gracias!	*Very well I thank you.*
Ya me voy. Ya me voy.	*Run away. Run away.*

❀ To the same tune, you can also try this movement activity:

Caminando,	*walking, walking*
A brincar,	*hop, hop, hop*
Corre, corre, corre	*Running, running, running*
Para ya.	*now we stop.*

Other

❀ Make flannel pieces of various parts of the body, such as the body parts introduced in one of the songs. For example, you could have flannel pieces of a head, shoulder, knee, toe, eye, ear, mouth, and nose. Introduce each body part and have the children find their own: "*¡Muevan las cabezas!* Everyone move your head!" Then have the group sing "*Cabeza, hombros, rodillas, pies.*" Afterward, ask the children to help you take each piece down in order to further reinforce the vocabulary: "*Cual es la nariz* / Which one is the nose?" This could be done with any of the movement songs that introduce body parts.

NIGHT/BEDTIME

Books

Gribel, Christiane. *No voy a dormer / I Am Not Going to Sleep.*

Mora, Pat. *Sweet Dreams / Dulces sueños.*

Weeks, Sarah. *Counting Ovejas.*

Wood, Audrey. *La casa adormecida.* Translated by Alma Flor Ada and F. Isabel Campoy.

Yolen, Jane. *¿Como dan las buenas noches los dinosaurios?*

Storytelling

❀ *Tengo miedo a la oscuridad* by Jacqueline East works as a flannel by making a dog who looks scared, a cat, a turtle, a horse, a tree, an owl, and a sleeping dog.

Songs/Fingerplays

❀ "Los pollitos" is a traditional lullaby. A nice version can be found on *De Colores and Other Latin-American Folk Songs* by José-Luis Orozco.

❀ "Habian diez en la cama" from *¡Todos, listos, canten! Canciones para niños y para aprender el español* by Sarah Barchas.

❀ "Twinkle, Twinkle Little Star / Brilla, brilla, estrellita"

Brilla, brilla, estrellita	*Twinkle, twinkle, little star*
En el cielo, tan bonita,	*How I wonder what you are.*
Deja el cielo y ven aca,	*Up above the world so high,*
A jugar, conmigo ya,	*like a diamond in the sky.*
Brilla, brilla, estrellita	*Twinkle, twinkle, little star*
En el cielo, tan bonita.	*How I wonder what you are.*

ANIMALS

Books

Beaton, Clare. *Cerdota grandota.* Translated by Yanitzia Canetti.

Carle, Eric. *La araña muy ocupada.*

Chaundler, Rachel. *Mariluz Avestruz.*

Gomi, Taro. *My Friends / Mis amigos.* This book is fun to extend with puppets, having the children each act as one of the animals and teaching the group what they can do.

Horáček, Petr. *La oca boba.*

Rathmann, Peggy. *Buenas noches gorila.*

Waddell, Martin. *Las lechucitas.* Translated by Andrea Bermúdes.

Storytelling

❀ *The Bossy Gallito / El gallo de bodas*, by Lucía González is a cumulative folktale that works perfectly for the flannelboard. Needed pieces are an elegant and beautifully dressed rooster, a patch of grass, a goat, a stick, a fire, a stream of water, and the sun. Let the children play with the pieces after storytime to retell the story themselves. Reinforces vocabulary and narrative skills.

❀ "Camping Out" drawing story from *Frog's Riddle and Other Draw-and-Tell Stories* by Richard Thompson. Two girls who are best friends go camping and have a great time swimming, until it begins to rain. They rush back to their tents, only to find something has gotten inside. What is it? As the drawing reveals, it's an owl.

❀ *Monkey Face* by Frank Asch works as a drawing story and is easily told bilingually.

Songs/Fingerplays

❀ "Cinco monitos" from *Ole! Ole! Ole! Dr. Jean en Español* by Jean Feldman. Make flannel pieces, puppets, or use fingerplay motions to make this song more interactive.

❀ "Follow the Leader/Sigue al lider" from *Bilingual Preschool: English-Spanish* by Sara Jordan.

❀ "Las hormiguitas" from *De Colores and Other Latin-American Folk Songs* by José-Luis Orozco.

❀ "Pajarito" from *Canto y Cuento: Lírica infantil* by José-Luis Orozco.

❀ "La araña pequeñita/The Itsy Bitsy Spider"

La araña pequeñita	*The itsy, bitsy spider*
Subió, subió, subió.	*Went up the water spout.*
Vino la lluvia	*Down came the rain*
Y se la llevo.	*And washed the spider out.*
Salio el sol	*Out came the sun*
Y todo lo seco,	*And dried up all the rain*
Y la araña pequeñita	*And the itsy, bitsy spider*
Subió, subió, subió.	*Went up the spout again.*

PETS

Books

Browne, Anthony. *Cosita linda.*

Falconer, Ian. 2004. *Olivia y el juguete desaparecido.*

Fox, Christyan, and Diane Fox. *Ratón, que te pilla el gato!*

Henkes, Kevin. *La primera luna llena de gatita.* Translated by Osvaldo Blanco.

Horáček, Petr. *Elefante.* Translated by Raquel Solà.

Masurel, Claire. *Un gato y un perro = A Cat and a Dog.*

Mora, Pat. *Here, Kitty, Kitty! = ¡Ven, gatita, ven!*

Morozumi, Atsuko. *Mi amigo Gorila.*

Serrano, Esteban. *Leonidas y su perro Luis.*

Storytelling

❁ *Cookie's Week* by Cindy Ward makes a great flannel. Cookie is a little kitten who gets into all types of mischief. Hopefully by the end of the week she will be ready to rest! Reinforces vocabulary for the days of the week.

❁ The easy reader classic *Biscuit* by Alyssa Capucilli works as a flannel. Biscuit needs many things before he's ready for bed, such as to play, a bone, some water, and, of course, a bedtime story.

Songs/Fingerplays

❁ "¿Dónde está mi perrito ahora?" from *Todos, listos, canten! canciones para niños y para aprender el español* by Sarah Barchas.

FAMILY

Books

Ada, Alma Flor. *I Love Saturdays y Domingos.*

Bertrand, Diane Gonzales. *We Are Cousins / Somos primos.*

Cisneros, Sandra. *Hairs / Pelitos.*

Cumpiano, Ina. *Quinito, Day and Night / Quinito, día y noche.*

Dorros, Arthur. *Papá and Me.*

Guy, Ginger Foglesong. *My Grandma / Mi abuelita.*

McNelly McCormack, Caren. *The Fiesta Dress: A Quinceañera Tale.*

Storytelling

❁ *Are You My Mother?* by P. D. Eastman and *My Mother Is Lost* by Bernice Myers both work well on the flannelboard.

Songs/Fingerplays

❁ "Don't Touch the Baby / No toques al bebé."

Here is the baby.	*Aqui es el bebé.*
(TELLER POINTS TO CENTER OF A CHILD'S PALM)	
Mama says: "Don't touch the baby."	*Mama dice, "no toques al bebé."*
(TELLER POINTS TO LISTENER'S THUMB)	
Daddy says: "Don't touch the baby."	*Papa dice, "no toques al bebé."*
(TELLER POINTS TO LISTENER'S INDEX FINGER)	

Grandfather says: "Don't touch the baby."	*Abuelo dice, "no toques al bebé."*
(TELLER POINTS TO LISTENER'S MIDDLE FINGER)	
Grandmother says: "Don't touch the baby."	*Abuela dice, "no toques al bebé."*
(TELLER POINTS TO LISTENER'S RING FINGER)	
Sister says: "Don't touch the baby."	*Hermana dice, "no toques al bebé."*
(TELLER POINTS TO LISTENER'S LITTLE FINGER)	
Now, do you remember where is the baby?	*Recuerdes, ¿donde esta el bebé?*
(TELLER WAITS. LISTENER WILL USUALLY REACH OUT AND TOUCH PALM)	
Don't touch the baby!	*¡No toques al bebé!*
(SHAKE FINGER AT LISTENER, AS IF SCOLDING)	

COUNTING

Books

Bang, Molly. *Diez, nueve, ocho.*

Blackstone, Stella. *Abuelita fue al mercado: Un libro en rima para contar por el mundo.*

Gorbachev, Valeri. *Nico y los lobos feroces.*

Guy, Ginger Foglesong. *¡Fiesta!*

Jenkins, Emily. *Cinco criaturas.*

Masurel, Claire. *Diez perros en la tienda: Un libro para contar.* Translated by Elena Moro.

Morales, Yuyi. *Just a Minute: A Trickster Tale and Counting Book.*

Walsh, Ellen Stoll. *Cuenta ratones.*

Songs/Fingerplays

❀ "Diez deditos" from *Diez Deditos: Ten Little Fingers and Other Play Rhymes and Action Songs from Latin America* by José-Luis Orozco.

❀ "Los deditos" from *¡A bailar! Let's dance! Spanish Learning Songs* by Jorge Anaya.

Other

❊ Practice higher numbers by counting together by 5's and 10's in both languages.

COLORS

Books

Andricaín, Sergio. *Arco iris de poesía: Poemas de las Américas y España.*

Crews, Donald. *Freight Train/Tren de carga.*

Desmazières, Sandra. *Emma y sus amigos: Un libro sobre los colores.*

Gonzalez, Maya Christina. *Mis colores, mi mundo/My Colors, My World.*

Guy, Ginger Foglesong. *Siesta.*

Walsh, Ellen Stoll. *Pinta ratones.*

Storytelling

❊ *Dog's Colorful Day* by Emma Dodd makes a great drawing story. On a large piece of paper, draw Dog/*Perrito* as he starts out at the beginning of the day. Have different colored spots that the children can tape on Dog as he gets into various messy items. When he gets his bath at the end, the children can take off each spot by color.

❊ *Brown Bear, Brown Bear, What Do You See?* by Bill Martin, Jr., works well as a flannel story by making each of the animals with the corresponding color.

PROFESSIONAL RESOURCES

Print

Avila, Salvador. *Crash Course in Serving Spanish-Speakers.* Westport, CT: Libraries Unlimited, 2008.

Flint Public Library. *Ring a Ring O'Roses: Fingerplays for Preschool Children.* Flint, MI: Flint Public Library, 2008.

Kranwinkel, S., and Ekberg, M. H. *Spanish Piggyback Songs.* Totline books. Everett, WA: Warren Publishing, 1995.

Schiller, P. B., R. Lara-Alecio, and B. J. Irby. *The Bilingual Book of Rhymes, Songs, Stories, and Fingerplays/El libro bilingue de rimas, canciones, cuentos y juegos.* Beltsville, MD: Gryphon House, 2004.

Treviño, Rose Zertuche. *Read Me a Rhyme in Spanish and English/Léame una rima en español e inglés.* Chicago: American Library Association, 2009.

Online

American Library Association. "Every Child Ready to Read in Practice: Translations." http://www.ala.org/ala/mgrps/divs/alsc/ecrr/ecrrinpractice/translations/languages. cfm (accessed November 2009). Find translations and information on pre-literacy skills in various languages, including Spanish.

Bonet, Elida Guardia, Paola Ferate-Soto, Josefina Rodriguez-Gibbs, Nohemi Lopez, and California State University San Marcos. "Baharona Center for the Study of Books in Spanish for Children and Adolescents." http://www2.csusm.edu/csb/ (accessed November 2009).

Cunningham, Katie. "¡Es divertido hablar dos idiomas!" http://www. bilingualchildrensprogramming.blogspot.com (accessed November 2009). Includes programming ideas, flannel patterns and scripts, suggested books for bilingual storytime, and links to other useful Web sites.

Moreyra-Torres, Maricela. "Dígame un cuento / Tell Me a Story: Bilingual Library Programs for Children and Families." http://www.tsl.state.tx.us/ld/pubs/ bilingual/ (accessed November 2009).

REFORMA. "Children and Young Adult Services. http://www.reforma.org/CYASC. htm (accessed November 2009). Find plans for bilingual and Spanish storytimes, along with other resources for libraries serving Latino children and families.

Webjunction. "Spanish Language Outreach Program." http://www.webjunction. org/slo (accessed November 2009). Find research, archived webinars, and case studies on bilingual storytime and other topics relating to outreach to the Spanish speaking.

WETA. "Reading Rockets." http://www.readingrockets.org/ (accessed November 2009). Information on literacy and learning to read for parents and educators. Also available in Spanish.

REFERENCES

American Library Association. "Every Child Ready to Read at Your Library." http:// www.ala.org/ala/mgrps/divs/alsc/ecrr/index.cfm (accessed November 2009).

Diamant-Cohen, B. *Mother Goose on the Loose: A Handbook and CD-ROM Kit with Scripts, Rhymes, Songs, Flannelboard Patterns, and Activities for Promoting Early Childhood Development.* New York: Neal-Schuman.

King, K. A., and A. Mackey. *The Bilingual Edge: Why, When, and How to Teach Your Child a Second Language.* New York: Collins, 2007.

Payne, R. K. *A Framework for Understanding Poverty.* Highlands, TX: Aha! Process, 2005.

Tabors, Patton O. *One Child, Two Languages: A Guide for Preschool Educators of Children Learning English as a Second Language.* Baltimore, MD: Paul H. Brookes Publishing, 1997.

❀ **CHAPTER 10**

Using Bilingual Music Programming to Improve Preliteracy

Amy Olson

Exposure to and eventual fluency in the English language is necessary for academic success in U.S. schools. Conservative estimates suggest there are more than 5.5 million students attending U.S. public schools whose first language is not English; of this group, 80 percent are fluent in Spanish (McCardle et al. 2005). When ELL (English Language Learner)[1] children attend school, they face the daily challenge of learning to communicate and read in a language that is different from the one spoken at home (Lindsey et al. 2003; Páez et al. 2007). Unfortunately, statistics consistently show that ELL children are at risk for poor reading outcomes, and that even proficient bilingual[2] children begin kindergarten with language and preliteracy skills that are below expectation (Hammer et al. 2007; Páez et al. 2007).

Where can ELL and bilingual children go to improve their literacy skills prior to entering kindergarten? The most obvious choices are preschools and Head Start centers. However, the local public library and elementary school library can also play an integral role in developing and fostering language and literacy skills. The Latino community is the largest and fastest-growing minority in the United States, exceeding 46.9 million people. Therefore, the ability to offer bilingual programming has become an essential part of the work of a children's librarian (U.S. Census Bureau 2008). Outside the classroom, music may be the only major source of English that an ELL child will hear; therefore the integration of music into a preliteracy learning setting, such as a school or library, can assist children's language development and academic learning while

---

1   As the focus of this volume is on serving Latino children, the term *ELL* (English Language Learner) will refer to Latinos learning English.

2   For the sake of clarity throughout this chapter, the term *bilingual* will be defined as the ability to speak both English and Spanish.

simultaneously allowing them to develop musically (Bolduc 2009; Wiggins 2007).

This chapter discusses how music can help ELL children with language and preliteracy development, the *musical tale*, and ways in which children's librarians can use the musical tale in bilingual musical literacy-based programming. Useful Web sites for bilingual music-oriented programming are provided at the end of this chapter, and the extensive bibliography later in this book includes musical tale titles and CDs that will assist children's librarians and other educators in creating valuable learning experiences for children.

MUSIC AND PRELITERACY SKILLS

Historically, songs and oral poetry have been used to pass cultural history and lore down from generation to generation. Over time, written language has overtaken oral language as the primary means of communication. Music is one sure form of communication that crosses the gap between oral and written language skills (Wiggins 2007). Infants and young children rely on their aural and oral skills for language acquisition. At the same time, infancy and early childhood are critical periods for the development of musical abilities and the formation of musical identities. Children as young as four years of age are able to remember random digits, letters, words, and even multiplication tables through song or rhythmic groupings (Anvari et al. 2002). For example, toddlers learn their ABCs to a tune long before they are able to read or even recognize letters. Interestingly enough, while the tune used for the ABCs is the same tune used for "Baa, Baa, Black Sheep" and "Twinkle, Twinkle Little Star," it is actually an old French tune made popular by Mozart in his Twelve Variations on "Ah! Vous dirai-je, Maman." Thus, the ABCs tune is a phenomenal way to introduce children to different styles of music, composers, languages, cultures, and countries.

A young child's introduction to text often occurs through songs, chants, jingles, or rhymes. We hum and sing all the time: in the car, while walking, in the shower, or when putting a baby to sleep. During playtime, it is common, almost innate, for a child to sing, "Nyah-nah-nah-nyah-nah, you can't get me" to get attention. Children experience music throughout their daily lives and enjoy having opportunities to represent what they know, playing with both language and lyrics (Yopp and Yopp 2009). Singing without the aid of instruments or technology is natural for them. Singing alone, *a cappella*, allows children to listen to their own voices and to create new sounds.

Music can prepare children for the different experiences they will encounter, allowing them to explore diversity and cultures that are not their own (Kirmani 2007).

Music also allows ELL children to have pride in and celebrate their own culture, to become empowered rather than remain hidden, and to participate in their community. It enables children to investigate the world around them, to imagine, to encourage others, and to be encouraged in their own personal creativity (Yopp and Yopp 2009).

Music can introduce children to cultural proverbs and idioms. Proverbs and idioms can be hard for children to understand, and often require an adult's explanation. English proverbs and idioms are incredibly difficult for ELL children to comprehend as many expressions do not cross cultures well ("in the nick of time, a piece of cake, out of the blue, for example"). Acquisition and use of idioms and proverbs are some of the last language skills that a new language-learner masters.

Involvement with music allows children's auditory and discrimination skills to improve naturally. Through music, children can experience different methods of listening: reflective (where children are encouraged to think for themselves) and active (where children listen to participate). Music and songs help to increase these listening skills in an entertaining and relaxed manner. Children who are unable to listen are unable to participate. Children instinctively listen to music in order to identify familiar melodies and rhythms, just as beginning readers look for words that sound alike, that have patterns, or contain rhyme. Listening to music teaches children to identify variances in pitch or tone, to differentiate between sounds, to identify rhythmic patterns, to describe sounds accurately, and to articulate personal responses to what they hear.

Children's librarians and parents/caregivers should remember to focus on children's process of learning—it is far more vital to encourage children to compose and improvise than to worry about how the music sounds. This takes the pressure off the parent/caregiver or librarian; they don't have to "prepare the child to sing" by getting out specific instruments or electronics . . . the child can just sing spontaneously. And when children are enjoying themselves, it is likely that their attitude will be positive. It is much easier for children to learn if they are having fun in a positive environment. A negative attitude or environment can prevent a child from learning; if a child is frightened or feeling unaccepted, he or she is less likely to participate. Music, fortunately, tends to be a pleasant experience for children. Through song, children can find ways to convey their feelings and thoughts fluently and freely while learning new forms of self-expression in a positive environment (Wiggins 2007). Ultimately, children will have their confidence augmented through their participation, even if their involvement is solely through body movements or clapping out rhythms (Bolduc 2009).

PHONOLOGICAL AWARENESS

Music can also play an important role in helping ELL children develop phonological awareness. A child's development of such awareness happens in two stages: when the child learns to match individual speech sounds to the letters of the alphabet (phonemic awareness), and when the child understands what graphemes represent (graphemic awareness). Phonemic and graphemic awareness are the precursors to phonological awareness.

Phonemic Awareness

A phoneme is the smallest unit of speech that, when replaced, results in a change of meaning—*mop* becomes *map* or *los* becomes *las*. The phonemes in each of these examples are *o* and *a*. Phonemic awareness occurs when a child can hear or see the word (for example, *bug*) and can match the individual sounds of the word to the corresponding letters (/*b*/-/*u*/-/*g*/). Children who can isolate and manipulate phonemes have greater success with reading than those who have difficulty with phonemes (Lamb and Gregory 1993). In addition, children who can recognize the beginning and ending sounds of words are more successful in school than children who cannot.

Monolingual[3] children are likely to develop their skills at a faster rate than ELL or bilingual children (Uccelli and Páez 2007). Music is one tool that can help to equalize educational instruction among these monolingual, ELL, and bilingual children, as phonemic awareness allows children to demonstrate greater ease with oral and written language, both inside and outside the classroom (Favila et al. 1999; Herrera et al. 2007; Lamb and Gregory 1993).

Children can also be taught about phonemes through various forms of rhythmic clapping. For instance, if children clap each syllable of the names below, the first two names would have three claps and the last two names would have two claps (Hansen and Bernstorf 2002; Stuart-Hamilton 1986):

---

3   For the sake of clarity in this chapter, the term *monolingual* will refer to those who only speak English.

Tor -i-ah   An-ge-la   An-drés   Mi-chael

Rhythmic clapping enables children to reproduce speech patterns while physically experiencing the musical and literary concepts of phrasing (Hansen and Bernstorf 2002). Teaching phrasing in this way allows children to grasp how a word is read, how to group words together smoothly, and how to make a transition from one word to another word within a sentence.

If the children have difficulty clapping simultaneously with the leader, they can be encouraged to echo-clap instead. Echo-clapping is where the adult initiates the clapping pattern and the children imitate it, as if they were the echo (Hansen and Bernstorf 2002). When the children begin to feel more comfortable with the concept of rhythmically clapping out words and syllables through imitation, they can return to group syllabic clapping. And as they become more confident with syllabic/phrase clapping in a group, they can be further challenged to accent syllables within a word. This accenting can be done in two ways: by clapping louder on the accented syllable or by clapping higher in the air for accented syllables.

Both rhythmic clapping and accentuating accented syllables help ELL children greatly because Spanish is a language where typically the second-to-last syllable receives the accent or the accent mark is visible in a word. These accent rules are not as consistent in English, where accenting is far more random and physical accent marks much less common (Herrera et al. 2007).

Graphemic Awareness

Graphemes are symbols, typically letters, used to represent certain sounds. For instance, in the word *box*, the *x* sounds like *k* and *s* together, so the grapheme for *x* is *ks*. A child who has difficulty with graphemes will tend to spell phonetically, such as writing *nee* instead of *knee* and *froot* instead of *fruit*. When a child has difficulty with graphemes, this will become evident through their spelling tests. For ELL children, graphemic awareness becomes all the more difficult—the English language has approximately forty-four different vowel and consonant sounds, whereas the Spanish language has only twenty-four (Yopp and Yopp 2009).

Achieving Phonological Awareness

Phonological awareness, the most important step in a child's ability to read, is directly related to the development of his or her reading skills. Phonological awareness happens when a child is able to distinguish and be sensitive to individual sounds and syllables, combining both phonemic and graphemic awareness (Lamb and Gregory 1993). At the phonological awareness stage of learning, it is all the more important to introduce ELL children to varying songs and books that encourage them to explore rhyme, meter, and musical poetry.

THE MUSICAL TALE

The musical tale[4] is a children's picture book that features the lyrics of a song along with illustrations that enhance the lyrics. The musical tale reinforces a child's phonemic, graphemic, and phonological awareness skills through lyrics and through rhythm using all five senses—seeing, hearing, touching, tasting, and smelling. Musical tales provide a way for children to see illustrations and print in English and in Spanish, to hear the tales as they are sung, and to touch, taste, and smell the instruments and books as they are used.

Rather than sitting down and officially learning how to read (which could be perceived by the child and even their parent/caregiver as work), the musical tale offers an opportunity for the child to do something they enjoy—playing with music—in order to learn. This is not to suggest that musical play is only a game; songs have intrinsic, instructional value. A child's ability to embrace musical play and the opportunities for imagination provide a foundation for learning preliteracy skills.

Note: I have found that many musical tales are available only in English or are out of print when previously they were available either in Spanish or bilingually. This need not be a deterrent; I have dealt with this situation successfully in four ways:

1. I make color copies of the books that are in English and add the Spanish text onto each page in order to make a bilingual tale—this has worked the best for me in programming.

2. I hold up a book that is available in English, and sing the words in Spanish (so that the children still have the visual context).

3. I use felt that I have cut out to recreate the visual illustrations on a flannel board and add the text to the flannel board using velcro.

4. I use PowerPoint to display the illustrations and remove all text. I then send the text home with the parents, along with copies of the illustrations so that the parents/caregivers can work with the children to recreate the musical tale in their own home.

---

4   It is presumed that the musical tale will be performed bilingually whenever possible.

Lyrics and Musical Tales

Lyrics in musical tales tend to be children's songs or nursery rhymes, chants, finger plays, poetry set to a melody, or other songs that have become well-known classics. Lyrics allow children to explore language through repeated exposure to words—singing is a celebration of language. Lyrics enable children to experience and celebrate diversity not only of other cultures, but of other singing styles. Ideas and emotions, both those of the children and those of the songwriter, can be explored through melody and lyrics, combining music with meaning.

Musical tales are useful to demonstrate to children how a book is read in English or Spanish. As a musical tale is sung, the words can be pointed out to the children; the children watch as the words are read from left to right and top to bottom, learning important literary skills (McIntosh et al. 2007; Wiggins 2007).

Musical tales can help children who are attempting to learn. To learn a song requires practice and memorization, which is essentially the repetition of vocabulary, fine-tuning pronunciation and intonation, and reinforcing grammatical and rhyming patterns (Jalongo and Ribblett 1997; Paquette and Reig 2008). Repetition is essential for children; hearing sounds, words, and phrases over and over is a necessary part of language acquisition, as is learning to recognize words that make the same sounds and how to manipulate those sounds to create new words (Paquette and Reig 2008). Vocabulary knowledge is an important precursor to preliteracy for children (Dickinson et al. 2003; Uccelli and Páez 2007). ELL children with slower vocabulary development are less able to comprehend information at the same level as their monolingual peers (August et al. 2005). Through repetition, however, ELL children can overcome their risk of early preliteracy difficulties and not lag as far behind their monolingual peers (Uccelli and Páez 2007).

For instance, in the musical tune *In My Face/En mi cara* children reinforce their vocabulary skills as they point to the parts of their faces:

In my face, my little round face	*En mi cara redondita*
I have two eyes and a nose	*Tengo ojos y nariz*
I have two ears	*Tengo orejas*
And lots of hair	*Tengo pelo*
And a mouth	*Y una boca*
Here's how it goes (BLOW KISSES).	*Pa' hacer así* (SOPLA BESOS).

Additional examples of musical tales that reinforce repetition and vocabulary skills are Maurice Sendak's *Chicken Soup with Rice* which helps children to learn the months of the year through catchy rhymes and song; Eric Carle's *Today Is Monday* which allows children to explore the days of the week through song; Bill Martin's *Chicka Chicka 1, 2, 3* which encourages children to rhythmically chant their numbers.

In *Over in the Meadow/Allá en la pradera* by Olive Wadsworth, children are not only able to sing about animals, but they describe what sounds animals can make in English and in Spanish. Animal sounds are very different in English versus Spanish; children will delight in their differences. For example, in Spanish a sheep says "*be be*" but in English it says "baa, baa"; in Spanish a rooster says "*kikiri, ki*" whereas in English it says "cockadoodledoo." In the musical tale *Come and See My Farm/Vengan a ver mi granja*, children are able to play with different animals sounds while improving their vocabulary skills:

Come and see my farm, it is lovely.	*Vengan a ver mi granja que es hermosa.*
Come and see my farm, it is lovely.	*Vengan a ver mi granja que es hermosa.*
The cow, the cow says this: moo, moo	*La vaca, la vaca hace así: mu, mu*

CHORUS:	**CORO:**
Oh, come my friends	*O, vengan amigos*
Come my friends	*Vengan amigos*
Come and see my farm.	*Vengan amigos, vengan.*
Come my friends	*Vengan amigos*
Come my friends	*Vengan amigos*
Come and see my farm.	*Vengan amigos, vengan.*

OTHER VERSES:	**OTROS VERSOS:**
The sheep, the sheep says this: baa, baa	*La oveja, la oveja hace así: be, be*

The duck, the duck says this: quack, quack	El pato, el pato hace así: cuá, cuá
The chicks, the chicks say this: cheep, cheep	Los pollitos, los pollitos hacen así: pío, pío
The rooster, the rooster says this: cockadoodledoo	El gallo, el gallo hace así: kikiri, kí
The pig, the pig says this: oink, oink	El cerdo, el cerdo hace así: oinc, oinc

Rhythm and Musical Tales

Children experience language through rhythm as well as lyrics. Good readers need good rhythm. As we emphasize rhythmic chant, we are helping children to become rhythmic readers. Children spontaneously respond to rhythm, learning volume, tempo, duration, and percussive pitch. Clapping, nodding, and/or walking to the beat, playing rhythm instruments, and chanting all allow children to anticipate patterns both in rhythm and in language (Hurwitz et al. 1975).

Rhythmic chanting is an especially powerful tool for ELL children. When a children's librarian chants a musical tale, the children can focus solely on the words and rhythm, without having to navigate a tune, making it possible for them to participate almost immediately in the music (Paquette and Reig 2008).

Movement to rhythmic musical tales encourages development of both large and small motor skills through creative physical movement. A safe environment that encourages physical movement and expression can help the children maintain attention, retention, and enjoyment of learning. For instance, if children must sit on the story carpet during storytime, they may have difficulty focusing on what the children's librarian is doing. Encouraging them to move, to get off the storytime carpet, and to participate in a group grabs their attention and allows their minds to be more receptive to what is being taught. And, once a child feels at ease with rhythm and movement, he or she will be able to demonstrate the kind of thinking, action, and interaction that embraces the multifaceted nature of active learning.

For example, in the cumulative musical tale *Juanito cuando baila/When Little Johnny Dances* the child is taught to first move his finger in rhythm. As the song is sung a second time, the child moves his foot and then his finger. These movements gradually get more and more complicated as the song is sung repeatedly and include moving the knee, hip, hand, elbow, shoulder, and finally the head:

Juanito cuando baila,	When Little Johnny dances	
Baila, baila, baila,	Dances, dances, dances.	
Juanito cuando baila	When Little Johnny dances	
Baila con el dedito,	He dances with his finger	(MOVE THE FINGER)
Con el dedito, ito, ito	With his finger, inger, inger	
Así baila Juanito.	And that is how he dances.	
Juanito cuando baila,	When Little Johnny dances	
Baila, baila, baila,	Dances, dances, dances.	
Juanito cuando baila,	When Little Johnny dances	
Baila con el pie,	He dances with his foot	
Con el pie, pie, pie . . .	With his foot, foot, foot . . .	(MOVE THE FOOT)
Con el dedito, ito, ito	With his finger, inger, inger	(MOVE THE FINGER)
Así baila Juanito.	And that is how he dances.	

OTROS VERSOS:	**OTHER VERSES:**	
Con la rodilla, illa, illa . . .	With his knee, knee, knee . . .	(MOVE THE KNEE)
Con la cadera, era, era . . .	With his hip, hip, hip . . .	(MOVE THE HIP)
Con la mano, ano, ano . . .	With his hand, hand, hand . . .	(MOVE THE HAND)
Con el codo, odo, odo . . .	With his elbow, elbow, elbow . . .	(MOVE THE ELBOW)
Con el hombro, ombro, ombro . . .	With his shoulder, oulder, oulder . . .	(MOVE THE SHOULDER)
Con la cabeza, eza, eza . . .	With his head, head, head . . .	(MOVE THE HEAD)

The musical tale *Ring Around the Rosie / Juguemos en la fronda* encourages children to hold hands to form a circle and walk together:

Ring around the rosie,	*Juguemos en la fronda*	(WALK IN CIRCLE)
A pocket full of posie,	*Cantemos una ronda*	
Ashes, ashes, we all fall down.	*Baila, baila, ¡siéntate!*	(FALL DOWN)
The cows are in the meadow	*Las vacas en el prado*	(PRETEND TO EAT)
Eating buttercups	*Comiendo el fardo*	
Ashes, ashes, we all stand up!	*Canta, canta, ¡párate!*	(STAND UP)

If a child does not participate, the circle is broken. Children are naturally encouraged by their peers to move together and make the musical tale work. Children learn to work cooperatively and to share the same space without bumping or crashing into each other, and they develop confidence, social bonds, and self-esteem as they see their creative expressions having value and being accepted (Jalongo and Ribblett 1997; Kirmani 2007).

Woody Guthrie's "Let's Go Ridin' in My Car" is a fantastic song for getting children to participate, sitting down in their "vehicle," even if they cannot speak the language. Prior to singing the song, ask the children:

- ❋ Can you show me how to drive a car? *¿Puedes mostrarme cómo manejar un carro?* (MAKE A MOTION OF TURNING A STEERING WHEEL)
- ❋ Can you fly a plane? *¿Puedes volar un avión?* (MAKE A MOTION OF WINGS IN THE AIR)
- ❋ Can you ride on a train? *¿Puedes viajar en tren?* (MAKE A MOTION OF A TRAIN: CHUG, CHUG, CHUGGING)
- ❋ Well great, then you can sing with me! *¡Fantastico, entonces puedes cantar conmigo!*

Asking these questions before singing the musical tale allows the children to feel confident that they know the movements and allows them to anticipate what is going to happen throughout the duration of the musical tale.

Let's go ridin' in my car, car	*Vamos en mi carro*
Let's go ridin' in my car, car	*Vamos en mi carro*
Let's go ridin' in my car, car	*Vamos en mi carro*
Let's go ridin' in my car.	*Vamos en mi carro.*

Let's go flyin' in my plane, plane	*Vamos en mi avión*
Let's go flyin' in my plane, plane	*Vamos en mi avión*
Let's go flyin' in my plane, plane	*Vamos en mi avión*
Let's go flyin' in my plane.	*Vamos en mi avión.*
Let's go chuggin' in my train, train	*Vamos en mi tren, tren*
Let's go chuggin' in my train, train	*Vamos en mi tren, tren*
Let's go chuggin' in my train, train	*Vamos en mi tren, tren*
Let's go chuggin' in my train.	*Vamos en mi tren.*

Establishing a sense of rhythm through movement and the use of percussive instruments (for example, shakers, maracas, drums, and jingle bells) can also be achieved through musical tales. When singing "Al tambor / The Drum," the librarian should bring out several drums and pass them out to various children in the group. Throughout the musical tale, the children should be encouraged to experiment and play with the drum while singing. Each time the musical tale is completed, the drums should be passed on to other children. When this musical tale is done successfully, the children will have learned to share and work cooperatively. If the children are unwilling to share, the musical tale cannot continue and the group's interaction becomes broken.

The drum, the drum	*Al tambor, al tambor*
The drum of happiness	*Al tambor de alegría*
I hope that you will share with me	*Yo quiero que tú me lleves*
The drum of happiness.	*Al tambor de alegría.*

Combining lyric recognition and movement can be encouraged through singing "Chocolate." Before starting, create four differently colored, cardstock signs and write one syllable—CHO, CO, LA, and TE—on each sign. Give each sign to a different child and have them hold up their syllable each time it is sung. Before starting, make sure each child without a sign has their imaginary spoon (*cuchara*) and bowl (*tazón*) ready to "mix" up their chocolate!

Uno, dos, tres CHO	(HOLD UP THE "CHO" SIGN)
Uno, dos, tres CO	(HOLD UP THE "CO" SIGN)
Uno, dos, tres LA	(HOLD UP THE "LA" SIGN)
Uno, dos, tres TE	(HOLD UP THE "TE" SIGN)

CORO:

Chocolate, chocolate, baté, baté chocolate   (HAVE ALL THE CHILDREN STIR
THEIR BOWLS)
Chocolate, chocolate, baté, baté chocolate

Simply doing an occasional musical tale or music-oriented program will not, however, lead to the positive preliteracy results for children suggested by research. The following section describes how a librarian can apply knowledge of music and preliteracy practices to create an engaging program that will assist ELL children with their language and preliteracy development using the musical tale.

IMPLEMENTING A BILINGUAL MUSICAL TALE PROGRAM

To make a difference in a child's preliteracy development and musical appreciation, a long-term (lasting at least seven months) daily musical tale program is recommended. Children will not improve their language or reading skills through music, nor will they have a true understanding of these skills, without participating in a more rigorous musical program (Barwick et al. 1989; Butzlaff 2000; Lamb and Gregory 1993; Riding and Simmons 1989; Stuart-Hamilton 1986). The level of preliteracy and musical education that children receive prior to kindergarten will influence their academic performance both in kindergarten and throughout elementary school (Dickinson et al. 2003; Riding and Simmons 1989; Turan and Gül 2008). In addition, the children who have had musical training are far better at verbal (oral) recall than those who have not had musical training (Anvari et al. 2002). Both public libraries and school libraries are excellent venues for a musical tale program that supports preschools and the educational system as a whole.

Most public libraries will be unable to maintain a daily musical tale program because of other programming requirements, time limitations, and spatial constraints. Parents/caregivers are also unlikely to be unable to commit to bringing their children to the public library on a daily basis. A weekly musical tale program is much more practical.

It is far more likely that an elementary school can offer a daily musical tale program—the children are already present, the program can be offered in a classroom, and it can easily be adapted to fit curriculum requirements.

Five Musical Steps Toward Preliteracy

The structure of a basic musical tale program is very simple—it is made up of songs, chants, and rhymes combined with musical tales. At the beginning of the program, it is important for the children's librarian to select musical tales and other songs that are familiar to the children, only interspersing one or two new, unfamiliar songs. Then, as the newer songs are learned, additional untried or less recognizable songs can be added to the repertoire. As long as a program is fun and exciting, the children will want to come and participate; learning will follow naturally.

Parental participation is beneficial, and even essential; the children's librarian should encourage parents to join their children as often as possible—even if they are unable to speak English and/or Spanish. In addition, the children's librarian should send bilingual lyrics, including pronunciation, home with the parents/caregivers whenever possible. This allows the adults to participate during the program when they can attend, and to sing and reinforce the songs at home.

A musical tale program can be implemented through five steps:

1. **Sing the same musical tale daily until the children become comfortable with it.** Repeatedly singing a song will bring about phonological awareness. Remember, the song should be lyrically and melodically repetitive, short, and simple. For the sake of discussion, we will use "The Itsy Bitsy Spider / La araña pequeñita":

The itsy bitsy spider	*La araña pequeñita*
went up the water spout	*subió, subió, subió*
Down came the rain and	*Vino la lluvia y se la llevó*
washed the spider out	
Out came the sun and washed	*Salió el sol y todo lo secó*
away the rain	
And the itsy bitsy spider	*Y la araña pequeñita*
went up the spout again.	*subió, subió, subió.*

Encourage the children to sing along as the librarian points to the words on each page, allowing the children to use their visual, aural, and oral skills. In this manner, the children get a general concept of what the words look like (word recognition) while imitating the librarian. As the children become more comfortable with the musical tale through constant repetition, start to leave out key words and let them fill in the blanks:

<table>
<tr>
<td>

The itsy bitsy spider
went up the water _____

The itsy bitsy _____
went up the water spout

</td>
<td>

La araña pequeñita
subió, subió, _____

La _____ *pequeñita*
subió, subió, subió

</td>
</tr>
</table>

2. **Begin to experiment with basic musical concepts by adjusting the singing style of the group. Many basic musical concepts are common adjectives, used daily on the playground:**

   🌸 VOLUME
   - soft vs. loud
   - *suave* v. *fuerte* (Spanish)
   - *piano* v. *forte* (Italian)

   🌸 SPEED
   - fast vs. slow
   - *rápido* v. *lento* (Spanish)
   - *allegro* v. *largo* (Italian)

   🌸 PITCH
   - high vs. low
   - *tono alto* v. *tono bajo* (Spanish)
   - *acuta* v. *sottovoce* (Italian)

   Start the musical tale at higher or lower on the musical scale. Initially make sure that the tonal change is obvious, even extreme, until the children truly comprehend the concept of tonal variation.

   Use the appropriate musical terms. While musical terms are typically in Italian, they can be comforting to ELL children as many Italian words are very similar to, or identical to, the Spanish words.

3. **Write the musical tale title and lyrics down on paper, cardstock, dry erase board, or other medium.**

   Begin to accent certain syllables, according to their pronunciation, by clapping louder for accented syllables and quieter for those which are not emphasized.

   Have the children attempt to identify the letters of the sounds they are singing. The children's librarian should pronounce and name the letters as the children try to identify them. Creating an integrated curriculum that incorporates reading, writing, and song exposes children to the fact that the words they are singing are similar to the words they see every day—words are not just sung or read in a book, but together can form a sentence or a paragraph and have meaning. Understanding this seemingly simple concept is actually a step forward in a child's reading development. Again referring to "The Itsy Bitsy Spider / La araña pequeñita":

❀ Ask the children to look carefully at the title of their musical tale.

❀ Ask them which word is *spider,* which is *araña.*

❀ Ask "How do you know?"

❀ Ask "Are you sure?"

It is most common for children to see the first letter in a word, such as the *s* in *spider* or the *a* in *araña.* Make the sounds of the other letters in the word *spider* and *araña* and have the children imitate these sounds.

4. ***Begin to sound out each word by syllable.*** Encourage the children to echo-clap or clap each syllable. Begin to accent certain syllables, according to their pronunciation, by clapping louder for accented syllables and more quietly for those that are not emphasized.

5. ***Using cardstock squares (similar to flash cards), print each word from the musical tale on a separate square.***

❀ Help the children sound out letters; removing the words from their context or illustrations may be difficult for the children initially.

❀ Help them to discover that individual words have meaning, even when taken out of a sentence.

❀ Mix up the words. Play a game to help children recognize the words out of context. Have the children place the words back in order, then string the words together again. Once the musical tale is reconstructed, it can be displayed in the program area.

❀ Continue to select strong nouns or verbs from the children's musical tale until the children are consistently able to recognize more and more words.

As the children learn to recognize words from their musical tale, they will discover that these words can be found in other musical tales as well. Of course, *The Itsy Bitsy Spider / La araña pequeñita* used in this five-step process would only be one of many musical tales sung throughout a long-term musical tale program. Once the children are comfortable with one musical tale, a second one may be chosen and the five-step process begun anew.

BILINGUAL PROGRAMMING ALTERNATIVES

It may not be possible or realistic to implement a daily musical tale program into your library's programming; other types of bilingual programming may be more acceptable or realistic. Consider doing the musical tale program on a weekly basis, rather than a daily basis—the preliteracy benefits of this format may not be as significant but the children (and parents/caregivers) will still learn and benefit.

Below is a list of additional suggestions for programming that incorporates music with visual art, multicultural literature, writing, and dancing or acting. Just as music is a wonderful tool to help children with the various facets of language: listening, speaking, memorizing, reading, and writing, it is also an inherently creative activity and relates well to other creative activities, such as visual art, multicultural literature, creative writing, and dance or drama. These cross-curricular programming alternatives for incorporating music and musical themes range from the simple to the more complex, thereby accommodating your scheduling needs.

Music

- ❈ Play music and invite students to illustrate what they hear.
- ❈ Create a shelf of CDs and DVDs that represent different cultures and languages (not necessarily just in English or Spanish) from all over the world.
- ❈ Expose children to multiple musical genres.
- ❈ Play music that demonstrates a feeling. Ask the children to describe how the music makes them feel.
- ❈ Use different musical instruments. Let the children experiment and make noise just for the sake of making noise.
- ❈ Have durable musical instruments available for the children to play and/or check out to take home.
- ❈ Encourage children to sing and hum not only during programming, but at home, too.
- ❈ Ask children "discovery" questions: How is music part of our lives? Does a sink make music? What about a vacuum cleaner? What sound does the rain make?
- ❈ Read the children a book about a composer and play that composer's music. Have the children create their own music that imitates the composer's style or that evokes similar feelings.

❀ Translate some currently unavailable musical tale books from English into Spanish. Make sure that the rhythm of the translation matches that of the original.

❀ Translate some musical tale books that are only available in Spanish into English. Again make sure that the rhythm of the translation matches that of the Spanish.

❀ Invite musicians (parents or professionals) to perform, talk to the children, and support your program.

Visual Art

❀ Use books with illustrations that depict the action in the tale. Talk to the children about the images and how they work together with the words to create meaning.

❀ Listen to bits of music (from different genres) and use different artistic media to create pictures. What colors will they choose? Why?

❀ Create masks, puppets, or musical instruments that complement the music sung in the program, so the children can conduct their own program at home.

❀ Choose a strong noun and have the children draw what that word means to them. Post the images in a special "Word of the Week" area.

❀ Invite visual artists to display their art, talk to the children, and support your program.

Multicultural Literature

❀ Make a shelf of multicultural books available to read or borrow.

❀ Emphasize English and Spanish musical tales, poetry, and folklore (poetry and folklore are often easy to write songs for).

❀ Create a quiet reading corner where multicultural music can be played while the children are reading.

❀ When appropriate, encourage children to talk about situations in their lives that are similar to situations in the multicultural books and musical tales.

❀ Invite multicultural authors and illustrators to talk to the children and support your program.

Writing

❀ Create a "Word Wall" with all the vocabulary words that the children have learned through the program.

🏶 Make up songs. Use spelling words, math facts, names of states, or the ABCs.

🏶 Post words from lyrics, and have children practice printing, cursive, and calligraphy.

🏶 Using lined poster paper, create a chart of all the songs children have learned.

🏶 Create a rebus song sheet to help children remember more difficult songs.

🏶 Invite writers and poets to talk to the children and support your program.

Dancing and Acting

🏶 Use puppets to let the children act out the song lyrics.

🏶 Act out or dance to a song. Incorporate percussive instruments into the song.

🏶 Use a song that the children are comfortable with and change its setting.

🏶 Invite dancers and actors to perform, talk to the children, and support your program.

CONCLUDING REMARKS

Children's librarians can alter the direction of a child's educational career with musical tale programming. When children listen, sing, interact, experiment, and create, they develop important building blocks of knowledge that they will use when reading and writing. Through daily, long-term musical tale programming children are able to enhance their reading skills, facilitating the development of simple concepts, memory, basic vocabulary, reading comprehension, and eventual fluency. The preliteracy skills gained in such programming are especially beneficial for ELL children, those who are already entering the U.S. school system at a linguistic deficit.

This chapter ends with lists of suggested Web sites, musical tales, and music CDs that should be helpful to librarians and educators interested in creating their own bilingual music programming.

REFERENCES

Anvari, Sima H., Laurel J. Trainor, Jennifer Woodside, and Betty Ann Levy. "Relations Among Musical Skills, Phonological Processing, and Early Reading Ability in

Preschool Children." *Journal of Experimental Child Psychology* 83, no. 2 (October 2002): 111–130.

August, Diane, Maria Carlo, Cheryl Dressler, and Catherine Snow. "The Critical Role of Vocabulary Development for English Language Learners." *Learning Disabilities Research and Practice* 20, no. 1 (February 2005): 50–57.

Barwick, Julia, Elizabeth Valentine, Robert West, John Wilding. "Relations Between Reading and Musical Abilities." *British Journal of Educational Psychology* 59, (June 1989): 253–257.

Bolduc, Jonathan. "Effects of a Music Programme on Kindergartners' Phonological Awareness Skills." *International Journal of Music Education* 27, no. 1 (February 2009): 37–47.

Butzlaff, Ron. "Can Music Be Used to Teach Reading?" *Journal of Aesthetic Education* 34, no. 3/4 (Autumn–Winter 2000): 167–178.

Dickinson, David K., Allyssa McCabe, Louisa Anastasopoulos, Ellen S. Peisner-Feinberg, and Michele D. Poe. "The Comprehensive Language Approach to Early Literacy: The Interrelationships Among Vocabulary, Phonological Sensitivity, and Print Knowledge Among Preschool-Aged Children." *Journal of Educational Psychology* 95, no. 3 (September 2003): 465–481.

Favila, Alejandra, Guillermina Yáñez, Jorge Bernal, Juan Silva, Erzsebet Marosi, Mario Rodríguez, and Thalia Fernández. "La conciencia y la memoria fonológicas son factores predictores del nivel de lectura y escritura alcanzado en niños de primer grado de primaria." *Revista Mexicana de Psicología* 16, no. 1 (June 1999): 57–63.

Hammer, Carol Scheffner, Frank R. Lawrence, and Adele W. Miccio. "Bilingual Children's Language Abilities and Early Reading Outcomes in Head Start and Kindergarten." *Language, Speech, and Hearing Services in Schools* 38, no. 3 (July 2007): 237–248.

Hansen, Dee, and Elaine Bernstorf. "Linking Music Learning to Reading Instruction." *Music Educators Journal* 88, no. 5 (March 2002): 17–21, 52.

Herrera, Lucía, Sylvia Defior, and Oswaldo Lorenzo. "Interventión educativa en conciencia fonológica en niños prelectores de lengua materna española y tamazight. Comparación de dos programas de entrenamiento." *Infancia y Aprendizaje* 30, no. 1 (2007): 39–54.

Hurwitz, Irving, Peter H. Wolff, Barrie D. Bortnick, and Klara Kokas. "Nonmusical Effects of the Kodaly Music Curriculum in Primary Grade Children." *Journal of Learning Disabilities* 8, no. 3 (March 1975): 45–51.

Jalongo, Mary Renck, and Deborah McDonald Ribblett. "Using Song Picture Books to Support Emergent Literacy." *Childhood Education* 74, no. 1 (Fall 1997): 15–23.

Kirmani, Mubina Hassanali. "Empowering Culturally and Linguistically Diverse Children and Families." *Young Children* 62, no. 6 (November 2007): 94–98.

Lamb, Susannah J., and Andrew H. Gregory. "The Relationship Between Music and Reading in Beginning Readers." *Educational Psychology* 13, no. 1 (March 1993): 19–27.

Lindsey, Kim A., Franklin R. Manis, and Caroline E. Bailey. "Prediction of First-Grade Reading in Spanish-Speaking English-Language Learners." *Journal of Educational Psychology* 95, no. 3 (September 2003): 482–494.

McCardle, Peggy, Joan Mele-McCarthy, Laurie Cutting, Kathleen Leos, and Tim D'Emilio. "Learning Disabilities in English Language Learners: Identifying the Issues." *Learning Disabilities Research and Practice* (Blackwell Publishing Limited) 20, no. 1 (February 2005): 1–5.

McIntosh, Beth, Sharon Crosbie, Alison Holm, and Barbara Dodd. "Enhancing the Phonological Awareness and Language Skills of Socially Disadvantaged Preschoolers: An Interdisciplinary Programme." *Child Language Teaching and Therapy* 23, no. 3 (October 2007): 267–286.

Páez, Mariela M., Patton O. Tabors, and Lisa M. López. "Dual Language and Literacy Development of Spanish-speaking Preschool Children." *Journal of Applied Developmental Psychology* 28, no. 2 (March 2007): 85–102.

Paquette, Kelli R., and Sue A. Rieg. "Using Music to Support the Literacy Development of Young English Language Learners." *Early Childhood Education Journal* 36, no. 3 (December 2008): 227–232.

Riding, R. J., and L. Simmons. "Instruction in Pre-Reading Skills in Preschool Children and Its Effect on the Subsequent Rate of Reading Attainment." *Educational Psychology* 9, no. 3 (1989): 247–252.

Stuart-Hamilton, Ian. "The Role of Phonemic Awareness in the Reading Style of Beginning Readers." *British Journal of Educational Psychology* 56, no. 3 (1986): 271–285.

Turan, Figen, and Gözde Gül. "Early Precursor of Reading: Acquisition of Phonological Awareness Skills." *Educational Sciences: Theory and Practice* 8, no. 1 (January 2008): 279–284.

Uccelli, Paola, and Mariela M. Páez. "Narrative and Vocabulary Development of Bilingual Children from Kindergarten to First Grade: Developmental Changes and Associations Among English and Spanish Skills." *Language, Speech, and Hearing Services in Schools* 38, no. 3 (July 2007): 225–236.

U.S. Census Bureau. "Population Estimates: National Sex, Age, Race, and Hispanic Origin: 2008." http://www.census.gov/popest/national/asrh/NC-EST2008-asrh. html (cited December 9, 2009).

Wiggins, Donna Gwyn. "Pre-K Music and the Emergent Reader: Promoting Literacy in a Music-Enhanced Environment." *Early Childhood Education Journal* 35, no. 1 (August 2007): 55–64.

Yopp, Hallie Kay, and Ruth Helen Yopp. "Phonological Awareness Is Child's Play!" *Young Children* 64, no. 1 (January 2009): 12–18.

APPENDIX: WEB SITES

Web sites are a valuable source of information for those creating musical programs for children. Not only is it possible to get regularly updated material, but song lyrics are readily accessible and often linked to audio files. It is no longer necessary to read music to learn a tune; one can quickly and conveniently listen to the song on the Internet and learn the melody.

Children's Music Web. "Resources for Teachers."
http://www.childrensmusic.org.

Educational Media Collection and the University of Wisconsin in Oshkosh. "Music for Children of All Ages."
http://www.uwosh.edu/library/emc/Bibliographies/musicbib.htm.

ESL Partyland. "Teaching ESL with Music."
http://www.eslpartyland.com/teachers/nov/music.htm.

National Institute of Environmental Health Sciences (NIEHS), the National Institutes of Health (NIH), and the Department of Health and Human Services (DHHS). "Young and Young at Heart."
http://www.niehs.nih.gov/kids/musicchild.htm.

National Storytelling Network. "National Storytelling Network: Connecting People to and through Storytelling."
http://www.storynet.org.

Songs for Teaching. "Songs for Teaching: The Definitive Source for Educational Music."
http://www.songsforteaching.com.

CHAPTER 11

The Spirit of Día:
Celebrating Cuentos Every Day

Irania Patterson and Jamie Campbell Naidoo

El día de los niños/El día de los libros (Children's Day/Book Day), known as Día, is a celebration of children, families, and reading that culminates each year on April 30. The celebration emphasizes the importance of advocating literacy for children of all linguistic and cultural backgrounds, and connecting all children to books, languages, and cultures. Founded in 1996 by Latino children's book author Pat Mora, Día is housed at the Association for Library Service to Children (ALSC), a division of the American Library Association. In February 1997 REFORMA (the National Association to Promote Library and Information Services to Latinos and the Spanish Speaking) voted to endorse this family literacy initiative and celebrate Día throughout the United States and Puerto Rico. The first annual Día celebration was held on April 30, 1997.

Mora's idea for Día came from the concept of expanding Children's Day (recognized on April 30 in Mexico) to include a celebration of literacy and culture. Since the celebration's inception, many organizations, especially library systems, have joined and supported Día initiatives throughout the United States. All of these initiatives include a commitment to honoring children and childhood, promoting literacy and linking children from all cultures and language to books, celebrating bilingual and multilingual literacy, fostering global understanding through reading, involving parents as partners in literacy education, and emphasizing library collections that reflect a culturally pluralistic society (Mora 2009). See Figure 11.1 for an interview with Día founder Pat Mora.

In 2009 more than 400 libraries and schools in almost every state were participating in Día activities and sharing the details on the official Día Web site (www.ala.org/dia). Thousands of Latino and non-Latino children and their families attending these programs enjoyed annual festivities and small celebrations honoring children, books, cultures, and languages.

UNA FIESTA OF BOOKS & BOOKJOY: A CONVERSATION WITH PAT MORA ABOUT HER DÍA PICTURE BOOK BOOK FIESTA!

By Dr. Jamie Campbell Naidoo

"Hooray! Today is our day / ¡Viva! Hoy es nuestro día. ¡El día de los niños! Let's have fun today reading our favorite books." From these opening lines of Pat Mora's and Rafael López's award-winning book *Book Fiesta!*, it is apparent that today is indeed Children's Day as we follow blazing images, suffused with magical realism, of children celebrating and reading books in a myriad of places: on the moon, tucked away in the clouds; from atop stone lions and very real elephants; within trains, planes, hot air balloons, and submarines; and even inside the mouth of a whale! Children from diverse cultural heritages practically leap off these vibrant pages and can barely contain their bookjoy! Indeed, I was scarcely able to control my own bookjoy as I finished this delightful new picture-book *celebración* of El día de los niños/El día de los libros (Día). Armed with this enthusiasm and gusto, I engaged in a lively conversation with the book's author and Día creator and advocate Pat Mora to learn more about this amazing book, Día celebrations, and how librarians can spread their own bookjoy!

Immediately I wanted to know where Pat got the idea of creating a book about Día. She explained that the seed was first planted back in 1998 by Jeanette Larson, then Director of the Library Development Division at the Texas State Library and Archives Commission. Jeanette offered to create a small booklet of stapled pages to advertise Día and encouraged Pat to create a Día song for the booklet. The author recalls, "It was a challenge, but I was grateful to Jeanette for offering to produce this booklet to give it out at the Texas Library Association meeting that spring. I wrote the song for the booklet and it eventually went up on my Web site and the Texas State Library and Archives Commission Web site." A while later, Pat was scheduled to visit a campus in Pennsylvania to talk about multicultural children's literature. The professor who coordinated the visit wanted to play the Día song as a way to welcome to the author to their campus; unfortunately, the song did

not have a tune. Again, it was a librarian at the Texas State Library and Archives Commission that came to the rescue and prompted a melody for the song. Librarian Belinda Boone had an idea for the tune and offered to sing it over the

FIGURE 11.1. *Reprinted with permission from Naidoo, J. C. (2008). Una fiesta of books & bookjoy: A conversation with Pat Mora about her Día picture book* Book Fiesta!. *REFORMA Newsletter, 26 (3/4), 10–11.*

phone for a music professor on the Pennsylvania campus. The work began and when Pat visited the campus she was serenaded with a musical rendition of her Día song (to listen to the song's tune visit: http://www.patmora.com/dia/dia_song.htm).

The seed for Pat's Día book began with a song, fertilized by the performance, and would blossom under the direction of Adriana Domínguez, then editor for Rayo HarperCollins. "She was a quick, intense Día supporter who, having grown up in Uruguay, knew," Pat says, "what it was like speak Spanish at home and long to speak English in the classroom in order to interact with the teacher and other students." Adriana understood the power of Día and suggested to Pat that she create a narrative to celebrate the importance of books and Día. Initially, Pat was not sure that a story would be the best format and suggested that she expand the Día song for the book. Adriana agreed and prompted that the book should be bilingual. After that, the magic began; Rafael López joined the project with what Pat calls his "boundless imagination," and *Book Fiesta!* was born.

Interestingly, Pat and Rafael were not in communication directly with each other during the creation of the text and illustrations. Of this, Pat remarks, "It always amazes people, particularly those from outside the country, that in the U.S. publishing world, the illustrator and author do not speak." The reasoning is that the illustrator needs to be given "the breadth, quiet, and freedom to produce a vision from reading the manuscript many times. Writing a children's book is more like writing a play but you, the author, aren't part of staging the play. You write it but you must then trust the editor, illustrator, marketing team, art editor, etc." Pat's trust was well placed. Rafael's acrylic mural illustrations explode with action, magic, *sabor*, and, of course, books. Much to Pat's delight, Adriana sent Rafael's illustrations to her for insight into his vision for the Día book. Pat reminisces, "I got to see the book evolve. Receiving each of the illustrations was a wonderful surprise. I have said to him, 'I wish that I could live in the imagination of Rafael López!' The wonder of the book's illustrations can't be understated. Librarians and parents can allow children to aesthetically experience the book. The book is a visual experience, typical of Rafael's work, and children should be allowed to delight in the art. When they are ready, then the children will move on to thinking about how great books are and why we'd want to celebrate children, books and have a children and book day."

In addition to talent and magic of Rafael, Pat admits the book would not be near as beautiful were it not for Adriana Domínguez. "I cannot say enough about how meticulous and enthusiastic Adriana was as an editor. She worked on every spread, lovingly deciding how it would appear to children and readers. It is very sad to me that Adriana is no longer at HarperCollins, although I am confident that Harper is still supportive of the Día book." Agreeably, Adriana's hard work can certainly be experienced by any reader, young or old, who has the pleasure of falling into the amazing pages of *Book Fiesta!* and being enveloped by bookjoy.

With bookjoy still in my head and heart, I asked Pat to tell me a little about the importance of Día and where she sees the celebration going in the future. The author admits she never intended on being a literacy advocate; rather, it was the work that found her. As a Latina author and mother, she had experienced the resistance to books in other languages or books about the non-mainstream U.S. culture as being for the "other," not for everyone. It made me keenly aware that many children didn't feel part of the reading experience or the reading family. Maybe they came from a home that wasn't print rich with books and magazines because of educational and economic issues. Those of us blessed in knowing to the marrow of our bones what bookjoy is . . . want to share it." It was in 1996 that Pat first had the idea of linking El día de los niños to her passion for bookjoy—the desire to share the joy and love of reading books with everyone, to connect all children to books, languages, and cultures. With help from REFORMA friends and the support of Dr. Dan Moore at the W. K. Kellogg Foundation, Día began to evolve into a national celebration celebrated not only on April 30th (the traditional day for Día celebrations in Mexico) but every day. Eventually, Día planning initiatives would be housed at the ALA's Association for Library Service to Children.

"Día is a culmination of the notion that every day is book day. We need to inspire libraries, schools, campuses, and parents to realize the importance of literacy and undertake Día celebrations. . . . We can't have a democracy without a literate electorate. We have a right and obligation to promote reading."

According to Pat, Día feels like her baby that keeps growing and changing. She stresses that developing of partnerships—between schools and libraries, libraries and nonprofit organizations, and so forth, strengthens Día and strengthens communities. "We all have our ways of working, and for Día to grow, all of us who are literacy advocates must work together respectfully to reach our common goal. It is a case study: what happens when an exciting, energetic grassroots effort such as Día, initially a partnership between REFORMA, the W. K. Kellogg Foundation and me, is invited into

Author Pat Mora. Used with permission.

a complex, national organization such as the American Library Association. I believe in Día's potential . . . My hope remains that one day we will have an active partnership between REFORMA, ALSC, me, and other media and corporate sponsors working together as a national team, engaged in steady communication to assist the concept of Día to grow and flourish. Currently, I'm investing a lot of my energies, as I did at the beginning, in encouraging local libraries and communities to start Día events of their own and make them an annual tradition." To help local libraries and communities with the funding of Día programs, Pat will donate a percentage of the proceeds from *Book Fiesta!* to support Día celebrations and thus honor children and family literacy. Indeed, she ended our conversation stating, "I hope the book spreads bookjoy!" The picture book has certainly left bookjoy within me and I am sure it will do the same for librarians and educators sharing the book in programs, making everyday a joyful Día day. For more information on Día celebrations and activities, consult Larson's Día programming book published by the American Library Association in 2010. Please also see Pat's article on Día:

❀   Mora, Pat. "Gratitude as a catalyst: One of ALA's newest honorary members calls on us to invest ourselves in the young." *American Libraries* 39.7 (August 2008): 52–53.

PLANNING DÍA PROGRAMS

Planning a Día program or celebration might seem a daunting task for children's and school librarians, particularly those who do not speak Spanish or know much about Latino cultures. Fortunately, many free resources are available online to help with the planning, development, promotion, execution, and evaluation of Día programs. These resources include lists of recommended books celebrating Latino cultures, finger rhymes and songs from Latin American countries, craft activities, thematic storytime suggestions, and interviews with Latino authors and illustrators of children's books. Figure 11.2 provides a list of recommended resources.

RESOURCES FOR PLANNING DÍA PROGRAMS

❇ **Official El día de los niños/El día de los libros (Day of the Child/ Day of the Book)** Web site—This comprehensive Web site contains a plethora of resources relating to planning and promoting your Día program as well as links to booklists and free publisher posters highlighting Día. Available: www.ala.org/dia.

❇ **Día de los niños/Día de los libros: A Celebration of Childhood and Bilingual Literacy**—Created by the California State Library and sponsored by an IMLS grant, this comprehensive Web site contains a Día planning checklist, downloadable graphics, bookmarks, press releases, and activity suggestions. Available: http://www.diacalifornia.org/.

❇ **Dígame un cuento / Tell Me a Story: Bilingual Library Programs for Children and Families**—Created by the Texas State Library and Archives Commission, this useful online manual suggests bilingual story hour programs for Latino children and their families. Librarians can use this resource to plan activities using Latino children's books. Available: http://www.tsl.state.tx.us/ld/pubs/bilingual/index.html.

❇ **El día de los niños/El día de los libros: A Celebration of Childhood and Bilingual Literacy**—Created by the Texas State Library and Archives Commission, this Web site contains a variety of information related to planning a Día celebration including: fingerplays, downloadable Spanish/ English rhymes and songs, suggested activities, bookmarks, a bibliography of recommended bilingual books and a list of helpful resources. Available: http://www.tsl.state.tx.us/ld/projects/ninos/contents.html.

❇ **El día de los niños/El día de los libros (Day of the Child/Day of the Book) Toolkit** is a 100-page online document describing booktalks, author visits, storytelling, and other programming ideas that can be used to celebrate El día de los niños/El día de los libros on April 30. These suggestions can be used for library programs throughout the entire year. The comprehensive document is available at: http://www.texasdia.org/toolkit. html.

❀ **¡Colorín Colorado!'s El día de los niños/El día de los libros** Web page—This page, part of ¡Colorín Colorado!'s comprehensive Web site celebrating children's literature, includes Día video interviews with Latina children's book creators Pat Mora and Lulu Delacre, activities and reproducibles, a Día e-card, and lists of recommended Latino children's books. Available: http://www.colorincolorado.org/calendar/celebrations/día.

❀ **Pat Mora's Día: El día de los niños/El día de los libros** Web site— This comprehensive Web site includes information on the history of Día, the Día song, Mora's Día picture book, and resources and articles about the celebration. Available: http://www.patmora.com/dia.htm.

FIGURE 11.2. *Recommended resources for school and public children's librarians planning Día programs. Compiled by Dr. Jamie C. Naidoo for the Día educational program "Cuentos de las Americas: Celebrating Latino Cultures and Día with Recent Outstanding Latino Children's Books" for the American Library Association 2009 Annual Conference.*

FUNDING DÍA PROGRAMS

*L*ibraries interested in finding funds to support a Día celebration should consider contacting their local REFORMA chapter, which may provide small funds for Día programs. Another option for libraries is to "toot their own horn" and apply for the Mora Award.

In 2000 Pat Mora and her siblings established the Estela and Raúl Mora Award in honor of their parents. This annual award, designed to promote Día and encourage organizations to plan Día celebrations, is presented to the library system, community organization, or school that held the most exemplary Día program during the calendar year. Members of REFORMA serve as judges for the Mora Award, which consists of a disbursement of $1,000 and a plaque donated by the Mora grandchildren. Past winners of the Mora Award include El Paso (TX) Public Library, Multnomah County (OR) Library, Corvallis-Benton (OR) Public Library, Providence (RI) Public Library, REFORMA de Utah, Kenton County (KY) Public Library, Broward County (FL) Library, Riverside County (CA) Library System, the Public Library of Charlotte and Mecklenburg County (NC), San Francisco (CA) Public Library, and Topeka and Shawnee County (KS) Public Library. For detailed information on the Mora Award, guidelines, and application process, visit http://www.reforma.org/ and click on Mora Award.

EMBRACING THE SPIRIT OF DÍA

To succeed in Día programming, librarians should embrace the spirit of the celebration. Día SPIRIT includes the following:

Spread the Día seed—Make literacy across languages and cultures an everyday intention.

Personal commitment—Make your organization believe, as you do, that this is an incredible way to serve the community at large.

Involvement—Spread the love for reading in many languages to many children in and outside your system by using volunteers, community resources, and political power.

Renaissance of the arts—Fight with the power of writers, storytellers, musicians, poets, actors, dancers, and illustrators, against stereotypes, apathy, and lack of vision.

Innovation—Study the success of other Día initiatives, adapt them, and create your own new flavor.

Transcend—Overcome any barriers to the love of reading beyond languages, colors, and cultures.

The SPIRIT of Día at PLCMC

Regardless of whether Día is a new term for you or you have celebrated it for more than ten years, the next step is to ask yourself: Is my organization really engaged in the Día spirit? And what does that spirit mean?

For the Public Library of Charlotte and Mecklenburg County (PLCMC), the Día spirit means "Diversity in Action." In 2008 PLCMC was the recipient of the Mora Award, which recognized the library's proven track record for producing outstanding Día celebrations in the community and making a commitment to celebrate literacy and culture. From the first Día celebration in 1998 to the present, PLCMC has sought to promote literacy in the Charlotte community by advocating for Día. The celebrations began as small storytelling sessions in local branches and have evolved into month-long programs and a statewide initiative with a grand finale featuring Latino authors as well as local artists. Día has been a tool to reach the Spanish and international community and to promote literacy and multicultural authors.

Thanks to the advocacy efforts of Meryle Leonard, outreach manager at PLCMC, Día is now a statewide initiative in North Carolina. In the following interview excerpt, Leonard shares with Irania Patterson her insights on successful Día programming.

WHAT ARE THE MOST SUCCESSFUL APPROACHES IN CELEBRATING DÍA?

The most successful approach to celebrating Día is one that works within the capacity of the organization. Create a celebration that is comfortable to your organization and budget. Anyone can celebrate and honor the spirit of Día. If you have a small library or organization, create a small celebration that concentrates on literacy and culture. Storytelling can be a small event that tells a powerful story. Storytelling can take a group of children to several different countries and allow them to experience various cultures in less than 60 minutes! Collaborating with community organizations and enlisting volunteers can make a small celebration go very far.

> ❀ Another successful approach is engaging the community. Your planning process should include your target audience. Not only will you offer a celebration that is relevant and accurate, but you will also have a team that can help market your celebration to the target audience.

> ❀ Plan your event. Give yourself enough time to plan an event that allows you to create a planning team, involve the target audience, secure space and funding, and develop an evaluation plan.

HOW CAN LIBRARIANS AND EDUCATORS EXTEND DÍA TO MORE THAN ONE DAY?

I love to quote Pat Mora when she says, "Plant a Día seed." Your April Día celebration should be a catalyst to year-long literacy experiences that honor all children and cultures. May to March can be used as a build-up to the next April celebration. Libraries and families can regularly include books and activities that introduce children to different cultures. They can also share books that honor different languages. When children participate in the April celebration, they will be excited to share their knowledge and have fun and relevant experiences related to literacy, language, and culture. Planting a Día seed also gives you the opportunity to offer long-term projects. Children can engage in projects that include picture-book clubs, writing books, craft projects, and communications with an author that all lead to the April celebration.

DÍA AS DIVERSITY IN ACTION

From its inception, Día was designed to honor home languages and cultures and not just the Latino culture. Any Día celebration can include books, art, music, and literature that celebrate a variety of cultures. Storytelling, puppetry, and arts and crafts can be a fun and educational way to reach a variety of audiences. These activities should be geared to children of all ages, languages, and cultures.

How Día Evolved at PLCMC

Winning the Mora Award in 2008 was the icing on the Día cupcake for PLCMC. As mentioned above, the library has promoted the celebration for more than ten years, during which it has evolved into a program that truly connects communities, cultures, families, and literacy. Following is a timeline of Día celebrations at PLCMC:

1998 (Celebrate Children Celebrate Books!)—The library celebrated Día for the first time. The small celebration was hosted at the main library, and community volunteers read to children representing 50 families. Other activities included Tía Panchita's Storytime and a mini piñata made from children's books.

1999 (Bingo Libro)—Día was again celebrated at the main library location. More than 100 families participated in Bingo Libro, a library game that introduced patrons young and old to library resources. The celebration also included fiestas and puppet shows.

2000—The library celebrated Día at Mecklenburg County Park and Recreation's Grady Cole Center. Mayor Pat McCory proclaimed the last Saturday in April as Día de los niños/Día de los libros in Charlotte, North Carolina. The celebration was supported by several local agencies including Mecklenburg County Park and Recreation Department, the Chemical Dependency Center, Programa Esperanza, Catholic Social Services, the National Conference for Community and Justice, Bilingual Preschool, Mi Casa Su Casa, the Mint Museum, Burger King, and Discovery Place. The activities honored several cultures through plays, puppet shows, music, and games from around the world. More than 300 families participated.

2001—PLCMC celebrated Día at the main library location and expanded to 22 additional library branches. Each branch developed a unique Día de los niños bookmark and hosted a bilingual book display. The main library's celebration was a children's festival with a farm animal theme. More than 100 families enjoyed plays featuring animals and made animal books to take home. Ki Kirikis, a group composed of library staff members, performed Latino-themed plays at both the main library and several library branches.

2002—Día was again celebrated at the main library and 22 branches. During this year's celebration, the library sponsored a five-month project, "La Fiesta de Enriqueta," with the Bilingual Preschool. The result was a published book created by the parents and children from the preschool. One hundred copies of the book were printed and distributed. In addition, the library's performing group Ki Kirikis presented two bilingual plays, *The Lizard and the Sun* by Alma Flor Ada, and *Borreguita and Coyote* by Verna Aardema. More than 150 families enjoyed the performances. The library also began its commitment to promoting Día statewide by presenting a Día workshop at the North Carolina Library Association regional conference.

2003—Twenty-three branches participated in the Día celebration, which took the form of a traditional festival, including book displays, bilingual storytelling, piñatas, and arts and crafts. Mecklenburg County Park and Recreation Department and a local radio station, Radio Lider, were the library's community partners; through their generous donations, all participants received an age-appropriate book along with other prizes, and two lucky participants won a new bicycle. Five hundred people attended the event.

2004—Again, PLCMC celebrated Día at the main library and 22 branches. The library received a $500 grant from El Pueblo Foundation, and funds were used to buy books for all program participants. Educational workshops were added to the festival, and community agencies such as Child Care Resources, Discovery Place, and the Nature Museum supported the celebration with a variety of children's craft activities. Five hundred families participated.

2005—The library celebrated Día at its new ImaginOn facility, a special location just for kids and teens. With a strong effort to embrace all nationalities, the celebration reflected the diversity in the Charlotte community. Puppet shows, crafts, storytelling, and music had an international theme, and all participants received a free age-appropriate book. More than 1,000 people enjoyed the celebration.

2006—The library again celebrated Día at ImaginOn and continued incorporating themes of community diversity with internationally themed puppet shows, crafts, storytelling, and music. The celebration featured two local literary artists: author Irania Patterson and illustrator Catherine Courtlandt-McElvane. Through a generous grant from Target, all participants received a free age-appropriate book. More than 1,000 people attended.

2007—The library celebrated Día at ImaginOn on April 28. Thanks to funding from Target, the celebration featured author Lulu Delacre, who conducted several teacher workshops and was the guest speaker at the main celebration. The day-long celebration included drama workshops, dancing, crafts, and storytelling from around the world, plus a presentation from the Gray Seal Puppets. More than 1,000 families participated.

2008—The library celebrated Día at ImaginOn on April 27. The celebration featured author Yuyi Morales. Born and raised in Veracruz, Mexico, Morales is an artist, author, and puppet maker. The festivities included a citywide illustration contest that honored family traditions. There were also several multicultural activities, including dancers from India, China, Japan, and Latin America; Arabic writing and crafts; and a karate and mime performance. Public television characters Maya and Miguel made a special guest appearance. More than 1,000 families took part.

2009—Día was celebrated at ImaginOn on April 25 and featured Arthur Dorros, author of 24 books including *Abuela*, winner of the Parent's Choice Award. The entire library system joined Día's mission and conducted creative activities in each location. Five storytellers— from France, Japan, Peru, Guatemala, and South Africa—performed on April 25. Chinese and Indian dancers made folkloric performances, and karate and Zumba classes, promoting health and fitness, were offered. Children's Theatre of Charlotte offered a drama class for children and families. In 2009 PLCMC demonstrated the commitment to make Día a statewide initiative, by delivering multiple conferences, webinars, and workshops across the states of North Carolina and South Carolina. Community organizations such as the Census, institutions in the field of education and special needs, and other media organizations were involved in Día 2009. More than 1,000 families were involved.

CONCLUDING REMARKS

B ecoming a multicultural institution requires fostering opportunities to promote multicultural readers, and Día is a great way to do it. Día has been successfully celebrated in small institutions with very limited resources, as well as in big systems that partner with for-profit and nonprofit organizations. Día can be seen as an outreach opportunity, a cultural and literary event, a kickoff for summer reading, a multi-linguistic festival, a way to promote bilingual authors and books, and a way to tell the world that books are essential in the lives of all children, regardless of language and background.

Libraries hosting Día celebrations embark on a journey to reach all children, not only the Spanish-speaking children. For some library systems, finding support to promote services to the international community is a challenge, whether the challenge comes from funding problems, lack of support by managers or supervisors, lack of bilingual staff, or simply the excuse that "We can only do so much." Día is a solution for those challenges and it is definitely one of the best and most practical ways to bring all languages, cultures, and ethnic groups together for the love of reading, or for what Pat Mora calls "bookjoy." There is little excuse not to engage in El día de los niños/El día de los libros.

REFERENCES

Mora, Pat. "Pat's History of El Día de los niños/El Día de los libros, Children's Day/ Book Day." http://www.patmora.com/dia/dia_history.htm (accessed November 25, 2009).

Public Library of Charlotte and Mecklenburg County. "The history of Día de los Niños/Día de los Libros: Children's Day/Book Day." http://www.plcmc.org/ programs/diaarchive.asp (accessed November 25, 2009).

❀ CHAPTER 12

Storytelling and Recently Arrived Latino Children

Lucía M. González, with interview by Jamie Campbell Naidoo

In 2006 I visited schools in Fort Collins, Colorado, as part of a grant-funded program called Art in the Sky. I spent one full day in a school where the majority of the students came from migrant working families. A fifth-grade student named Carlos was especially interested in the stories I told. Carlos, who was described to me as a "problem student," surprised the teachers that day. He was glued to my stories, and later he shared with his teacher what he knew about the characters and how to pronounce their names. Carlos asked to be allowed to attend my other presentations that day. The school personnel could not believe his transformation or his distinct interest in my stories.

The day ended with a family performance and book signing. At 7 P.M. I was ready for my presentation, waiting for the audience to arrive. It was a very cold and rainy evening. Five minutes before the start of the program, the principal approached me and said, "Don't worry if they don't come. It's always like this. It's very hard to get the parents in." And then, as if they had been waiting to come together all at once, they came! The children arrived dragging their parents, grandparents, little brothers and sisters. Lines of parents and children waited to purchase my books. In the distance, I heard Carlos telling his father, "*Mire a'pá! Ella es!* The lady of the stories!"

The story above illustrates the effectiveness of including library and literacy programs that are culturally relevant to students and their families. In this example, the students listened to stories from their culture, told in English, by a storyteller who spoke their language and the language of the host culture. The parents felt appreciated and empowered. They were participants in a school activity that validated their culture by showcasing their stories and their language.

This chapter focuses on the art and technique of sharing stories orally and their effective use in classrooms and libraries with large numbers of recently arrived, Spanish-speaking Latino children. It is a manifold process in which the teacher/librarian storyteller will need to master some basic skills of storytelling, create a special space and environment for telling, know what stories to select, and coach and encourage students to tell their own stories. Hopefully, this chapter will serve as a springboard for teachers and librarians as they embark on the journey of the storyteller.

RECENTLY ARRIVED SPANISH-SPEAKING LATINO CHILDREN

Most Latino children live between two cultures, balancing integration of values, beliefs, and behaviors of both the home and the host cultures; recently arrived Latino children differ in that they have lost the connection with everything familiar and are suddenly immersed in an environment where everything is foreign and incomprehensible. Within the context of this chapter, we refer to children who have been in the country for five years or less as *recently arrived*. These children are in a stage transition, of non-belonging, of cultural homelessness.

Unlike their parents, the children didn't have the opportunity to fully grow and develop in their native culture. They were truncated from that home culture. During this period of adaptation they feel alone, unappreciated, and isolated while they struggle with self-expression in a new language and new environment.

Cultural adaptation is a lengthy, difficult process that can be a vulnerable time for new immigrant children without appropriate cultural support and intervention. It can take at least five years for these children to be able to communicate with confidence and comprehend many aspects of the host culture. They grapple with academic pressure while experiencing a variety of other stressors relating to adaptation. Studies show that a child's failure to cope effectively may result in major learning difficulties, behavioral problems, poor social adjustment, or low academic achievement (Canino and Spurlock 2000; Cárdenas, Taylor, and Adelman 1993).

Teachers and librarians working with recently arrived children need to become knowledgeable about the children's home culture, traditions, language, and literature in order to create culturally responsive environments where the students feel welcomed and appreciated as they acquire the skills and knowledge needed for cultural adaptation (Nieto 2008). Resources such as this book are a great way for non-Latino educators to learn how to connect with Latino children and their families. In addition, storytelling that reflects the culture, traditions, and language of Latino children is another highly effective way for teachers and librarians to make these critical connections with their students.

WHY STORYTELLING

Storytelling can serve as an effective means of building bridges across cultural identities, helping to create a space in classrooms and libraries that is supportive, inclusive, and affirming. It provides a tremendous level of confidence and intimacy for both teller and listener. It is different from reading aloud in that it is a visual and auditory experience in which the teller uses voice, movement, facial expressions, and hand gestures as vehicles to convey the story.

Much has been written about the art of storytelling and its many applications and benefits. Ruth Sawyer, Augusta Baker, Ellin Greene, and our own Pura Belpré are among the leading names in the field. Among the many reasons for using storytelling in classrooms and libraries are the following:

1. It is empowering for a child to be able to express his/her thoughts and feelings through oral language.

2. The art of storytelling can be an enjoyable tool for practicing both listening skills and verbal expression.

3. Teachers and librarians can effectively model expressive language for students to emulate.

4. New vocabulary can be introduced and easily comprehended within a story's context.

5. Diverse ways in which language is used can be depicted in folktales, including recipes, riddles, warnings, questions, and explanations.

6. Stories are the best means of explaining and passing on the moral values a family or people wishes to retain.

7. Students learn new skills when they are interested in the topic. Finding folktales to tell can stimulate reading and research interest.

8. Storytelling is a way to emphasize the uniqueness of each person's imagination. Imagination can generate language.

9. Comprehension, or the ability to make sense of a story's plot, is facilitated by being able to mentally map the story's main events.

10. Storytelling is fun!

11. Within the context of the classroom, the teacher can use storytelling as a way to expand the students' ability to visualize the action beneath the words and enhance their imagery-building practice. This is a very important skill for language learners.

CONNECTING WITH CUENTOS

Latin American culture is very rich in its oral traditions, in particular children's folklore. We share many of the same stories, games, songs, *dichos* and *refranes* (sayings and proverbs). We learn basic lessons about social relationships and behavior through those cuentos and *dichos*. The dominant themes of traditional cuentos are universal to the childhood experience. Their characters learn the power of sharing, they learn to overcome grief, and they learn the value of wit and cleverness.

Cuentos that are passed down from generation to generation transcend language. They speak to the heart of the listener helping to build the ethnic identity of the child. The characters are memorable for their unusual names and traits. They are used as cultural points of reference and are as important as *dichos*. Cuentos are part of the child's literary heritage.

Recently, I came across cuento therapy, an intervention therapy using Puerto Rican folktales as a way to help children model the adaptive behavior depicted in the stories (Constantino et al. 1986). The study of this therapy shows that the oral transmission of folktales is compatible with the Latino child's cultural background, language, values, and auditory learning style, thus providing a familiar cultural experience in which children are eager to participate. Listed as a secondary benefit of cuento therapy is the positive interaction between parents and school when parents are invited to share/tell the stories, becoming equal partners with school personnel in the acculturation of the children.

Cuentos from the oral tradition are the best stories to learn and to tell aloud to children. The language of the folktale is poetic and has an internal music. In his classic *The Uses of Enchantment: The Meaning and Importance of Fairy Tales*, Bruno Bettelheim (1976) explains how folk and fairy tales are unique, not only as a form of literature, but as works of art that are fully comprehensible to the child, as no other form of art can be (p. 12).

Many authentic renditions of traditional cuentos are available in bilingual picture books. These bilingual renditions are perfect to use with recently arrived Latino children because the texts have a clear structure and tend to use repetition, encouraging children to develop their memories and expand their vocabularies as they join in repeating ever-lengthening refrains. *The Bossy Gallito* by Lucía González and Lulu Delacre (1994) and *Perez and Martina* by Pura Belpré and Carlos Sanchez (1932) are classic examples of these cumulative tales that are fun to learn and tell.

ILLUMINATING THE IMAGINATION:
A WORD WITH THE CREATORS OF
THE STORYTELLER'S CANDLE/LA VELITA DE LOS CUENTOS.

By Dr. Jamie Campbell Naidoo

A match gently lights a lone candle. In the warm glow of the room a puppet stage has been set. Juan Bobo and el coquí patiently await their performance. Illustrator Lulu Delacre has strategically positioned these visual elements to invite readers into the magnificent, bilingual picture book that she and author Lucía González have lovingly crafted as a tribute to puppeteer, storyteller, author, and librarian Pura Belpré.

As I grab the storyteller's candle and push aside the curtains, join me as we revisit the early years of the Great Depression in New York City. It is an icy winter afternoon as we follow young Hildamar and Santiago on their brisk journey home from school. Both children long for the soft warm breeze of their Puerto Rican village and wonder if the Kings will find them in time for El Dia de los Reyes. The following day, like every day, they pass an expansive building with huge windows. The children sense the inviting presence of the public library but their Titi informs them that libraries are not for people who do not speak English. Fortunately, that afternoon Hildamar and Santiago have a very special guest in their classroom—a tall slender woman who tells stories with puppets, in English *and* Spanish. The storyteller is none other than Pura Belpré, who has come from the public library to spread the glorious news that "The library is for everyone, *la biblioteca es para todos.*" The excited children share this magical secret with all their neighbors throughout El Barrio. A few days later Santiago and Hildamar, accompanied by several friends and family members, eagerly climb the library stairs where they are welcomed in the story room by Ms. Belpré.

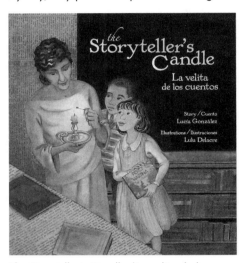

The Storyteller's Candle / La velita de los cuentos © 2008 by Lucía González and Lulu Delacre. Published by Children's Book Press. Used with permission. All rights reserved.

The librarian lights a storyteller's candle and begins a cuento the children have heard several times from their *abuela,* a story about beautiful Martina and her brave Pérez. As the story ends, the candle is extinguished with the instructions to "close your eyes and make a wish." Then, to the amazement of everyone, Ms. Belpré announces that the library will be hosting a big fiesta in honor of El Dia de los Reyes. The entire community is encouraged to help create costumes, decorations, and a stage for the library celebration. A while later on January 6th, 1930, Hildamar, Santiago, their family, and many members from El Barrio have transformed the story room into a Caribbean island blazing with warmth. Anxiously the children participate in a play of *Pérez y Martina* and are surprised by the arrival of the Kings just in time for El Dia de los Reyes.

In our interview, both the author Lucía and the illustrator Lulu described the extensive research needed to create this historical account of New York Public Library's first Puerto Rican librarian, and disclosed serendipitous incidents that suggested the spirit of Pura Belpré had a hand in the creation of her story.

Lucía González, author of The Storyteller's Candle. *Used with permission.*

Lucía dedicated weeks to original research and went to New York City for the first time when she started work on the book. From the moment she arrived, she experience good fortune with the spirit of Belpré guiding her. The author recalls, "I stayed at the YMCA in Harlem because I couldn't find another affordable place at the time. As I walked out of the YMCA the next morning and asked for the nearest New York Public Library, a man who was leaning against the dark brick wall just lifted his hand and pointed across the street. There, across from the room where I stayed, was the Schomburg Library, the first library where Pura Belpré worked in 1921. My heart pounded with emotion when I entered the place where Ms. Belpré first told the story of Pérez and Martina to an eager group of children by the light of the storyteller's candle." While in the heart of El Barrio in New York City, Lucía visited the library branches where Belpré worked, spoke with the storyteller's acquaintances, listened to recordings of Belpré's stories, and examined original letters written to the librarian by children who attended her programs, as well as letters written by Belpré herself.

Lucía shared her research with Lulu, who studied it before beginning her detailed collage illustrations. Lulu remarks that she wanted to ensure complete historical accuracy in her illustrations and used many online images from the New York Public Library's Digital Gallery to assist her in recreating the atmosphere of the 115th Street library and its surrounding neighborhood during the 1930s. She also wanted to enrich the book and make it historical. Lulu notes, "I kept thinking, how can I bring the history into the illustrations without simply reproducing the pictures from the 1930s?" She had an idea about using an original *New York Times* newspaper distributed on the actual day of Pura Belpré's El Dia de los Reyes celebration.

At first she wanted to use bits of newspaper to tell readers about the time period of the book without conflicting with the story. Then the spirit of Belpré again offered a helping hand in this project of love. Lulu began noticing news articles from the paper that supported the story on specific pages. "I was just going to use the color of the paper, but then I noticed that the paper actually supported the text," Lulu remembers. For instance, on pages 4 and 5, readers will note the newspaper contains a listing of ships arriving with immigrants.

Lulu Delacre, illustrator of
The Storyteller's Candle.
Used with permission.

Behind the elbow of the cat is a listing for San Juan with immigrants from Porto Rico. On page 6, the second column tells the story of the Three Kings tradition. Lulu acknowledges that, "readers may not pick up the information at first, but then they can go back and make the connection." The inclusion of the newspaper puts the story into a historical context. Page 26 provides a weather report, page 27 details reviews of plays, and page 29 (in the king's robe) lists radio programming during the time. History and culture are embedded throughout the book's illustrations. The bodega on page 14 depicts product brands and labels that were available during that era, and the big jar of *pilonnes* candy would have been enjoyed by Puerto Rican children of the time. In fact, the only place where the illustrator uses artistic license is on the book's cover, where she depicts Hildamar holding a copy of Belpré's *Pérez and Martina.* Although the title was released a few years after 1930, Lulu wanted the image included to "show Pura Belpré as the puppeteer, storyteller, and writer that she was."

On the final page of the book, Pura Belpré concludes the El Dia de los Reyes celebration by blowing out her candle and reminding everyone, "Today, with everyone's help, we brought the warmth and beauty of Puerto Rico to New York. Remember, the library belongs to you all." As the smoke from the storyteller's candle rises, we are gently reassured that the library indeed belongs to everyone. Through the creative talents of Lucía González and Lulu Delacre, generations of *niños* reading *The Storyteller's Candle/La velita de los cuentos* will accompany Hildamar and Santiago as they encounter the warmth of Puerto Rico in the midst of a cold Nueva York City through the light of Belpré's candle. *Colorín colorado este cuento se ha acabado.*

FIGURE 12.1. *Reprinted with permission from J. C. Naidoo (2007). "Illuminating the Imagination: A Word with the Creators of* The Storyteller's Candle / La velita de los cuentos." REFORMA Newsletter, *25 (3/4), 12–13.*

Rhythmic, cumulative tales work well with children who are learning English. Flannelboards, stick puppets, and masks serve as visual and memory aids while encouraging active participation from the children. Included at the end of this chapter is a list of recommended storytelling resources intended to aid with the selection of stories and with learning basic storytelling techniques.

SELECTING READY-TO-TELL STORIES

The 1990s saw a boom in the publication of high-quality Latino children's books, partly brought to the forefront by the establishment of national literary awards such as the Pura Belpré and Américas awards (see Chapter 5 for more information on these). Versions of folktales from all over Latin America populate the shelves of library collections in both school and public libraries. Most are ready-to-tell tales of exceptional literary value written in Spanish and English.

There are classic retellings and collections that, although out of print, should be considered when searching for appropriate stories to tell. The best examples of these out-of-print classics still available in libraries are Pura Belpré's renditions of traditional tales such as *The Tiger and the Rabbit and Other Tales* (1965), *Pérez and Martina* (1932), and *Oté* (1969). The following are additional recommended print and out-of-print cuentos for telling.

Baila, Nana, Baila/Dance, Nana, Dance: Cuban Folktales in English and Spanish by Joe Hayes, illustrated by Mauricio Trenard Sayago.

This savory collection of Cuban folktales is framed with an introduction about the author's quest to gather the stories, and an all-important "note to readers and storytellers" that describes the origins of each story. The storytelling is clear and amusing, capturing the rhythm of Cuban culture. Two of my favorite cuentos to tell from this collection are "Compay Monkey and Comay Turtle" and "The Fig Tree."

"The Bed" in *The Tiger and the Rabbit* by Pura Belpré, illustrated by Tomie dePaola.

This is a wonderful participation story about a grandmother who puts one animal after another into the bed of a child who's frightened by the sound of the old squeaky bed. The outrageous exaggeration is delightfully comic; the repetitions invite spontaneous bilingual telling.

The Blacksmith and the Devils by María Cristina Brusca, illustrated by Tona Wilson.

This is an Argentinean retelling of a familiar folktale about a clever man, Pedro Pobreza, who outwits the devil. The theme of outwitting the devil is a common motif in stories from many countries. Considering its active, visual language, this folktale would be ideal for 5th- and 6th-grade students.

Borreguita and the Coyote: A Tale from Ayutla by Verna Aardema, illustrated by Petra Mathers.

In this fun-to-tell trickster tale a cute little lamb tricks a very hungry but gullible coyote. Elementary children will quickly comprehend the humor in this story in which it is not always clear who is the real underdog.

The Bossy Gallito/El gallo de bodas: A Traditional Cuban Folktale by Lucía González, illustrated by Lulu Delacre.

A bossy rooster dirties his beak on his way to the wedding of uncle the parrot (*su tio el perico*), starting a chain of events in this cumulative folktale from Cuba that is ideal for bilingual telling.

Cuentos de espantos y aparecidos (Tales About Ghosts and Spectres) ed. by Verónica Uribe.

The richness of this collection lies in its mixture of mysterious and spine-chilling tales and legends carefully selected by country, respectful of the stories' most original versions. This treasure for storytellers will also be loved by upper elementary and middle school students who will delight in learning and retelling stories from this collection.

Cuentos populares de Iberoamérica by Carmen Bravo-Villasante.

This anthology of Latin American folklore is an outstanding compilation of stories from the Pampas to the Andes, from the mainland continent to the islands. The stories are well told in a format perfect for oral narration.

Doña Flor: A Tall Tale About a Giant Woman with a Great Big Heart by Pat Mora, illustrated by Raúl Colón.

Great to pair with tall tales such as Paul Bunyan from other cultures, this magical story describes a strong woman whose heart is as large as her enormous hands and feet. The language has the flavor and vividness of a story from the oral tradition, ready to be told and enjoyed.

From the Winds of Manguito: Cuban Folktales in English and Spanish/Desde los vientos de Manguito: Cuentos folklóricos de Cuba, en inglés y español by Elvia Pérez, illustrated by Victor Francisco Hernández Mora, ed. by Margaret Read MacDonald, translated by Paula Martín.

This lovely and lively collection of stories retold by one of Cuba's most beloved storytellers will let tellers and listeners enjoy the sounds and feeling of Cuba and the Afro-Hispanic Caribbean cultures. Great introductions to Cuban folklore, these stories are fun to tell and include singing refrains.

"The Goat in the Chile Patch" in *Multicultural Folktales: Stories to Tell Young Children* by Judy Sierra and Robert Kaminski.

This is the Mexican variant of a cumulative story in which an awful and stubborn goat tramples over a garden while a number of animals try and fail to scare it away. As is true in many folktales, it is the most insignificant ant or bee that finally succeeds in scaring the goat. This bilingual rendition is fun to tell as a participation story and the flannelboard figures provided at the end of the story are great visuals to use with younger children.

"How Uncle Rabbit Tricked Uncle Tiger" in *Señor Cat's Romance and Other Favorite Stories from Latin America* by Lucía M. González, illustrated by Lulu Delacre.

Tío Conejo is Latin America's most famous trickster. He loves to play tricks on his powerful rivals, Tío Tigre (the tiger) and Tía Zorra (the fox), and always manages to get away with it. He makes children laugh with his ingenuity. The tales of Tío Conejo are most popular in places where there were large slave plantations.

Juan Bobo: Four Folktales from Puerto Rico by Carmen Bernier-Grand, illustrated by Ernesto Remos Nieves.

In Puerto Rico, Juan Bobo is the most popular folk hero. He represents the humor, innocence, and wisdom of the country folk. Variants of these stories are also told throughout most Latin American countries.

Juan Bobo Goes to Work by Marisa Montes, illustrated by Jose Cepeda.

This is another hilarious and easy-to-tell rendition of the adventures of our most famous fool, Juan Bobo. Pair this with other noodlehead or "fool" stories from other countries for a multicultural celebration.

Just a Minute: A Trickster Tale and Counting Book written and illustrated by Yuyi Morales.

Perfect for *Día de los muertos* or any other time of the year, this original trickster tale contains all the elements of folklore and is a joy to tell. The younger children may not catch the humor behind the old woman outwitting death, but they will certainly enjoy the story just the same.

"The Little Crab and the Magic Eyes" in *Twenty Tellable Tales: Audience Participation Tales for the Beginning Storyteller* by Margaret Read MacDonald, illustrated by Roxane Murphy.

Multiple variants of this tale are available in different sources. In this retelling, MacDonald offers a straightforward and easy-to-tell story that will keep children mesmerized while also engaging them in the telling of the story. There is a Venezuelan version, *El cangrejo y el tigre*, published in Spanish by Ekare-Banco del libro that is also fun and easy to tell. The Venezuelan variant retains more elements of the cultural traits and flavor of the original tale.

"The Little Half Chick" in *Señor Cat's Romance and Other Favorite Stories from Latin America* by Lucía M. González, illustrated by Lulu Delacre.

Widely known in Spain and Latin America, this story follows a willful and adventurous little chick who, in spite of his many limitations, sets out to see the world and meet the king. In his quest, he learns a very important lesson but still grows up to become a very helpful and important half-chick. Excellent for audience participation.

The Lizard and the Sun / La lagartija y el sol: A Folktale in English and Spanish by Alma Flor Ada, illustrated by Felipe Dávalos.

A nontraditional, bilingual retelling, this Mexican folktale follows a determined lizard who won't stop looking for the sun when it disappears. Eventually she discovers a glowing rock and runs to tell the emperor, who orders her to move it. But when the lizard is unable to move the rock, the emperor and the woodpecker must work together to help the lizard release the reluctant sun trapped inside. This story can be easily adapted for telling and demonstrates the power of cooperation to complete a task.

Martina, the Beautiful Cockroach by Carmen Agra Deedy, illustrated by Michael Austin.

This is a very original and humorous retelling of the story of Martina, the beautiful cockroach, a tale that is part of the children's folklore of almost all Spanish-speaking countries. It came to the Americas from Spain, where there are other stories told about the adventurous Ratoncito Perez and Cucarachita Martina. This lively tale is Agra Deedy's original retelling of the traditional story.

Pedro Fools the Gringo and Other Tales of a Latin American Trickster by María Cristina Brusca, illustrated by Tona Wilson.

Here are twelve humorous and lively stories about a character who would feel right at home with Brer Rabbit, Coyote, and Anansi the Spider. Pedro Urdemales, also known as Pedro Malasartes in Colombia and Venezuela, is a clever trickster who appears in tales throughout Latin America. He is able to convince outlaws that money grows on trees, outsmarts the devil, and even gets San Pedro (Saint Peter) to let him into heaven.

Prietita and the Ghost Woman/Prietita y la Llorona by Gloria Anzaldúa, illustrated by Maya Christina Gonzalez.

In this nontraditional, feminist interpretation intended for very young children, a female ghost guides a young girl to safety. This original telling is a good introduction to the tragic figure of La Llorona, who roams the rivers of the Américas in an eternal search for her drowned children. The traditional stories of La Llorona are best for children in grades 4 and up.

CREATING A STORYTELLING SPACE AND MOOD

*A*fter stories have been selected, librarians and teachers need to create a space for them within the hectic routine of their students' lives. When using storytelling in the classroom, the story space must be clearly defined and differentiated from instructional and other areas. It should be a special place in the room where children expect to enter a circle of magic. The storytelling space can be simply created by shifting chairs to face in the opposite direction. A semicircle (or theater) arrangement is recommended as it is conducive to intimacy and allows the full attention of the audience to be focused on the teller as well as permitting the teller to have eye contact with the audience. There should be no distractions behind the teller. In this way, children learn to respect the teller, and the teller feels the importance of his/her role.

Within the public library or school library media center, the storytelling space should be carefully selected and marked. Books relating to the culture, the country, or the subject should always be displayed. Storytelling will spark the interest of children about the country or the subject of the story. Having books on hand will allow children to extend the story and strengthen their research skills as they seek new information to connect with the story they heard.

The children should be able to hear, taste, and sense the place where the stories originate. Music is perfect to set the mood. Librarians and teachers should consider playing music from the storyteller's country or from the story's country as the children settle. Decorations that are specific to the culture of the story or the teller are also important. As mentioned in other chapters of this book, these decorations can include *papel picado*, native textiles, papier-mâché items, artwork, *alebrijes*, and so forth. Serving special treats that originate from the culture of the story or storyteller will also give children an opportunity to taste the stories.

EVERY CHILD HAS A STORY TO TELL

Once storytelling has become a part of the classroom or library experience and the teacher or librarian has modeled techniques, students, particularly the upper elementary students, will be ready to tell their own stories. Some will share stories they have heard from their parents or grandparents. Others will tell stories they have read. As they listen to stories told to them by the teacher, librarian, or guest storyteller, the students can work on preparing their stories to present and share with the group. Students with limited English can be encouraged to illustrate or draw their stories. They should also be encouraged to tell the story in the language of their preference. Compiling the students' stories in written form, with drawings, is always a rewarding project that can be shared with the entire school and the children's families.

The best way to encourage story sharing is to select a theme that is particularly relevant to the experiences of recently arrived children such as the departure from their countries. This is a universal experience for all recently arrived children. Each child will have a very different story to tell, and each child will have a different perspective.

Cuentos Make Magic!

The phrases *Habia una vez* (once upon a time) and *Colorín colorado* are music to the ears of Spanish-speaking children. These are the phrases with which Latin American storytellers always start and end a story. Upon hearing *Habia una vez . . .* , children's faces light up with expectations of wonderful things to come. These phrases are cultural points of reference that are universal to the oral traditions of all Spanish-speaking children. The listeners are immediately transported to a magic circle, a faraway place where they feel at home.

As recently arrived Latino children embark on the journey of language acquisition and cultural adaptation, they need connecting links between their home and the host cultures of school, library, and community. They need to feel that they and their families are active participants in the process, and that they are not just receiving but also giving and contributing. Telling stories is among the least costly and most effective means of achieving this. Preparation and long-term commitment are essential to the success of a storytelling program. The teller needs to become familiar with the rituals of childhood that are part of the oral traditions from which the stories come. Children and their parents are primary providers of this information. Inviting them to share their stories or their memories of childhood as follow-up activities encourages the participation of the entire *familia*.

There is also a wealth of literature from which to select stories. It is the teller's responsibility to research the story, to know its many variants and to tell the version that most authentically depicts the culture of origin and that retains the internal rhythm and cadence of its language. Storytelling, when executed effectively, transcends language barriers to offer teachers and librarians the opportunity to have an everlasting effect in the lives of recently arrived Latino children. Connect cultures and celebrate cuentos @ your library with rich stories from the Latino cultures. *Colorín colorado!*

REFERENCES

Bettelheim, Bruno. *The Uses of Enchantment: The Meaning and Importance of Fairy Tales.* New York: Knopf, 1976.

Canino, Ian A., and Jeanne Spurlock. *Culturally Diverse Children and Adolescents: Assessment, Diagnosis, and Treatment.* 2nd ed. New York: Guilford Press, 2000.

Cárdenas, Jose, Linda Taylor, and Howard Adelman. "Transition Support for Immigrant Students." *Journal of Multicultural Counseling and Development* 21, no. 4 (1993): 203–210.

Constantino, Giuseppe, Robert G. Malgady, and Lloyd H. Rogler. "Cuento Therapy: A Culturally Sensitive Modality for Puerto Rican Children." *Journal of Consulting and Clinical Psychology*, 54 (1986): 639–645.

Nieto, Sonia. *Language, Culture, and Teaching: Critical Perspectives for a New Century.* Boston: Pearson/Allyn and Bacon, 2008.

CHAPTER 13

Bailando ante el espejo literario: Responses to Culturally Familiar Themes in Picture Books

Ruth E. Quiroa

Ana's (all names are pseudonyms) pony-tail bobbed up and down and her eyes sparkled as she previewed the illustrations in *My Very Own Room/Mi propio cuartito*, a Mexican American-themed bilingual picture book by Amada Pérez and Maya Gonzalez. This text depicts an eight-year-old girl whose family helps her create a little bedroom of her own within their tiny home filled with family and visitors. One of the illustrations shows the protagonist and her mother embracing, and when Ana came across this picture, she exclaimed, *"¡Ohhh, mi mamá así me abraza!"* ("Ohhh, this is the way my mother hugs me!") Her small literary group of six first-graders, all of Mexican heritage, began discussing this page, noting how the protagonist looked just like her mother, as if they were twins with the same lips, eyes, and eyebrows. Yolanda commented, *"A mi me gusta el pelo de ella"* ("I like her hair"), as she shook her head dramatically and pulled a lock of her own shiny dark hair out to inspect. The three girls in the group then decided that several of their classmates had hair like that of the protagonist and her mother.

The children's personal responses to a text they found to be culturally familiar poignantly illustrate the manner in which culturally relevant multicultural children's literature can serve as a mirror that reflects the readers' own lives as part of the larger human experience (Bishop 1990a). Such books can present to students of parallel cultures their own histories and cultural identities, as well as a sense of pride in who they are. Sharing such books in the classroom or library setting may set the stage for students to access personal, community, and transnational knowledge, while at the same time giving the teacher or librarian the opportunity to gain insight into children's thinking about books. The resulting "poem" of such textual transactions (Rosenblatt 1978) may produce joyous, spontaneous celebrations reflected in dramatic, even comical responses to texts.

227

This chapter focuses on how the children in the opening vignette responded to the cultural reflections they saw in Mexican American-themed picture books portraying distinct life experiences within the larger picture of this culture in the United States. It also highlights ways in which teachers and librarians can facilitate discussions and offer opportunities for students to verbalize, write, or visually represent their thinking about such books.

ROLES AND FUNCTIONS OF CHILDREN'S LITERATURE

Children's literature can be *"una forma de la alegría"* ("a form of joy") (Borges 2000 as cited in Benda, Hernández de Lamas, and Ianantuoni 2000), providing "literary pleasure and intellectual stimulation" (Nodelman 1996, p. 209). Literature also serves as a way of "knowing" (Short 1997), and texts read over time can form an inner encyclopedia deep within one's memory, crucial to the construction of identity: *"A tal punto ellas terminan construyendo nuestra mismidad"* ("At some point, these [readings] end up constructing our identity") (Benda et al. 2000, p. 14). In addition, Margarita Dobles Rodríguez (2000, p. 14) calls children's literature a *"vacuna espiritual"* ("spiritual vaccine") against pedagogical currents solely valuing this literary art as a tool to teach specific literacy skills or content-based concepts. She states that the function of children's literature is one of cultivating the inner world of the child as a creative human being.

Children's literature provides windows for students to view real or imagined worlds that can open like sliding glass doors and allow them to walk into the story worlds and participate in those worlds (Bishop 1990a). Under the right lighting conditions such windows turn into mirrors:

> Literature transforms human experience and reflects it back to us, and in that reflection we can see our own lives and experiences as part of the larger human experience. Reading, then, becomes a means of self-affirmation, and readers often seek their mirrors in books (p. ix).

Children from parallel cultures and diverse peoples often have been deprived of the validating and other salutary effects of books with mirror-like potential (Harris 1993, 1997; Horning, Kruse, and Schliesman 2002; Larrick 1965). Multicultural children's literature has the potential to offer literary mirrors to children traditionally marginalized, misrepresented, and deprived of cultural identities in books (Cai 2002). In particular, *culturally specific* books with ethnic themes detailing recognizable "specifics of daily living" (Bishop 1993, p. 44), as opposed to generic or neutral cultural content, provide familiar, self-affirming images for members of that ethnic group. Thus, Latino-themed literature with its mirror-like potential for children of similar cultural backgrounds can provide opportunities for admiration of the familiar images in the literary mirror, and even occasions for students to dance in front of that mirror.

READ-ALOUDS WITH YOUNG CHILDREN OF MEXICAN HERITAGE

The students described in the opening paragraphs were all children of immigrant parents, originally from seven different states of Mexico. These families settled in the western suburbs of a large midwestern city between six months and thirteen years before spring 2004 when this four-month, qualitative study was conducted. The children were all members of one first-grade bilingual classroom in which the primary language of instruction was Spanish; they varied in generational status, experiential background, English language proficiency, and Spanish literacy development. There were three boys and three girls, some of whom also received special services including speech, Title I, and gifted and talented classes. The group met at least twice a week with the author to participate in dialogic Spanish-language read-alouds of several Mexican American-themed picture books. The classroom teacher's guided reading groups and independent literacy centers met at the same time as this focal group of students.

In addition to responding to *My Very Own Room / Mi propio cuartito*, these students also reacted to another Mexican-themed picture book *Grandma and Me at the Flea / Los Meros Meros Remateros*, referred to by the Spanish portion of the title hereafter. This book was written by the renowned poet and award-winning children's author Juan Felipe Herrera and was illustrated by Anita DeLucio-Brock. It was recognized by the Américas Award for Children's and Young Adult Literature in 2003, and appears on the Cooperative Children's Book Center bibliography of recommended Spanish/English bilingual books. Brightly colored, humorous illustrations depict one of protagonist Juanito's weekly Sunday trips with his grandmother to the local flea market or *remate*. Here his *abuelita* sells old clothes and is an integral member of the community due to her generosity and support for others. Readers follow Juanito and two of his friends through a maze of stands as he runs errands for his *abuelita*, bartering for needed items in a community where hope prevails in spite of difficulties. The illustrations and storyline incorporate many aspects of the Mexican and

Cover image from Grandma and Me at the Flea / Los Meros Meros Remateros. *Story © 2002 by Juan Felipe Herrera. Illustrations © 2002 by Anita DeLucio-Brock. Reprinted with permission of the publisher, Children's Book Press, San Francisco, CA, www. childrensbookpress.org.*

Mexican American culture including foods (chiles, churritos), a Mexican flag, and a reference to Cantínflas, a famous Mexican actor/comedian. In addition, the illustrations provide visual narratives that stand alongside the text—a baby stealing items from different booths, and customers and vendors interacting with one another.

The focal students participated in pre-reading activities during which they previewed illustrations and made story predictions to activate background knowledge and interest in the book. This was followed by a read-aloud in Spanish with frequent pauses to hear students' comments, as well as open-ended questions to elicit thinking in relationship to the book. Talk around the book often began with simple responses to very general questions such as: "What are you thinking about the book at this moment? Why are you smiling/laughing?" These prompts were often followed by intensive group conversations with overlapping speech, all of which was recorded through audio and video tapes that were later transcribed and augmented with the nonverbal responses captured in the videos. Students also created written and pictorial responses for each book.

CULTURAL INTERSECTIONS AND STUDENT RESPONSES

Personal Connections: Looking into the Mirror

One of the children's most common responses to *Los Meros Meros Remateros* was to share their own personal connections to this story, which were often linked to culture. These responses provided windows into the children's own lives, particularly family stories that were loosely linked to the textual content or illustrations. The students were especially intrigued by two illustrations of the "thieving" baby being held by its mother. In the first picture, the baby is eating a hot chile stolen from a chile stand, and in the second, on the back cover, he or she is smiling delightedly at an orange stolen from a fruit stand. During the read-aloud, on the page depicting the chile stand, María began smiling broadly. This child was generally silent during previous read-alouds, but this particular story and its visual images sparked vivid personal connections that she readily shared when asked about her smile.

María: *Mi hermano chiquito . . . cuando mi mamá hizo chiles, mi hermano le agarró un montón de chiles y se los comió.*	**María**: My younger brother . . . when my mom made chiles, my brother grabbed a lot of chiles and ate them.
Ruth: Ahh (INTAKE OF BREATH). *¿Qué pasó después?*	**Ruth**: Ahh (INTAKE OF BREATH). What happened next?
María: *Le quitaba y luego le hizo así . . .* (STICKING TONGUE OUT AND MAKING A PANTING NOISE WHILE MOVING A HAND BACK AND FORTH IN FRONT OF HER MOUTH) *. . . y mi mamá le dio agua.*	**María**: He took it out and then he went like this and my mother gave him water.

(All translations are the author's.)

José was another child who remained silent during many of the oral group response sessions, except during readings of *Los Meros Meros Remateros*. The following example of his personal connection begins with another child's analytical comment, followed by a specific prompt directed to José's, and then his personal response:

Jorge: *El niño está robando una naranja.*	**Jorge**: The boy is stealing an orange.
Ruth: *¡Ahh! ¡El bebé está robando una naranja! Es como tu hermano, ¿verdad?* (TO JOSÉ). *El es como la edad de tu hermano* (PUTTING THE PICTURE CLOSE FOR HIM TO SEE).	**Ruth**: Ahh! The baby is stealing an orange! It's like your brother, right? (TO JOSÉ). He is about the same age as your brother (PUTTING THE PICTURE CLOSE FOR HIM TO SEE).
José: (SMILING AND NODDING HIS HEAD). *El siempre agarra cosas.*	**José**: (SMILING AND NODDING HIS HEAD). He is always grabbing things.
Ruth: *¿Cómo?*	**Ruth**: What?
José: *Mi hermano siempre agarra cosas, así* (USING HAND TO SHOW HIS BROTHER GRABBING SOMETHING).	**José**: My brother is always grabbing things, like this (USING HAND TO SHOW HIS BROTHER GRABBING SOMETHING).

José's thoughts remained with the baby throughout the oral readings and discussions of the book, as evidenced in the lengthy, detailed written narrative produced at the end of the readings (see Figure 13.1).

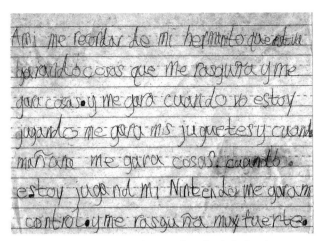

FIGURE 13.1. *José's story about his baby brother.*

The transcription and translation for his written narrative are:

A mi me recuerda de mi hermanito que estaba agarrando cosas, que me rasguña y . . . agarra cuando yo estoy jugando, me agarra mis juguetes y cuando [en la] mañana me agarra cosas. Cuando estoy jugando mi Nintendo me agarra mi control. Y me rasguña muy fuerte. (It reminded me of my little brother who was grabbing things, that he scratched me and . . . when I play he grabs my toys and [in the] morning he grabs things. When I am playing my Nintendo he grabs my control. And he scratches me very hard.)

Another personal, visual response with the theme of *chiles picosos* (spicy chilies) occurred when Jorge shared his drawing (Figure 13.2) relating to this book, describing it simply as his older sister eating chiles in a market in Mexico. Queries by his peers prompted a longer story in which Jorge revealed that the chile was very spicy and that his sister cried when she ate it. The group also discovered that the figure behind her was that of a peacock, an animal depicted on a *zarape* (blanket) sold in one of the flea market stands in the text. Jorge said he chose to include this animal in his picture because his sister liked them. Notably, his ten-year-old sister did not immigrate to the United States with the family, and although she remained in Mexico, she was an important person in Jorge's life.

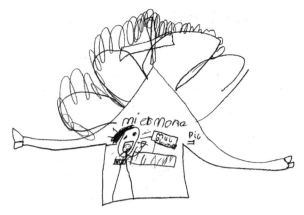

FIGURE 13.2. *Jorge's sister eating a very spicy chile.*

DANCING IN FRONT OF THE MIRROR: THE "WILD RUMPUS"

Cultural intersections with *Los Meros Meros Remateros* were also evident in students' "performative" responses, when the children seemed to spontaneously enter the world of the text by acting it out or embellishing it orally. Sipe (2000) refers to this as a "carnivalesque romp" (p. 267), and notes that such responses allow children to manipulate or steer the storyline toward their own creative purposes. The children took a situation or event in the book and used it for a "flight of their own imagination" (p. 267) that often involved spontaneous theatrical outbursts replete with movement or long, creative group stories. Thus children worked together to manipulate the textual world toward their own creative storyline, or to dramatize the textual story or illustrations. The results seemed similar to the "wild rumpus" of Max and the Wild Things in Sendak's (1963) fantasy picture book *Where the Wild Things Are*. In some of the performative stories, the children chose to code-switch between Spanish and English to convey their messages fully. For example, they responded to Jaime's comment about a woman bending over her table at a fruit stand seemingly to adjust a rectangular-shaped sign with the word *"fruta"* ("fruit") on it. Jaime thought the picture was *"bien chistoso"* ("very funny") and Jorge took off in a new direction that involved hand motions and movement as follows:

Jorge: *Como jugamos con las skateboards in the gym eeeehhhh! Que hacemos carreras* (MOVING HANDS WILDLY).	**Jorge**: Like when we play with the skateboards in the gym eeeehhhh! We race each other (MOVING HANDS WILDLY).

Ruth: ¿*Ella parece cómo que está jugando* skateboards?	**Ruth**: She looks like she is playing skateboards?
Jorge: (NODS HIS HEAD YES).	
Jaime: *Lo que me gusta más jugar es cuando, es en* gym *es* spiders.	**Jaime**: What I like best to play in gym is spiders.
Jorge: *A mi* skateboards	**Jorge**: For me, it's skateboards
(MORE BODY AND HAND MOTIONS)	

Thus, the fruit sign reminded Jorge of a skateboard, which then reminded him of gym class, a clearly logical line of thinking for a seven-year-old. The boys' conversation, which included "code-switching" of English words into a primarily Spanish-language conversation, evidenced the cultural/linguistic borders they crossed daily from their Spanish-language classroom to their English-language gym class. Their hand and body motions served to accentuate their ideas, as well as indicating a strong tendency to perform their thoughts.

In another response to *Los Meros Meros Remateros,* a lengthy performative group story involved declarations of what children would like to purchase at the used toy booth. Every child participated and the list of desired toys was quite lengthy. Embedded within this conversation was José's statement listing almost everything on the page, *"Pero menos mal las muñecas"* ("Except the dolls"), to which Jaime chimed in "Me, too." A similar response pattern occurred toward the end of the text when Juanito returned to his grandmother's clothing booth. Here the children inserted themselves into the story by stating which type of clothing they liked. After reciting a long list of desired clothing depicted in this illustration, Ana was asked to explain why she liked these clothes. She answered unequivocally, stating: *"Porque es la ropa de México"* ("Because it is clothing from Mexico"). Yolanda even chose specific clothes for herself and for her younger sister. In both instances the students completely took over the text and entered its world. It was as if they were standing with Juanito in the flea market, choosing what to purchase.

PROMOTING CULTURAL INTERSECTIONS IN RESPONSIVE READ-ALOUDS

Young children love to look at themselves in mirrors—to admire their reflections, make faces, and even watch their images as they dance to music. The humorous tone of *Los Meros Meros Remateros,* with its familiar cultural images, created a literary mirror for the students in this study. They greatly enjoyed analyzing and interpreting a story in which a baby eats a spicy chile and steals an orange, while also including references to Michoacán, Mexico. In essence, this text wove all these images into a storyline that the children were able to identify with and enjoy. In particular, their written and artistic responses paralleled this text, as they told personal stories of their siblings and families. In fact, when the students were asked at the end of the study to select their favorite and least favorite texts, Jaime chose *Los Meros Meros Remateros* as his favorite stating: "*. . . porque me hace recordar a mis aguelitos* (sic)" (". . . because it made me remember my grandparents"). This was important to him because his grandmother died right at the beginning of the study.

Cultural and personal connections are critical in children's enjoyment of, and participation in interactive read-alouds. Certain books have distinct appeal for children of Mexican origin, particularly books with Mexican American themes presenting some of the specifics of daily living and familial relationships. When such content is coupled with a humorous tone in the text or the illustrations, students seem to absorb the books, basking in the familiarity reflected in them. Images of younger siblings, favorite foods, and Mexican clothing and flags seem to promote extended literary conversations and even theatrical *bailes*.

Students' responses do not happen in a vacuum. The ways in which adults conduct and participate in read-alouds are equally important components in literary transactions. This study included the use of open-ended prompts to start book discussions, and encouragement of open expression of students' thoughts. Effective questioning in such instances involved knowledge of students' cultural and personal backgrounds, sensitivity to their nonverbal cues (smiles, laughter, and so forth), and provision for multiple response modes (including oral, written, and pictorial). The use of these three instructional aspects provided comfortable, safe spaces that helped scaffold the expression of personal stories, creative thought, and even theatrical movement.

The remainder of this chapter includes a list of recommended fiction and informational Mexican American-themed books that can be used in classrooms and libraries in much the same way as I used *Los Meros Meros Remateros* in the study described above. Also included in Figure 13.3 are guidelines for implementing dialogic read-alouds with such texts. This information may serve as a springboard for the implementation of such books in K–3 classrooms and libraries.

GUIDELINES FOR IMPLEMENTING DIALOGIC READ-ALOUDS

❋ After text selection, closely review all textual illustrations and read the story multiple times.

❋ Check pronunciation of any Spanish words or phrases with a proficient Spanish-speaking individual; incorrect pronunciations can result in missed meanings for young children. Many books are now available in audio format, and listening to the audio read by a native Spanish speaker is another way to improve pronunciation.

❋ Use post-it notes to mark points to pause and allow for spontaneous conversations to emerge, or to provide prompts to spur discussion.

❋ Plan multiple pre-reading activities, starting with the allotment of adequate time for students to simply preview all illustrations.

❋ Provide students with multiple text copies to view in pairs, or use a document camera to enlarge the book for all to see.

❋ During the previews of illustrations, ask students to provide input regarding their thoughts about the images, which may result in predictions or connections to personal, local, or transnational knowledge in terms of geographical settings, physical objects, foods, religious artifacts, and so forth. Be prepared to discuss the students' ideas.

❋ Other possible pre-reading activities include: a K-W-L graphic organizer (Ogle, 1986) to list what students already know (K), and want to learn (W) about a book prior to reading, and then what they learned (L) after reading; prompts to promote predictions/discussions of the meaning of vocabulary that will be encountered during the read-aloud; or an activity in which artifacts representing story themes or events are removed one by one from a box or sack. Students make predictions about the book based on these objects.

❋ Read the book aloud with expression, stopping at each double-page spread or predetermined part of the book so to ask students to share their thinking about the book. Start with general prompts such as "What do you notice in the story?" or "What are you thinking about the story right now?"

❋ Use follow-up prompts based on students' behaviors or comments during and after textual readings. This is particularly important to gain clarification of their initial responses, as well as to gain further information or the reason behind student laughter or other nonverbal cues during the read-aloud. Some of these follow-up prompts may include: "I see you're smiling, tell me why" or "You seem to have some thoughts at this point, does this (refer to the storyline or illustration) remind you of anything? Why?"

❋ Accept students' story-related questions and risky narratives that focus on difficult or painful issues (immigration, death, etc.), as well as joyous "wild rumpuses," even if these take the form of parallel, non-linear story formats related by individuals or created by the group as a whole.

❋ Allow for multiple response modes during and after the readings so students have different ways to express and explain their thinking. Children should have opportunities to discuss books orally, as well as in writing, drawing, and other art forms; they should have the opportunity to present their work (Author's Chair) and entertain questions from their peers.

> ❊ Monitor your comfort level with students' responses, and note when these cause you to feel uncomfortable so that you can later reflect on and analyze your own responses to the students' thoughts. Such reflections may serve as the basis for assessment and shifts in instruction, and even your own participation in future literary conversations.

FIGURE 13.3. *Guidelines for Implementing Dialogic Read-Alouds.*

MEXICAN AMERICAN-THEMED PICTURE STORYBOOKS FOR READ-ALOUDS

The books on this selected list are recommended as read-alouds for younger children based on the aesthetic beauty presented in the illustrations coupled with often repeating text, or visual and textual narratives filled with humor and, at times, mischief. Although Mexican American-themed books also exist with important historical and social topics, the texts below represent a joyous starting point from which to move into other types of books.

Andrews-Goebel, Nancy, and David Diaz. *The Pot that Juan Built.*

Deedy, Carmen A., and Michael Austin. *Martina: Una cucarachita muy linda/Martina the Beautiful Cockroach: Un cuento cubano/A Cuban Folktale.* (Although not specifically Mexican-themed, the story of Martina the Cockroach is told throughout Latin America and will be highly relevant to Mexican or Mexican American students.)

Herrera, Juan Felipe, and Anita DeLucio-Brock. *Grandma and Me at the Flea/Los Meros Meros Remateros.*

Mora, Pat, and Raúl Cólon. *Doña Flor: A Tall Tale About a Giant Woman with a Great Big Heart.*

———. *Doña Flor: Un cuento de una mujer gigante con un gran corazón.*

Mora, Pat, and Magaly Morales. *Piñata in a Pine Tree: A Latino Twelve Days of Christmas.*

Morales, Yuyi. *Just a Minute: A Trickster Tale and Counting Book.*

———. *Just in Case: A Trickster Tale and Spanish Alphabet Book.*

Pérez, Amada Irma, and Maya Christina Gonzalez. *My Very Own Room/Mi propio cuartito.*

Rosa-Casanova, Sylvia, and Robert Roth. *Mama Provi and the Pot of Rice.*

Ryan, Pam Muñoz, and Joe Cepeda. *Arroz con frijoles y unos amables ratones.*

———. *Mice and Beans.*

REFERENCES

Benda, Ana, Graciela Hernández de Lamas, and Elena Ianantuoni. "El libro y la identidad." In *La importancia del uso del libro en la educación,* ed. by Anna Benda et al., pp. 14–53. Buenos Aires, Argentina: Ediciones Santillana, 2000.

Bishop, Rudine Sims. "Mirrors, Windows, and Sliding Glass Doors." In *Collected Perspectives: Choosing and Using Books for the Classroom* 6 (1990a): ix–xi.

———. "Multicultural Literature for Children: Making Informed Choices. In *Teaching Multicultural Literature in Grades K–8,* ed. by V. J. Harris (pp. 27–53). Norwood, MA: Christopher-Gordon, 1993.

Cai, Mingshui. *Multicultural Literature for Children and Young Adults: Reflections on Critical Issues.* Westport, CT: Greenwood Press, 2002.

Dobles Rodríguez, Margarita. *Literatura infantil* (3rd ed.). Costa Rica: EUNED (Editorial Universidad Estatal a Distancia), 2000.

Harris, Violet J. *Teaching Multicultural Literature in the K–8 Classroom.* Norwood, MA: Christopher-Gordon, 1993.

———. *Using Multiethnic Children's Literature in Grades K–8.* Norwood, MA: Christopher-Gordon, 1997.

Horning, Kathleen T., Ginny Moore Kruse, and Megan Schliesman. *CCBC Choices 2002.* Madison: University of Wisconsin–Madison, 2002.

Larrick, Nancy. "The All-White World of Children's Books." *Saturday Review* 48 (1965): 84–85.

Nodelman, Perry. *The Pleasures of Children's Literature* (2nd ed.). White Plains, NY: Longman, 1996.

Ogle, Donna M. "K-W-L: A Teaching Model that Develops Active Reading of Expository Text." *Reading Teacher* 39 (1986): 564–570.

Quiroa, Ruth E. "Literature as Mirror: Analyzing the Oral, Written, and Artistic Responses of Young Mexican-Origin Children to Mexican American-Themed Picture Storybooks." Ph.D. diss., University of Illinois, Urbana-Champaign, 2004.

Rosenblatt, Louise M. *The Reader, the Text, the Poem: The Transactional Theory of the Literary Work.* Carbondale and Edwardsville: Southern Illinois University Press, 1978.

Sendak, Maurice. *Where the Wild Things Are.* New York: HarperCollins, 1963.

Short, Kathy Gnagey. *Literature as a Way of Knowing.* York, MN: Stenhouse, 1997.

Sipe, Lawrence R. "The Construction of Literary Understanding by First and Second Graders in Oral Response to Picture Storybook Read-Alouds." *Reading Research Quarterly* 35 (2000): 252–275.

CHAPTER 14

Developing and Enriching Comunidad: Reaching out to Latino Communities via Public and School Libraries

Jamie Campbell Naidoo

"¡Vamos! Let's go to the library!"
Tomás said to his family.
He showed them his favorite books
and his cozy reading nooks.

"¡Vamos! Let's go to the library!"
Tomás said to his friends. "Hurry!"
They saw libros in stacks and rows.
They laughed at funny puppet shows.

"¡Vamos! Let's all go to the library!"
Join the fun, a treasure house that's free.
Bring your friends and family.
Stories, computers, maps and more,
facts, fun. Enter the magic door.
Like Tomás, open books and soar.
Be a reader. Explore galore.

("Library Magic," Pat Mora, 2005)

PUBLIC AND SCHOOL LIBRARIES SERVING LATINO COMMUNITIES

A s Mora's poem indicates, the library has a wealth of resources to offer Latino children and their families. The role of any public or school library is to serve the informational, cultural, and literacy needs of its local community with free access to print and electronic materials. Generally, public libraries serve either an entire county or specific area of a county or city. They provide literacy programs, library services, and material collections (books, movies, music, audiobooks, and so forth) to all ages from cradle to grave. School libraries usually serve a specific population of teachers and students enrolled at a particular school. They provide many of the same services as public libraries but within the constraints of a school setting. Some school libraries also open their collections and services to the parents of their children, making many valuable resources available to Latino families that may not have the transportation available to utilize the services of the local public library.

This chapter describes the opportunities and challenges for serving Spanish-speaking and Latino children and their families in both school and public libraries. Suggestions and considerations for planning library services and collections to this diverse population are discussed along with ideas about Latino literacy organizations and programs that are perfect for community outreach partnerships.

OPPORTUNITIES FOR SERVING SPANISH-SPEAKING AND LATINO CHILDREN AND THEIR FAMILIES IN THE LIBRARY

P ublic and school libraries situated within communities with large Latino populations have the potential to play an integral role in the literacy development, education, and socialization of this diverse cultural group. Libraries attuned to their local Latino community can develop library programs and services that encourage *family literacy* or the combined understanding of the importance of reading, information evaluation, and life-long learning within the extended Latino family. Latinos can use the public library for a variety of reasons: to learn how to read (traditional literacy); to learn or improve their English (if English is not their first language); to use the Internet and computer programs to obtain employment, contact family members back home, or find answers to personal problems (health questions, citizen information for immigrants, and so forth); to find recreational reading materials for themselves, their children, or other family members; or to meet and socialize with other members of their local community.

School libraries can provide Latino students with ESL (English as a Second Language) resources (for children whose first language is not English); information literacy skills (the ability to seek and examine information to determine its relevancy and usefulness); and recreational reading materials including books, magazines, audiobooks, and music about the Latino cultures, books in Spanish, and other materials that promote reading enjoyment and life-long learning. School libraries that reach beyond the walls of their schools to provide services to the local community can provide parenting resources and English classes for Latino parents as well as early literacy materials for preschool Latino children.

The school and public libraries most successful in reaching their Latino communities work with the local Latino community leaders to advertise and promote library programs and events such as bilingual storytimes, Latino holiday programs, visits from Latino/a authors and illustrators, and English classes. Likewise, these libraries promote events being held within the Latino community even if they are non-library related. The development of partnerships between libraries and the local Latino community is integral to the success of library services and programs for Latinos. For libraries that do not have Spanish-speaking staff, community partnerships can provide volunteers from the Latino community willing to assist in selecting culturally accurate books about Latinos as well as grammatically correct Spanish-language materials. Additional information about successful libraries serving Latino communities can be found in Judith Rosen's (2008) article "Se habla español—How Librarians Are Overcoming the Language Divide." For a current look at how Latinos view the public library and its services, consult the report created by the Tomás Rivera Policy Institute (2008) entitled "Latinos and Public Library Perceptions."

CHALLENGES FACED BY LIBRARIES SERVING SPANISH-SPEAKING AND LATINO CHILDREN AND THEIR FAMILIES

Some public and school libraries do not realize their full potential when it comes to serving their local Latino communities and often face obstacles when planning library programs, services, or developing material collections. These challenges can be attributed to a variety of reasons including cultural misconceptions, immigration legislation, and a limited understanding of how to adequately serve Latino populations.

Cultural misconceptions occur when a person relies upon preconceived notions and stereotypes about a particular cultural group rather than developing their own understanding based upon facts and reliable information. Often the media and anecdotal accounts influence a person's perception of a culture. In relation to the Latino cultures, it is thought that Latinos are a monolithic group with the same customs, physical appearances, and traits. General misconceptions about Latinos include the beliefs that all Latinos are Mexican, speak Spanish, and are undocumented or illegal immigrants. In reality, Latinos are a richly diverse group of people from a variety of cultural and ethnic backgrounds who speak English, Spanish, Portuguese, and indigenous languages in varying degrees. Not all Latinos are immigrants and many of the Latinos who are immigrants are documented or hold the necessary papers to reside legally in the United States. In the report "Latino Children: A Majority Are U.S.-Born Offspring of Immigrants," the Pew Hispanic Center (Fry and Passel 2009) provides a current snapshot of Latino children in the United States, detailing immigration and generational status as well as specific needs.

Misconceptions about Latino cultures influence the attitudes of librarians developing programs, collections, and services for local Latino communities. If a librarian believes that all Latinos in the community are from Mexico and speak Spanish, then material collections and library programs will be marketed to Spanish-speaking Mexicans. However, if the local Latino community consists mainly of third-generation Cubans who speak only English, then the library will have failed in serving the needs of the local Latino community. Another way in which misconceptions can hinder library services to Latinos relates to the opinions of the local non-Latino citizens served by the library. If the local community erroneously believes that all Latinos are undocumented immigrants who are taking advantage of government and social resources, then they may challenge or attack the library for developing Spanish-language collections or services and programs for the Latino community.

Local, state, and federal immigration legislation can also create challenges for libraries serving Latinos. Anti-immigration sentiment—the opposition to immigrants within the United States or within a particular region—can be spurred by legislation passed at the various levels of government ranging from local to federal. If particular legislation is passed that prohibits tax-supported agencies from serving undocumented immigrants or distributing materials in Spanish, then a library that aims to serve Latinos can be adversely affected. Because libraries are supported by tax dollars, they may not be allowed to develop library services or collections for Latinos for fear of losing funding or participating in illegal activity. Some libraries have avoided providing library services to legal Latino citizens because of concerns that local and state governments may misconstrue their practices. Additional information on anti-immigration sentiment and how it influences libraries can be found in Loida García-Febo's (2007) article "U.S. Libraries and Anti-Immigrant Sentiment— How Librarians Are Coping with Discrimination to Better Serve Hispanic Communities," and in Jamie Campbell Naidoo's (2009) article "Puentes de la comunidad," which describes how libraries in South Carolina are adversely influenced by local government attitudes and state immigration legislation.

A further hindrance to libraries serving Latinos is a limited understanding of how to plan services, programs, and collections for this diverse cultural group. Some libraries desire to serve their local Latino community but, due to a lack of resources, have difficulty connecting with Latinos. This lack of resources can range from limited material budgets to deficient staff expertise. Some library staff may feel intimidated about creating services, programs, and material collections for a cultural group different from their own, fearing they will provide inaccurate information. Likewise, some libraries are not knowledgeable about how to reach out to their Latino community to develop partnerships to strengthen their offerings. Fortunately, numerous print and electronic resources are available to assist these libraries in developing library collections, services and programs, and community outreach partnerships.

DEVELOPING LIBRARY COLLECTIONS FOR LATINOS

*W*hen developing school and public library collections for Latinos, libraries need an understanding of the rich cultural heritage of Latinos as well as knowledge of the qualities of good books about Latino cultures. It is important to remember that the Latino cultures are uniquely different, with their own customs and beliefs. Librarians should also strive to develop material collections that represent their local Latino community as well as other Latino cultures. Criteria for selecting quality materials about Latinos include: (1) examining the personal traits of Latino characters to determine if they are multidimensional, can solve their own problems without the help of Anglo Americans, and embrace their cultural heritage; (2) analyzing texts and illustrations for cultural stereotypes of Latinos such as lazy Mexicans taking siestas; (3) identifying cultural elements within the texts and illustrations consistent with Latino cultural values such as a strong sense of family; and (4) evaluating the experiences of the author to determine whether they are Latino or have knowledge of Latino cultures. Figure 14.1 presents Guidelines for Evaluating Children's Books About Latinos and Figure 14.2 provides an Individual Title Evaluation Sheet to use when evaluating children's books about Latinos. For a more detailed evaluation guide for evaluating Latino children's books, see Appendix B.

When selecting Spanish-language materials, libraries should consider the quality of the Spanish translation (is the Spanish a literal translation of the English text or a parallel translation keeping the same ideas as the English text?); the accuracy in spelling, punctuation, and grammar; the placement and formatting of the Spanish text in relation to English text in bilingual materials— Is the Spanish text written in a different color or font that is difficult to read? Is the Spanish text always secondary to the English text?; the type of Spanish used (formal, regional, etc.); and the credentials of the translators (are they native Spanish speakers and writers?). For more information on Spanish bilingual book publishing, consult "Descubriendo el sabor: Spanish Bilingual Book Publishing and Cultural Authenticity" (Naidoo and López-Robertson 2007).

Librarians developing Latino and Spanish material collections have several tools available to assist them. *Críticas* (Reed Elsevier 2009) is an online magazine that reviews Spanish-language materials for children and adults, suggesting the best titles for libraries to purchase. The resource also includes information on various aspects relating to developing material collections for Latinos. Tim Wadham's (2006) *Libros Esenciales: Building, Marketing, and Programming a Core Collection of Spanish Language Children's Materials* contains several lists of recommended books about Latinos and in Spanish for libraries developing collections for Latino children and young adults. Isabel Schon has been publishing lists of recommended Latino and Spanish-language children's books since the 1970s. Her *Best of Latino Heritage* and *Recommended Books in Spanish for Children and Young Adults* series are invaluable resources for librarians and educators developing collections of Latino-themed and Spanish-language children's books. In addition, the Barahona Center for the Study of Books in Spanish for Children and Adolescents, started by Schon, offers a helpful online database of recommended books in Spanish and about Latinos for children and young adults (available at http://www2.csusm.edu/csb/english/ California State University, San Marcos). For libraries developing collections for Latino families, America Reads Spanish has published the "Essential Guide to Spanish Reading: Librarians' Selections," which contains more than 500 recommended Spanish-

GUIDELINES FOR EVALUATING CHILDREN'S BOOKS ABOUT LATINOS

Image © Maya C. Gonzalez, 2008. Used with permission.

Examine the Personal Traits of the Character

❖ Are the Latino characters portrayed as having a broad range of emotions similar to characters from other cultures?
❖ Can Latinos solve their own problems or do they rely upon Anglos for help?
❖ Do Latinos abandon some aspect of their culture in order to achieve happiness?
❖ Do Latinos move to the U.S. where everything is "perfect" and everyone is happy?

Examine the Role of Various Characters

❖ Do Latino characters actively participate in the story (main characters) or are they only secondary characters? Do they have leadership roles?
❖ Do Latinos spend their time taking siestas and putting off things until mañana?
❖ Are Latino characters in culturally stereotyped roles such as newly arrived immigrants, men full of machismo, shy girls, mothers of many children, or gang members?
❖ Is a strong sense of community and family expressed in the illustrations and text? Do elders help care for the children?

Examine and Identify Cultural Stereotypes

❖ Are Latinos only depicted as poor low class citizens often living in barrios (Latino neighborhoods)?
❖ Are cultural stereotypes present in the illustrations such as sombreros, piñatas, cacti, mariachi bands, donkeys, and palm trees?
❖ Are females depicted outdoors and as active as male characters?
❖ Do Latinos lapse into Spanish when excited or use broken English?

Examine the Diversity of Representation in Text and Illustrations

❖ Are positive role models of both genders provided for Latino children?
❖ Do all of Latino characters have the same appearance? OR Is the diversity in skin tones, hair styles and textures, and clothing presented? Not all Latinos have a "Latin Look" of dark skin, hair, and eyes.
❖ Are varied cultural experiences of Latinos represented? Is the diversity of the Latino cultures represented such as Central and South America, Mexico, the Dominican Republic, Puerto Rico, Cuba, etc.?

Examine the Experience of the Author and Illustrator

❖ Does the author/illustrator have experience with the Latino subculture that he/she is representing? OR Is the book written/illustrated by someone who has briefly visited a Latin American country? How qualified is the author/illustrator to write the book?

* Many of the ideas for these evaluation criteria are my own and other are adapted from: Council on Interracial Books for Children. "Latinos or Hispanic Americans." *Guidelines for Selecting Bias-free Textbooks and Storybooks.* New York, 1980.

FIGURE 14.1. *Guidelines for Evaluating Children's Books About Latinos, created by Jamie Campbell Naidoo, printed with permission.*

SELECTING CHILDREN'S BOOKS ABOUT LATINOS

Individual Title Evaluation Sheet

Title of Book:		Publication Date:		Publisher:
Author:		**Illustrator:**		
Book Characteristics:		**Please Circle ONE Answer**		

Book Characteristics:	Please Circle ONE Answer		
1. What is the genre of the book?	Fiction		Nonfiction
2. Is the author of the book Latino or non-Latino?	Latino	Non-Latino	Don't Know
3. Is the illustrator of the book Latino or non-Latino?	Latino	Non-Latino	Don't Know
4. Is the text of the book bilingual, interlingual, or written only in English?	Bilingual	Interlingual (English with few Spanish words)	English Only
5. What supplemental linguistic features are present in the text? **Select all that apply.**	Glossary / Pronunciation Guide	Author Notes	None

Examine the Personal Traits of the Character

6. Are the Latino characters portrayed as having a broad range of emotions similar to characters from other cultures?	Yes	No
7. Do Latinos need the help of Anglos to solve their problems?	Yes	No
8. Do Latinos have to abandon some aspect of their culture in order to achieve happiness?	Yes	No
9. Do Latinos move to the U.S. where everything is "perfect" and everyone is happy? (Do they leave their home country to find success in America?)	Yes	No

Examine the Role of Various Characters

10. Do Latino characters actively participate in the story (main character) or are they only secondary characters?	Main Characters	Secondary Characters
11. Do Latinos spend their time taking siestas and putting off things until mañana (<u>lazy</u>) or do they have <u>active</u> roles like other characters in the narrative?	Lazy	Active
12. Are Latino characters in culturally stereotyped roles such as newly arrived immigrants, men full of machismo, shy girls, mothers of many children, or gang members?	Yes	No

FIGURE 14.2. *Individual Title Evaluation Sheet, created by Jamie Campbell Naidoo, printed with permission.*

13. Is a strong sense of community and family expressed in the illustrations and text? (Community and extended family are very important in the Latino cultures).	Yes	No

Examine and Identify Stereotypes

14. Are Latinos only depicted as poor, low class citizens living in barrios or migrant communities?	Yes	No
15. Are cultural stereotypes present in the illustrations such as sombreros, piñatas, cacti, mariachi bands, donkeys, and palm trees?	Yes	No
16. Are females depicted outdoors and as equally active as male characters?	Yes	No
17. Do Latinos lapse into Spanish when excited, or use broken English?	Yes	No

Examine the Diversity in Text and Illustrations

18. Are positive role models of both genders provided for Latino children in the book's illustrations and text?	Yes	No
19. Do all of Latino characters have the same physical appearance? (The diversity in skin tones, hair styles and textures, and clothing should be presented. Not all Latinos have a "Latin Look" of dark skin, hair, and eyes.)	Yes	No
20. Are varied cultural experiences of Latinos represented? (The diversity of the Latino cultures – such as Central and South America, Mexico, the Dominican Republic, Puerto Rico, Cuba, etc. – should be represented in the books available in your collection. One book will probably not contain all the diversity of the Latino cultures but, collectively, your books should represent the various cultural differences.)	Yes	No

21. Which Latino culture is represented in the book? (If a culture is not specified, select the Generic Latino category.)	Puerto Rican	Cuban	Central America	South American
	Caribbean (Non-Puerto Rican or Cuban)	Mexican/ Mexican American	Generic Latino	

Comments and Recommendations

language books for both adults and children, as well as the "Essential Guide to Spanish Reading for Children and Young Adults," which includes more than 400 recommended titles in Spanish for children and young adults. The three awards for Latino children's literature—the Tomás Rivera Mexican-American Children's Book Award, the Américas Award, and the Pura Belpré Award—also highlight the best in Latino literature for youth since the early 1990s and honor high-quality books that should be in library collections. More information on these can be found on the respective award Web sites.

LIBRARY SERVICES AND PROGRAMS FOR LATINOS

In addition to developing collections of quality literature about Latinos and in Spanish, libraries striving to reach their Latino community should consider developing library programs and services of interest to Latinos. These programs and services can have a broad range of appeal and format ranging from traditional storytimes with Latino children's literature to English classes to computer training in Spanish. Many libraries have begun to offer programs relating to Latino cultures during Hispanic Heritage Month (September 15–October 15); however, it is important to remember to celebrate Latinos throughout the year. Traditionally, library programs about Latinos have focused on foods (tacos, chile peppers, etc.), clothing (sombreros, serapes, etc.), and fiestas (usually piñata parties). It is essential for libraries to go beyond these cultural symbols and emphasize other features of Latino cultures, particularly those that highlight the achievements as well as everyday lives of Latinos. For wonderful suggestions for library programs and storytimes celebrating the Latino cultures, consult Ana-Elba Pavon and Diana Borrego's (2002) *25 Latino Craft Projects*, Rose Treviño's (2009) *Read Me a Rhyme in Spanish and English / Léame una rima en español e inglés*, and Treviño's (2006) *The Pura Belpré Awards: Celebrating Latino Authors and Illustrators*.

Besides choosing appropriate content for library programs, librarians should also consider program format and time. The importance of family is a very strong cultural trait of Latinos. Often when Latinos visit the library, they attend as a family group and use library services collectively. If a library program is planned for a select age group (preschool storytime, for example), then Latinos will most likely not attend if other family members are not welcomed. Similarly, if the programs are offered at times that do not fit with the schedule of Latino families, they will be poorly attended by Latinos. For instance, if a program is offered on Wednesdays at 10 A.M. and most Latino families have members working during that time, then the program will most likely not be attended by Latinos. Typically, the best types of programs for Latinos are intergenerational programs held at night or on the weekend. However, each library developing programs for Latinos should survey its local community to determine special needs and schedules.

Information to assist libraries in developing programs and services for Latinos is readily available. A nonprofit organization dedicated to assisting libraries with planning services and programs to Latinos is REFORMA, The National Association to Promote Library and Information Services to Latinos and the Spanish Speaking. The association includes a network of librarians, library-educators, publishers, and advocates devoted to sharing information on developing culturally authentic Latino material collections and programs, overcoming anti-immigration sentiment in libraries, and providing equity of information access to Latinos and Spanish-speaking residents of the United States. Visit the REFORMA Web site (http://www.reforma.org/) for more information about this organization and its services.

Other exemplary resources for libraries serving Latinos include Camila A. Alire and Jacqueline Ayala's (2007) *Serving Latino Communities: A How-to-do-it Manual for Librarians,* Salvador Güereña's (2000) edited book *Library Services to Latinos: An Anthology,* Barbara Immroth and Kathleen de la Peña McCook's (2000) *Library Services to Youth of Hispanic Heritage,* Sharon Chickering Moller's (2001) *Library Services to Spanish Speaking Patrons: A Practical Guide,* and Salvador Avila's (2008) *Crash Course in Serving Spanish-Speakers.* For libraries seeking information relating to library services for immigrant groups, the best resources are Rick J. Ashton and Danielle Patrick Milam's "Welcome, Stranger: Public Libraries Build the Global Village" and the U.S. Citizenship and Immigration Services' "Library Services for Immigrants: A Report on Current Practices."

COMMUNITY OUTREACH AND PARTNERSHIPS

High-quality collections of Latino materials and culturally relevant library programs are steps towards serving the informational and recreational needs of Latinos. However, if Latinos do not visit the library to take advantage of programs, services, and collections, then all of the energy and resources expended to serve the Latino community will be futile. Latinos need to attend the library to reap all the benefits it has to offer. Creating outreach programs in the Latino community and forging partnerships with other agencies serving Latinos or with Latino businesses is important to the success of library services to Latinos. Libraries should find ways to "plug in" to the local Latino community to market their offerings. Creating alliances with churches that have a large percentage of Latinos in the congregation is one way to do this. A wonderful resource for librarians seeking community programs for partnerships is the U.S. Department of Education's "What Works for Latino Youth," a 62-page document that details more than 60 successful programs for Latino youth across the nation, noting the effectiveness of each program.

Another opportunity is for libraries to work with ESL teachers at local schools. Many ESL teachers who work with young Latino children make home-visits to communicate information to Latino families. Libraries can send outreach or youth librarians to accompany the ESL teachers, or they can have the ESL teacher distribute information about library programs and services to the Latino families. For more ideas on how the library, particularly a school library, can work with the ESL teacher and ELL (English language learner) children, consult Naidoo's (2005) article "Informational Empowerment: Using Informational Books to Connect the Library Media Center with Sheltered Instruction."

Scheduling the library's bookmobile (a portable library similar to a bus full of books that travels to various parts of the community) to visit Latino communities and offer culturally relevant programs in Latino community centers is yet another outreach prospect to connect the library and local Latinos. If the library is visible in the Latino community and if Latinos understand what the library has to offer, then they are more likely to make the most of its services, programs, and collections.

Partnerships between public and school libraries are an additional prospect for libraries serving Latinos. School librarians have a captive audience of Latino children through the classes that visit the library, so public librarians could visit schools and advertise their services in the school library. Public librarians could also perform storytimes and other programs using Latino children's literature. School librarians could work with the public library to plan joint programs centered around various literacy-related programs and events.

The following section describes a few Latino literacy programs, projects, and resources that could be beneficial to both school and public librarians.

LATINO LITERACY PROGRAMS, PROJECTS, AND RESOURCES

¡Colorín Colorado! and Lee y serás

Taking advantage of early literacy materials specifically for Latino families, such as Reading Rockets' ¡Colorín Colorado! and Scholastic's Lee y serás, librarians can invite Latino parents into the library in order to teach them more about the importance of literacy in the lives of young children. ¡Colorín Colorado! (http://www.colorincolorado.org/) is a reading literacy program that provides information on the importance of reading in the lives of English Language Learner (ELL), Spanish-speaking, and Latino children, and highlights literature by and about Latinos. Activities, reports, and links are available on numerous topics concerning children's literature about Latinos—using culturally responsive teaching practices in instruction, helping Latino families understand the importance of literacy, reaching out to Latino families, and understanding the needs of recently arrived immigrant children. Librarians and educators can use the myriad activities, the free 92-page planning booklet, and the Latino author/illustrator video clips to launch their services and programs to Latino children and their families.

Sponsored by Scholastic, Verizon, and the National Council of La Raza, Lee y serás (Read and You Will Be) is a reading and cultural literacy initiative aimed at helping Latino parents and educators understand the keys to helping Latino children achieve optimal literacy development. The program provides support for Latino parents with training about early literacy, offers educators and librarians resources that will create print-rich learning environments for Latino children, and supplies information to public agencies on how to support Latino literacy in the community. Online activities, games, and e-stories, along with downloadable program and activity booklets, help both librarians and educators succeed in fostering the literacy development of Latino children and their families. More information about Lee y serás is available at http://www. leeyseras.net/.

El día de los niños/El día de los libros

The Latino literacy celebration El día de los niños/El día de los libros (Day of the Child/Day of the Book), or Día for short, offers an opportunity for collaborations between public and school libraries and between libraries and community organizations. Created in 1996, Día promotes bilingual literacy and "bookjoy" (the intense love of reading) and was initiated by Latina author and poet Pat Mora. Many libraries feature Día only on April 30th, but the ideas behind the celebration are relevant throughout the year. Libraries can partner with Latino organizations to create programs that meet Día's goals to honor children, promote literacy and cultural understanding, celebrate home languages, encourage parental involvement in early literacy, and endorse library collection development that reflects all heritages, including the myriad Latino cultures (Mora 2010).

Numerous free online resources are available to libraries creating Día programs. Some of these resources include the Texas State Library and Archives Commission's Dígame un cuento / Tell Me a Story: Bilingual Library Programs for Children and Families, the American Library Association's official Día Web site, and the Texas Library Association's El día de los niños/El día de los libros (Day of the Child/Day of the Book) Toolkit. Any of the ideas suggested in these resources can be used by librarians to promote Latino culture and heritage in programs all year long. Pat Mora and Rafael López have also created a picture book, *Book Fiesta! Celebrate Children's Day/Book Day/Book Fiesta! Celebremos El día de los niños/El día de los libros,* which highlights Día and provides suggestions for literacy activities. (Additional information about Día can be found in Chapter 11.)

Noche de Cuentos @ mi biblioteca

Another opportunity to engage the local Latino community while collaborating with various community organizations is the family literacy program Noche de Cuentos @ mi biblioteca. Established in 2009 by REFORMA and first implemented in 2010, Noche de Cuentos @ mi biblioteca is a family literacy/ storytelling program that encourages families from Latino communities to gather in libraries across the United States on March 20th, World Storytelling Day, to share cultural stories, songs, and experiences from their families, communities, and native countries. Part of Camila Alire's ALA Presidential Initiative "Libraries: The Heart of All Communities," Noche de Cuentos addresses the family literacy focus instituted by the first Latina president of the American Library Association. According to Lucía González, "the mission of the celebration of Noche de Cuentos @ mi biblioteca is to help promote and preserve the art of storytelling within immigrant Latino communities in the United States. Our language and our stories bind us together and make us stronger" (personal communication).

Libraries can reach members of the Latino community who might not otherwise attend a library program through the intergenerational storytelling and sharing component of Noche de Cuentos. By targeting immigrant Latino communities, the program highlights the importance of literacy in the United States and provides an avenue for Latino families to learn more about the programs, services, and collections offered by libraries. At the same time, the program encourages libraries to work with Latino literacy organizations in the community to promote oral and cultural literacy among Latino families. Additional information about Noche de Cuentos can be found on the REFORMA Web site—http://www.reforma.org.

Cuentos y Más

Cuentos y Más (Stories and More) is a bilingual (Spanish and English), Latino literacy television program that promotes reading, literacy, and cultural appreciation among both English- and Spanish-speaking children. Produced by the Arlington Virginia Network (AVN) and Arlington Public Library, this early literacy program shares stories, songs, games, and more relating to the Latino cultures. It also promotes the importance of books and libraries in the daily lives of children and their families. Think of a bilingual Reading Rainbow and you have Cuentos y Más. Free Webstreams of programs are available from http://www.arlingtonva.us/cuentos. Libraries can show these programs during storytimes or direct children and their families to the Web site using library computers. The program could also be helpful for librarians considering planning and implementation of bilingual programs for Latino children as it provides examples of successful storytelling and literacy strategies to use with bilingual children.

Connecting Cultures and Celebrating Cuentos: National Latino Children's Literature Conference

Connecting Cultures and Celebrating Cuentos is a national conference celebrating Latino children's literature and literacy. Initiated in 2007 by Jamie Campbell Naidoo and Julia López-Robertson as the University of South Carolina's Annual Celebration of Latino Children's Literature, the conference invites librarians, teachers, educators, child-care workers, and others interested in Latino literacy, literature, and education to come together to share successful strategies for meeting the informational, cultural, recreational, and traditional literacy needs of Latino children. In 2010 the conference made a permanent move to the University of Alabama's School of Library and Information Studies and changed its name to Connecting Cultures and Celebrating Cuentos, broadened to a more national scope, and began a more concerted effort to focus on the role of the library as the cultural institution to meet all the literacy needs of today's Latino children and families.

Each year several award-winning Latino authors and illustrators visit the conference and present programs at a local community event for Latino families at the public library in celebration of Día. Latino children attending the event receive free high-quality books representing the Latino cultures and have an opportunity to visit with the Latino artists. The conference is situated within one of the states in the "New Latino South" with the fastest-growing Latino populations. Local educators, librarians, and teachers, many just beginning to work with Latino children and their families, have an opportunity to collaborate with professionals from across the United States who have been serving the literacy needs of Latino children for many years. In addition, participants learn about the latest and best in Latino children's literature along with ideas on how to incorporate the books into their classrooms and library programs. Many ideas from participants are shared on the conference Web site (http://www.latinochildlitconf.org/) and on the Imagínense Libros: Celebrating Latino Children's Literature, Literacy, and Libraries blog (http://imaginenselibros.blogspot.com/).

CONCLUDING REMARKS

As the Latino population continues to increase in the United States, the need for pertinent information on how to successfully meet the informational and recreational reading needs of the fastest-growing minority is crucial. The role of any public or school library is to serve the informational, recreational, cultural, and literacy needs of its local community. Some libraries face challenges when providing services and material collections to their Latino patrons. These problems can be attributed to cultural misconceptions, immigration legislation, and a limited understanding of how to adequately serve Latino populations.

Numerous print and online resources are available to assist both school and public librarians in planning collections, library services, and literacy programs for Latinos and Spanish-speaking patrons. However, the best way for public and school libraries to serve their local Latino populations is to develop partnerships among themselves and within the Latino community. Latino literacy organizations often offer many free resources to librarians planning services and programs for Latino children and their families, including information on handling anti-immigration sentiments. Libraries that use these resources have the potential to make a significant impact within their local communities.

REFERENCES

Alire, Camila A., and Jacqueline Ayala. *Serving Latino Communities: A How-to-Do-It Manual for Librarians.* 2nd ed. New York: Neal-Schuman, 2007.

America Reads Spanish. "Essential Guide to Spanish Reading: Librarians' Selections." http://www.americareadsspanish.org/libro/pdf.pdf (accessed December 29, 2009).

———. "Essential Guide to Spanish Reading for Children and Young Adults." http://www.americareadsspanish.org/libro/ARS_Essential_Guide_to_Spanish_Reading_for_Children_and_Young_Adults.pdf (accessed December 29, 2009).

American Library Association. "Belpré Medal." http://ala.org/ala/mgrps/divs/alsc/awardsgrants/bookmedia/belpremedal/index.cfm (accessed December 4, 2009).

———. "Celebrate El día de los niños/El día de los libros (Children's Day/Book Day)." http://www.ala.org/dia (accessed December 29, 2009).

Arlington Virginia Network and the Arlington Public Library. "Cuentos y Más." http://www.arlingtonva.us/cuentos (accessed December 29, 2009).

Ashton, Rick J., and Danielle Patrick Milam. "Welcome, Stranger: Public Libraries Build the Global Village." http://urbanlibraries.org/associations/9851/files/ULC_WS.pdf (accessed December 29, 2009).

Avila, Salvador. *Crash Course in Serving Spanish-Speakers.* Westport, CT: Libraries Unlimited, 2008.

California State University, San Marcos. "Barahona Center for the Study of Books in Spanish for Children and Adolescents." http://www2.csusm.edu/csb/english/ (accessed December 29, 2009).

Fry, Richard, and Jeffrey S. Passel. "Latino Children: A Majority Are U.S.-Born Offspring of Immigrants." Washington, DC: Pew Hispanic Center, May 2009. http://pewhispanic.org/files/reports/110.pdf (accessed December 29, 2009).

García-Febo, Loida. "U.S. Libraries and Anti-Immigrant Sentiment—How Librarians Are Coping with Discrimination to Better Serve Hispanic Communities," *Críticas Online* (October 1, 2007). http://www.criticasmagazine.com/article/CA6487725.html?industryid=48434 (accessed December 29, 2009).

Güereña, Salvador, ed. *Library Services to Latinos: An Anthology.* Jefferson, NC: McFarland, 2000.

Immroth, Barbara, and Kathleen de la Peña McCook. *Library Services to Youth of Hispanic Heritage.* Jefferson, NC: McFarland, 2000.

Moller, Sharon Chickering. *Library Services to Spanish Speaking Patrons: A Practical Guide.* Englewood, CO: Libraries Unlimited, 2001.

Mora, Pat. "Library Magic, 2005." http://www.patmora.com/book_pages/tomas.htm (accessed December 29, 2009).

———. "Pat's History of El día de los niños/El día de los libros, 2010." http://www.patmora.com/dia/dia_history.htm (accessed December 29, 2009).

Naidoo, Jamie Campbell. "Informational Empowerment: Using Informational Books to Connect the Library Media Center with Sheltered Instruction." *School Libraries Worldwide*, 11 no. 2 (2005): 132–152.

———. "Puentes de la comunidad: Exploring the Impact of LIS Service Learning on Library Services to Latino Youth in the Carolinas." In *Service Learning: Linking Library Education and Practice,* ed. by L. Roy and A. Hershey, pp. 83–94. Chicago: American Library Association, 2009.

Naidoo, Jamie Campbell, and Julia López-Robertson. "Descubriendo el sabor: Spanish Bilingual Book Publishing and Cultural Authenticity." *Multicultural Review*, 16 no. 4 (2007): 24–37.

Pavon, Ana-Elba, and Diana Borrego. *25 Latino Craft Projects.* Chicago: American Library Association, 2002.

Reading Rockets. "¡Colorín Colorado!: A Bilingual Site for Families and Educators of English Language Learners." http://www.colorincolorado.org/ (accessed December 28, 2009).

Reed Elsevier Inc. "Críticas: An English Speaker's Guide to the Latest Spanish-Language Titles." http://www.criticasmagazine.com/ (accessed December 29, 2009).

REFORMA. "The National Association to Promote Library & Information Services to Latinos and the Spanish Speaking." http://www.reforma.org/ (accessed December 29, 2009).

Rosen, Judith. "Se habla español—How Librarians Are Overcoming the Language Divide." *Críticas Online* (November 1, 2008). http://www.criticasmagazine.com/article/CA6606945.html (accessed December 29, 2009).

Scholastic. "Lee y serás (Read and You Will Be)." http://www.leeyseras.net/ (accessed December 28, 2009).

Schon, Isabel. *The Best of Latino Heritage: A Guide to the Best Juvenile Books About Latino People.* Lanham, MD: Scarecrow Press, 1996.

———. *The Best of Latino Heritage, 1996–2002: A Guide to the Best Juvenile Books About Latino People.* Lanham, MD: Scarecrow Press, 2003.

———. *Recommended Books in Spanish for Children and Young Adults.* Lanham, MD: Scarecrow Press, 2000.

———. *Recommended Books in Spanish for Children and Young Adults: 2000–2004.* Lanham, MD: Scarecrow Press, 2004.

————. *Recommended Books in Spanish for Children and Young Adults: 2004–2008.* Lanham, MD: Scarecrow Press, 2008.

Texas Library Association. "El día de los niños/El día de los libros (Day of the Child/ Day of the Book) Toolkit." http://www.texasdia.org/toolkit.html (accessed December 27, 2009).

Texas State Library and Archives Commission. "Dígame un cuento / Tell Me a Story: Bilingual Library Programs for Children and Families." http://www.tsl.state.tx.us/ ld/pubs/bilingual/ (accessed December 28, 2009).

Texas State University College of Education. "Tomás Rivera Mexican American Children's Book Award." http://www.education.txstate.edu/departments/Tomas-Rivera-Book-Award-Project-Link.html (accessed December 28, 2009).

Tomás Rivera Policy Institute. "Latinos and Public Library Perceptions." Dublin, OH: Webjunction/OCLC Online Computer Library Center, Inc., September 2008. http://www.webjunction.org/latino-perceptions/articles/content/10860971 (accessed December 29, 2009).

Treviño, Rose. *The Pura Belpré Awards: Celebrating Latino Authors and Illustrators.* Chicago: American Library Association, 2006.

————. *Read Me a Rhyme in Spanish and English / Léame una rima en español e inglés.* Chicago: American Library Association, 2009.

U.S. Citizenship and Immigration Services. "Library Services for Immigrants: A Report on Current Practices." http://www.uscis.gov/files/ nativedocuments/G-1112.pdf (accessed December 29, 2009).

U.S. Department of Education. "What Works for Latino Youth." http://permanent. access.gpo.gov/lps15113/whatwrks2Ed.pdf (accessed December 29, 2009).

Wadham, Tim. *Libros Esenciales: Building, Marketing, and Programming a Core Collection of Spanish Language Children's Materials.* New York: Neal-Schuman, 2006.

CHAPTER 15

Culturally Relevant Literature Pedagogies: Latino Students Reading in the Borderlands

Carmen L. Medina and Carmen Martínez-Roldán

In this chapter we explore the notions of borderlands as ways to understand how students and authors from diverse Latino backgrounds construct in richly imaginative ways a sense of borderlands lived as narratives, social and political realities that intersect and diverge in literature discussions. Drawing from data in two interpretive studies, we analyze how these borderlands or "border crossings" are constructed as children read Latino literature and bring to their readings multiple experiences and ways of knowing across cultural worlds, identities, politics, and languages to mediate (Vygotsky 1978, 1987) and make sense not only of authors' literary works but also of theirs and others' identities. We use this concept not to make universal claims about Latino students and their cultural backgrounds but to understand students' and authors' ways of knowing and experiences, "as people with certain histories of engagement with specific cultural activities" (Gutierrez and Rogoff 2003). If, as Sumara (2002) suggests, engagement with literary texts "can become a productive site for the continued interpretation of culture and the way culture is historically influenced" (p. 29), we want to examine: What are the everyday experiences, histories, and ways of knowing that Latino children bring to literary events to make sense of texts? How, through their engagement with texts, do they make sense of their lives as borderlands where cultures, ethnicities, languages, politics, gender, and other ideological discourses meet? What is the relationship between students' interpretations of texts and their constructions of identities as children "in between"—culturally, linguistically, geographically, gendered—borderlands?

DEFINING BORDERLAND SPACES IN CLASSROOM LITERARY EVENTS

The borderlands, according to Chicana feminist theorist and writer Anzaldúa (1987, 1998) constitute a way of making sense of the rich physical, psychological, and imaginative spaces where forms of identities emerge through hybrid constructions of languages, gender, race, and class, among others. Migratory movements seem to frame these new forms of theorization to help us understand the realities lived by those who move across nations, languages, and cultures.

Our understanding of the work done for young audiences by many Latino authors is situated in a borderland where writers share complex aspects of their lives. In books such as *Super Cilantro Girl / La niña del supercilantro* by Juan Felipe Herrera and Honorio Robleda Tapia (2004), *Friends from the Other Side / Amigos del otro lado* by Gloria Anzaldúa and Consuelo Mendez (1993), *The Circuit: Stories from the Life of a Migrant Child* by Francisco Jiménez (1997), and *A Movie in My Pillow / Una película en mi almohada* by Jorge Argueta and Elizabeth Gomez (2001), the authors perceive their writing as a way of recreating forms of witnessing life experiences across borders and sharing these with larger communities. These forms of sharing stories reflect the authors' experiences across borders in the "borderlands" (Medina and Enciso 2002; Medina 2006a). Each telling of an experience represents a borderland that "mirror[s] how we live life in our memories, with our past and our present juxtaposed and bleeding, seeping back and forth, one to another in a recursive dance" (Cantú 1995, p. xii).

In the research that has been conducted with Latino students in elementary schools to examine responses in literature discussions, it is possible to identify how the students also create a borderland space where language, gender, race, and culture intersect in unique ways (DeNicolo and Fránquiz 2006; López-Robertson 2004). These intersections become visible to us as researchers and educators in the process of supporting children as they speak, read, and write about their unique cultural experiences. Through the process of what Delgado-Bernal (1998) calls "cultural intuition" and drawing from the experiences of subordination through "such methods as storytelling, family histories, biographies, scenarios, parables, cuentos, testimonies, chronicles and narratives [it is possible to focus on] the racialized, gendered and classed experiences as sources of strength" (Solórzano and Yosso 2002, p. 26). We perceive the spaces created in literature discussions as locations where children bring their "cultural intuition" as they construct narratives and interpret aspects of their identities and social movements as strengths and not deficits (Martínez-Roldán 2003; Medina 2010) and where the past is interpreted in the present. In a sense, through their responses, the students are co-constructing stories in the borderlands that were unique to that particular present moment, which reflected on the past and collectively redefined the present.

Classroom #1: Border Crossings in Literary Interpretation

The first example we share comes from a group of students from Latino backgrounds who, at the time the study took place, had recently moved to a town in the U.S. Midwest. The students participated in bilingual literature discussions in an ESL classroom with Carmen Medina and their teacher, Mrs. Richardson. The group met twice a week for eight months to read and respond to bilingual books, focusing on creative response strategies (see Medina 2006b; Medina 2010 for other examples of the students' work). The group read books such as *Tomás and the Library Lady/Tomás y la señora de la biblioteca* by Pat Mora and Raúl Colón (1997), *My Diary from Here to There/Mi diario de aquí hasta allá by* Amada Irma Pérez and Maya Christina Gonzalez (2002), and *Prietita and the Ghost Woman/Prietita y la Llorona* by Gloria Anzaldúa and Christina Gonzalez (1996). In our meetings we read, discussed, and made verbal, dramatic, written, and visual responses. Among the curricular activities we worked on were graffiti boards. The graffiti board is an activity to respond to literature created by Short, Harste, and Burke (1996) in which students meet in small groups, and during and/or after the reading they respond to the story on a large piece of paper using words and images. The curricular activity facilitates the students' individual thinking about the book while simultaneously creating a context for the small group to share ideas and comments about the book. The effectiveness of this curricular engagement lies in the openness it creates for the students to express individual ideas while collectively crafting a response. In Carmen Medina's experiences using graffiti boards, she finds the students not only enjoy the work but also create powerful interactions as they simultaneously write, draw, and talk.

In the classroom we used graffiti boards when we read the Spanish and English versions of *Tomás and the Library Lady/Tomás y la señora de la biblioteca*. This story is based on writer Tomás Rivera, a highly regarded Latino author, and his life as a child of migrant farm workers moving across the United States. The text centers on Rivera's passion for stories and storytelling. His experiences sharing and listening to his *abuelo's* stories are highlighted in a way that allows the reader to get a sense of how the role of storytelling in Rivera's everyday life connects to his identity as a reader and work as a writer. Figure 15.1 is a representation of a graffiti board that three girls created. At the time of the study, these girls—Alma, Ivonne, and Yolanda (all names are pseudonyms)—had recently moved to the United States from Mexico. All of them were Spanish speakers and were already mastering aspects of the English language.

The graffiti board is an example of how students who had recently immigrated to the United States participated in the activity and included their life experiences moving across nations (U.S./Mexico) and languages (Spanish/English). Yolanda, Ivonne, and Alma created a written and visual representation illustrating their perceptions and connections to the story, while simultaneously sharing aspects of their personal narratives relating to their own memories of storytelling. They describe their experiences negotiating "border crossings" that are made visible in their transition from using personal memories of storytelling, the intertextual practices in telling stories from oral or popular traditions in Mexico, their relationships with people across spaces, the ways those are connected to Rivera's bilingual story, and their bilingual work on the graffiti board in a school in the United States.

Alma begins her graffiti board by affirming her enjoyment reading the text. Here she uses Spanish, her dominant language, to share her impressions of the book and the main character's imagination. As we read both the English and Spanish versions of the book, she follows her comments with rewriting an excerpt of the book in English. While she can't yet write complex ideas in English because English is a new language for her, having access to a bilingual text helps her identify an important passage that represents her ideas from the book and she decides to rewrite this in English. In this moment Alma creates a linguistic borderland space where English and Spanish intersect and coexist within a powerful negotiation of languages.

Moving into a personal experience Alma writes "*A mi me gusta esta historia porque me recuerda unas cosas*" ("I like this story because it reminds me of some things"). She then makes her knowledge about different literary genres visible. Here the texts and the group dynamic provide a context for her to demonstrate that she has literary knowledge. She talks about *cuentos, leyendas* (legends), and *historias de terror* (horror stories). What she shares about literary knowledge makes visible an aspect of herself as a reader and storyteller. This interaction with the text challenges common beliefs that immigrant children do not know or possess literary knowledge. She resituates her knowledge as an immigrant child and puts it at the center of her engagement with the text, creating a borderland between her cultural practices and school practices. Furthermore she merges this knowledge with a connection to her life experiences leaving the

Alma: *A mi me gustan la historia y las imaginaciones de Tomas.* [Rewrites excerpt in English from the book on "graffiti board":] "It was midnight. The light of the full moon followed the tired old car. Tomas was tired too. Hot and tired." *A mi me gusta esta historia porque me recuerda unas cosas. A mi me gustan los cuentos y más las leyendas y cuentos de terror y también porque un día salí de la ciudad y eso me recordó.*

Alma: I like the story and Tomas' imaginations. [Rewrites excerpt in English from the book on graffiti board:] "It was midnight. The light of the full moon followed the tired old car. Tomas was tired too. Hot and tired."
I like the story because it reminds me of things in my life. I like the short stories and especially the legends and horror stories and also it reminds me of one day when I left the city.

Ivonne: *A mi me gustó la historia porque me fascinan las fantasías y las historias de aventuras pero me gustan más las historias de terror. En una parte Tomas se parece a un niño que se llama Francisco. Y en México mi abuelita me contaba historias de antes como la llorona, los chanecos y otras historias. Todas las tardes nos sentábamos en el corredor de mi casa y me contaba las historias. También cuando íbamos al rancho de mi papá habían muchas historias, mis primos y mis tíos.*

Ivonne: I liked the story because I'm fascinated with fantasies and adventure stories but what I like most are horror stories. In one part Tomas looks like a boy called Francisco. And in Mexico my grandmother told me old stories, like The Weeping Woman and "los chanecos." Every afternoon we sat on my house balcony and she told me stories. When we went to my father's ranch, there were also lots of stories, with my cousins and aunts and uncles.

Yolanda: *A mi me gusta que me lean libros. Los cuentos de terror me gustan mucho. Mucho menos de fantasia.* I love his stories.

Yolanda: I like being read to. I like horror stories very much. Fantasies much less. I love his stories.

Graffiti Board 12-16-03

FIGURE 15.1. *Example of text from a graffiti board created by three young Latina girls as they interact with the book* Tomás and the Library Lady / Tomás y la señora de la biblioteca *as part of an ESL pull-out program.*

city in Mexico, *"y también porque un día salí de la ciudad y eso me recordó"* ("and also it reminds me of one day when I left the city"). In her engagement with the text and the space for interaction created in the graffiti board, she rewrites aspects of her life history and trajectory as she simultaneously interprets the author's life as represented in the literary text. This response is not distant from what the other students also shared in their graffiti boards.

Ivonne connects the book to her literary preference for fantasies, adventure stories, and horror stories. *"A mi me gustó la historia porque me fascinan las fantasías y las historias de aventuras pero me gustan más las historias de terror"* ("I liked the story because I'm fascinated with fantasies and adventure stories but what I like most are horror stories"). Her engagement with the text becomes a location to travel back and reinterpret her experiences with her family, retelling stories from the popular imaginary. Here Ivonne creates a borderland space where her location in Mexico intersects with the one in the school in the United States. Ivonne also begins to explore her experiential knowledge with the literary text by making a connection between the visual representation of Tomás Rivera in the book and a student in the classroom. Collectively, all three students—Ivonne, Yolanda, and Alma—use the response engagement to create a bridge between their personal lives and their literary genre knowledge such as fantasies, adventures, horror stories, cuentos, and legends.

Looking back and analyzing the students' work, it is possible to see that the graffiti boards provided an opportunity for the students to share knowledge and experiences; they also provided a context where they could play and engage with both English and Spanish. In a school where English is the dominant language (like most schools in the United States) where children are immersed in learning English and are expected to learn it without using their linguistic and cultural resources as they learn and negotiate a new language, their experiences with Latino literature become a political act. Situating Tomás Rivera's story and experiences at the center of the reading curriculum allows for the students to demonstrate and share their literary knowledge, and for their voices to be heard. These ways of knowing are directly connected to their community cultural practices.

Classroom #2: Recreating Borderland Experiences Through Personal Stories

Like Medina's students, the Latino children in Martínez-Roldán's study (2000) also had powerful transactions with culturally specific texts in addition to multicultural books representing other cultures. Given the focus of this chapter, what is presented here are the students' responses to only the Latino literature; however, the students in this classroom had access to a broad selection of multicultural literature in both English and Spanish.

This primary bilingual classroom had 21 students, 11 Spanish-dominant students, mostly first-generation immigrants, and 10 English-dominant students, mostly second-generation immigrants. The children had their first small group literature discussions by the end of first grade when they responded to what Latino writers and scholars characterize as *literatura fronteriza* or border literature (Benito and Manzanas 2002; Castillo and Tabuenca-Córdoba 2002; Trujillo 1998), dealing with border crossing experiences such as the explicit act of crossing the United States/Mexico border but also other forms of border crossings such as cultural, linguistic, and identity crossings. These texts generated 13 small group literature discussions that were audio-recorded. The study continued in second grade when the children discussed many books for a total of 75 small group discussions.

The children offered a wide repertoire of responses to literature—they focused on the characters, on events within the stories, they paid attention to illustrations, and especially they made connections to their lives and engaged in storytelling. Beginning the literature discussions with *literatura fronteriza* provided a context in which the literature mediated, in the Vygotskyan (1978) sense, the students' discussions in various culturally relevant ways. Given the focus of such literature and the children's experiences, the students were able to move between borderlands through the narratives they created in response to the texts. The power of Latino literature to make sense of past experiences was evident in an interview with the mother of Isabela, one of the storytellers in the class. Her mother described how the girl asked her to read some books to her many times and in her opinion, Isabela particularly liked the stories that she could relate to:

> *A Isabela le gustan más, por decir, un cuento que ella haya vivido algo atrás. Por decir cuando los libros de los tamales, ella, como que le hacen recordar atrás cuando uno hace las cosas, cuando la navidad, cuantos que a ella le queden. Los quiere juntar como con su vida, así.*

(Isabela likes more, let's say, stories that she has lived something [similar] before. Let's say, like with the stories of tamales, they made her remember the past, like things that one has done, like Christmas; stories that remain in her. She wants to make them part of her life, like that.)

Stories such as those they were reading, which reminded children of their past and that they could relate to their present, prompted a high level of participation in the literature discussions through the construction of new narratives. The stories told in the Latino literature seemed to provide a sense of history and belonging. Relatives were a main focus in many of their stories across literature discussions, independent of the focus of the picture book. If the book was about family, the family stories were endless such as in Helena's responses to the book *In My Family/En mi familia* by Carmen Lomas Garza (1997):

> I like this part because they're dancing and that's what happened to me once when we went to a party. My *tata* Steve, my-Steve, my *tata*, and then I have two *tatas*, my *tata* Steve and my *tata* Manuel. They both, first my *tata* Manuel, took me up to dance. And then my *tío* [uncle] and I didn't know who to choose. And I chose my *tata* Manuel and he said that he was going to pick me up. And that reminded me that I had a dress too, and he lifted me up in his arms and I was really dancing.

Grandparents or *tatas*, as the children called them, were central figures in many of the narratives shared by them in response to the literature. Helena told with excitement how she had two *tatas* and an uncle and she remembered dancing with them. Other students also shared stories about relatives even if family was not a salient focus of the book.

The students narrated both happy and sad experiences in the literature discussions. The *literatura fronteriza* prompted narratives that seemed to support the students in making sense of the tensions and possibilities relating to the borderland experiences that some of them or their families had experienced. For instance, in response to *Friends from the Other Side/Amigos del otro lado* in which a group of boys call the character Joaquín, who had recently crossed the border, a *mojado* (wetback), seven-year-old Isabela responded:

> *Una vez un niño nos dijo: "mojados, se están mojando, cochinos . . ." Porque eso es malo que le digan a los demás "mojados" porque todos somos hijos de Dios y no le deben decir nada a él [a Joaquín]. . . . Porque esa palabra mata el sentimiento con la lengua . . . Porque la lengua, la lengua también mata.*

> (Long ago, a boy called us "wetbacks, you are getting wet, pigs . . ." Because it is wrong that they called the others "wetbacks" because we are all God's children and they shouldn't say anything to him [to Joaquín]. . . Because that word kills your feelings with the tongue . . . . Because the tongue, the tongue also kills.)

Isabela rejected the *mojado* identity that some want to impose on recent immigrants from Mexico and instead claimed an identity as *Atilena* as we illustrate in the next section. Some of the children's narratives reflected not only their negotiations of identities but the complex relationships between language and identity and their negotiation of linguistic borderlands.

NEGOTIATING LINGUISTIC BORDERLANDS

The children had plenty of opportunities to use Spanish, English, and Spanglish in the literature discussions. Spanglish served as a *linguistic borderland* that the students drew on to position themselves as bilingual speakers in the literature discussions and where they could bring the linguistic resources from their communities to mediate their discussions. In a previous discussion on *La mariposa* by Francisco Jiménez and Simon Silva (1998), the students were discussing whether Francisco, the boy in the story, felt that he belonged to that school. The children had different opinions. Mario said that Francisco did not feel he belonged to that school because he spoke Spanish and he was not allowed to speak Spanish at school. In the context of these comments, Isabela claimed her sense of belonging as tied to Atil, the little town in Mexico where she was born:

> *Yo creo que* I—*yo* belong *a mi casa del Atil* . . . I said that I belong to my
> *pueblito* . . . *porque allí yo nací y allí yo tengo que estar* (to my little town
> . . . because I was born there and there is what I need to be.)

Isabela shared her sense of belonging in a discussion about bilingualism. She identified her sense of belonging with the place she was born, a place, she explained later, where no one laughed at her for not knowing English. Isabela connected both country of origin and language. Through her stories she was remembering past experiences in Mexico and making sense of them in her present in the United States. Also, through hybrid literacy practices in which the boundaries of Spanish and English seemed to disappear, the literature discussions became a linguistic borderland context in which English language learners and bilingual students seemed to move smoothly and effortlessly from one language to the next.

Isabela was not the only one resolute about making connections between language, identity, and place of origin. In response to the book *Pepita Talks Twice/Pepita habla dos veces* by Ofelia Dumas Lachtman (1995), Sandy, English dominant, stated her stance toward being bilingual:

I like the book because it's good to talk both languages, and then she [Pepita] talked in both languages, and then, I wouldn't stop talking in both languages because I'm Mexican. . . . I like to talking Spanish and English because I'm Mexican and then my family is Mexican and they came from there except for me and my sister.

This excerpt shows an English-dominant speaker making statements in favor of being bilingual—which in her situation meant to also speak Spanish—and she expressed that stance in English. Although she could not produce Spanish, she understood when her peers shared in Spanish and seemed attentive to their participation; Sandy was developing an identity as a bilingual person. She connected her intentions to keep being bilingual to ethnicity: "because I'm Mexican," although she and her sister were born in the United States. Like students in Pease-Alvarez (1993), Sandy and other children in the classroom felt that ethnicity played an important role in determining their decision to keep speaking Spanish and English.

In the discussions around Latino literature that dealt with language issues, some students found a context where they could negotiate not only identities but also contradictory ideological discourses they were learning about being bilingual, sometimes within their families. The personal stories of some reflected those tensions. In response to *In My Family/En mi familia*, Dayanara brought those tensions to the surface: "My cousin, we need to hide from her too so I can speak in Spanish because if she hears me speaking Spanish she'll go tell her mom and her mom won't let her play with me any more."

Latino literature addressing bilingualism and reflecting hybrid linguistic practices supported these Latino students as they engaged in the negotiation of linguistic borderlands and ideologies of language.

In sum, the children's narratives in this classroom in response to Latino literature were about their lives between the borderlands of their previous homes and their new ones, of their past and their present, of Spanish and English. Through negotiating these borderlands the children positioned themselves as students who used their voices, experiences, and linguistic resources to participate successfully in literacy events at school. These linguistic resources—their narratives and hybrid linguistic practices—were important funds of knowledge (Martínez-Roldán 2003; Mercado 2005; Moll 1994) that mediated students' discussions of Latino literature.

SUPPORTING A RICH LITERARY EXPERIENCE

Notwithstanding the power of culturally specific literature in which students may see aspects of their lives reflected, we are not arguing for limiting Latino students' literary experience to the reading of *literatura fronteriza*. Books in which the children could not see themselves so evidently also prompted not only narratives but a rich range of literary responses that led them to approach the stories and the texts as cultural objects to be questioned. In response to the book *A Handful of Seeds* by Monica Hughes (1993), in which a group of homeless children from Central America try to survive by planting seeds, Luis shared personal experiences about working in his garden. His participation in this literature discussion was characterized by the many questions he asked about the book and the story. Although this text can be characterized as Latino literature because of its characters and setting, it was close to Luis's experience but not in relation to the main theme, in the sense that he had a home and did not have to work like the homeless children in the story. This led Luis and others to engage in inquiry questions to make sense of the story:

> *Yo también quería saber quién es su mama.* (I wanted to know who her mother is.)
> *Yo quería saber si ellos cuatro son hermanos y qué comían también.* (I wanted to know if the four of them are siblings, and also what they ate.)
> *Yo quería saber si se cansaba [de trabajar].* (I wanted to know whether she got tired [from working].)
> *¿Y qué país es ese? ¿Y de dónde viene el libro?* (And what country is that one? And where the book comes from?)

By not being able to identify with the main aspects of the story, the students adopted an analytical stance that led them to focus on details of the story they wanted to grasp better. They showed an interest in understanding how the story was created. It is plausible that the children were able to engage in these inquiries with texts that were not so close to their lives because they were already familiar with literature discussions and had learned to talk about books as a literary experience and to explore meanings.

BEYOND THE REPRESENTATIONAL POWER OF LATINO LITERATURE

We believe that culturally specific Latino literature should hold a special place in classrooms, and libraries for that matter, because it mediates not only students' representation of past and present experiences, but they also have the potential to engage students in rewriting and co-authoring those stories through their own personal narratives. In doing so, possibilities are created for the children to position themselves as children with agency, children who reinvent themselves through narratives and borderlands in literature discussions. The narratives produced by the children in response to Latino literature have the potential to mediate not only their understandings of texts and life; they also have the potential to mediate their identities in complex ways.

Additionally, we believe that the roles of discussion and creative engagement play an important part in developing meaningful literature pedagogies with Latino literature. As is shown in our examples, engagements such as the graffiti board or a student-led literature discussion, allow children to openly express their ideas and honor their linguistic resources. These situate children at the center of the meaning-making process rather than allowing the teacher to completely control the process. It is powerful when students are provided with non-scripted open response practices where correct answers are not anticipated and openness exists for self and text to merge in dynamic ways.

Finally, as with the children we work with, it is important for us to acknowledge that our lives as readers have been enriched in complex ways by the works of Latino authors. We see our lives mapped in the lives of characters and plots and this serves as a reaffirmation of who we are. We also admit that through Latino literature we are able to discover the worlds and lives of other *hermanos y hermanas* (brothers and sisters) who we do not know. We may not know what it means to move around and live the life of migrant farm workers and we are grateful to those writers who make those realities visible through their stories. In this sense the bottom line for us is to see the potential of Latino literature in classrooms as stories that all children should have access to, particularly Latino children who can find a space to which they can bring their knowledge and experiences and, as a result, discover a place to belong, connect, imagine, and reaffirm their identities.

REFERENCES

Anzaldúa, Gloria. *Borderlands/La frontera: The New Mestiza*. San Francisco: Aunt Lute Books, 1987.

———. "Chicana Artists: Exploring Neplanta, el lugar de la frontera." In *The Latino Studies Reader*, ed. by Antonia Darder and Rodolfo Torres, pp. 161–169. Malden, MA: Blackwell, 1998.

Benito, Jesús, and Ana María Manzanas. *Literature and Ethnicity in the Cultural Borderlands*. Amsterdam, Netherlands: Rodopi, 2002.

Bishop, Rudine. "Selecting Literature for a Multicultural Curriculum." In *Using Multiethnic Literature in the K–8 Classroom*, ed. by Violet J. Harris, pp. 1–20. Norwood, MA: Christopher-Gordon, 1992.

Cantú, Norma. *Canícula: Snapshots of a Girlhood en la frontera*. Albuquerque: University of New Mexico Press, 1995.

Castillo, Debra, and María-Socorro Tabuenca Córdoba. Maria Socorro. *Border Women: Writing la frontera*. Minneapolis: University of Minnesota Press, 2002.

Delgado-Bernal, Dolores. "Using a Chicana Feminist Epistemology." *Harvard Educational Review* 68 (1998): 555–582.

DeNicolo, Christina, and María Fránquiz. "Do I Have to Say It? Critical Encounters with Multicultural Literature." *Language Arts* 84 (2006): 157–170.

Gutiérrez, Kris, and Barbara Rogoff. "Cultural Ways of Learning: Individual Traits or Repertoires of Practices." *Educational Researcher* 32 (2003): 19–25.

Ladson-Billings, Gloria. "Toward a Theory of Culturally Relevant Pedagogy." *American Educational Research Journal* 32 (1995): 465–491.

López-Robertson, Julia. "Making Sense of Literature Through Story: Young Latinas Using Stories as Meaning-Making Devices During Literature Discussions." Unpublished doctoral dissertation, University of Arizona, 2004.

Martínez-Roldán, Carmen. "Building Worlds and Identities: A Case Study of the Role of Narratives in Bilingual Literature Discussions." *Research in the Teaching of English* 37 (2003): 491–526.

Medina, Carmen. "Identity and Imagination of Immigrant Children: Creating Common Place Locations in Literary Interpretation." In *Process Drama: An Educational Tool for Developing Multiple Literacies*, ed. by Jenifer Jasinski Schneider, Thomas P. Crumpler, and Theresa Rogers, pp. 53–69. Mahwah, NJ: Lawrence Erlbaum (2006b).

————. "Latino/a Children's Literature as Critical Fictions." *ALAN Review* 33 (2006a): 71–77.

————. "Reading Across Communities in Biliteracy Practices: Examining Translocal Discourses and Cultural Flows in Literature Discussions." *Reading Research Quarterly* 45 (2010): 40–60.

Medina, Carmen, and Patricia Enciso. "Some Words Are / Hay palabras mensajeras: Interpreting Sociopolitical Themes in Latino/a Children's Literature." *The New Advocate* 15 (2002): 35–47.

Mercado, Carmen. "Seeing What's There: Language and Literacy Funds of Knowledge in New York Puerto Rican Homes." In *Building on Strength: Language and Literacy in Latino Families and Communities*, ed. by Ana Celia Zentella, pp. 134–147. New York: Teachers College, 2005.

Moll, Luis. "Literacy Research in Community and Classrooms: A Sociocultural Approach." In *Theoretical Models and Processes of Reading*, 4th ed. Ed. by Robert B. Ruddell, Martha Ruddell, and Harry Singer, pp. 208–230. Newark, DE: International Reading Association, 1994.

Pease-Alvarez, L. "Moving In and Out of Bilingualism: Investigating Native Language Maintenance and Shift in Mexican-Descent Children." (Report No. 6). Santa Cruz, CA: National Center for Cultural Diversity and Second Language Learning, 1993. (ERIC Document Reproduction Service No. ED 354 779).

Short, Kathy, Jerome Harste, and Carolyn Burke. *Creating Classrooms for Authors and Inquirers*. Portsmouth, NH: Heinemann, 1996.

Solórzano, Daniel, and Tara Yosso. "Critical Race Methodology: Counter-Storytelling as an Analytical Framework for Education Research." *Qualitative Inquiry* 8 (2002): 23–44.

Sumara, Dennis. *Why Reading Literature Still Matters: Imagination, Interpretation and Insight*. Mahwah, NJ: Lawrence Erlbaum, 2002.

Trujillo, Carla. *Living Chicana Theory*. Berkeley, CA: Third Woman Press, 1998.

Vygotsky, Lev Semenovich. *Mind in Society: The Development of Higher Psychological Processes*. Cambridge, MA: Harvard University Press, 1978.

————. "Thinking and Speech." In *Collected Works of L. S. Vygotsky: Vol. 1. Problems of General Psychology*, ed. by Robert W. Rieber, and Aaron S. Carton, pp. 239–289. New York: Plenum Press, 1987.

❀ CHAPTER 16

Using Latin American Folktales in Literacy and Library Programming

Amy Olson

Folktales are a valuable way to promote cultural awareness, diversity, normalization, and compassion in both classroom and library settings. This chapter emphasizes significant Latin American folklore and the influential power of storytelling while also providing concrete examples of simple ways for children's, youth, and school librarians to incorporate folktales into bilingual programs and lesson plans for both Latino[1] and non-Latino children.

Folktales reflect people past and present. They answer the who, what, where, when, why, and how of a people's cultural origins, traits, composition, belief systems, and so forth. Folktales are the tales, games, superstitions, *dichos* (proverbs), riddles, and songs of a culture. They are tools of instruction, collections of wisdom, and examples of core values that are passed down from generation to generation. Simple yet picturesque, folktales convey traditions, medicinal cures, customs, myths, values, and important stories.

WHY USE FOLKTALES IN PROGRAMMING?

Folktales are educational entertainment. Our elders knew that we are more likely to remember things that we enjoy learning. Retention has been enhanced for centuries through songs, melodic rhymes, rhythmic chants, and especially through repetition. Stories have been told over and over to teach a culture's ethics, to celebrate life, to offer hope, to bring cohesion to a tribe, and simply to pass the time. Folktales are used to teach life lessons, humanize the

---

1   Throughout this chapter, the term *Latino* refers to people who are from Mexico, Puerto Rico, Cuba, Central America, and South America by origin or descent, regardless of their race (U.S. Census Bureau 2008).

past, pass on tribal history, affirm heritage, explain natural phenomena, ease fears about the unknown, explore new perspectives, and embrace unfamiliar ideas (Zuñiga 1992; Oring 2004). Folktales cross barriers that may exist between culture, ethnicity, geography, and time, as well as the spiritual and philosophical worlds (Hearne 1999; Strong 2003). Experiencing folklore enables the satisfaction of basic human needs: a desire to love and be loved, a sense of belonging and security, a desire for justice, a need to laugh.

As folklore became more complex and continued to develop over time, folktales were used to enhance religious practices, introduce darker spiritual figures such as witches, demons, and cryptozoids (*la chupacabra* and Bigfoot), and to celebrate heroes and heroines. Geography, history, ecology, science, health, archaeology, art, religion, agriculture, math, and many other subjects were taught and shared through folklore (Pedersen 1993; Smolen and Ortiz-Castro 2000).

Even today, both children and adults can learn—outside a textbook-driven, sterile educational system—through well-chosen folktales. Children, their caregivers, and educators can become engaged, motivated, and even entertained while listening to the tales of their own and other cultures. On some level, the listener is able to experience the world of days gone by and to gain knowledge about beliefs, values, and behaviors.

In addition, if listeners are entertained, they are more likely to remember what they have been told and to pass that knowledge on to someone else. The hearing and retelling of folktales allows the listener's language and literacy skills to develop successfully (Smolen and Ortiz-Castro 2000).

Active listening to folklore also aids participants with the integration and implementation of crucial pre-literacy and literacy skills—helping them to discriminate, identify, and pronounce sounds (phonemic awareness), words (graphic awareness), and phrases (phonological awareness). Folklore also enables participants to explore and strengthen a variety of language learning strategies such as identification of basic concepts, cross-curricular integration from other content areas, observation, imagery and symbolism, interpretation of facts vs. the identification of opinions, cause and effect, sequencing, comparing and contrasting of materials, brainstorming to explore related concepts, and problem solving (Pedersen 1993; Zuñiga 1992).

Folktales can be shared through oral storytelling, a performance art form based on sounds and actions, or print versions found in singular children's books or in collected volumes. When a folktale is shared through oral storytelling, the listener is naturally given the opportunity to explore and imagine. There are no illustrations to limit or alter the listeners' visions, nor are there printed words to limit what is said. The storyteller can embellish or expand upon the bones, or crucial basic elements, of a folktale (Hearne 2005). The story's bones may be gently adapted and improvised to fit the needs of the age group(s) listening to the tale, thereby allowing the tale to transcend age barriers and meet the needs of a combined audience of children and adults, enabling the creation of an ideal family-oriented program (Hearne 1999, 2005).

Folktales, especially those appropriate for children, have been lovingly gathered by folklorists and carefully written down for other cultures to experience and learn from. They have been part of children's literature since the beginning of children's publishing and continue to be an integral part of a library's collection development. Children who have heard a folktale told will enjoy accessing the print version and revisiting the world they remember hearing about (Hearne July 1993).

The popularity of folktales has increased over the years; in fact, the illustrated children's book is perhaps the best-known folktale format today. Children's, youth, and school librarians can now introduce children to print forms of diverse multicultural tales that previously were only available orally (stories heard around a fire, before bedtime, or at a time of celebration and gathering). By offering these tales, librarians broaden the range of subjects and cultures that are typically presented to their patrons (Hamer 2000). It is unlikely that folktales will ever be tested as valuable core content in a curriculum, yet the need to share them—to help children see that there is more than one way to do something—is vitally important regardless of whether it is test material or not.

FOLKTALES FROM LATIN AMERICA

Folktales considered Latino originate from the Spanish-speaking areas of South and Central America, Mexico, Puerto Rico, Cuba, and the American Southwest, where the U.S.-Mexico border has fluctuated over the years (Smolen and Ortiz-Castro 2000). Aztec, Inca, Maya, Guaraní, Olmec, Taíno, Toltec, many other Central/South American indigenous tribes, and Apache and Pueblo Indian folktales are all considered to be part of Latino folklore (Norton 2008).

Spain, too, has influenced Latino folklore through the tales left behind by Spanish adventurers, *conquistadors,* and slave traders as well as by the Moors, Romany, and Jews who fled Spain in order to find a life free of persecution. Further enriching this multifaceted tradition, African cultural influences, due primarily to the slave trade, can also be found within Latino folklore (Raffaelli et al. 2005).

To our great misfortune, however, much of the indigenous tribal folklore that has been collected for today's access has been received, and often indoctrinated or otherwise altered, through various sources. Even when the preserver of folklore was well intentioned, the tales today often have been influenced by empires, subcultures, conquerors, historians, and even language barriers. It is very difficult to find a folkloric tale from a pure source, especially when indigenous tribes such as the Inca, Maya, and Aztec have been decimated, assimilated, dispersed, or have otherwise disappeared (Strong 2003).

Whenever possible, it is important to verify the source of a folktale. Having just an author's and illustrator's name is insufficient. Each folktale must be placed in its proper cultural context. Librarians should ask: What culture is the tale from, who shared the tale, when was the tale written down, what was the context for the tale, and have any known adaptations been made to the folktale (Hearne August 1993). Citing and respecting the source of a folktale are essential if a librarian is to provide culturally responsible programming (Hearne August 1993).

NORMALIZATION OF CULTURES THROUGH LATINO FOLKTALES

Children respond strongly to a welcoming, caring environment regardless of their background; feeling cared for will greatly alter a child's performance, prompting academic accomplishments and increased effort as well as the growth of healthy interpersonal relationships. In addition, children who participate with their families in celebrating their cultural traditions and background have been proven to have better childhood behavior, improved academic achievement, a better sense of identity, and an enhanced ability to adjust to varying circumstances (Fritz 2004). Librarians can help to facilitate this participation by encouraging families to read folklore from their cultures, to celebrate their rituals, and to share their folklore with others. Librarians will be remembered for many years to come by the children whom they welcome and accept and whom they serve with kindness and gentleness.

Acceptance—and support—of Latino cultures and experiences is essential for a children's librarian in today's world. Nearly one out of six residents in the United States, or approximately 46.9 million people, identify as Latino (U.S. Census Bureau 2008). And while the majority of Latinos in the United States are Mexican or of Mexican descent, librarians must be extremely careful to pay attention to the cultural diversity within the Latino population they serve (Raffaelli et al. 2005), including whether a Latino is a long-term resident or a more recently arrived immigrant.

Folklore allows librarians to share the voices of people from diverse cultures, especially of those who are unable to do so: the poor, the underrepresented, those without power (Oring 2004). By acting as advocates, librarians can help to create a more humane and peaceful world through culturally responsive programming, thereby aiding in eliminating confusion and misunderstandings that can bring about friction and injustice. To create this culturally responsive programming, librarians must be informed not only about Latino cultures, although this is important, but also about the world in which they live. Librarians must consciously incorporate into bilingual programming the understanding that all cultures are worthy of study and deserve respect.

UNIQUE NEEDS OF LATINO CHILDREN AND THEIR FAMILIES

Librarians also must continue to educate themselves about their patrons' cultures while taking time to discover, comprehend, and share their patrons' stories within an appropriate cultural context (Oring 2004). They must be vigilant about understanding and carefully representing the cultural context of folktales, remembering that their own personal context will influence how they hear and later share folktales with their patrons (Hamer 2000; Hearne 2005). Librarians should also monitor the demographics of the neighborhoods and patrons served by their library in order to best meet the needs of those patrons. When working with Latino children, librarians must remember that each Latino child has a unique history and special needs. See Figure 16.1 for a list of common stress factors that can greatly affect a Latino child's academic achievement, ability to participate in entertaining programs, family dynamics, self-esteem, and overall mental health.

Rather than reinforcing stereotypes or demanding cultural assimilation and/or the superiority of hegemony, folktales can help a Latino child to make sense of their world, thereby alleviating many stressors and normalizing experiences (Chappell and Faltis 2007; Hamer 2000). Folktales help children to take complex abstract and concrete concepts and place them within a culture and context that is understandable to them.

Fortunately, folktales typically are of high interest to children, with lots of action and strong emotions such as humor, anger, and sadness. They tend to be highly visual and descriptive, and start and end in familiar ways, thereby

STRESS FACTORS INFLUENCING SOCIAL AND ACADEMIC FUNCTIONING OF LATINO CHILDREN AND THEIR FAMILIES

❋ **Inability to Relax:** Recently arrived Latino children may not be able to relax or feel fully at home in the United States for a long time. People here dress differently, smell differently, eat differently, etc.

❋ **Feelings of Rejection:** Latino children may feel lonely, vulnerable, and/or misunderstood by the dominant culture. This can lead to feelings of rejection and potential future problems such as academic failure, affiliation with gangs, dropping out of school, and so forth.

❋ **Resentment about Leaving Home Culture:** Recently arrived Latino children may not have wanted to leave their homeland, but may have been forced to for political, religious, or economic reasons. They also may want to move back to their homeland and cannot.

❋ **Fear of Authoritarian Figures and the Government:** Recently arrived Latino children may be victims of oppression, famine, torture, murder, loss of family, or other atrocities of war. As a result of their experiences, they may fear authority and have a lack of trust in the "system."

❋ **Conflicting Academic/Professional Standards:** Some recently arrived Latino children may have been highly educated in their previous domicile, and their parents may have had high professional standing; however, once here in the United States their education/professional standing is often viewed as being sub-par.

❋ **Illiteracy:** Recently arrived Latino families may be working class or poor, with little or no education. If they can't read or write in their own language, it will be all that more complicated to learn to speak, read, and write a new one.
- 47 percent of Latinos who are first-generation residents of the United States have parents who have had less than a high school education (Fry 2009).

❋ **Poverty or Life Complications:** Latino children may currently be living in poverty or facing other life complications.
- 34 percent of first-generation Latino residents, 26 percent of second-generation Latino residents, and 24 percent of third-generation Latino residents in the United States live in poverty (Fry 2009).

❋ **Language Learning:** Latino children and their families may presently be learning English and/or Spanish.
- 43 percent of first-generation, 21 percent of second-generation, and 5 percent of third-generation Latino residents are not fluent in English (Fry 2009).
- Just because a Latino can speak Spanish doesn't necessarily mean he or she can read and write in Spanish.
- Although a Latino child is from a country where Spanish is the first language, he or she may not speak Spanish. Hundreds of languages are spoken throughout Latin America.

❋ **Complications with Verbal and Nonverbal Communication:** Latino children and/or their family members may be confused by intonations, gestures (nonverbal communication), sarcasm, joking behavior toward them, physical distances between people, customs surrounding food or drink, and interactions with the opposite sex.

- Latinos, in general, speak more softly than non-Latinos.
- Looking down is a sign of respect and is not necessarily a sign of inattention.
- Hand gestures mean different things in different cultures. A wave is often a way to say goodbye or "go away" in English-speaking cultures. A wave in Latino cultures, however, tends to be a request for a person to come closer.

FIGURE 16.1. *Common stress factors that can greatly affect a Latino child's academic achievement, ability to participate in library programs, family dynamics, self-esteem, and overall mental health.*

creating an atmosphere of magic and mystery that is outside time. Beginning and ending folktales in a way that can be anticipated by Latino children helps to create a comfortable and secure environment for their imaginations and allows the tale to live on in their memories. Below are a few sayings that are useful for librarians sharing folktales with Spanish-speaking Latino children:

- ❁ In a land far, far away . . . / *En un país muy lejano* . . .
- ❁ Once upon a time . . . / *Había una vez* . . .
- ❁ . . . *esto es verdad y no miento.* / . . . and that's the truth and I'm not lying.
- ❁ . . . *y colorín colorado este cuento se ha acabado.* / . . . snip, snap, snout this tale's told out.

Folktales are also a perfect way for librarians to engage the families of Latino children. Sharing folktales through text or storytelling is a way to form community, including both creating and sustaining that community (Hearne 2005). As Latinos often prefer to participate in groups, rather than individually, this style of programming would fit well into their cultural paradigm (Isom and Casteel 1997). The only limiter on whether a tale is shared orally or through a book will be the size of the group, as a text can be difficult to share well with a larger number of people unless projection devices are introduced.

SELECTING FOLKTALES USING LATINO CHILDREN'S BOOK AWARDS

Finding the perfect folktale to share with Latino children and their families should not be a hard task for librarians. Book award lists routinely provide a convenient starting point for finding high-quality folktales to add to collections and use in library programming. Books winning the Américas Book Award for Children's and Young Adult Literature or the Pura Belpré Award often include rich folktales celebrating the diversity of the Latino cultures.

The Américas Book Award is given annually by the University of Wisconsin–Milwaukee to honor books written in English or Spanish that authentically portray Latino culture (MW-Milwaukee 2009). One or more folktales generally appear on the list of award winners. In 2009 several folklore and folklore-esque titles were recognized:

- ❀ Yuyi Morales won for her folklore-esque title, *Just in Case: A Trickster Tale and Spanish Alphabet Book.*

- ❀ Julia Alvarez received an honorable mention for *The Best Gift of All: The Legend of La Vieja Belén / El mejor regalo del mundo: La leyenda de la Vieja Belén.*

- ❀ Joe Hayes received a commendation for *Baila, Nana, Baila / Dance, Nana, Dance: Cuban Folktales in English and Spanish.*

The Pura Belpré Award is given to a Latino or Latina children's author and illustrator whose work best celebrates the Latino cultural experience (ALA/ALSC 2009). Folklore and folklore-esque books that have won the Belpré in the past are:

- ❀ 2009: Yuyi Morales received the medal for her illustrations and was honored for her writing in her folklore-esque title, *Just in Case: A Trickster Tale and Spanish Alphabet Book*

- ❀ 2008: Carmen Agra Deedy was honored for her writing in *Martina the Beautiful Cockroach: A Cuban Folktale*

- ❀ 2006: Raúl Colón's illustrations in *Doña Flor: A Tall Tale About a Giant Woman with a Big Heart* won the medal, and Pat Mora was honored for her narrative in the book

- ❀ 2006: Lulu Delacre's *Arrorró, mi niño: Latino Lullabies and Gentle Games* was honored for her illustrations

- ❀ 2004: Yuyi Morales won the medal for best illustration for *Just a Minute: A Trickster Tale and Counting Book*

- ❀ 2002: Joe Cepeda was honored for his illustrations in *Juan Bobo Goes to Work* by Marisa Montes

- ❀ 2000: Carmen Lomas Garza received the medal for her illustrations in *Magic Windows.*

- ❀ 2000: Felipe Dávalos was honored for his illustrations in the folklore-esque title *The Secret Stars*, written by Joseph Slate

- ❀ 1998: Enrique Sánchez was honored for his illustrations in *The Golden Flower: A Taino Myth from Puerto Rico* written by Nina Jaffe

❀ 1996: Lucía González was honored for her writing and Lulu Delacre was honored for her illustrations in *The Bossy Gallito / El gallo de bodas: A Traditional Cuban Folktale*

SABORS OF FOLKLORIC STORYTELLING

It may be daunting at first to think about incorporating storytelling into programming. However, the folkloric tale doesn't necessarily have to be memorized (Hearne 2005). Apprehension about misrepresenting a folktale or forgetting the words can impede the power of a memorized story, but librarians who suffer from such apprehension can read illustrated books, short stories, and other tales to an audience just as a performer would read a tale in reader's theatre. Good librarianship and instruction is about telling the story; sharing stories enables group cohesiveness and the ability to form community within a library setting (Hearne 2005).

On delving into the world of Latino folklore, librarians will find that there are two broad categories: *cuentos* and *mitos*. *Cuentos* are religious tales, magical tales, romantic tales, trickster tales, cumulative tales, and scary tales. *Mitos* are tales that explain why things happen or how things came about, otherwise known as *pourquoi* tales; they take place in a time long past.

Throughout Latino folklore, certain Latino core values are demonstrated. *Espiritualismo, familismo, fatalismo,* and *harmonia* are unique identifiers that resonate across most, if not all, Latino cultures. These four core values will be discussed at further length below.

RELIGIOUS TALES / CUENTOS RELIGIOSOS

When religious beliefs and faith intermix and infuse folktales in a quest to find meaning and patterns in all that is said and done, the outcome is referred to as *espiritualismo*. *Espiritualismo* is when religion is unable to be separated from everyday life: what is experienced by the mind is also experienced by the body, and what is real and what is unreal blend together in everyday life. Miracles happen and are anticipated and expected. The imaginary line between the natural world and the supernatural world is blurred. Religious tales, in particular, embrace the core value of Latino *espiritualismo*. Folktales about how the world was made, the great flood, the afterlife, and religious icons or saints all are considered to be examples of religious tales. For instance, Nina Jaffe's

The Golden Flower: A Taino Myth from Puerto Rico / Flor de oro: Un mito taíno de Puerto Rico describes how the seas and all that is within them were formed by the smashing of a pumpkin from a mountaintop.

Almost every culture appears to have tales about a great worldwide flood. Peru's tale is retold by Ellen Alexander in *The Llama and the Great Flood: A Folktale from Peru.* The llama was a sacred animal to the Incans (Strong 2003); llamas were used to travel to the underworld and were symbols of life and harvest as well. The llama in this tale saves his master and the master's family by warning them about the flood that is to come, allowing them to escape to the top of a mountain and wait out the flood. Venezuela's version of the worldwide flood is told in Maria Elena Maggi's *The Great Canoe: A Karina Legend,* in which Kaputano plays the role of Noah, saving four couples, numerous pairs of animals, and seeds from destruction.

Folktales commonly explore death and the afterlife, sharing what is viewed as mystical and adding flavor to the tale (Hearne 2009). In her folktale *Mother Scorpion Country / La tierra de madre escorpión,* Harriet Rohmer shares a traditional folktale of the Miskito tribe of Central America (Nicaragua/ Honduras regions). Kati, the much loved wife of Naklili has just died. Naklili desires to be buried with her and join her in her travels to the land of death; yet while there, Naklili is unable to share in the joys of the land as he is still living.

Below are a few other examples of *cuentos religiosos* that describe miracles, religious icons, and saints. Figure 16.2 provides a programming idea and recommended books relating to religious cuentos, or folktales embodying *espiritualismo.*

* ❀ Tomie dePaola's *Nuestra Señora de Guadalupe / Our Lady of Guadalupe* honors one of the best-known Mexican icons, the Virgin of Guadalupe, by retelling the story of her appearance to a poor Mexican farmer and the sign she left behind on the farmer's clothing in 1531.

* ❀ *Spirit Child: A Story of the Nativity* is a phenomenal Mexican folktale about Jesus' birth composed originally in the Aztec language by Fray Bernadino de Sahagun and unnamed Aztec poets and musicians during the early 1500s. It was originally performed as a rhythmic chant to the accompaniment of toned drums in Mexico City. Fortunately John Bierhorst rediscovered the tale and has republished it with beautiful illustrations by Barbara Cooney.

* ❀ Dorothy Sharp Carter's "The Purchased Miracle," from *The Enchanted Orchard: And Other Folktales of Central America,* is a tale from Honduras about a wealthy gentleman who felt that those who went on pilgrimages in search of miracles were mad or too lazy to work. Because of his disbelief, Don Juan became blind. His family and friends told him to go on a healing pilgrimage, and out of desperation

PROGRAMMING IDEA — PAPEL PICADOS

Papel picados are literally "pecked paper"—tissue paper rectangles that are cut in ways similar to the paper snowflakes created at Christmastime. Latinos use papel picados to decorate during times of celebration and religious festivals. Each rectangle is strung on a piece of string to make a colorful banner; the more banners, the more festive the atmosphere.

The following books are additional programming suggestions. Note that some of these titles (followed by an *) are not pure folklore; rather, they are tales that incorporate folkloric themes and iconic characters:

❊ Alvarez, Julia. *The Best Gift of All: The Legend of La Vieja Belén / El mejor regalo del mundo: La leyenda de la Vieja Belén*

❊ dePaola, Tomie. *The Night of Las Posadas*

❊ Garza, Carmen Lomas. *Magic Windows / Ventanas mágicas*

❊ Garza, Carmen Lomas. *Making Magic Windows: Creating Cut-Paper Art with Carmen Lomas Garza**

❊ Oppenheim, Joanne. *The Miracle of the First Poinsettia*

❊ Robbins, Sandra. *The Firefly Star: A Hispanic Folktale*

❊ Shahan, Sherry. *Fiesta!**

❊ Slate, Joseph. *The Secret Stars*

FIGURE 16.2. *Example of a programming idea with recommended books relating to religious cuentos or folktales embodying espiritualismo.*

he went. A miracle happened and he was healed. However, instead of crediting the miracle, Don Juan acknowledged luck. Almost immediately, Don Juan became blind again.

MAGICAL TALES / CUENTOS MÁGICOS

Magical tales, like religious tales, often incorporate concepts of *espiritualismo*, especially where the boundaries between what is real and what is imaginary are blurred through the genre of magical realism. The concept of *magical realism*, perhaps best demonstrated by authors Gabriel Garcia Marquez of Colombia, Julio Cortázar of Argentina, Mario Vargas Llosa of Peru, and Carlos Fuentes of Mexico, merges magical, spiritual, and even illogical elements into everyday scenarios, thereby revealing the magic that is in our world.

Julia Alvarez's folktale from the Dominican Republic tells of a secret tribe, the Ciguapas, who live under the ocean and are able to keep themselves secret from the rest of the world because their feet face backward. Thus, in *The Secret Footsteps / Las huellas secretas*, the footprints left behind by the tribe always appear to be heading toward the water even though, in truth, the tribe is coming up from under the water.

Keith Polette's colorfully illustrated, Latino-flavored Jack tale, *Paco and the Giant Chile Plant / Paco y la planta de chile gigante*, retells the Jack and the Beanstalk story through the eyes and experiences of Paco. In a library program it would be interesting to pair this title with another Jack and the Beanstalk tale in order to compare and contrast the cultures and the characters' experiences.

Caroline Pitcher's *Mariana and the Merchild: A Folk Tale from Chile* is reminiscent of the selkie tales of Ireland. *La vieja* Mariana discovers a merbaby on the beach after a horrible storm. She is asked by the baby's mother to care for the merchild. The villagers initially are greatly frightened by the merchild, but as time passes they adapt and overcome their fears. When the merbaby's mother comes to reclaim her baby, it is the village children who comfort Mariana for her loss. A book for older children with many of the same elements is *Milagros: Girl from Away* by Meg Medina. Although the book is too long to be read aloud or told, older children can tell portions of the story or share the *espiritualismo* and magical realism elements with their families. Figure 16.3 provides a programming idea and recommended books relating to magical realism in folktales embodying *espiritualismo*.

PROGRAMMING IDEA — TIN ORNAMENTS

Tin ornaments are a decorative craft performed by artisans throughout Latin America. The tin is cut into a variety of shapes and sizes, including those of magical creatures. Simple tools, such as scissors, pencil, and stained glass paints and/or markers, are used to create the colorful, decorative hangings.

The following books are additional programming suggestions. Note that some of these titles (followed by an *) are not pure folklore but do contain relevant concepts:

❈ Delacre, Lulu. *De oro y esmeraldas: Mitos, leyendas y cuentos populares de latinoamérica / Golden Tales: Myths, Legends, and Folktales from Latin America*

❈ Mora, Pat. *Doña Flor: A Tall Tale About a Giant Woman with a Big Heart / Doña Flor: Un cuento de un mujer gigante con un gran corazón*

❈ Pavón, Ana-Elba. *25 Latino Craft Projects: Celebrating Culture in Your Library* *

❈ VanLaan, Nancy. *The Magic Bean Tree: A Legend from Argentina*

FIGURE 16.3 *provides an example of a programming idea with recommended books relating to magical realism in folktales embodying espiritualismo.*

ROMANTIC TALES / CUENTOS ROMÁNTICOS

The Latino core value of *familismo* is repeatedly demonstrated throughout romantic folktales. *Familismo* is simply defined as "family first." It is the collective loyalty to an extended family that outranks the needs of the individual. When a family member has a need, whether great or small, the individual will immediately drop everything to help. A daughter's obedience to her father, a son's disregard for his mother's advice, and disaster ensuing when pride exceeds all other concerns or when familial advice is not heeded—these are all examples of situations and outcomes that are explored through romantic folklore.

Cuban storyteller and writer Carmen Agra Deedy has written a *cuento romántico* in her version of the well-known Latin American folktale Martina and Perez entitled *Martina the Beautiful Cockroach: A Cuban Folktale / Martina una cucarachita muy linda: Un cuento Cubano*. In this rambunctious tale, Martina has decided that she is going to marry, and her *abuela* suggests how she should go about finding a husband. Unfortunately, Martina is quite fickle and suitor after suitor fails to impress her until she meets her one true love. A superb audio version of the tale, performed by Deedy, is available and sure to delight audiences of both Latino and non-Latino children and families.

Jacaltec Mayan author Victor Montejo sets the traditional Spanish tale of Blanca Flor into a Mayan setting in his *Blanca Flor: Una princesa maya / White Flower: A Maya Princess,* which tells of a young prince who has lost his memory. The prince must complete several impossible tasks set for him by the Lord of the Forest. In doing so, the prince falls in love with Blanca Flor, but the Lord of the Forest, Blanca Flor's father, demands they stay apart. Rather than obey her father, Blanca Flor helps the prince to successfully finish his tasks through her magic and wit so that they may marry. Figure 16.4 provides a programming idea and recommended books relating to *familismo* and romantic tales.

TRICKSTER TALES / CUENTOS DE ASTUCIA

What is going to happen will happen, especially when there is a trickster involved. *Fatalismo* is the belief that man cannot control his destiny, as a person's destiny is determined by God's will and other unknown variables. *Fatalismo* is a core value within the Latino culture that is repeatedly explored within trickster tales, where individuals can do little or nothing to alter their fate.

Tricksters are specialists in manipulating scenarios to get what they want, often through cleverness. Tricksters can also take that which is bad or evil

PROGRAMMING IDEA —
TISSUE PAPER FLOWERS/DUCT TAPE ROSES

Flowers are colorful symbols of romance. Children can make flowers for the ones they love, similar to those illustrated in these romantic tales.

Tissue paper flowers are literally just that, flowers made out of tissue paper.

❀ Layer 4 to 5 sheets of tissue paper on top of each other, making sure that the tissues are rectangular in shape (not square)

❀ Starting with the longest side, accordion-fold the layered tissue paper

❀ Then attach the middle of the tissue paper to a green wooden floral stem with green masking tape

❀ Slowly and gently separate each layer

Roses made out of colored duct tape will have teens clamoring for more.

❀ Tear pieces of duct tape

❀ Fold down two corners (on the same side) of each piece

❀ Wrap the pieces around a green wooden floral stem

❀ Keep wrapping the folded squares around the stem until you have the size of flower desired

The following books tie into this activity. Note that some of these titles (followed by an *) are not pure folklore but contain related concepts.

❀ Gerson, Mary-Joan. *Fiesta Femenina: Celebrating Women in Mexican Folktale/Fiesta femenina: Homenaje a las mujeres a través de historias tradicionales mexicanas*

❀ González, Lucía. *Señor Cat's Romance and Other Favorite Stories from Latin America*

❀ Perl, Lila. *Piñatas and Paper Flowers: Holidays of the Americas in English and Spanish/Piñatas y flores de papel: Fiestas de las Américas en ingles y español**

FIGURE 16.4 *provides two examples of programming ideas with recommended books relating to* familismo *and romantic tales.*

and remove it, often by taking the trouble upon themselves in order to save the greater good (Strong 2003). The suspense over whether the trickster is going to be selfish or caring—and the humor surrounding the trickster—is what is so irresistibly intriguing in Latino folktales.

Pat Mora's *La carerra de sapo y venado / The Race of Toad and Deer* is a retelling of a Guatemalan trickster folktale. A race is arranged between Toad and Deer. Deer, the strongest runner in the jungle, always wins—yet this time Toad's friends trick Deer into running as hard as he can the entire race. In his zeal, Deer is unable to finish, and falls exhausted to the ground while Toad hops on by to win.

Jabutí the Tortoise: A Trickster Tale from the Amazon by Gerald McDermott is a story about the consummate trickster. Jabutí has tricked everyone, yet he is about to meet his match. Vulture is jealous of Jabutí's ability to play music (Vulture cannot sing but a note). It is only the intervention of the King of Heaven that saves Jabutí from Vulture's trap.

Love and Roast Chicken: A Trickster Tale from the Andes Mountains / Amor y pollo asado: Un cuento de estafadores de enredos y engaños is another folktale in which the trickster is tricked. Fox wants to eat Cuy, a spunky guinea pig, yet Cuy outsmarts the trickster Fox over and over again. To enhance the flavor of the tale, not only does Barbara Knutson incorporate both English and Spanish into the text, but she adds Quechua (typically spoken in Bolivia, Ecuador, and Peru), as well. Figure 16.5 provides a programming idea and recommended books relating to *fatalismo* and trickster tales.

CUMULATIVE TALES / *CUENTOS CUMULATIVOS*

Latinos live in a nuanced world that has many layers of meaning, yet these layers are all interconnected. Conversations are non-linear, tangential. Themes are less defined; story topics blend. Folktales allow multiple subjects to be presented and shared at once through association or *harmonia*. *Harmonia*, another core value within Latino culture, exists where the emotional, physical, and social facets of an individual are in balance, in harmony. Latino culture is unlike Western culture, which is very black and white in thought and conversation. For instance, it is common in Western cultural conversations to make "either" and "or" statements, whereas in Latino culture the conjunctions used tend to be "and" and "but," allowing more flexibility and emphasizing the underlying assumption that things are rarely black and white, but often gray. Living in the "gray" is living in *harmonia*. Because of this flexibility, Latino folklore might

PROGRAMMING IDEA — ALEBRIJES

Alebrijes is a wooden art form associated with Oaxaca, Mexico. Animalistic body parts are mixed and matched to create a fantastical, imaginary creature much like those seen in the illustrations of *Jabutí the Tortoise: A Trickster Tale from the Amazon* and *ABeCedarios: Mexican Folk Art ABCs in English and Spanish.* Insulation panels, such as Foamular, can be cut with plastic knives, shaped and sculpted with sticks, toothpicks, wooden dowels, and glue guns, and then painted with acrylic paints to form fantastic, imaginary three-dimensional shapes.

The following books tie into this activity. Note that some of these titles (followed by an *) are not pure folklore; rather they incorporate folkloric themes and iconic characters.

❀ Loya, Olga. "The Monkey and the Crocodile / *El mono y el cocodrilo*," "Opossum and Coyote / *La zarigüena y el coyote*," "The Alligator and the Dog / *El perro y el caiman*," and "Uncle Rabbit and Uncle Tiger / *El tío Conejo y el tío Tigre*" from *Momentos mágicos / Magic Moments: Tales from Latin America*

❀ Morales, Yuyi. *Just a Minute: A Trickster Tale and Counting Book* *

❀ Morales, Yuyi. *Just in Case: A Trickster Tale and Spanish Alphabet Book* *

❀ Weill, Cynthia. *ABeCedarios: Mexican Folk Art ABCs in English and Spanish* *

❀ Weill, Cynthia. *Opuestos: Mexican Folk Art Opposites in English and Spanish* *

FIGURE 16.5 *provides an example of a programming idea with recommended books relating to* fatalismo *and trickster tales.*

be viewed by those culturally unfamiliar with it as rambling, over-emotional, repetitious, contradictory, and even impossible. Getting "to the point" takes a while as stories tend to unfold in a circuitous fashion; going directly "to the point" is often lauded in Western culture, but viewed as rude or dishonorable by Latinos.

Cumulative tales contain themes or experiences that continue throughout the tale. Each cumulative tale is connected from start to end; as the same thread continues throughout a tale, however, the characters often have difficulty reaching the end. It is this very lack of productivity that makes cumulative folklore some of the most humorous to experience.

Marisa Montes's *Juan Bobo Goes to Work: A Puerto Rican Folktale / Juan Bobo busca trabajo: Un cuento Puertorriqueño* is a typical Jack tale that is cumulative and full of humor, misunderstandings, and giggles. Poor Juan's misadventures abound as he tries to get a job, but every single thing that can go wrong does go wrong. Yet, somehow, against all odds and very unexpectedly, Juan triumphs.

Margaret Read MacDonald's *A Hen, a Chick, and a String Guitar: Inspired by a Chilean Folktale / Algarabia en la granja* is a folktale that should be sung through chant. Full of animal sounds, it tells the story of a little boy who receives the gift of a chicken from his grandma. Day after day, two by two, new animals keep arriving until the little boy has sixteen pets.

In Margaret Read MacDonald's *Conejito: A Folktale from Panama*, Conejito is trying to get to his Tía Mónica's house on the other side of the mountain. To get there he has to pass many obstacles, namely Sr. Fox, Sr. Tiger, and Sr. Lion. Poor Conejito! All he wants is to eat Tía's treats and all the Señores want to do is eat Conejito! Figure 16.6 provides a programming idea and recommended books relating to *harmonia* and cumulative tales.

SCARY TALES / *CUENTOS DE MIEDO*

Teens are often overlooked in programming. Yet, some of the most powerful and meaningful programming that can be done for teens will scare the pants off them. Teens adore having chills sent up and down their spines; folklore enables that to happen.

Few would disagree that being a teenager is a difficult time. Latino teens must adapt to the changes that are happening in their lives while simultaneously deciding whether to reflect different aspects of their heritage and meeting societal expectations and combating stereotypes (Northrup and Bean 2007).

PROGRAMMING IDEA — FELTED ANIMALS AND ART

South America is known for the fiber of its llamas, vicuñas, guanacos, and alpacas. As the majority of the indigenous tribes around the Andes Mountains incorporate this fiber into their products, making felted animals and art would be a perfect artistic activity linking folktales and culture.

The following books are suggestions for ideas and information on how to felt.

❀ Heckman, Andrea. *Woven Stories: Andean Textiles and Rituals*

❀ Horvath, Marie-Noelle. *Little Felted Animals: Create 16 Irresistible Creatures with Simple Needle-Felting Techniques*

❀ Sharp, Laurie. *Wool Pets: Making 20 Figures with Wool Roving and a Barbed Needle*

❀ Thompson, Angela. *Textiles of Central and South America*

The following titles tie in with this program; those (followed by an *) are not pure folklore; rather they incorporate folkloric themes and iconic characters.

❀ Ada, Alma Flor. *Mamá Goose: A Latino Treasury / Mamá Goose: Un tesoro de rimas infantiles*

❀ Ada, Alma Flor. *¡Pío Peep! Rimas tradicionales en español / Traditional Spanish Nursery Rhymes with CD*

❀ Hayes, Joe. *Tell Me a Cuento / Cuéntame un Story*

❀ Orozco, José-Luis. *De Colores and Other Latin-American Folksongs for Children*

FIGURE 16.6 *provides an example of a programming idea with recommended books relating to* harmonia *and cumulative tales.*

What better way to appease the teens while honoring their cultural background than through scary Latino folktales?

It is easy to fear and to project fears into that which is not seen, the unknown, the disgusting. The mutation of that which is human with that which is beast, such as *la chupacabra, la cegua,* or *el cucuy*, allows Latino teens to explore what it is to be human by contrasting it with an abnormality (Chappell and Faltis 2007). Tensions that occur within the real world—the desire to disobey those in authority, feelings of being misunderstood, the overwhelming sense of rage that occurs randomly in the daily life of a teen—can all be explored from a safe distance through that which is supernatural or hybridized.

However, limiting the use of scary tales to just teen programming would be a great loss to the younger child. Even early elementary-aged children, when asked, will say that they like to be scared. The level of fear to be experienced by a child will have to be determined by the librarian; it is a simple matter to tone the fear factor of the tale back a bit. Thus, I say, don't be afraid—scare them all!!!

La Llorona

The folktale about La Llorona has been told and retold for generations throughout Latin America; it is so old that the source of the tale is lost to present-day storytellers. Pretty much every Latino, adult and child, has either personally seen La Llorona, heard her cries, or knows someone who claims they have. The tale of La Llorona begins as a Cinderella story: a poor woman meets a handsome rich man who falls in love with her and takes her away from her troubles to marry her. They are very happy and have two children. Yet, their joy is short-lived; the man finds a new younger, rich woman and goes off to marry her,

La Llorona, illustrated by Drew Scott Noffsinger. Permission provided by Drew Scott Noffsinger.

leaving his first family behind and unacknowledged. Overcome by madness, the jilted wife takes her two children down to the river and drowns them. Now and forevermore, La Llorona is destined to walk along the riverside calling out for the souls of her children, *los chaneques*, *"Ay, mis hijos, Ay, mis hijos,"* deeply regretful for her actions. La Llorona is never reunited with her children, but at times *los chaneques* can be seen or heard playing with other children along the river, or so say *los ancianos*. Joe Hayes's *La Llorona/The Weeping Woman: A Hispanic Legend* is a fantastic retelling of the classic La Llorona tale. John Bierhorst has edited a book, *The Hungry Woman: Myths and Legends of the Aztecs*, that contains three additional weeping woman tales. These tales aren't illustrated; they would add to the fullness of a scary tale program, however, offering other *sabores* on the La Llorona folktale.

El Cucuy

El Cucuy is another folkloric character well known throughout Latin America. Sometimes spoken of as El Cucó, El Cucuy is equivalent to the North American boogeyman who hides in closets and under beds in order to catch children who are *malcriados* (badly behaved) and refuse to obey their parents. Parents tell their children, "You better be good or I'll call El Cucuy to come and take you away." When El Cucuy hears through his enormous ear a parent calling his name or disobedient, disrespectful voices of children, he comes for the horrible children and takes them away, deep into his mountain, never to be seen again.

Joe Hayes's *¡El Cucuy! A Bogeyman Cuento in English and Spanish* is a wonderful way to share this tale. In Hayes's tale, the two elder daughters who are taken to El Cucuy's lair are saved by a herder in the mountains and returned to their father and younger sister, who have never stopped looking for them all the time they were with El Cucuy. The two returned daughters are never disrespectful again.

El Cucuy illustrated by Drew Scott Noffsinger. Permission provided by Drew Scott Noffsinger.

La Chupacabra

La chupacabra is another classic Latino cryptozoid figure used to elicit fear and to explain that which is unexplainable. La chupacabra or the "goat sucker" is a creature that comes out when the moon is full and lives in the middle of the desert or open plains, far from established populations. La chupacabra survives by sucking the blood out of unprepared animals, including distracted humans who happen to cross their path.

The grandfather in Xavier Garza's bilingual book *Juan and the Chupacabras/Juan y el chupacabras* tells the tale of the chupacabra to his grandchildren. Luz and Juan are unsure as to whether to believe their *abuelo's* stories, so they arm themselves with different household items they believe will protect them from the chupacabra's attack. Garza, also, in his short story collection *Creepy Creatures and Other Cucuys*, tells of how Lupe and Leo's dog saves them from the attack of *"Los Chupacabras."*

The following are additional scary programming title suggestions. Note that some of these titles (followed by an *) are not pure folklore, but rather tales that incorporate folkloric themes and iconic characters. Figure 16.7 provides a programming idea and a further list of related tales.

- 🏵 Anaya, Rudolfo *Curse of the Chupacabra**
- 🏵 Belting, Natalia. "Ghosts and Souls" a poem from *The Moon Was Tired of Walking on Air: Origin Myths of South American Indians*
- 🏵 Carter, Dorothy Sharp. "The Cegua" from *The Enchanted Orchard: And Other Folktales of Central America*
- 🏵 Loya, Olga. "The Flying Skeleton/El esqueleto volador," "La Llorona," "La madrina muerte/Godmother Death," "The Rooster's Claw/La pata de gallo" from *Momentos mágicos/Magic Moments: Tales from Latin America*

La chupacabra illustrated by Drew Scott Noffsinger. Permission provided by Drew Scott Noffsinger.

PROGRAMMING IDEA — SUGAR SKULLS

Every year, Latinos celebrate the Day of the Dead or *El día de los muertos* starting October 31st and culminating November 2nd. It is believed that during this time, once a year, the deceased are able to return to the land of the living, to keep company with their loved ones and to enjoy the ordinary pleasures of life—food, smells, movements, emotions, and so forth. As a way of honoring this traditional belief, families go to tend the graves of family members. They bring food and drinks, sing songs, play instruments, and share memories. Thus, the folklore of each generation is passed on to the next, and those who have died are not forgotten.

Sugar skulls are easy to make, although they do take some time.

RECIPE

1 cup sugar

1 teaspoon meringue powder

1 teaspoon water

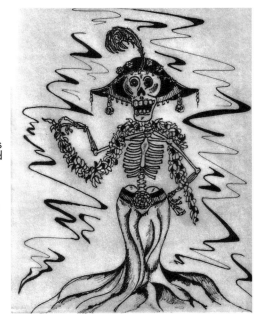

❋ Crunch ingredients in a bowl with your hands until the sugar starts to feel light and fluffy, then push mixture into molds

❋ If you have a mold that has multiple skulls on it, I would recommend doing one skull at a time rather than all the skulls at once

❋ Let sit for ten minutes in the mold

❋ Take skull out of mold by flipping it onto a piece of cardboard

❋ Let skulls harden completely on cardboard before storing them

   • NOTE: Sugar skulls have difficulty hardening when it is humid or rainy outside.

La Catrina, illustrated by Drew Scott Noffsinger.
Permission provided by Drew Scott Noffsinger.

❋ Put molds into cardboard boxes for storage

   • NOTE: Do not use plastic containers to contain molds, the skulls will fall apart

❋ Decorate skulls with frosting or as desired

The following books are additional programming suggestions. Note that some of these titles (followed by an *) are not pure folklore but incorporate folkloric themes and iconic characters.

❋ Arquette, Kerry, et al. *Day of the Dead Crafts: More than 24 Projects**

❋ Galindo, Claudia. *Do You Know the Cucuy? / ¿Conoces al Cucuy?*

❀   González, Ada Acosta. *Mayte and the Bogeyman/Mayte y el cuco*
❀   Keep, Richard. *Clatter Bash! A Day of the Dead Celebration* *
❀   Perales, Alonso M. *Brujas, lechuzas y espantos/Witches, Owls and Spooks*
❀   San Vicente, Luis. *Festival of Bones/El festival de las calaveras: The Little-Bitty Book for the Day of the Dead* *
❀   Winter, Jeanette. *Calavera Abecedario: A Day of the Dead Alphabet Book* *

FIGURE 16.7 *provides an example of a programming idea with recommended books relating to other scary tales.*

POURQUOI MYTHS / MITOS

Why does it rain? Where did our food come from? Why is there a moon in the sky? Why do certain animals only come out at night and not during the day? Why? Why? Why? Toddlers are notorious for their questions, but they are not the only ones who are curious. Asking *why* is a form of learning that was encouraged by the elders. *Pourquoi* myths or *mitos* are a genre of tale that was specifically created to answer questions, to educate, and to set minds at ease.

Alma Flor Ada's *Mediopollito/Half-Chicken*, for instance, explains how the weather vane came into existence. Lois Ehlert's *Moon Rope/Un lazo a la luna: A Peruvian Folktale* shares the Peruvian version of why moles only come out at nighttime. Ehlert's *Cuckoo/Cucú: A Mexican Folktale* tells why the cuckoo has a dry, raspy cry and cannot sing.

The following are additional programming suggestions. Note that some of these titles (followed by an *) are not pure folklore, but rather tales that incorporate folkloric themes and iconic characters. Figure 16.8 provides a programming idea and further books relating to *mitos*.

❀ Belting, Natalia. *The Moon Was Tired of Walking on Air: Origin Myths of South American Indians*

❀ Brusca, María Cristina. *When Jaguars Ate the Moon and Other Stories about Animals and Plants of the Américas*

❀ McDermott, Gerald. *Musicians of the Sun*

❀ McManus, Kay. *Land of the Five Suns: Looking at Aztec Myths and Legends*

❀ Mohr, Nicholasa. *La canción del coquí y otros cuentos de Puerto Rico / The Song of el Coquí and Other Tales of Puerto Rico*

PROGRAMMING IDEA — SALT DOUGH CREATIONS

Salt dough is used throughout Latin America to create colorful figures and decorative ornaments. Salt dough is very versatile, long-lasting, and easy to make. *Pourquoi* myths may be re-enacted or displayed through a child's salt dough creations.

RECIPE

1 cup salt

1 ¼ cup water (dissolve salt in water before adding flour)

3 cups flour

❀ Dissolve salt in water prior to adding the flour one cup at a time

❀ Mix until doughy consistency

❀ Shape as desired and let harden

❀ Bake at 200°

❀ Paint with acrylics

❀ Shellac item for protection and longevity

FIGURE 16.8 *provides a programming idea with recommended books relating to other* mitos.

ADDITIONAL PROGRAMMING IDEAS

Figure 16.9 lists supplementary programming ideas along with corresponding Latino folklore/folkloric literature. I have used the programs and books with Latino families in libraries and can attest to their success.

ADDITIONAL PROGRAMMING SUGGESTIONS FOR FOLKLORE

Become Cultural Ambassadors

❋ Learn about a different country and share

❋ Empower patrons to come and tell their own stories from their own cultures in a program such as REFORMA's Noche de Cuentos / Evening of Stories.

❋ Explore multiculturalism

Celebrate Different Latino Holidays

❋ January 1st Happy New Year / *Feliz Año Nuevo*

❋ January 6th Day of the Three Kings / *Día de los Tres Reyes*

❋ February 14th Valentine's Day / *Día de San Valintín*

❋ Holy Week / *Semana Santa and Carnaval*

❋ Easter / *Pascua*

❋ April 30th Day of the Child / Día del niño
This holiday has been adapted by Latina author Pat Mora to become El día de los niños/El día de los libros or Children's Day/Book Day

❋ October 31st–November 2nd (especially November 2nd) Day of the Dead / *Día de los muertos*

❋ December 16th–24th *Las Posadas*

❋ December 24th Christmas Eve / *La Nochebuena*

❋ December 25th Christmas / *Navidad*

Make Footprints in Plaster

❋ Alvarez, Julia. *The Secret Footsteps / Las huellas secretas*

Make a Mosaic of the Nighttime Sky/Milky Way

❋ Mora, Pat. *The Night the Moon Fell: A Maya Myth Retold / La noche que cayó la luna: mita maya*

Make a Rain Stick

❋ Belting, Natalia. "Daughter of Rain" from *The Moon Was Tired of Walking on Air: Origin Myths of South American Indians*

❋ Wisniewski, David. *Rain Player*

Make Tortillas

❋ Anaya, Rudolfo. *The First Tortilla: A Bilingual Story*

❋ Griego, Margot. *Tortillitas para Mamá and Other Nursery Rhymes*

❋ Hayes, Joe. *The Day It Snowed Tortillas / El día que nevo tortillas*

Make a Volcano

❋ Arguenta, Mario. *Magic Dogs of the Volcanoes / Los perros mágicos de los volcanes*

Plant Seedlings

❋ Polette, Keith. *Paco and the Giant Chile Plant / Paco y la planta de chile gigante*

❋ VanLaan, Nancy. *The Magic Bean Tree: A Legend from Argentina*

FIGURE 16.9. *Suggestions for incorporating folklore into everyday library programming.*

FINALLY, AN ENCOURAGEMENT

As children's, teen, and school librarians, it is our responsibility to incorporate multiculturalism into our programming. Folktales are an ideal tool to promote cultural awareness, diversity, normalization, and compassion. It is through these stories that we learn about people: who they are, what they are, where they come from, when they lived, why they believe what they do, and how they are as they are. As librarians, we are able to engage families through sharing folktales by way of written tales and oral storytelling, thereby forming a healthy, accepting community within the borders of the library—a community that may positively alter a child's life forever.

REFERENCES

American Library Association (ALA), "Día de los Niños," http://www.ala.org/ala/mgrps/divs/alsc/initiatives/diadelosninos/index.cfm (cited December 20, 2009).

American Library Association (ALA)/Association for Library Services to Children (ALSC), "The Pura Belpré Award," http://www.ala.org/ala/mgrps/divs/alsc/awardsgrants/bookmedia/belpremedal/belpreabout/index.cfm (cited December 20, 2009).

Chappell, Sharon, and Christian Faltis. "Spanglish, Bilingualism, Culture, and Identity in Latino Children's Literature." *Children's Literature in Education* 38, no. 4 (December 2007): 253–262.

Dendle, Peter. "Cryptozoology in the Medieval and Modern Worlds." *Folklore* 117, no. 2 (August 2006): 190–206.

Fritz, Gregory K. "Children and Adults Need Family Traditions." *Brown University Child & Adolescent Behavior Letter* 20, no. 1 (January 2004): 8.

Fry, Richard. "Latino Children: A Majority Are U.S.-Born Offspring of Immigrants." Pew Hispanic Center, 2009. http://pewhispanic.org/files/reports/110.pdf (cited December 20, 2009).

Hamer, Lynne. "Folklore in Schools and Multicultural Education." *Journal of American Folklore* 113, no. 447 (Winter 2000): 44.

Hearne, Betsy. "The Bones of Story." *Horn Book Magazine* 81, no. 1 (January 2005): 39–47.

———. "Cite the Source." *School Library Journal* 39, no. 7 (July 1993): 22–27.

———. "Introduction." *Library Trends* 47, no. 3 (Winter 1999): 341–345.

————. "Nobody Knows . . . " *Horn Book Magazine* 85, no. 5 (September 2009): 457–462.

————. "Once There Was and Will Be: Storytelling the Future." *Horn Book Magazine* 76, no. 6 (November/December 2000): 712–719.

————. "Respect the Source." *School Library Journal* 39, no. 8 (August 1993): 33–37.

————. "Swapping Tales and Stealing Stories: The Ethics and Aesthetics of Folklore in Children's Literature." *Library Trends* 47, no. 3 (Winter 1999): 509–528.

Isom, Bess A., and Carolyn P. Casteel. "Hispanic Literature: A Fiesta for Literacy Instruction." *Childhood Education* 74, no. 2 (1997): 83–89.

MW-Milwaukee: Center for Latin American and Caribbean Studies, "Américas Book Award for Children's and Young Adult Literature," http://www4.uwm.edu/clacs/aa/index.cfm (cited December 20, 2009).

Northrup, Jason C., and Roy A. Bean. "Culturally Competent Family Therapy with Latino/Anglo-American Adolescents: Facilitating Identity Formation." *American Journal of Family Therapy* 35, no. 3 (May 2007): 251–263.

Norton, Donna E. *Multicultural Children's Literature: Through the Eyes of Many Children*, 3rd ed. New Jersey: Merrill Prentice Hall, 2008.

Oring, Elliott. "Folklore and Advocacy." *Journal of Folklore Research* 41, no. 2/3 (May 2004): 259–267.

Pedersen, E. Martin. "Folklore in ESL/EFL." *Curriculum Materials*. Paper presented at Annual Meeting of the Teachers of English to Speakers of Other Languages (1993): 1–10.

Raffaelli, Marcela, Gustavo Carlo, Miguel A. Carranza, and Gloria E. Gonzales-Kruger. "Understanding Latino Children and Adolescents in the Mainstream: Placing Culture at the Center of Developmental Models." *New Directions for Child and Adolescent Development* 2005, no. 109 (Fall 2005): 23–32.

Smolen, Lynn Atkinson, and Victoria Ortiz-Castro. "Dissolving Borders and Broadening Perspectives Through Latino Traditional Literature." *Reading Teacher* 53, no. 7 (April 2000): 566–578.

Strong, Mary. "Powers Within: Artists and Anthropologists Work Together to Create Andean Mythic Beasts and Elements of Nature in Their Own Image." *Visual Anthropology* 16, no. 2/3 (April 2003): 117–158.

U.S. Census Bureau. "Population Estimates: National Sex, Age, Race, and Hispanic Origin: 2008," http://www.census.gov/popest/national/asrh/NC-EST2008-asrh.html (cited December 20, 2009).

Zuñiga, Maria E. "Using Metaphors in Therapy: *Dichos* and Latino Clients." *Social Work* 37, no. 1 (January 1992): 55–60.

❀ CHAPTER 17

Using Print and Digital Latino Children's Books to Promote Multiple Literacies in Classrooms and Libraries

Jamie Campbell Naidoo

"In a few weeks, they'll be back," Abuelote broke the silence. It took me a second to realize what he was talking about. "We wait and wait," Abuelota agreed. "And our hearts are not complete till we see those *golondrinas* coming back, filling the sky." "As numerous as stars," Abuelito observed. I knew then how much my grandparents had missed us, how a part of their very own hearts had been missing until now. How we were the ones they had been waiting for. We all grew quiet again, looking up, feeling the specialness of this night before we would fly apart (Alvarez 2009, p. 318).

As he concludes the final lines of Julia Alvarez's *Return to Sender*, an unnatural hush falls upon Frank's sixth-grade classroom. His students are left momentarily speechless by this contentious novel that grapples with illegal immigration, patriotism, and the human condition. After a moment, Kaylee blurts out, "It's not fair! Mari and her family should be able to stay in the U.S." Her comment is instantly followed by Blake's, "Yes it is! They have to come to the U.S. legally like everyone else. That is the price they have to pay!" Jorge, who has expressed a keen interest in the book's subject, remarks, "It's not that simple. Didn't you listen as Mr. Frank read the story to us? There is so much to think about. Being a Mexican in the U.S. is not easy." Picking up on Jorge's cue, Frank suggests that the class take a trip to the school library to research more about U.S. immigration laws, migrant farming, "Operation Return to Sender," and Latinos in the United States. He divides the class into two teams that represent the opposing viewpoints on the issue of illegal immigration and asks that each team research information that will allow them to construct arguments for and against the deportation of immigrant families that have members with both legal and illegal citizenship status. He has already collaborated with the school librarian to locate a list of useful Web resources relating to all of these topics. The students will be using information from the U.S. Department of Homeland Security as well as a list of immigration and other resources available on Julia Alvarez's *Return to Sender: Further Research* Web page (Alvarez 2010). Frank and the school librarian have also created a Webquest on "U.S. Immigration Concerns and Migrant Farmers" to guide students' online learning as they watch archival video footage of speeches, research selected Web sites, and listen to oral histories from the children of migrant farmers. In addition to working with electronic resources such as San Diego's Media Arts Center's Digital Story Station (http://digitalstorystation.com/), which houses many personal stories from immigrants and Latinos, students will also locate both fiction and nonfiction books relating to migrant farm workers, the National Farm Workers Association, Dolores Huerta, César Chávez, illegal immigration, and immigration legislation in the United States. Frank's students will use these books along with Francisco Jiménez's award-winning novel *The Circuit* and Michelle Mulder's international book *After Peaches* to construct additional background information that will assist them as they develop a Web site that provides opposing viewpoints on the issues that they have been researching. This Web site will also include digital storytelling and book trailers where they booktalk their fiction and nonfiction resources and explain the information they have found in their research.

LATINO CHILDREN'S LITERATURE NURTURING NEW LITERACIES

The preceding lesson is a perfect example of incorporating multimodal learning with Latino children's literature to facilitate intercultural understanding while also engaging multiple new literacies. The children in Frank's class are engaged in visual, auditory, and hand-on activities that require competency in multiple 21st-century literacies such as information literacy, media literacy, Web literacy, visual literacy, and cultural literacy. They are learning how to navigate *new literacies*[1] such as locating, evaluating, synthesizing, and recre-

---

1   The terms *new literacies*, *multiliteracies*, and *multiple literacies* are used interchangeably throughout this chapter depending on the field of research being referenced. All three of these terms indicate multiple literacies that go beyond traditional reading and writing literacies to include informational, Web, cultural,

ating information in order to understand a highly relevant, contentious issue. At the same time, the majority of these students (81 percent non-Latino U.S. citizens) are reaching beyond the scope of their cultural experiences in Atlanta, Georgia, to learn about historical and recent events relating to migrant farming and U.S. immigration. Frank has specifically chosen a Latino novel (*Return to Sender*), which has won awards for Latino children's literature including the Pura Belpré and the Américas, because he knows it will spark discussion. He has also provided students with copies of an international novel (*After Peaches*) that highlights political refugees from Mexico and their lives as immigrants in Canada; this book will provide an entirely different perspective on Mexican immigration in an entirely different context. His choice of *The Circuit* is also purposeful in providing yet another angle on immigration and migrant farming. These three books, along with the Internet resources and students' self-selected texts, provide a rich learning environment for examining the intersections of race, class, culture, patriotism, and immigration in two diverse countries. Student-generated knowledge from these resources can be applied to U.S. history to better understand the complexities of immigration. In turn, students may research their own family history to determine how their ancestors arrived in the United States.

LATINO CHILDREN'S LITERATURE: FOSTERING MULTICULTURAL LITERACY AND INTERCULTURAL CONNECTIONS

Educators, teachers, and librarians serving in today's classrooms are charged with creating a forum for facilitating understanding and acceptance of student differences based upon culture, ethnicity, linguistic ability, religion, physical ability, immigration status, and sexual orientation. If schools are to become bridges between academic learning, students' home cultures, and world cultures (Moore-Hart, Diamond, and Knapp 2003), then intercultural connections must be forged. An excellent way to build these cultural bridges between home, school, and the world is to integrate culturally authentic, contemporary Latino children's literature into the classroom to promote *multicultural literacy* of the Latino cultures. According to Diamond and Moore (1995), multicultural literacy (1) links home and school cultures to promote traditional literacy, (2) activates silenced voices while opening closed minds,

---

media, and other literacies needed to function in today's high-tech, culturally pluralistic society.

(3) promotes academic achievement, and (4) empowers students' thinking and abilities to function in a culturally pluralistic society.

Research indicates that it is important for Latino children to encounter accurate and positive representations of diverse cultures in the books they read (Fox and Short 2003; Harris 1993; Rogers and Soter 1997). For children from Latino backgrounds, positive images of their culture in children's literature increase their self-esteem, assist with their ethnic identity development, provide positive role-models, and support richer connections with the text. For non-Latino children, authentic and accurate literature about "other" cultures fosters acceptance of diversity, challenges stereotypes, and encourages stronger relationships with Latino classmates. Such encounters help students to become multiculturally literate.

Moore-Hart, Diamond, and Knapp (2003) urge educators to incorporate multicultural literature into the daily learning experiences of all students in all areas of the curriculum rather than adopting an ad hoc approach. More than 20 years ago, Derman-Sparks and the A.B.C. Task Force (1989) found that by preschool age, young children exhibit stereotypes and negative behaviors toward those who are perceived as being different or "other." These attitudes are learned from many different sources: parents, the media, and peers, to name a few. Fortunately, children can learn to develop favorable attitudes toward those perceived as the "other" when they are introduced to authentic, high-quality literature about diverse cultures through an *anti-bias curriculum*. This type of curriculum is similar to a multicultural curriculum except that it avoids the "tourist approach" to learning about diverse cultures that is common in many culturally oriented lesson plans. A *tourist curriculum* highlights the food, clothing, and celebrations of a culture rather than exploring the daily interactions of people within that culture. The result is a curriculum that is both patronizing and trivializing. "Children 'visit' non-white cultures and then 'go home' to the daily classroom, which reflects only the dominant culture" (Derman-Sparks and the A.B.C. Task Force, 1989, p. 7).

Going one step further, Cotton (2007) proposes that teachers and librarians promote intercultural connections in the education curriculum. These connections extend beyond multicultural literacy by "inviting comparisons, exchanges, and cooperation between groups" and incorporating "aspects of identity and disability, in addition to the values of tolerance, respect, and celebration of racial and ethnic differences highlighted within multiculturalism" (pp. 77–78). Teachers and librarians, who encourage intercultural connections, strive for an anti-bias curriculum that uses multicultural and international children's literature to foster multicultural literacy while providing a forum for examining issues of class, race, and culture. The vignette at the beginning of this chapter is a perfect example of such a curriculum promoting intercultural understanding and fostering multicultural literacy.

BEYOND TRADITIONAL BOOKS: MULTIMODAL TEXTS, READER RESPONSE, TEXTUAL GAPS

Culturally responsive teachers, librarians, and other educators who are attuned to the needs of their students have been using multicultural and international children's literature in the classroom and educational curriculum for years. The concept of multicultural literacy is familiar to them, as is the use of traditional (print) materials to promote understanding of other cultures. However, with each passing year, more children's books are published that exemplify "radical change" by defying tradition and using multiple modes for communicating meaning such as nonlinear organization and format, moving images, hypertext, and sound (Dresang 1999; Unsworth, Thomas, Simpson, and Asha 2005). These *multimodal texts* hold multiple layers of meaning and often possess a digital design—"the presentation of pictures and text in a juxtaposition that requires, or at least promotes, a hypertextual approach to thinking and reading" (Dresang 1999, p. 105). One of my students, interacting with multimodal informational books, summarized Dresang's sentiments when he exclaimed, "It's almost like the books are designed as Web pages without the long blocks of text" (personal communication). Indeed, multimodal texts embody both print and electronic forms, encompassing books exhibiting "radical change," magazines and newspapers, graphic novels, film and video, computer and video games, Internet sites, and digital books (Walsh 2005).[2]

The concepts for understanding the cultural meanings children glean from both print and electronic multimodal texts are best understood through a lens that combines ideas of visual literacy, reader response theory, textual gaps, and Vygotsky's sociocultural theory. The interconnectedness of these theories explains how children's past and present visual experiences work with incoming knowledge to create basic meaning and understanding of concepts described in the text and/or illustrations in a piece of literature (Arizpe and Styles 2003; Nodelman 1990; Sinatra 1986). In the context of interactions with the illustrations in Latino children's picture books, the concept of visual

---

2   For additional information on radical change and how it applies to culturally specific books, consult Dresang (2000).

literacy suggests that children use their past and present experiences, and images of Latinos in the media and throughout society, to develop an understanding of how society views that particular culture. Roethler (1998) indicates that children develop their schemata of social norms through their encounters with picture books; negative picturebook images of cultures can stay with children for their entire lives.

In most picture books, gaps exist between the information provided in the verbal text and the information provided in the illustration (Barthes 1974; Nikolajeva and Scott 2001; Sipe 2008). These gaps are "filled in" by the reader using past experiences and cultural influences. Therefore, if a child has a preexisting negative schemata relating to Latinos, then he/she will inadvertently rely upon it when filling in these gaps (García 2003). This can result in the reinforcement of cultural bias by non-Latino children and the development of negative ethnic identity by Latino children.

Many of the same skills used by children to interpret the text and illustrations of a traditional picture book are necessary for interpreting the images and text on screen. Walsh (2005) suggests that the past experiences of the reader as well as the social purpose of the text influence the meaning that is taken from both print-based and multimodal texts. She notes, "The way we interpret any new text, whether words or images, will then produce new interpretations, new responses, and new meanings. We go through . . . an interactive process as we read words or look at images, negotiate electronic screens and hyperlinks" (p. 9).

As previously mentioned, books that exhibit characteristics of Dresang's "radical change" hold multiple layers of meaning and often possess a digital design that helps prepare students to work in virtual environments and function in a digital world. An example of a Latino children's book that exhibits qualities of radical change is Mora and López's *Yum! ¡MmMm! ¡Qué rico! Americas' Sproutings*. Children are exposed to multiple layers of meaning, throughout the text and illustrations of this vibrant picture book, as they engage with two non-linear printed texts and multiple visual images. On the left-hand side (verso) of each two-page spread, an informational text describes the origins of foods throughout North, Central, and South America. The right-hand side (recto) of the double-page spread provides haikus celebrating the sensations that various foods induce. Children can read the informational text only, the haikus only, or both. Their choice will influence the meaning that they glean from the text. Through the informational texts, non-Latino children will make intercultural connections as they realize that many of the foods they enjoy originate from cultures throughout Latin America. Children reading only the haikus will encounter onomatopoeias and alliteration that will appeal to their senses as they are invited to "taste" various foods. Read collectively, the informational text and haikus provide cultural facts as well as energetic odes that encourage children to play with language.

Created by Rafael López, the bold and blazing illustrations in the picture book virtually leap from the page, creating a visual fiesta. Vibrantly painted images, overflowing with magical realism, provide a sensory *celebración* that allows children to almost taste the foods, feel the heat of the sun, and hear the cranberries popping. The illustrations are suffused with hues and symbols relating to Latino cultures and contain references to various art forms including Mexican folk art, naïve art, and surrealism. Children examining the illustrations can gain cultural insights not mentioned in the text.

The non-linear, dual texts in *Yum! ¡MmMm! ¡Qué rico! Americas' Sproutings* help prepare children to read the non-linear texts such as menus, pop-up windows, and hypertexts found on Web sites. The multiple layers of meaning found in the text and illustrations prepare children to navigate through the textual and visual messages they will encounter simultaneously while using social media and other Web resources. The cultural elements of the book encourage non-Latino children to make intercultural connections between their culture and their experiences with the cultures and experiences represented. At the same time, the particular cultural elements will resonate with Latino children who see their cultural experiences being mirrored in the text and illustrations. The next section extends the ideas of radical change in children's literature to include new literacies that are mediated by various technologies. It is through the concept of mediated technologies that we can better understand how Latino children's literature securely fits into new literacies classrooms.

LATINO CHILDREN'S LITERATURE, NEW LITERACIES, AND MEDIATED TECHNOLOGIES

New mediated technologies are continuously changing the types of learning activities in contemporary classrooms and libraries, resulting in the need for new literacies to assist in the navigation of multimodal texts. The International Reading Association (2001) and the New London Group (1996) urge educators to reach beyond traditional classroom literacies such as reading and writing and embrace new literacies that will allow students to crucially evaluate and use technology. A growing body of research is available that enumerates the many ways in which children's literature can be used with technology to support the curriculum and encourage new literacies (Castek et al. 2006; Coiro et al. 2008; Cummins et al. 2007; Eagleton and Dobler 2007; Leu et al. 2004).

This topic is also prominently featured in the "Exploring Literacy on the Internet" and "New Literacies in Action" columns of the practitioners' journal *Reading Teacher*. Many of these articles are available for free on the International Reading Association's Reading Online Web site (www.readingonline.org). Another resource of particular interest to educators is the Multiliteracy Project (http://www.multiliteracies.ca/), which describes actual projects initiated in schools throughout Canada to promote new literacies in the classroom.

There are several ways for educators to incorporate new literacies and intercultural understanding into classrooms and library programs interested in supporting cultural literacy of Latinos. These include: (1) moving fluidly in a two-way process between traditional and online multimodal texts that represent Latino themes; (2) utilizing WebQuests to learn additional information about Latino cultures; (3) engaging in social networking, blogging, and online collaborative projects; (4) creating Web sites devoted to intercultural understanding through Latino children's literature; and (5) exploring digital books about/by Latinos. Each of these strategies will be highlighted in the following sections.

Moving Fluidly from Traditional and Online Multimodal Texts Representing Latino Themes

High-quality Latino children's literature can be a catalyst for new learning with new technologies. Children use children's books about/by Latinos to access background information about a specific Latino cultural group and then navigate to the Internet to further research the culture, watch video clips, chat with students in different regions, and so forth. Using the new knowledge and schemata created through these interactions, children then go back to traditional, print Latino literature to develop an even better understanding of the specific culture being explored. The interaction between traditional print texts and online multimodal texts becomes a two-way process whereby children use newly created meaning from one source to gain a richer comprehension of the information in the other source. Children can then use this new information to create their own online multimodal texts—digital stories, book trailers, Web sites, blogs, and Wikipedia entries for example—that become part of the collective knowledge of the classroom or library.

In addition to the lesson on immigration and migrant farming that opened this chapter, an example of the two-way process between traditional print texts and online multimodal texts can be found in using Yuyi Morales's *Just in Case: A Trickster Tale and Spanish Alphabet Book.* In this picture book, readers are introduced to many elements of the Mexican cultures via simple text and vibrant images bursting with magical realism. Through the charming story of Señor Calavera's search for the perfect gift for Grandma Beetle's birthday, children encounter many Spanish words whose meaning can be deciphered using contextual and visual clues. However, it is the glowing illustrations that ultimately lead readers of this book to online multimodal resources and engage them in new literacies. From the first to the last endpaper, Morales's illustrations include layers of meaning imbued with cultural content and literary allusions. Many of the images in the Mexican *Lotería* cards on the endpapers are hidden within the pages of Morales's humorous tale. The title page invites readers to Grandma Beetle's birthday *celebracíon* and includes a picture of Grandma and Señor Calavera from Morales's previous book, *Just a Minute.* On the first two-page spread, Señor Calavera (who represents death) is ironing while Chilean author Babriel García Márquez's book *Cien Años de Soledad (100 Years of Solitude)* rests under his hat on the stool, which is quite appropriate for someone who spends his days (and years) alone. Another spread depicts the skeleton, Zelmiro (the ghost of Grandfather), and a jaguar pouring over a comic book version of Morales's *Just a Minute.* The endpages at the back of the book depict a *Lotería* card that reads "El Libro" and includes the cover of another one of Morales's books, *Little Night.* Other cultural objects are depicted in the illustrations— such as the Mexican wrestling card, Quinceañera doll, and Señor Calavera's skull, which is a candy skull created for *El día de los muertos* celebrations. When children first read this book, they may not notice all of these little details if they are unfamiliar with Mexican culture. But, with guidance from an astute teacher or librarian, children can be directed to the Internet to gain background information on these objects/symbols, and then return to the book to develop a richer understanding.

At this point, they can return to the Internet to create their own multimodal texts such as Wikipedia articles or blog posts on Señor Calavera, the Day of the Dead, or Yuyi Morales. They can go to the illustrator's Web page (http://www.srcalavera.com/) and print Señor Calavera masks or stick puppets. Children can use the masks/puppets to dramatize portions of the text, incorporating supplemental information about the historical/cultural allusions. This performance could be recorded on video and uploaded on YouTube (http://www.youtube.com/), StoryTubes (http://www.storytubes.info/drupal/), or TeacherTube (http://www.teachertube.com/) to share with other children around the world. Students might also view Morales's online Webstreams that describe the origins of Señor Calavera and depict the skeleton attending various *celebracions*. Students can even download and create their very own *Lotería* cards with images from *Just in Case* or with various Mexican cultural symbols. Librarians and teachers could enrich this study by including additional information on *Lotería* or sharing Latino children's books that feature the game, such as Contreras and Lindmark's *Braids/Trencitas*, Laínez and Arena's *Playing Lotería/El juego de la lotería*, and *The King of Things/El rey de las cosas* by Rodriguez.

Through these activities, children have an opportunity to experience the two-way flow between traditional and multimodal texts and to make intercultural connections between their own culture and that of the Mexican culture represented by the myriad cultural references. Simultaneously, the children are engaging their knowledge of new literacies—such as visual literacy to understand the cultural allusions, Web literacy to navigate the Internet, informational literacy to determine acceptable sources of information, cultural literacy to understand the significance of the allusions to Mexican culture, and general technology literacy to create a Wikipedia article or blog or to record and upload a video to YouTube, StoryTubes, or TeacherTube.

WebQuests

Educators can also create literature-based WebQuests to facilitate multicultural literacy and intercultural connections via multimodal and traditional print Latino children's literature. WebQuests are inquiry-based approaches that offer rich, mediated environments for solving problems and processing information. Using this strategy encourages collaboration among the students as they use the Internet to answer questions and explore settings, topics, and plots highlighted in classroom texts (teacher-assigned Latino children's books). If a teacher were to create a WebQuest to go along with a novel such as Calcines's *Leaving Glorytown: One Boy's Struggle Under Castro*, she could create higher-order thinking questions relating to the book's setting (Cuba), topic (growing up under the Castro regime/ political refugees), and plot (trying to escape the harsh living conditions created by a communistic government). Either while reading the novel or after finishing it, students could use a teacher-generated WebQuest to learn more, using new literacies and developing their intercultural understanding of Cubans under Castro's regime. An excellent resource for locating examples of WebQuests is Annette Lamb's "Literature-based WebQuests" (http://eduscapes.com/ladders/themes/webquests.htm).

A wonderful example of using WebQuests in the school library can be found in a primary school in Birmingham, Alabama, where the librarian had students in first and fifth grades collaborating together to learn more about *El día de los muertos* (The Day of the Dead). To prepare the students for the expansive Day of the Dead festival that would be held in the city, Matt shared Morales's children's picture book *Just a Minute: A Trickster Tale and Counting Book* with his first-grade students and Canales's *The Tequila Worm* with his fifth-grade students. He then had the students work collaboratively together at the end of the week to finish a Day of the Dead WebQuest (http://its.guilford.k12.nc.us/webquests/dayofdead/dodead.htm). Through this collaboration, the fifth-grade students were able to share their Web navigational and informational literacy skills with the first-grade students, allowing the younger counterparts to evaluate information about the celebration that they might not find on their own. At the same time, both groups of students were able to learn more about the holiday while making deeper connections with the Mexican cultures represented in the books they read.

Online Collaborative Projects and Social Networking

U.S. students can work with children from Latin American countries to better understand each others' culture and create intercultural connections. One way to accomplish this is to have children publish their own stories, poems, and letters in sources such as the international multicultural magazine *Skipping Stones* (http://www.skippingstones.org/), which highlights children's letters and other writing from around the world. Students could respond to the writing of students from other countries with their own letters, poems, and stories. The only drawback to this idea is that there would be quite a time lapse between the responses. To receive instant feedback from other students, children can (1) use Web sites such as Kidscribe (http://www.brightinvisiblegreen.com/kidscribe/) and Bookhooks http://www.bookhooks.com/note.cfm) where students write their own books about their cultures, (2) interact in social networking environments via wikis and blogs, or (3) utilize traditional online communication sources such as email or chat.

Blogs that allow children and young adults to respond to the various issues of class, race, culture, and patriotism raised by Latino children's literature are easy to create using the many free blogging sites available on the Web. Teachers and librarians can create a blog space for their students and then have students write reviews of Latino books or blog their reactions to an assigned discussion book. The option is also available for students from around the world to comment on the posts, and a forum for dialog on the books can be constructed.

The Web site ePals (http://www.epals.com/) also provides ways for educators and students to connect with other classrooms around the world to discuss various world topics. Latino children's books such as Omar Castañeda's *Among the Volcanoes* open up new windows concerning the lives of children and teens in Guatemala. After reading the book, researching the location of Guatemala, and gathering other information about the country, U.S. children are better positioned to use ePals to contact students from schools in Guatemala to learn more about their daily experiences. Students could initiate inquiry projects to benefit children in Guatemala as well.

Creating Latino-Themed Web Sites

Another example of how students can use Latino children's literature and online multimodal texts that promote understanding of diversity and intercultural understandings is the Web site "Breaking Down Walls." Fourth- and fifth-grade students in Wisconsin created this Web site in the ThinkQuest library (http://library.thinkquest.org/CR0212302/index.html), which describes the importance of learning about and accepting cultures that are different from one's own. The Web site includes an example of using children's literature to learn about diversity, and contains a PowerPoint presentation relating to acceptance. To create something similar relating to Latino cultures or themes, U.S. students would begin by reading international or multicultural literature about a specific Latino culture, navigate online to learn more about the culture and to connect with U.S. Latino or Latin American students from that culture, and then create a Web site that provides opportunities for other students to learn about cultural acceptance and issues faced by Latinos from the highlighted culture. The interaction with students from other cultures helps to foster U.S. students' sense of intercultural understanding. Creating the Web site requires higher order thinking skills and also leaves a lasting resource that can be updated as children learn more about the culture.

Exploring Digital Books About and By Latinos

Exploring digital books, particularly digital picture books about the Latino cultures, is an excellent way to integrate Latino children's literature into the new literacies classroom to cultivate intercultural understanding. Castek et al. (2006) assert that digital picture books "build students' understanding of story structures [traditional literacies] and introduce new opportunities to develop online navigational skills [new literacies]" (p. 717). By using digital picture books, teachers and librarians are able to easily supplement their physical book collection with U.S. and international titles about Latinos that might not be readily available in a print format.

Numerous profit and nonprofit resources are available and contain a varying range of digital books about the Latino cultures. Some of the more notable ones that offer Latino titles are TumbleBooks, International Children's Digital Library, and Scholastic BookFlix. Each of these sources contains digital books that can facilitate intercultural understanding and incorporate new literacies.

One subscription service for animated, digital picture books that include sound and music is TumbleBooks (http://www.tumblebooks.com/). Three of their books about Latino cultures are Elya and Salerno's *Bebé Goes Shopping*, Smith and Jones's *The Best Mariachi in the World*, and Ada and Savadier's *I Love Saturdays y Domingos*. Children interacting with these digital picture books use Web literacies to navigate through the books and have the option of selecting English, Spanish, or French as the language of the story. This allows the books to be navigated by students who are English-language learners.

Another subscription, digital book service is Scholastic BookFlix (http://teacher.scholastic.com/products/bookflixfreetrial/index.htm), which pairs fiction picture books with nonfiction or informational books on a similar topic. Much like TumbleBooks, these digital books include sound and animation. However, whereas TumbleBooks include minimal animation and sound, the digital books from BookFlix are actually Webstreams of Scholastic's Weston Woods book videos and deviate to a certain extent from the original title. Examples of Latino-themed digital books from BookFlix are Soto and Guevara's *Chato's Kitchen* and *Too Many Tamales* by Soto and Martinez. An excellent, free resource including U.S. and international picture books that feature Latino themes and cultures is the International Children's Digital Library (http://www.icdlbooks.org/). Books from all around the world, representing many different cultures and written in several different languages, are included on this Web site. While animation and sound are lacking, this resource does allow classroom teachers and librarians to supplement their collection of international books. Children using this site have the opportunity to use Web, cultural, informational, visual, and traditional literacies as they navigate the collections of books, selecting a topic, language, type of book, and so forth. Two examples of Latino-themed books in this vast online collection are Carling's *Mama and Papa Have a Store*, an American book that represents several cultures in Guatemala, and Lihón's *Los Cuatro Hermanos Ayar*, a Peruvian book describing an origin myth of Tahuantinsuyo.

SPECIFIC EXAMPLES OF SUCCESSFUL CHILDREN'S LITERATURE AND NEW LITERACIES PROJECTS

Educators are often more inclined to adopt new ideas and teaching strategies when they observe successful examples. There are many resources available for locating successful projects that integrate children's literature with new literacies and technology. The "New Literacies" Web site (http://ctell.uconn.edu/cases/newliteracies.htm), part of a collaborative research project entitled Case Technologies to Enhance Literacy Learning, provides a plethora of examples of teachers successfully integrating children's literature with new literacies. Included on the Web site are professional articles, lesson plans, and Webstreams. Latino children's literature is not specifically mentioned in all of the examples, but the concepts and strategies can be applied toward lessons integrating Latino children's books into the curriculum.

Katz and Rimon (2006) describe another example of a research project that included multimodal learning using children's literature and new literacies to connect globally with other children. In this project, the researchers had their students read a particular translated book from a country and culture different from their own. The students then interacted online with other students from the country, comparing and contrasting their responses to the book and discussing how the translation changed the meaning of the book. Students also explored differences in culture and created intercultural connections. Although the project did not use Latino children's literature, many of the ideas and concepts can be applied to using multimodal learning to help children learn about the Latino cultures.

CONCLUDING REMARKS

It has been reiterated throughout this book that literature can provide windows into a different cross-culture or mirror a child's own culture. Books illuminate the social, political, and cultural mores that underlie our world. It is through the illustrations and texts of books that children encounter these messages and discern the dominant culture's views of Latinos. The potency of the visual image and its effects on a child's construction of reality can assist or prevent a Latino child's ethnic identity development. The creators of Latino children's literature are purveyors of cultural heritage and it is through these cultural moderators that Latino children learn to value and respect their own culture and that non-Latino children learn to make intercultural connections with the cultures of their classmates, community members, and the world around them.

Connecting Latino children's literature with new literacies and technology empowers educators to explore issues of class, race, culture, and patriotism with their students. At the same time, mediated learning environments that incorporate new literacies and technology encourage even the most reluctant child and reader to engage in educational activities and instruction. Adding Latino children's books to a mediated environment encourages all children from all cultural backgrounds to learn more about the fastest-growing minority in U.S. classrooms and libraries, and celebrate its rich cultural cuentos and traditions.

REFERENCES

Alvarez, Julia. *Return to Sender.* New York: Random House, 2009.

———. "Return to Sender: Further Research." http://return-to-sender.juliaalvarez.com/research-links.php (accessed February 19, 2010).

Arizpe, Evelyn, and Morag Styles. *Children Reading Pictures: Interpreting Visual Texts.* New York: Routledge, 2003.

Barthes, Roland. *S/Z.* Translated by Richard Miller. New York: Farrar, Straus and Giroux, 1974.

Castek, Jill, Jessica Bevans-Mangelson, and Bette Goldstone. "Reading Adventures Online: Five Ways to Introduce the New Literacies of the Internet Through Children's Literature." *Reading Teacher* 59, no. 7 (2006): 714–728.

Coiro, Julie, Michele Knobel, Colin Lankshear, and Donald Leu, Jr., eds. *Handbook of Research on New Literacies.* Mahwah, NJ: Lawrence Erlbaum Associates, 2008.

Cotton, Penni. "Intercultural Approaches to Using Children's Literature Websites." *New Review of Children's Literature and Librarianship* 13, no. 1 (2007): 77–100.

Cummins, Jim, Kristin Brown, and Dennis Sayers. *Literacy, Technology, and Diversity: Teaching for Success in Changing Times.* Boston: Allyn & Bacon, 2007.

Derman-Sparks, L., and the A.B.C. Task Force. *Anti-Bias Curriculum: Tools for Empowering Young Children.* Washington, DC: NAEYC, 1989.

Diamond, Barbara, and Margaret Moore. *Multicultural Literacy: Mirroring the Reality of the Classroom.* White Plains, NY: Longman, 1995.

Dresang, Eliza T. "Outstanding Literature: Pura Belpré and Américas Selections with Special Appeal in the Digital Age." In *Library Services to Youth of Hispanic*

Heritage, ed. by Barbara Immroth and Kathleen de la Peña McCook, pp. 69–87. Jefferson, NC: McFarland & Company, Inc., 2000.

———. *Radical Change: Books for Youth in a Digital Age*. New York: H. W. Wilson, 1999.

Eagleton, Maya, and Elizabeth Dobler. *Reading the Web: Strategies for Internet Inquiry*. New York: Guilford, 2007.

Fox, Dana L., and Kathy G. Short, eds. *Stories Matter: The Complexity of Cultural Authenticity in Children's Literature*. Urbana, IL: National Council of Teachers of English, 2003.

García, Georgia. "Giving Voice to Multicultural Literacy Research and Practice." In *Multicultural Issues in Literacy Research and Practice*, ed. by Arlette Willis, Georgia García, Rosalinda Barrera, and V. J. Harris, pp. 1–9. Mahwah, NJ: Lawrence Erlbaum Associates, 2003.

Harris, Violet. J., ed. *Teaching Multicultural Literature in Grades K–8*. Norwood, MA: Christopher-Gordon Publishers, 1993.

International Reading Association. "Integrating Literacy and Technology into the Curriculum, 2001" http://www.reading.org/resources/issues/positions_technology.html (cited February 2, 2008).

Katz, Yaacov, and Ofer Rimon. "The Study of Literature and Culture in a Web-Based Environment." *Educational Media International* 43, no. 1 (2006): 29–41.

Leu, Donald, Jr., Jill Castek, Laurie Henry, Julie Coiro, and Melissa McMullan. "The Lessons That Children Teach Us: Integrating Children's Literature and the New Literacies of the Internet." *Reading Teacher* 57, no. 5 (2004): 496–503.

Moore-Hart, Margaret, Barbara Diamond, and John Knapp. "The Implementation of a Multicultural Literacy Program in Fourth- and Fifth-Grade Classrooms." In *Multicultural Issues in Literacy Research and Practice*, ed. by Arlette Willis, Georgia García, and Rosalinda Barrera, pp. 223–261. Mahwah, NJ: Lawrence Erlbaum Associates, 2003.

New London Group. "A Pedagogy of Muliliteracies: Designing Social Futures 1, 1996." http://wwwstatic.kern.org/filer/blogWrite44ManilaWebsite/paul/articles/A_Pedagogy_of_Multiliteracies_Designing_Social_Futures.htm#11 (cited February 1, 2008).

Nikolajeva, Maria, and Carole Scott. *How Picturebooks Work*. New York: Garland, 2001.

Nodelman, Perry. *Words About Pictures: The Narrative Art of Children's Picture Books*. Athens: University of Georgia Press, 1990.

Roethler, Jacque. "Reading in Color: Children's Book Illustrations and Identity Formation for Black Children in the United States." *African American Review* 32, no. 1 (1998): 95–105.

Rogers, Theresa, and Anna O. Soter. *Reading Across Cultures: Teaching Literature in a Diverse Society.* New York: Teachers College Press, 1997.

Sinatra, Richard. *Visual Literacy Connections to Thinking, Reading, and Writing.* Springfield, IL: Charles C. Thomas, 1986.

Sipe, Lawrence. *Storytime: Young Children's Literary Understanding in the Classroom.* New York: Teachers College Press, 2008.

Unsworth, Len, Angela Thomas, Alyson Simpson, and Jennifer Asha. *Children's Literature and Computer-Based Teaching.* New York: Open University Press, 2005.

Walsh, Maureen. "Reading Visual and Multimodal Texts: How Is 'Reading' Different?," 2005. http://www.literacyeducators.com.au/docs/Reading%20 multimodal%20texts.pdf (cited March 14, 2006).

❀ *AFTERWORD*

I Am All That I See: The Power of Reflection

Maya Christina Gonzalez

IMAGINE

I love my imagination! It is wide and inclusive and powerful. It allows me to play with seeing myself as a young girl:

> In every direction I turn, I am met with sights and sounds that reflect who I am. All of this conspires to tell me that I am a competent resource for my community, holding gifts that are uniquely mine to claim and develop and explore without limitation! In my home, in the town that I live, in my school, in the public library and the books I hold, in the movies I see, in the songs that I hear, I understand my courage and strong-girl stature. It is with great ease that I grow like a flower towards the expanse of the sky. I can grow as far as the sky can hold me. My roots dig into the earth as deep as I need them to. I am all that I see. This is how I experience myself, how I experience the potential and the beauty in all others and how we fit together to create our world.

I hold this imagined reflection like a yardstick and recall the life I have lived. I grew up in the Mojave Desert in the 1960s and 1970s. I remember a lot of beige: the empty lots, the sandstorms, the stucco houses. The desert wind would blow so hard I had to push against it to make my way home. It picked up the dust and the sand, and stung my face with its force, covering everything the color of the desert. Everything beige.

I don't think I fully understood it at the time, but that's how a lot of life felt when I was growing up: as if everything was the same color and I had to push against some invisible force to make it home. I grew up Chicana and biracial in what seemed like a white, white world. I would not have had those words then. All I knew was that I could never find books at the library that felt like me and I often found myself drawing my image onto the blank pages in the backs of books, seemingly because I needed some place to draw. Now, of course, I imagine that I wanted to see myself there; my round, Chicana, girl face inside the covers of a real book: hard cover, library shelf, label on the spine. It's as if I knew my image belonged there reflected in the "real world."

REFLECTIONS

When I had the opportunity to both author and illustrate my first children's book, I wrote about where I did finally find my reflection as a child. It was not in the few Latino faces I saw on television or in movies as gang members, maids, or prostitutes. It was also not in the pages of books and magazines or on billboards. It was nearly nowhere to be found in the "real world." I found it in the sky. I grew up on a cul-de-sac. Our house was the one at the very end that you would have driven into if it was a through street. I used to say we lived at the "dead" end. But, if you walked out in front of our house at dusk, right there straight ahead, you could see the sun set. It was in perfect line. In my child's mind it was as if each day the sun positioned itself for its finest moment of glory just for me to see. Sunset became my favorite time of day. The sky would smear hot pink, blood red, and purple with orange edges. There in the center, the sun burned, a singular eye of fire. The power of the sunset was so fierce, it turned everything in my world pink, *hot pink*. It transformed the beige of the day into something that made sense to me, that felt more like me—color!

"Sunset" from My Colors, My World / Mis colores, mi mundo, *©2007 Maya Christina Gonzalez. Permission granted by the artist.*

As an adult and an artist, I have worked to reconcile the effects of not seeing myself reflected in the "real world" as a child. I have painted my round, Chicana, woman face as well as my girl face in my fine art, using the power of creativity to claim my face and place in the *here and now*. As an extension of this personal work, I have had the opportunity to paint my round, Chicana, girl face in book after book as an illustrator, no longer relegated to scratching myself onto the blank pages at the back of someone else's book. I now fill all the pages with my own paintings *and* words, exactly where long ago and far away I intuited that I belonged, fully reflected page upon page. Doing this over and over has changed me. I still do it for the child that I was, for the girl in the desert. But I know very deeply now that I belong. So now I paint for every child who is invisible, excluded, denied: girls, all children of color, LGBT (lesbian, gay, bisexual, transgender) and gender-variant (sissies and tomboys) children, and differently abled children. I have learned the importance of seeing myself authentically reflected in my media. It is the wordless, intrinsic acknowledgment that I am here. I exist. I belong. I contribute in my presence and my experience. Clearly, this is not my story alone. I believe all children need to hold a book in their hands that feels true . . . a book in which they will find themselves, their faces . . . a book in which to land and rest and then to dream.

One of my favorite things to do is to go to the library, although it is still tricky to find a book that reflects the child that I was. Around 1 percent of the children's books published each year are written and illustrated by or about Latinos and our experience (Cooperative Children's Book Center 2009). But we *are* still here, and now in ever-increasing numbers. As we reach more than 20 percent of the population, our persistent presence is creating slow but expanding change. I recently went to the National Latino Children's Literature Conference to lecture about reflection. I spoke about the girl in the desert and the sunset. I knew the majority of attendees were students who would be in the classroom soon. Their faces were mostly white and female. Soon they would be teaching in classrooms filled with brown and cinnamon faces. I spoke about what it was like to grow up invisible, and how as an artist I had worked to resolve that very complicated experience. I wondered if this experience was familiar territory to any of them—if they had ever felt that they did not belong, that this country was in any way not their own.

It is valuable for us to acknowledge the truth that we *are* all equal, *and* that our current power structures and school systems reflect that we are not all treated equally. This is a conflict that is palpable and uncomfortable, however wordless to the children who are not authentically reflected in the world around them. As I have experienced, it has a very real effect. What I know is that this situation creates discomfort on both sides. Without adequate representation, we continue to stand as the unknown, the different, the other, and humans are often unsure and uncomfortable with the unknown. I imagine also that it is challenging to acknowledge a privileged position in the current power structure and that there are feelings I cannot know. How do we begin? How can we be in right relationship?

While I love my own books and love the beautiful and amazing Latino-focused books that *are* produced every year, I want to acknowledge and accept what is true now. My opening vision "I am all that I see" does not yet exist. In fact, despite all the awesome and necessary efforts to use the resources we currently have available, we still land far short of any genuine reflection in our country. Specifically I speak here about our children of color, primarily Latino children. The children's book industry alone would have to produce 190 percent more Latino-relevant books per year. I sense that achievement may be a ways off. It is clearly important that we continue to join together and support the good work being done by many authors, illustrators, educators, and librarians on this front. It is also appropriate to allow ourselves to wonder. How can we equip ourselves as we slowly become more visible in our books? How can children best be empowered? And how can educators, often white, model sincere equality? Can white educators serve as reflections in any way for our children of color?

We all learn from example, but children do especially. Without word or thought we look to the primary figures in our lives to set an example. From talking to educators over the years, I have come to respect not only their position in our schools, but also the many stresses specifically attached to their jobs. As a child, I naturally used creativity as a tool to navigate some of the conflict I felt from not being reflected. I drew myself on the blank pages of books—I

"Reflection" from I Know the River Loves Me / Yo sé que el río me ama, *©2009 Maya Christina Gonzalez. Permission granted by the artist.*

created my own reflection. As an adult, I now understand how important it is for us to see ourselves reflected in our world. Yet, having had the great privilege of creating so much imagery like this, I find that I have not filled pages with images of Chicanas solely because I needed to know that I exist. I have created images because I needed to know myself, to explore and expand. I like the word reflection because of its double meaning. *Reflection is an image, representation, counterpart. But also, reflection is a fixing of the thoughts on something, careful consideration, a thought (or an image) occurring in consideration or meditation.* My personal work has led me to link the two meanings. I create reflections of myself so that I can reflect upon them.

CLAIMING FACE

Many educators know and value creativity and would like to bring it into their classrooms. But the pressures of their work make it difficult to gather the necessary resources to create new programs. As I've gone into classrooms and worked with hundreds of students, I have of course found that we all need to see ourselves in our world *and* we all need to know ourselves. No matter how old we are. The curriculum I call Claiming Face evolved slowly as I drew on my experience as an artist and my 15 years' experience in the classroom, working with kids like myself.

Creativity belongs to all of us. Focusing on this common ground unifies us. But creativity is also highly individual, and no matter what, it remains wholly our own. It is no secret that creativity is important. I could cite countless studies that say how fabulous creativity is, what the benefits are, how much we need

"Eye Seeing" from My Colors, My World / Mis colores, mi mundo, *©2007 Maya Christina Gonzalez. Permission granted by the artist.*

it, and how it supports our self-esteem and our ability to think new thoughts, make new connections, and expand beyond perceived limitations. But the truth is that we are losing our connection with creativity—through standards, testing, overcrowded schools, and much more. In this country, most adults' creative expression operates at a fourth-grade level at best. It's not that I dislike stick figures; in fact I like them very much. What I am more curious about is what contributes to the idea that one can only safely draw a stick figure and that only "artists" are creative. Around fourth grade, we begin to limit ourselves. We begin to distance ourselves from our own creative power and instead point to "the artist" in the classroom. We become more externally focused and indoctrinated into the systems surrounding us that convey what we can and can't do, who we are, and what is available to us. At times the messages are explicit; but it is the messages that are subtle and insidious, virtually invisible, that affect us the most. (One example is the fact that few books adequately reflect our presence and experience as Latinos.) We begin to believe on multiple levels what the world tells us about "the way things are."

Although I've spent a lifetime learning from Creativity and focus on my relationship with her every day, I have adjusted the Claiming Face curriculum to take as little as 20 minutes a day. I've found that there are a few basic elements that seriously compensate for the constant inundation of external messages. One is doing something, even a little something, every day. Two is having role models in our environment who are not only doing what we are doing, but who are being how we're trying to be. A third is to remove judgment and treat all things with a sense of curiosity and respect. With these basic elements as a backdrop, the curriculum explores reflection through creativity to develop emotional, mental, and psychological skills. Art skills will most likely develop also, but the goal of the curriculum is to create the powerful link between creativity and a sense of self. Using a vast and diverse sense of self-portraiture, we explore, empower, and express.

The Claiming Face curriculum has 26 basic projects, broken into categories of Reflection, Freedom, Empowering, Exploring, Expanding, and Expressing. In projects such as "Animal Self-Portrait," "Frida Mirror," and "Courage Portrait" we focus on reflection. In "Self-Portrait as Space" and "Map of Me" we explore ourselves, and in "What No One Can See" and "Touch Your Face Portrait" we expand. Our sense of self changes—we change as we engage with knowing ourselves more through our creative power. And since we are consistently using ourselves as our subject, an association naturally develops between our sense of self and this flowing creative force.

What we show about ourselves through our art is unique to us. I love to tell students "You are the boss of you. Only you can know you!" Through a steady and persistent engagement with creativity, a sense of self and empowerment grows until it is deep within us and becomes a part of who we are and how we navigate the world. When we have a strong sense of self and feel that we are our own agent, we are freer to learn. Our mind is unburdened from some of the external messages because our sense of self is securely rooted internally. The energy usually spent managing the constant external input can instead be put to whatever task is at hand. We can use our energy on what we care about and what best serves us. Often this is a quiet, progressive shift. It can be seen as an ability to focus easier, feel lighter, care more about the day, and share more about ourselves. Sometimes within a session there are profound shifts, quiet but dramatic. I once watched as one boy, completely frozen in an "I can't" moment, arrive at a place of powerful expression with a look of joy and self-respect in his eyes. The children are ready.

Most of us have stories and experiences of being invisible or un-empowered. We are all learning and exploring throughout our entire lives. When we take time for ourselves, we are silently communicating to our students that they, too, can benefit from taking time for themselves. It is a style of thinking and being; this is the "artist's way." When we focus on ourselves as "artists,"[1] we become equal. I do not feel separate from the students I work with. This feeling of connection is not just because we have the shared experience of growing up as children of color in this country at this time. More importantly, I feel unified with them, as I do with the adults I work with, because we are doing the same work. When we engage in creativity alongside our students, we are modeling equality. We all struggle. We all triumph. We all hit creative blocks. We all find our way through them. In this way, white educators become reflections for our children of color, in practice if not in image, and thus convey a powerful, unspoken message. An educator committing to modeling equality in the classroom can go a long way toward compensating for the limitations often reflected in the external world.

---

1   By "artists," I don't mean that you have to be a professional artist. We are all creative and by embracing our creativity we can become artists.

INTERNAL SELF-REFLECTIONS

It seems at this time that the strange gift is that we are not reflected. Most of us will not experience externally the vision I created with my imagination at the beginning of this chapter: "I am all that I see." But what may be more important is that our current situation forces upon us the opportunity to create that vision internally. This era challenges us to root our sense of self within, and it begs us to engage with one of the great teachers of all time—creativity.

I believe that one day I will see all of us reflected in the world as beautiful, valuable, equal, and strong, growing without limitation as high as the sky can hold us. Until then I support our children and educators in becoming the artists they are! Our schools and systems are in need of change. It doesn't have to be something dramatic or external. It can be something simple and slow from within. The power and effects of creativity are something steady to rise up through the schools and into our world. The children are already keen on seizing this opportunity, I believe we have only to help them on their way.

REFERENCES

Cooperative Children's Book Center. "Children's Books by and About People of Color Published in the United States," http://www.education.wisc.edu/ccbc/books/pcstats.asp (accessed December 14, 2009).

SELECTED ONLINE RESOURCES FEATURING MAYA'S WORK

Children's Book Press. "Children's Book Press: Many Voices, One World: Latino," http://www.childrensbookpress.org/our-books/latino (accessed December 22, 2009). Nonprofit publisher of many of Maya Gonzalez's books for children.

Gonzalez, Maya Christina. "Maya Christina Gonzalez Chicana Woman Artist." http://www.mayagonzalez.com/ (accessed December 22, 2009). Provides biographical information on Maya Gonzalez as well as samples of her fine artwork for adults.

Reflection Press. "Reflection Press: A People Should Not Long for Their Image." http://reflectionpress.com/ (accessed December 22, 2009). Highlights Maya Gonzalez's Claiming Face™ curriculum and provides information about her artwork and other projects.

❀ RECOMMENDED BIBLIOGRAPHY OF CHILDREN'S LITERATURE AND RELATED PROFESSIONAL RESOURCES

PICTURE BOOKS

Ada, Alma Flor, and Elivia Savadier. *I Love Saturdays y domingos*. New York: Atheneum, 2002.

Albert, Richard, and Sylvia Long. *Alejandro's Gift*. San Francisco: Chronicle Books, 1994.

Anaya, Rudolfo A., and Amy Códova. *The Santero's Miracle: A Bilingual Story*. Albuquerque: University of New Mexico Press, 2004.

Anaya, Rudolfo A., and Edward Gonzales. *Farolitos for Abuelo*. New York: Hyperion Books for Children, 1998.

———. *The Farolitos of Christmas*. New York: Hyperion Books for Children, 1995.

Anzaldúa, Gloria, and Consuelo Mendez. *Friends from the Other Side / Amigos del otro lado*. San Francisco: Children's Book Press, 1993.

Argueta, Jorge, and Elizabeth Gomez. *A Movie in My Pillow / Una película en mi almohada*. San Francisco: Children's Book Press, 2001.

Asch, Frank. *Monkey Face*. New York: Parents' Magazine Press, 1977.

Belpré, Pura, and Symeon Shimin. *Santiago*. New York: Frederick Warne, 1969.

Bernier-Grand, Carmen T., and David Diaz. *Cesar: Si, Se Puede! / Yes, We Can*. Tarrytown, NY: Marshall Cavendish, 2004.

Bertrand, Diane Gonzales, and Anthony Accardo. *The Last Doll / La última muñeca*. Houston: Piñata Books, 2000.

Bertrand, Diane Gonzales, and Alex Pardo Delange. *Sip, Slurp, Soup, Soup / Caldo, Caldo, Caldo*. Houston: Piñata Books, 1996.

Bertrand, Diane Gonzales, and Christina E. Rodriguez. *We Are Cousins / Somos primos*. Houston: Piñata Books, 2007.

Bertrand, Diane Gonzales, and Robert L. Sweetland. *My Pal, Victor / Mi amigo, Víctor*. Green Bay, WI: Raven Tree Press, 2004.

Brett, Jan. *The Umbrella*. New York: Putnam, 2004.

Brown, Margaret. *Goodnight Moon*. New York: Harper & Bros., 1947.

Brown, Monica, and Magaly Morales. *Chavela and the Magic Bubble.* Boston: Clarion Books/Houghton Mifflin Harcourt, 2010.

Brown, Monica, and Gabriela B. Ventura. *Butterflies on Carmen Street/Mariposas en la calle Carmen.* Houston: Piñata Books, 2007.

Carling, Amelia Lau. *Mama and Papa Have a Store.* New York: Dial/Penguin, 1998.

———. *Sawdust Carpets.* Toronto: Groundwood, 2005.

Castañeda, Omar S., and Enrique O. Sanchez. *Abuela's Weave.* New York: Lee & Low, 1993.

Cisneros, Sandra, and Terry Ybáñez. *Hairs/Pelitos.* New York: Knopf, 1994.

Cohn, Diana, and Amy Córdova. *Dream Carver.* New York: Chronicle, 2002.

Contreras, Kathleen, and Margaret Lindmark. *Trencitas/Braids.* New York: Lectorum, 2009.

Costales, Amy, and Martha Avilés. *Abuelita Full of Life/Abuelita llena de vida.* Flagstaff, AZ: Luna Rising, 2007

Costales, Amy, and Mercedes McDonald. *Hola noche/Hello Night.* Flagstaff, AZ: Luna Rising, 2007.

Cowley, Joy, and Joe Cepeda. *Gracias the Thanksgiving Turkey.* New York: Scholastic, 1996.

Cox, July, and Angela Dominguez. *Carmen Learns English.* New York: Holiday House, 2010.

Crews, Donald. *Freight Train/Tren de carga.* New York: Rayo, 2008.

Cumpiano, Ina, and José Ramírez. *Quinito, Day and Night/Quinito, día y noche.* San Francisco: Children's Book Press, 2008.

Davis, Katie. *Who Hops?/¿Quién salta?* Orlando, FL: Harcourt, 2005.

Delacre, Lulu. *Vejigante Masquerader.* New York: Scholastic, 1993.

De la Hoya, Oscar, and Lisa Kopelke. *Super Oscar.* New York: Simon & Schuster, 2006.

De Prieto, Marianna Beeching. *The Wise Rooster/El Gallo Sabio.* New York: John Day Co., 1962.

Dorros, Arthur, and Rudy Gutierrez. *Papá and Me.* New York: Rayo/Harper Collins, 2008.

Dorros, Arthur, and Elia Kleven. *Abuela.* New York: Dutton Children's Books, 1991.

———. *Isla.* New York: Dutton/Penguin, 1995.

Elya, Susan Middleton, and Steven Salerno. *Bebé Goes Shopping.* New York: Harcourt, 2006.

Ets, Marie H., and Aurora Labastida. *Nine Days to Christmas*. New York: Viking, 1959.

Fine, Edith Hope, and René King Moreno. *Under the Lemon Moon*. New York: Lee & Low, 1999.

Flatharta, Antoine, and Meilo So. *Hurry and the Monarch*. New York: Knopf, 2005.

Galindo, Mary Sue, and Pauline Rodriguez Howard. *Icy Watermelon / Sandía fría*. Houston: Piñata Books, 2001.

Gershator, David, Phillis Gershator, and Emma Shaw-Smith. *Bread Is for Eating*. New York: Holt, 1995.

Gomi, Taro. *My Friends / Mis amigos*. San Francisco: Chronicle Books, 2006.

González, Lucía, and Lulu Delacre. *The Storyteller's Candle / La velita de los cuentos*. San Francisco: Children's Book Press, 2008.

Gonzalez, Maya Christina. *I Know the River Loves Me / Yo sé que el río me ama*. San Francisco: Children's Book Press, 2009.

———. *My Colors, My World / Mis colores, mi mundo*. San Francisco: Children's Book Press, 2007.

González, Rigoberto, and Cecilia Álvarez. *Antonio's Card / La tarjeta de Antonio*. San Francisco: Children's Book Press, 2005.

Gribel, Christiane. *No voy a dormir / I Am Not Going to Sleep*. New York: Lectorum Publications, 2009.

Guy, Ginger Foglesong, and Vivi Escrivá. *My Grandma / Mi abuelita*. New York: Rayo/ HarperCollins, 2007.

Guy, Ginger Foglesong, and Sharon Glick. *¡Perros! ¡Perros! Dogs! Dogs! A Story in English and Spanish*. New York: Greenwillow, 2006.

Guy, Ginger Foglesong, and René King Moreno. *¡Fiesta!* New York: Greenwillow Books, 1996.

———. *Siesta*. New York: Greenwillow Books, 2005.

Herrera, Juan Felipe, and Elly Simmons. *Calling the Doves / El canto de las palomas*. San Francisco: Children's Book Press, 1995.

Herrera, Juan Felipe, and Honorio Robleda Tapia. *Super Cilantro Girl / La niña del supercilantro*. San Francisco: Children's Book Press, 2003.

Hoffman, Eric, and Celeste Henriquez. *Best Best Colors / Los Mejores Colores*. St. Paul, MN: Redleaf Press, 1999.

Hughes, Monica, and Luis Garay. *A Handful of Seeds*. Toronto: Lester Publishing, 1993.

Jiménez, Francisco, and Claire B. Cotts. *The Christmas Gift: El regalo de Navidad.* Boston: Houghton Mifflin, 2000.

Jiménez, Francisco, and Simon Silva. *La Mariposa.* Boston: Houghton Mifflin, 1998.

Johnston, Tony, and Susan Guevara. *Isabel's House of Butterflies.* San Francisco: Sierra Club Books for Children, 2003.

Johnston, Tony, and Yuyi Morales. *My Abuelita.* New York: Harcourt, 2009.

King-Pérez, L., and David Diaz. *First Day in Grapes.* New York: Lee & Low, 2002.

Lacámara, Laura, and Yuyi Morales. *Floating on Mama's Song/Flotando en la canción de mamá.* New York: Katherine Tegen Books/HarperCollins, 2010.

Lachtman Dumas, Ofelia, and Alex Pardo Delange. *Pepita Talks Twice/Pepita habla dos veces.* Houston: Piñata Books 1995.

Laínez, René Colato, and Jill Arena. *Playing Lotería/El juego de la lotería.* Flagstaff, AZ: Luna Rising, 2005.

Laínez, René Colato, and Fabricio Vanden Broeck. *My Shoes and I.* Honesdale, PA: Boyds Mills Press, 2010.

Laínez, René Colato, and Joe Cepeda. *From North to South/Del norte al sur.* San Francisco: Children's Book Press, 2010.

Laínez, René Colato, and Tom Lintern. *The Tooth Fairy Meets El Ratón Pérez.* Berkeley, CA: Tricycle Press, 2010.

Laínez, René Colato, and Fabiola Graullera Ramírez. *I Am René, the Boy/Soy René, el niño.* Houston: Piñata Books, 2004.

———. *René Has Two Last Names/René tiene dos apellidos.* Houston: Piñata Books, 2009.

Lessac, Frané. *My Little Island.* New York: Lippincott, 1985.

Levy, Janice, and Morella Fuenmayor. *The Spirit of Tío Fernando: A Day of the Dead Story.* Morton Grove, IL: A. Whitman, 1995.

Lewis, Thomas, and Joan Sandin. *Hill of Fire.* New York: Harper & Row, 1971.

Lomas Garza, Carmen. *Family Picture/Cuadros de familia.* 15th Anniversary Ed. San Francisco: Children's Book Press, 2005.

———. *In My Family/En mi familia.* San Francisco: Children's Book Press, 1997.

McCormack, Caren McNelly, and Martha Avilés. *The Fiesta Dress: A Quinceañera Tale.* Tarrytown, NY: Marshall Cavendish, 2009.

Machado, Ana Maria, and Rosana Faría. *Nina Bonita.* Brooklyn, NY: Kane Miller, 1996.

Manzano, Sonia, and Jon J Muth. *No Dogs Allowed.* New York: Atheneum, 2004.

Masurel, Claire, and Bob Kolar. *Un gato y un perro / A Cat and a Dog.* New York: Ediciones Norte-Sur, 2003.

Montes, Marissa, and Yuyi Morales. *Los Gatos Black on Halloween.* New York: Henry Holt, 2006.

Mora, Pat, and Raúl Colón. *Tomás and the Library Lady.* New York: Knopf, 1997.

Mora, Pat, and Cecily Lang. *A Birthday Basket for Tía.* New York: Macmillan, 1992.

Mora, Pat, and Rafael López. *Book Fiesta! Celebrate Children's Day/Book Day/Book Fiesta! Celebremos El día de los niños/El día de los libros.* New York: Rayo/ HarperCollins, 2009.

Mora, Pat, and John Parra. *Gracias / Thanks.* New York: Lee & Low, 2009.

Mora, Pat, and Maribel Suárez. *Here Kitty, Kitty / ¡Ven, gatita, ven!* New York: Rayo, 2008.

———. *Let's Eat! / ¡A Comer!* New York: Rayo, 2008.

———. *Sweet Dreams / Dulces sueños.* New York: Rayo, 2008.

Morales, Yuyi. *Just a Minute: A Trickster Tale and Counting Book.* New York: Chronicle, 2003.

———. *Just in Case: A Trickster Tale and Spanish Alphabet Book.* New York: Roaring Brook Press, 2008.

———. *Little Night.* New York: Roaring Brook Press, 2007.

Newman, Lesléa, and Adriana Romo. *Felicia's Favorite Story.* Ridley Park, PA: Two Lives Publishing, 2002.

Patterson, Irania Macías, and Catherine Courtlandt-McElvane. *Chipi Chipis: Small Shells of the Sea / Chipi chipis: Caracolitos del mar.* Charlotte, NC: CPCC Press, 2005.

Pérez, Amada Irma, and Maya Christina Gonzalez. *My Diary from Here to There / Mi diario de aquí hasta allá.* San Francisco: Children's Book Press, 2002.

———. *My Very Own Room / Mi propio cuartito.* San Francisco: Children's Book Press, 2000.

———. *Nana's Big Surprise / Nana, ¡Qué Sorpresa!* San Francisco: Children's Book Press, 2007.

Ramirez, Michael Rose, and Linda Dalal Sawaya. *The Little Ant / La Hormiga Chiquita.* New York: Rizzoli, 1995.

Reich, Susana, and Raúl Colón. *José! Born to Dance.* New York: Simon & Schuster, 2005.

Rivera-Ashford, Roni Capin, and Edna San Miguel. *My Nana's Remedies / Los remedios de mi nana.* Tucson: Arizona-Sonora Desert Museum, 2002.

Rodríguez, Artemio. *The King of Things / El rey de las cosas.* El Paso, TX: Cinco Puntos, 2006.

Rodriguez, Luis J. *It Doesn't Have to Be This Way.* San Francisco: Children's Book Press, 2004.

Rodriguez, Luis J., and Carlos Vázquez. *America Is Her Name.* Willimantic, CT: Curbstone Press, 1998.

Rosa-Casanova, Sarah, and Robert Roth. *Mama Provi and the Pot of Rice.* New York: Atheneum, 1997.

Skármeta, Antonio, and Alfonso Ruano. *The Composition.* Toronto: Groundwood, 2000.

Slate, Joseph. *The Secret Stars.* New York: Marshall Cavendish, 1998.

Smith, J. D., and Dani Jones. *The Best Mariachi in the World.* Green Bay, WI: Raven Tree, 2008.

Solomon, Sharon, and Pamela Barcita. *A Walk with Grandpa / Un paseo con abuelo.* McHenry, IL: Raven Tree Press, 2009.

Soto, Gary, and Susan Guevara. *Chato's Kitchen.* New York: Putnam, 1995.

Soto, Gary, and Ed Martinez. *Too Many Tamales!* New York: Putnam, 1993.

Soto, Gary, and Pam Paparone. *My Little Car.* New York: Putnam, 2006.

Tafolla, Carmen, and Amy Córdova. *What Can You Do With a Rebozo? / ¿Que puedes hacer con un rebozo?* Berkeley, CA: Tricycle Press, 2009.

Tafolla, Carmen, and Magaly Morales. *What Can You Do with a Paleta? / ¿Qué puedes hacer con una paleta?* Berkeley, CA: Tricycle Press, 2009.

Tonatiuh, Duncan. *Dear Primo: A Letter to My Cousin.* New York: Abrams Books for Young Readers, 2010.

Torres, Leyla. *Saturday Sancocho.* New York: Farrar, Straus and Giroux, 1999.

Vidal, Beatriz. *Federico and the Magi's Gift: A Latin American Christmas Story.* New York: Knopf, 2004.

Walsh, Ellen Stoll. *Mouse Count.* San Diego: Harcourt Brace, 1991.

Ward, Cindy. *Cookie's Week.* New York: Putnam, 1988.

Weeks, Sarah, and David Diaz. *Counting Ovejas.* New York: Atheneum, 2006.

Wellington, Monica. *Ana cultiva manzanas / Apple Farmer Annie.* Translated by Eida del Risco. New York: Dutton, 2004.

Williams, Vera B. *A Chair for My Mother.* New York: Greenwillow Books, 1982.

Yolen, Jane, and Mark Teague. *How Do Dinosaurs Say Good Night?* New York: Scholastic, 2000.

NOVELS—INTERMEDIATE TO UPPER ELEMENTARY

Ada, Alma Flor. *My Name Is María Isabel.* New York: Atheneum/Simon & Schuster, 1993.

Alvarez, Julia. *How Tía Lola Came to Stay.* New York: Dell Yearling, 2002.

———. *How Tía Lola Learned to Teach.* New York: Knopf, 2010.

———. *Return to Sender.* New York: Knopf, 2009.

Anaya, Rudolfo, and Amy Córdova. *My Land Sings: Stories from the Río Grande.* New York: Rayo/HarperCollins, 1999.

Belpré, Pura. *Firefly Summer.* Houston: Piñata Books, 1996.

Canales, Viola. *The Tequila Worm.* New York: Wendy Lamb/Random House, 2005.

Cofer, Judith Ortiz. *An Island Like You: Stories of the Barrio.* New York: Orchard Books/Scholastic, 1995.

Delacre, Lulu. *Salsa Stories.* New York: Scholastic, 2000.

Herrera, Juan Felipe. *Downtown Boy.* New York: Scholastic, 2005

Jiménez, Francisco. *Breaking Through.* New York: Houghton Mifflin, 2001.

———. *The Circuit: Stories From the Life of a Migrant Child.* Albuquerque: University of New Mexico Press, 1997.

Joseph, Lynn. *The Color of My Words.* New York: Joanna Cotler/HarperCollins, 2000.

Martínez, Claudia Guadalupe. *The Smell of Old Lady Perfume.* El Paso, TX: Cinco Puntos Press, 2008.

Mulder, Michelle. *After Peaches.* Victoria, BC: Orca Book Publishers, 2009.

Ryan, Pam Muñoz. *Becoming Naomi León.* New York: Scholastic, 2004.

———. *Esperanza Rising.* New York: Scholastic, 2000.

Ryan, Pam Muñoz, and Peter Sís. *The Dreamer.* New York: Scholastic, 2010.

Sanchez, Alex. *So Hard to Say.* New York: Simon & Schuster, 2004.

Soto, Gary. *Baseball in April and Other Stories.* Orlando, FL: Harcourt, 1990.

———. *The Skirt.* New York: Random House, 1992.

NOVELS—JR. HIGH AND YOUNG ADULT

Alegría, Malín. *Estrella's Quinceañera.* New York: Simon & Schuster, 2006.

Alvarez, Julia. *Before We Were Free.* New York: Knopf, 2002.

———. *In the Time of the Butterflies.* Chapel Hill, NC: Algonquin Books, 1994.

Anaya, Rudolfo. *Bless Me, Ultima.* New York: Warner Books, 1972.

Calcines, Eduardo F. *Leaving Glorytown: One Boy's Struggle Under Castro.* New York: Farrar, Straus and Giroux, 2009.

Cárdenas, Teresa. *Old Dog.* Toronto: Groundwood, 2006.

Carlson, Lori Marie, ed. *Voices in First Person: Reflections on Latino Identity.* New York: Atheneum, 2008.

Castañeda, Omar S. *Among the Volcanoes.* New York: Dutton, 1991.

Cisneros, Sandra. *House on Mango Street.* Houston: Arte Público Press, 1983.

Cofer, Judith Ortiz. *Meaning of Consuelo.* New York: Farrar, Straus and Giroux, 2003.

Dole, Mayra Lazara. *Down to the Bone.* New York: HarperCollins, 2008.

Ellis, Deborah. *I Am a Taxi.* Toronto: Groundwood, 2006.

———. *Sacred Leaf.* Toronto: Groundwood, 2007.

Flores, Carlos Nicolás. *Our House on Hueco.* Lubbock: Texas Tech University Press, 2006.

Hernández, Jorge F. *Sun, Stone, and Shadows.* San Diego: Fondo de Cultura Economica USA, 2008.

Hijuelos, Oscar. *Dark Dude.* New York: Atheneum, 2008.

Jiménez, Francisco. *Reaching Out.* New York: Houghton Mifflin, 2008.

López, Diana. *Confetti Girl.* New York: Little, Brown, 2009.

Martínez, Victor. *Parrot in the Oven: mi vida.* New York: HarperCollins, 1996.

Miller-Lachmann, Lyn. *Gringolandia.* Willimantic, CT: Curbstone, 2009.

———, ed. *Once Upon a Cuento.* Willimantic, CT: Curbstone, 2003.

Osa, Nancy. *Cuba 15.* New York: Delacorte/Random House, 2003.

Pellegrino, Marge. *Journey of Dreams.* London: Frances Lincoln, 2009.

Resau, Laura. *Red Glass.* New York: Delacorte/Random House, 2007.

Rodriguez, Luis. *Always Running—La Vida Loca: Gang Days in L.A.* New York: Touchstone, 2005.

Sáenz, Benjamin Alire. *He Forgot to Say Goodbye: The Things Our Fathers Left Unsaid.* New York: Simon & Schuster, 2008.

———. *Sammy and Juliana in Hollywood.* El Paso, TX: Cinco Puntos Press, 2004.

Saldaña, René, Jr. *Finding Our Way.* New York: Random House, 2003.

———. *The Jumping Tree.* New York: Random House, 2001.

Sanchez, Alex. *The God Box.* New York: Simon & Schuster, 2007.

Santiago, Esmeralda. *When I Was Puerto Rican.* New York: Random House, 1993.

Sitomer, Alan Lawrence. *The Secret Story of Sonia Rodriguez*. New York: Hyperion/ Jump at the Sun, 2008.

Soto, Gary. *Accidental Love*. New York: Harcourt, 2006.

Trujillo, Carla. *What Night Brings*. Willimantic, CT: Curbstone, 2003.

Valdes-Rodriguez, Alisa. *Haters*. New York: Little, Brown, 2006.

FOLKTALES

Aardema,Verna, and Petra Mathers. *Borreguita and the Coyote: A Tale from Ayutla*. New York: Knopf, 1991.

Ada, Alma Flor, and Felipe Dávalos. *The Lizard and the Sun / La lagartija y el sol*. New York: Doubleday Books for Young Readers, 1997.

Ada, Alma Flor, and Ana López Escrivá. *The Great-Great-Granddaughter of La Cucarachita Martina*. New York: Scholastic, 1993.

Ada, Alma Flor, and Kim Howard. *Mediopollito / Half Chicken*. New York: Doubleday Books for Young Readers, 1995.

Ada, Alma Flor, and Kathleen Kuchera. *The Rooster Who Went to His Uncle's Wedding: A Latin American Folktale*. San Diego: Del Sol Books, 1993.

Alexander, Ellen. *The Llama and the Great Flood: A Folktale from Peru*. Boston: T. Y. Crowell, 1989.

Alvarez, Julia, and Fabin Negrin. *The Secret Footsteps*. New York: Knopf, 2000.

Alvarez, Julia, and Ruddy Núñez. *El mejor regalo del mundo: La leyenda de la Vieja Belén / The Best Gift of All: The Legend of La Vieja Belén*. Miami, FL: Santillana USA, 2008.

Alvarez, Julia, and Beatriz Vidal. *A Gift of Gracias: The Legend of Altagracia*. New York: Knopf/Random House, 2005.

Anaya, Rudolfo. *Curse of the Chupacabra*. Albuquerque: University of New Mexico Press, 2006.

———. *Maya's Children: The Story of La Llorona*. New York: Hyperion, 1997.

Anaya, Rudolfo, Amy Córdova, and Enrique R. Lamadrid. *The First Tortilla: A Bilingual Story*, Albuquerque: University of New Mexico Press, 2007.

Anzaldúa, Gloria, and Maya Christina Gonzalez. *Prietita and the Ghost Woman / Prietita y la llorona*. San Francisco: Children's Book Press, 1996.

Argueta, Jorge, and Gloria Calderón. *Zipitio*. Toronto: Groundwood, 2003.

Argueta, Manilo, and Elly Simmons. *Magic Dogs of the Volcanoes / Los perros mágicos de los volcanes*. San Francisco: Children's Book Press, 1997.

Barchas, Sarah. *The Giant and the Rabbit: Six Bilingual Folktales from Hispanic Culture.* Sonoita, AZ: High Haven Music, 1996.

Belpré, Pura, and Tomie dePaola. *The Tiger and the Rabbit and Other Tales.* New York: J. B. Lippincott, 1965.

Belpré, Pura, and Paul Galdone. *Oté: A Puerto Rican Folk Tale.* New York: Random House, 1969.

Belpré, Pura, and Christine Price. *Juan Bobo and the Queen's Necklace: A Puerto Rican Folk Tale.* New York: Frederick Warne, 1962.

Belpré, Pura, and Carlos Sánchez. *Perez and Martina: A Portorican Folk Tale.* New York: Frederick Warne, 1932.

Belting, Natalia, and William Hillenbrand. *The Moon Was Tired of Walking on Air: Origin Myths of South American Indians.* New York: Houghton Mifflin, 1992.

Bernier-Grand, Carmen T., and Lulu Delacre. *Shake It Morena! and Other Folklore from Puerto Rico.* Minneapolis, MN: Millbrook Press, 2006.

Bernier-Grand, Carmen T., and Ernesto Ramos Nieves. *Juan Bobo: Four Folktales from Puerto Rico.* New York: HarperCollins, 1994.

Bierhorst, John, ed. *The Hungry Woman: Myths and Legends of the Aztecs.* New York: William Morrow, 1984.

———. *Latin American Folktales: Stories from Hispanic and Indian Traditions.* New York: Pantheon, 2003.

———. *The Monkey's Haircut and Other Stories Told by the Maya.* New York: William Morrow, 1986.

Brusca, María Cristina, and Tona Wilson. *The Blacksmith and the Devils.* New York: Henry Holt, 1992.

———. *Pedro Fools the Gringo and Other Tales of a Latin American Trickster.* New York: Henry Holt, 1992.

———. *When Jaguars Ate the Moon and Other Stories About Animals and Plants of the Américas.* New York: Henry Holt, 1995.

Campoy, F. Isabel, and Alma Flor Ada. *Tales Our Abuelitas Told: A Hispanic Folktale Collection.* New York: Atheneum, 2006.

Carter, Dorothy Sharp, and W. T. Mars. *The Enchanted Orchard: And Other Folktales of Central America.* New York: Harcourt Brace Jovanovich, 1973.

Deedy, Carmen Agra, and Michael Austin. *Martina the Beautiful Cockroach: A Cuban Folktale.* Atlanta, GA: Peachtree, 2007.

Delacre, Lulu. *Golden Tales: Myths, Legends, and Folktales from Latin America.* New York: Scholastic, 1996.

dePaola, Tomie. *The Lady of Guadalupe.* New York: Holiday House, 1980.

———. *The Legend of the Poinsettia.* New York: Putnam, 1994.

————. *The Night of Las Posadas.* New York: Putnam, 1999.

De Sauza, James. *Brother Anansi and the Cattle Ranch / El hermano Anansi y el rancho de Ganado.* San Francisco: Children's Book Press, 1998.

DeSpain, Pleasant, ed. *The Emerald Lizard: Fifteen Latin American Folktales to Tell.* Atlanta, GA: August House, 1999.

Ehlert, Lois, and Gloria de Aragón. *Cuckoo / Cucú: A Mexican Folktale.* New York: Harcourt Children's Books, 1997.

Ehlert, Lois, and Amy Prince. *Moon Rope / Un lazo a la luna: A Peruvian Folktale.* New York: Harcourt Children's Books, 1992.

Endredy, James, María Hernández de la Cruz, and Casimiro de la Cruz López. *The Journey of Tunuri and the Blue Deer: A Huichol Indian Story.* Rochester, VT: Bear Cub Books, 2003.

Galindo, Claudia, and Jonathan Coombs. *Do You Know the Cucuy? / ¿Conoces al Cucuy?* Houston: Piñata Books, 2008.

————. *It's Bedtime, Cucuy! / ¡A la cama, Cucuy!* Houston: Piñata Books, 2008.

Garza, Xavier. *Creepy Creatures and Other Cucuys.* Houston: Arté Publico, 2004.

Garza, Xavier, and April Ward. *Juan and the Chupacabras / Juan y el chupacabras.* Houston: Piñata Books, 2006.

Gerson, Mary-Joan, and Maya Christina Gonzalez. *Fiesta Femenina: Celebrating Women in Mexican Folktale.* Cambridge, MA: Barefoot Books, 2001.

González, Ada Acosta, and Christina Rodriguez. *Mayte and the Bogeyman / Mayte y el cuco.* Houston: Piñata Books, 2006.

González, Lucía, and Lulu Delacre. *The Bossy Gallito / El gallo de bodas: A Traditional Cuban Folktale.* New York: Scholastic, 1994.

————. *Señor Cat's Romance and Other Favorite Stories from Latin America.* New York: Scholastic, 1997.

Griego y Maestas, José, Rudolfo A. Anaya, and Jaime Valdez. *Cuentos: Tales from the Hispanic Southwest Based on Stories Originally Collected by Juan B. Baul.* Santa Fe: Museum of New Mexico Press, 1980.

Hayes, Joe. *Ghost Fever: Mal de Fantasma.* El Paso, TX: Cinco Puntos Press, 2004.

Hayes, Joe, and Joseph Daniel Fiedler. *Juan Verdades: The Man Who Couldn't Tell a Lie.* New York: Orchard Press, 2001.

Hayes, Joe, and Geronimo Garcia. *Tell Me a Cuento / Cuéntame un Story.* El Paso, TX: Cinco Puntos Press, 1998.

Hayes, Joe, and Vicki Trego Hill. *Watch Out for Clever Women! / ¡Cuidado con las mujeres astutas!* El Paso, TX: Cinco Puntos Press, 1996.

Hayes, Joe, Vicki Trego Hill, and Mona Pennypacker. *La Llorona/The Weeping Woman: A Hispanic Legend Told in Spanish and English*. El Paso, TX: Cinco Puntos Press, 2004.

Hayes, Joe, and Antonio Castro Lopez. *The Day It Snowed Tortillas/El día que nevo tortillas*. El Paso, TX: Cinco Puntos Press, 2003.

Hayes, Joe, and Honorio Robledo. *El Cucuy! A Bogeyman Cuento in English and Spanish*. El Paso, TX: Cinco Puntos Press, 2001.

Hayes, Joe, and Mauricio Trenard Sayago. *Dance, Nana, Dance: Cuban Folktales in English and Spanish*. El Paso, TX: Cinco Puntos Press, 2008.

Jaffe, Nina, and Enrique O. Sanchez. *The Golden Flower: A Taino Myth from Puerto Rico*. Houston: Piñata Books, 2005.

Johnston, Tony, and Tomie dePaola. *The Tale of Rabbit and Coyote*. New York: Putnam, 1994.

Knutson, Barbara. *Love and Roast Chicken: A Trickster Tale from the Andes Mountains*. Minneapolis, MN: Carolrhoda Books, 2004.

Lattimore, Deborah Nourse. *The Flame of Peace: A Tale of the Aztecs*. New York: Harper & Row, 1987.

Love, Hallie, and Bonnie Larson. *Love's Watákame's Journey: The Story of the Great Flood and the New World*. Santa Fe, NM: Clear Light Books, 1999.

Loya, Olga. *Momentos mágicos/Magic Moments: Tales from Latin America Told in English and in Spanish*. Atlanta, GA: August House, 1997.

MacCracken, Joan, and Augusto Silva. *Trisba and Sula: A Miskitu Folktale from Nicaragua/Una leyenda de los Miskitos de Nicaragua*. Brooksville, ME: Tiffin Press, 2005.

McDermott, Gerald. *Jabutí the Tortoise: A Trickster Tale from the Amazon*. New York: Sandpiper, 2005.

———. *Musicians of the Sun*. New York: Aladdin, 2000.

MacDonald, Margaret Read, and Sophie Fatus. *A Hen, a Chick, and a String Guitar: Inspired by a Chilean Folktale with CD*. Cambridge, MA: Barefoot Books, 2005. Reissued as *The Farmyard Jamboree*.

MacDonald, Margaret Read, and Geraldo Valéro. *Conejito: A Folktale from Panama*. Little Rock, AR: August House LittleFolk, 2006.

McManus, Kay. *Land of the Five Suns: Looking at Aztec Myths and Legends*. Lincolnwood, IL: NTC/Contemporary Publishing, 1997.

Martinez, Alejandro Cruz, Rosalma Zubizarreta, and Harriet Rohmer. *The Woman Who Outshone the Sun: the Legend of Lucia Zenteno/La mujer que brillaba aún más que el sol: La leyenda de Lucia Zenteno*. San Francisco: Children's Book Press, 1991.

Menchú, Rigoberta, and Domi. *The Honey Jar*. Toronto: Groundwood, 2006.

————. *The Secret Legacy*. Toronto: Groundwood, 2008.

Mohr, Nicholasa, and Antonio Martorell. *The Song of el Coquí and Other Tales of Puerto Rico*. New York: Viking Juvenile, 1995.

Montejo, Victor, and Wallace Kaufman. *The Bird Who Cleans the World: and Other Mayan Fables*. Willimantic, CT: Curbstone Press, 1995.

Montejo, Victor, and Rafael Yockteng. *White Flower: A Maya Princess*. Toronto: Groundwood, 2005.

Montes, Marisa, and Joe Cepeda. *Juan Bobo Goes to Work: A Puerto Rican Folk Tale*. New York: HarperCollins, 2000.

Montes, Marisa, and Maurie J. Manning. *Juan Bobo Goes Up and Down the Hill: A Puerto Rican Folk Tale*. Carmel, CA: Hampton-Brown, 2000.

Mora, Pat, and Charles R. Berg. *The Gift of the Poinsettia / El regalo de la flor de nochebuena*. Houston: Piñata Books, 1995.

Mora, Pat, and Raul Colón. *Doña Flor: A Tall Tale About a Giant Woman with a Big Heart*. New York: Knopf, 2005.

Mora, Pat, and Domi. *The Night the Moon Fell: A Maya Myth / La noche que se cayó la luna: Mito Maya*. Toronto: Groundwood, 2000.

————. *The Race of Toad and Deer*. Toronto: Groundwood, 2001.

Moreton, Daniel. *La Cucaracha Martina: A Caribbean Folktale*. New York: Turtle Books, 1997.

Ober, Hal, and Carol Ober. *How Music Came to the World: An Ancient Mexican Myth*. New York: Houghton Mifflin, 1994.

Oppenheim, Joanne, and Fabian Negrin. *The Miracle of the First Poinsettia*. Cambridge, MA: Barefoot Books, 2003.

Perales, Alonso M., and John Pluecker. *Brujas, lechuzas y espantos / Witches, Owls and Spooks*. Houston: Piñata Books, 2008.

Perez, Elvia, Victor Hernandez Mora, Margaret Read MacDonald, and Paula Martin. *From the Winds of Manguito / Desde los vientos de Manguito: Cuban Folktales in English and Spanish*. Santa Barbara, CA: Libraries Unlimited, 2004.

Philip, Neil, and Jacqueline Mair. *Horse Hooves and Chicken Feet: Mexican Folktales*. New York: Clarion Books, 2003.

Pitcher, Caroline, and Jackie Morris. *Mariana and the Merchild: A Folk Tale from Chile*. Grand Rapids, MI: William B. Eerdmans, 2000.

Pitre, Felix, and Christy Hale. *Juan Bobo and the Pig: A Puerto Rican Folktale*. New York: Lodestar Books, 1993.

Polette, Keith, and Elisabeth O. Dulemba. *Paco and the Giant Chile Plant / Paco y la planta de chile gigante*. Green Bay, WI: Raven Tree Press, 2008.

Robbins, Sandra, and Iku Oseki. *The Firefly Star: A Hispanic Folktale with CD*. New York: See-Mores Workshop, 2002.

Rohmer, Harriet, and Mary Anchondo. *How We Came to the Fifth World/Cómo vinimos al quinto mundo*. San Francisco: Children's Book Press, 1988.

Rohmer, Harriet, and Graciela Carrillo. *Legend of Food Mountain/La montaña de alimento*. San Francisco: Children's Book Press, 1982.

Rohmer, Harriet, Octavio Chow, Morris Viduare, and Joe Sam. *The Invisible Hunters/Los cazadores invisibles*. San Francisco: Children's Book Press, 1997.

Rohmer, Harriet, and Jesus Guerrero Rea. *Atariba and Niguayona: A Story from the Taino People of Puerto Rico*. San Francisco: Children's Book Press, 1988.

Rohmer, Harriet, and Mira Reisberg. *Uncle Nacho's Hat/El sombrero de Tío Nacho*. San Francisco: Children's Book Press, 1997.

Ryan, Pam Muñoz, and Claudia Rueda. *Nacho and Lolita*. New York: Scholastic Press, 2005.

Salinas, Bobbi. *The Three Pigs/Los tres cerdos: Nacho, Tito, and Miguel*. Houston: Piñata Books/Arte Público Press, 1999.

VanLaan, Nancy, and Beatriz Vidal. *The Magic Bean Tree: A Legend from Argentina*. New York: Houghton Mifflin, 1998.

Wisniewski, David. *Rain Player*. Logan, IA: Perfection Learning, 1995.

POETRY

Alarcón, Francisco X., and Maya Christina Gonzalez. *Angels Ride Bikes and Other Fall Poems/Los Ángeles andan en bicicleta y otros poemas de otoño*. San Francisco: Children's Book Press, 1999.

———. *Animal Poems of the Iguazú/Animalario del Iguazú*. San Francisco: Children's Book Press, 2008.

———. *From the Bellybutton of the Moon and Other Summer Poems/Del ombligo de la luna y otros poemas de verano*. San Francisco: Children's Book Press, 1998.

———. *Iguanas in the Snow and Other Winter Poems/Iguanas en la nieve y otros poemas de invierno*. San Francisco: Children's Book Press, 2001.

———. *Laughing Tomatoes and Other Spring Poems/Jitomates risueños y otros poemas de primavera*. San Francisco: Children's Book Press, 1997.

Argueta, Jorge, and Elizabeth Gómez. *A Movie in My Pillow/Una película en mi almohada*. San Francisco: Children's Book Press, 2001.

Argueta, Jorge, and Rafael Yockteng. *Sopa de frijoles: Un poema para cocinar/Bean Soup: A Cooking Poem*. Toronto: Groundwood, 2009.

Bernier-Grand, Carmen T. *Frida: ¡Viva la vida! Long Live Life!* Tarrytown, NY: Marshall Cavendish, 2007.

Bernier-Grand, Carmen T., and David Diaz. *César: ¡Sí, se puede! Yes, We Can!* Tarrytown, NY: Marshall Cavendish, 2004.

———. *Diego: Bigger Than Life.* Tarrytown, NY: Marshall Cavendish, 2009.

Carlson, Lori Marie, ed. *Cool Salsa: Bilingual Poems on Growing Up Hispanic in the United States.* New York: Henry Holt, 1994.

———. *Red Hot Salsa: Bilingual Poems on Being Young and Latino in the United States.* New York: Henry Holt, 2005.

Engle, Margarita. *The Surrender Tree: Poems of Cuba's Struggle for Freedom.* New York: Henry Holt, 2008.

———. *Tropical Secrets: Holocaust Refugees in Cuba.* New York: Henry Holt, 2009.

Engle, Margarita, and Sean Qualls. *The Poet Slave of Cuba: A Biography of Juan Francisco Manzano.* New York: Henry Holt, 2006.

Luján, Jorge, and Manuel Monroy. *Rooster/Gallo.* Toronto: Groundwood, 2004.

Medina, Jane, and Robert Castilla. *The Dream on Blanca's Wall/El sueño pegado en la pared de Blanca: Poems in English and Spanish.* Honesdale, PA: Wordsong/Boyds Mills Press, 2004.

Mora, Pat, and Paula Barragán. *Love to Mamá: A Tribute to Mothers.* New York: Lee & Low, 2001.

Mora, Pat, and Rafael López. *Yum! ¡MmMm! ¡Qué Rico! Americas' Sproutings.* New York: Lee & Low, 2007.

Mora, Pat, and Enrique O. Sanchez. *Confetti: Poems for Children.* New York: Lee & Low, 1996.

Soto, Gary. *Canto familiar.* San Diego, CA: Harcourt Brace, 1995.

———. *Neighborhood Odes.* San Diego, CA: Harcourt Brace, 1992.

SONGS, RHYMES, LULLABIES, AND MUSICAL RECORDINGS

Ada, Alma Flor, and F. Isabel Campoy. *Mamá Goose: A Latino Nursery Treasury/Mamá Goose: Un tesoro de rimas infantiles.* New York: Hyperion, 2004.

———. *Merry Navidad! Christmas Carols in English and Spanish/Merry Navidad! Villancicos en español e inglés.* New York: Rayo/HarperCollins, 2007.

Ada, Alma Flor, F. Isabel Campoy, and Alice Schertle. *¡Pío Peep! Traditional Spanish Nursery Rhymes.* New York: HarperCollins, 2003.

Ada, Alma Flor, and Tarry Ybáñez. *The Christmas Tree/El árbol de Navidad: A Christmas Rhyme in English and Spanish*. New York: Hyperion, 1997.

Anaya, Jorge. *¡A bailar! Let's Dance! Spanish Learning Songs*. Glen Echo, MD: Whistlefritz, 2008. (Music Recording)

Barchas, Sarah. *¡Piñata! and More! Bilingual Songs for Children*. Sonoita, AZ: High Haven Music, 1997. (Music Recording)

———. *¡Todos, listos, canten! Canciones para niños y para aprender el español*. Sonoita, AZ: High Haven Music, 1995. (Music Recording)

Bertrand, Diane Gonzales, and Alex Pardo Delange. *The Empanadas That Abuela Made/Las empanadas que hacía la abuela*. Houston: Piñata Books, 2003.

Campoy, F. Isabel, and Alma Flor Ada. *¡Muu, Moo! Rimas de animales/Animal Nursery Rhymes*. New York: Rayo/HarperCollins, 2010.

Children's Nursery Rhyme Songs in Spanish/Canciones infantiles para niños en español. Bilingual Beginnings, 2004. (Music Recording)

Deedy, Carmen Agra. *Growing Up Cuban in Decatur, Georgia*. Atlanta, GA: Peachtree, 2004. (Sound Recording)

Delacre, Lulu. *Arrorró, mi niño: Latino Lullabies and Gentle Games*. New York: Lee & Low, 2004.

———. *Arroz con leche: Popular Songs and Rhymes from Latin America*. New York: Scholastic, 1989.

Del Rey, Maria. *Universe of Song*. Redway, CA: Music for Little People, 1999. (Music Recording)

Feldman, Jean R. *Ole! Ole! Ole! Dr. Jean en Español*. Seabrook Island, SC: Jean Feldman, 2003. (Music Recording)

Gonzalez, Ralfka, and Ana Ruiz. *My First Book of Proverbs/Mi primer libro de dichos*. San Francisco: Children's Book Press, 1995.

Griego, Margot, Betsy Bucks, Sharon Gilbert, Laurel Kimball, and Barbara Cooney. *Tortillitas para mamá and Other Nursery Rhymes: Spanish and English*. New York: Henry Holt, 1981.

Hall, Nancy A., Jill Syverson-Stork, and Kay Chorao. *Los pollitos dicen/The Baby Chicks Sing: Juegos, rimas y canciones infantiles de países de habla hispana/Traditional Games, Nursery Rhymes, and Songs from Spanish-Speaking Countries*. Boston: Little, Brown, 1994.

Hinojosa, Tish. *Cada niño, Every Child: A Bilingual Album for Kids,* Rounder Kids, 1996. (Music Recording)

Hinojosa, Tish, and Lucia Angela Perez. *Cada niño/Every Child*. El Paso, TX: Cinco Puntos Press, 2002. (Song Book)

Jaramillo, Nelly P., and Elivia. *Las Nanas de abuelita: Canciones de cuna, trabalenguas y adivinanzas de Suramérica / Grandmother's Nursery Rhymes: Lullabies, Tongue Twisters, and Riddles from South America.* New York: Henry Holt, 1996.

Jordan, Sara. *Bilingual Preschool: English-Spanish.* St. Catharines, ON: Sara Jordan Publishing, 2007.

Mora, Pat, and Magaly Morales. *A Piñata in a Pine Tree: A Latino Twelve Days of Christmas.* New York: Clarion/Houghton Mifflin Harcourt, 2009.

Orozco, José-Luis. *Canto y cuento: Lírica infantil.* Berkeley, CA: Arcoiris Records, 2000. (Music Recording)

———. *De Colores and Other Latin-American Folk Songs.* Berkeley, CA: Arcoiris Records, 1996 (Music Recording)

Orozco, José-Luis, and Elisa Kleven. *De colores and Other Latin American Folk Songs for Children.* New York: Penguin Putnam, 1999. (Song Book)

———. *Fiestas: A Year of Latin American Songs of Celebration.* New York: Dutton/Penguin Putnam, 2002. (Song Book)

———. *Diez deditos and Other Play Rhymes and Action Songs from Latin America.* New York: Puffin, 2002. (Song Book)

Owen, Ann, and Sandra D'Antonio. *Las ruedas del camión / The Wheels on the Bus.* Mankato, MN: Picture Window Books, 2006.

Patterson, Irania Macias, Ana L. Divins, and Fred Figueroa. *Criss, Cross Mangosauce: A Fun Way to Learn Spanish.* Indian Trail, NC: Expresiones, 2007. (Music Recording)

Peek, Merle. *¡Dénse vuelta! Una canción de cuentas / Roll Over! A Counting Song.* New York: Clarion Books, 2008.

Rockwell, Anne. *El toro pinto and Other Songs in Spanish.* New York: Simon & Schuster, 1995.

Sol y Canto. *El doble de amigos / Twice as Many Friends.* Cambridge, MA: Rounder Kids, 2003. (Music Recording)

Tafolla, Carmen, and Amy Córdova. *Fiesta Babies.* Berkeley, CA: Tricycle Press, 2010.

INFORMATIONAL

Ada, Alma Flor. *Under the Royal Palms: A Childhood in Cuba.* New York: Atheneum, 1998.

Ada, Alma Flor, and Simón Silva. *Gathering the Sun: An Alphabet in Spanish and English.* New York: Lothrop, Lee & Shepard Books, 1997.

Alegre, Cesar. *Extraordinary Hispanic Americans.* New York: Children's Press/ Scholastic, 2007.

Ancona, George. *Capoeira: Game! Dance! Martial Art!* New York: Lee & Low, 2007.

———. *Fiesta U.S.A.* New York: Lodestar Books, 1995.

———. *Harvest.* New York: Marshall Cavendish, 2001.

———. *Mayeros: A Yucatec Maya Family.* New York: HarperCollins, 1997.

———. *Pablo Remembers: The Fiesta of the Days of the Dead.* New York: Lothrop, Lee & Shepard Books, 1993.

———. *The Piñata Maker/El Piñatero.* San Diego: Harcourt Brace, 1994.

Andrews-Goebel, Nancy, and David Diaz. *The Pot That Juan Built.* New York: Lee & Low, 2002.

Atkin, S. Beth. *Voices from the Fields: Children of Migrant Farmworkers Tell Their Stories.* Boston: Little, Brown, 1993.

Brown, Monica, and Joe Cepeda. *Side by Side: The Story of Dolores Huerta and Cesar Chavez/Lado a lado: La historia de Dolores Huerta y César Chávez.* New York: Rayo/HarperCollins, 2010.

Brown, Monica, and Rudy Gutierrez. *Pelé, King of Soccer: Pelé, El rey del fútbol.* New York: Rayo/Harper Collins, 2009.

Brown, Monica, and Rafael López. *My Name Is Celia: The Life of Celia Cruz/Me llamo Celia: La vida de Celia Cruz.* Flagstaff, AZ: Luna Rising, 2004.

Campoy, F. Isabel, and Alma Flor Ada. *Celebrate Cinco de Mayo with the Mexican Hat Dance.* Miami, FL: Santillana USA, 2006.

Carlson, Lori Marie, and Ed Martinez. *Hurray for Three Kings' Day!* New York: HarperCollins, 1999.

Celebrating History—Texas Style. Petersborough, NH: *Cobblestone*, March 1997.

Contró, Arturo. *Rafael Márquez.* New York: Rosen/PowerKids Press, 2008.

Cumpiano, Ina, and José Ramírez. *Quinito's Neighborhood/El vecindario de Quinito.* San Francisco: Children's Book Press, 2005.

de Fatima Campos, Maria. *Victoria Goes to Brazil.* London, England: Frances Lincoln Children's Books, 2009.

de Ruiz, Dana C., and Richard Larios. *La Causa: the Migrant Farmworkers' Story.* Austin, TX: Raintree Steck-Vaughn, 1993.

Doak, Robin. *Dolores Huerta: Labor Leader and Civil Rights Activist.* Mankato, MN: Compass Point Books/Capstone, 2008.

Doeden, Matt. *Autos lowriders/Lowriders.* Mankato, MN: Capstone Press, 2007.

Elya, Susan Middleton, Merry Banks, and Joe Cepeda. *N Is for Navidad*. San Francisco: Chronicle Books, 2007.

Flanagan, Alice K. *Cinco de Mayo*. Minneapolis, MN: Compass Point Books, 2004.

Garza, Xavier. *Lucha libre: the Man in the Silver Mask: A Bilingual Cuento*. El Paso, TX: Cinco Puntos Press, 2005.

Hoyt-Goldsmith, Diane. *Celebrating a Quinceañera: A Latina's 15th Birthday Celebration*. New York: Holiday House, 2002.

———. *Day of the Dead: A Mexican-American Celebration*. New York: Holiday House, 1994.

———. *Las Posadas: A Hispanic Christmas Celebration*. New York: Holiday House, 1999.

———. *Three Kings Day: A Celebration at Christmastime*. New York: Holiday House, 2004.

Hoyt-Goldsmith, Diane, and Lawrence Migdale. *Cinco de Mayo: Celebrating the Traditions of Mexico*. New York: Holiday House, 2008.

Johnston, Tony, and Jeanette Winter. *Day of the Dead*. New York: Voyager Books, 2000.

Keep, Richard. *Clatter Bash! A Day of the Dead Celebration*. Atlanta, GA: Peachtree, 2004.

Kroll, Virginia L., and Loretta Lopez. *Uno, dos, tres, posada!/Let's Celebrate Christmas*. New York: Viking, 2006.

Krull, Kathleen, and Yuyi Morales. *Harvesting Hope: The Story of Cesar Chavez*. San Diego, CA: Harcourt, 2003.

Lane, Kimberly. *Come Look With Me: Latin American Art*. Watertown, MA: Charlesbridge, 2007.

Lasky, Kathryn. *Days of the Dead*. New York: Hyperion Books for Children, 1994.

Levy, Janice. *Celebrate! It's Cinco de Mayo!/¡Celebremos! ¡Es el cinco de mayo!* Morton Grove, IL: Albert Whitman, 2007.

Lomas Garza, Carmen. *Magic Windows: Ventanas mágicas*. San Francisco: Children's Book Press, 1999.

MacMillan, Dianne M. *Mexican Independence Day and Cinco de Mayo*. Berkeley Heights, NJ: Enslow, 1997.

Menard, Valerie. *The Latino Holiday Book: From Cinco de Mayo to Día de los Muertos—The Celebrations and Traditions of Hispanic-Americans*. 2nd ed. New York: Marlowe & Co., 2004.

Menchú, Rigoberta, and Domi. *The Girl from Chimel*. Toronto: Groundwood, 2005.

Mohr, Nicholasa. *In My Own Words: Growing Up Inside the Sanctuary of My Imagination.* New York: Julian Messner/Simon & Schuster, 1994.

Mora, Pat, and Doug Cushman. *Marimba! Animales from A to Z.* New York: Clarion Books, 2006.

Mora, Pat, and Beatriz Vidal. *A Library for Juana: The World of Sor Juana Inés.* New York: Knopf, 2002.

Palacios, Argentina, and Alex Haley. *¡Viva México! The Story of Benito Juárez and Cinco de Mayo.* Austin, TX: Raintree-Steck Vaughn, 1993.

Ray, Deborah Kogan. *To Go Singing Through the World: The Childhood of Pablo Neruda.* New York: Farrar, Straus and Giroux, 2006.

Reed, Lynn Rowe. *Pedro, His Perro, and the Alphabet Sombrero.* New York: Hyperion, 1995.

Reich, Susanna, and Raúl Colón. *José! Born to Dance: The Story of José Limón.* New York: Simon & Schuster, 2005.

Rivera Marín, Guadalupe, and Diego Rivera. *My Papa Diego and Me: Memories of My Father and His Art / Mi papa Diego y yo: Recuerdos de mi padre y su arte.* San Francisco: Children's Book Press, 2009.

San Vicente, Luis. *The Festival of the Bones / El festival de las calaveras: The Little-Bitty Book for the Day of the Dead.* El Paso, TX: Cinco Puntos Press, 2002.

Sciurba, Katie, and Edel Rodriguez. *Oye, Celia! A Song for Celia Cruz.* New York: Henry Holt, 2007.

Serrano, Francisco, and Eugenia Guzmán. *Our Lady of Guadalupe.* Mexico City: CIDCLI, 1998.

Serrano, Francisco, and Pablo Serrano. *The Poet King of Tezcoco: A Great Leader of Ancient Mexico.* Toronto: Groundwood, 2007.

Shahan, Sherry, and Paula Barragán. *Fiesta!* Atlanta, GA: August House, 2008.

————. *Spicy Hot Colors: Colores picantes.* Atlanta, GA: August House, 2004.

Stewart, Mark, and Mike Kennedy. *Latino Baseball's Hottest Hitters / Los mejores bateadores del béisbol Latino.* Brookfield, CT: Twenty-First Century Books, 2002.

Weill, Cynthia, K. B. Basseches, Moisés Jiménez, and Armando Jiménez. *ABeCedarios: Mexican Folk Art ABCs in English and Spanish.* El Paso, TX: Cinco Puntos Press, 2007.

Weill, Cynthia, Quirino Santiago, and Martín Santiago. *Opuestos: Mexican Folk Art Opposites in English and Spanish.* El Paso, TX: Cinco Puntos Press, 2009.

Winter, Jeanette. *Calavera abecedario: A Day of the Dead Alphabet Book.* Orlando, FL: Harcourt, 2004.

Winter, Jonah, and Raúl Colón. *Roberto Clemente: Pride of the Pittsburgh Pirates.* New York: Atheneum, 2005.

SPANISH LANGUAGE BOOKS, K-12

Primary Age Books—Fiction and Informational

Aardema, Verna. *Por qué zumban los mosquitos en los oídos de la gente: un cuento de África Occidental.* New York: Dial Books, 1998.

Ada, Alma Flor, F. Isabel Campoy, Felipe Dávalos, and Susan Guevara. *Cuentos que contaban nuestras abuelas: Cuentos populares Hispánicos.* New York: Aladdin, 2007.

Ada, Alma Flor, F. Isabel Campoy, and Maribel Suarez. *Mamá Goose: Un tesoro de rimas infantiles.* New York: Hyperion, 2005.

Ada, Alma Flor, and Vivi Escrivá. *¿Pavo para la Cena de Gracias? ¡No gracias!* Miami, FL: Santillana USA, 1999.

Ada, Alma Flor, and Judith Jacobson. *El vuelo de los colibríes.* Beverly Hills, CA: Laredo, 1995.

Ada, Alma Flor, and Kathleen Kuchera. *El gallo que fue a la boda de su tío: Cuento popular Hispanoamericano.* New York: Putnam & Grosset Group, 1998.

Alvarez, Julia, and Fabin Negrin. *Las huellas secretas.* New York: Dragonfly Books, 2002.

Amado, Elisa. *Un barrilete para el día de los muertos.* Toronto: Groundwood, 1999.

Ancona, George. *Pablo recuerda: La fiesta del día de los muertos.* New York: Lothrop, 1993.

Andricaín, Sergio, and Olga Cuéllar Serrano. *Arco iris de poesía: Poemas de las Américas y España.* New York: Lectorum Publications, 2008.

Aranda, Charles. *Dichos y frases hechas.* Zaragoza, Spain: Edelvives, 2002.

Arrieta Munguía, Adriana. *Si entras al castillo.* Mexico City: Alfaguara, 2002.

Bang, Molly. *Diez, nueve, ocho.* New York: Greenwillow, 1997.

Barragán Santos, Salatiel. *Mi primer libro de convivencia en la naturaleza.* Mexico City: SM de Ediciones, 2005.

———. *Mi primer libro de plantas: Curativas y tóxica.* Mexico City: SM de Ediciones, 2005.

Beaton, Clare. *Cerdota grandota.* Translated by Yanitzia Canetti. Cambridge, MA: Barefoot Books, 2003.

Blackstone, Stella. *Abuelita fue al mercado: Un libro en rima para contar por el mundo.* Cambridge, MA: Barefoot Books, 2007.

———. *Una isla bajo el sol.* Translated by Yanitzia Canetti. Cambridge, MA: Barefoot Books, 2002.

Brown, Margaret Wise. *Buenas Noches Luna.* Harper Arco Iris, 1995.

Browne, Anthony. *Cosita linda.* Mexico City: Fondo de Cultura Económica, 2008.

———. *La feria de los animales.* Mexico City: Fondo de Cultura Económica, 2002.

Burr, Claudia, Krystyna Libura, and Ma C. Urrutia. *Doña Josefa y sus conspiraciones.* Mexico City: Ediciones Tecolote, 2000.

Bustos, Eduardo. *El panteón de la patria: Calaveras de la Independencia.* Mexico City: Artes de México, 2008.

Calles Vales, José. *Adivinanzas y trabalenguas.* Madrid, Spain: Edelvives, 2002.

Campoy, F. Isabel. *Mi día de la A a la Z.* Miami, FL: Alfaguara/Santillana USA, 2009.

Campoy, F. Isabel, and Alma Flor Ada. *Celebra el Cinco de Mayo con un jarabe tapatío.* Miami, FL: Santillana USA, 2006.

———. *Celebra el Día de Acción de Gracias con Beto y Gaby.* Miami, FL: Santillana USA, 2006.

———. *Cuentos que contaban nuestras abuela: cuentos populares hispánicos.* New York: Atheneum Libros Infantiles, 2006.

Carle, Eric. *La araña muy ocupada.* New York: Philomel, 2004.

———. *De la cabeza a los pies.* New York: HarperCollins, 2003.

Chaundler, Rachel. *Mariluz avestruz.* Pontevedra, Spain: OQO Editora, 2007.

Chavelas, Rosalía. *El señor cosquillas.* Mexico City: Alfaguara, 2004.

Cohn, Diana. *El tallador de sueños.* Mexico City: Editorial Planeta Mexicana, 2003.

Cronin, Doreen. *¡A tu ritmo!* Translated by Yanitzia Canetti. New York: Lectorum, 2007.

———. *Clic, clac, muu: Vacas escritoras.* Translated by Alberto Jimenez Rioja. New York: Lectorum, 2002.

Cuenca, Héctor. *La cucarachita Martina: Adaptación de un cuento popular.* New York: Lectorum, 2008.

Darío, Rubén, and Olga Lucía García. *Margarita.* Caracas, Venezuela: Ediciones Ekaré, 1979.

de Avalle-Arce, Diane. *Madonas de Mexico.* Santa Barbara, CA: Bellerophon Books, 2000.

Deedy, Carmen Agra, and Michael Austin. *Martina una cucarachita muy linda: Un cuento Cubano.* Atlanta, GA: Peachtree, 2007.

Del Paso, Fernando. *¡Hay naranjas y hay limones! Pregones, refranes y adivinanzas en verso.* Mexico City: CIDCLI, 2007.

dePaola, Tomie. *La leyenda de la flor de nochebuena.* New York: Putnam, 1994.

———. *Nuestra Señora de Guadalupe.* New York: Holiday House, 1980.

Desmaziéres, Sandra. *Emma y sus amigos: Un libro sobre los colores.* Milwaukee, WI: Gareth Stevens, 2007.

De Varona, Frank. *Miguel Hidalgo y Costilla: Father of Mexican Independence.* Brookfield, CT: Millbrook Press, 1993.

Diez, Carola. *Junta cosas.* Mexico City: Ríosdetinta, Contenidos Estudiantiles Mexicanos, 2007.

East, Jacqueline. *Tengo miedo de la oscuridad.* Bogotá, Colombia: Group Editorial Norma, 1997.

Ehlert, Lois. *A sembrar sopa de verduras.* Translated by Alma Flor Ada and F. Isabel Campoy. San Diego, CA: Red Wagon Books, 1996.

Falconer, Ian. 2004. *Olivia y el juguete desaparecido.* New York: Lectorum, 2004.

Fancy, Colin. *Los cocodrilos no se cepillan los dientes.* Barcelona, Spain: Editorial Juventud, 2005.

Ferri, Francesca. *Cucú—¡Te veo!* Hauppauge, NY: Barron's, 2007.

Fox, Christyan, and Diane Fox. *¡Ratón, que te pilla el gato!* Barcelona, Spain: Combel Editorial, 2003.

Gabán, Jesús. *El libro de los cuentos y leyendas de América Latina y España.* Barcelona, Spain: Ediciones B, 2000.

Garralón, Ana. *Cuentos y leyendas hispanoamericanos.* Madrid, Spain: Anaya, 2005.

Gerson, Sara. *Una nueva nación: México independiente.* Mexico City: Editorial Trillas, 1991.

Gnojewski, Carol. *Cinco de Mayo: Se celebra el orgullo.* Berkeley Heights, NJ: Enslow Elementary, 2005.

———. *El día de los muertos: Una celebración de la familia y la vida.* Berkeley Heights, NJ: Enslow Elementary, 2005.

Gorbachev, Valeri. *Nico y los lobos feroces.* New York: North South Books, 2000.

Granados, Antonio. *El cuentófago.* Mexico City: Ediciones El Naranjo, 2007.

Grejniec, Michael. *Buenos días, buenas noches.* Translated by Alis Alejandro. New York: Ediciones Norte-Sur, 1997.

Henkes, Kevin. *La primera luna llena de gatita.* Translated by Osvaldo Blanco. New York: Greenwillow, 2006.

Hinojosa, Francisco. *Yanka, yanka.* Mexico City: Alfaguara, 2004.

Hollinger, Valerie, and Crystal O'Connor. *Jake y la migración de la monarca.* Greenville, SC: Monarch, 2005.

Horáček, Petr. *Elefante.* Translated by Raquel Solà. Barcelona, Spain: Editorial Juventud, 2009.

———. *La oca boba.* Barcelona, Spain: Editorial Juventude, 2007.

Isol. *Tener un patito es útil.* Mexico City: Fondo de Cultura Económica, 2007.

Jaffe, Nina, Enrique O. Sanchez, and Gabriela Baeza Ventura. *Flor de oro: Un mito taíno de Puerto Rico.* Houston: Piñata Books, 2006.

Jaramillo, Ann. *La Línea.* New Milford, CT: Roaring Brook, 2006.

Jenkins, Emily. *Cinco criaturas.* Mexico City: Planeta Junior, 2002.

Knutson, Barbara, and Wendy A. Luft. *Amor y pollo asado: Un cuento de estafadores de enredos y engaños.* Minneapolis, MN: Ediciones Lerner, 2005.

Kohen, Clarita. *El conejo y el coyote.* Torrance, CA: Laredo, 1993.

Lázaro León, Georgina, and Morella Fuenmayor. *¡Ya llegan los reyes magos!* New York: Lectorum, 2001.

Lee, Claudia M., and Rafael Yockteng. *A la orilla del agua y otros poemas de América Latina.* Mexico City: Artes de México, 2002.

Leveroni, Gabriela. *Salvemos a nuestros monstruos.* Mexico City: Alfaguara, 2005.

Lihón, Danilo Sánchez. *Los Cuatro Hermanos Ayar.* Lima, Peru: Asociación Editorial Bruño, 1998.

Longo, Alejandra. *Trabalenguas.* New York: Scholastic, 2004.

Longo, Alejandra, and Daniel Chaskielberg. *Refranes.* New York: Scholastic, 2005.

MacDonald, Margaret Read, and Sophie Fatus. *Algarabia en la granja.* Cambridge, MA: Barefoot Books, 2009.

Machado, Ana María. *Camilón, comilón.* Madrid, Spain: Ediciones SM, 2008.

———. *Raúl pintado de azul.* Bogotá, Colombia: Editorial Norma, 2001.

Martí, José, and Lulu Delacre. *Los zapaticos de rosa.* New York: Lectorum, 1997.

Masurel, Claire. *Diez perros en la tienda: Un libro para contar.* Translated by Elena Moro. New York: Ediciones Norte-Sur, 2000.

Mike, Jan M. *Juan Bobo y el caballo de siete colores: Una leyenda Puertorriqueña.* Mahwah, NJ: Troll, 1997.

Millán, José Antonio. *¡Me como esa coma! ¡Glups! parece que la puntuación es importante.* Mexico City: Editorial Oceana de México, 2007.

Mohr, Nicholasa, and Antonio Martorell. *La canción del coquí y otros cuentos de Puerto Rico.* New York: Viking Juvenile, 1995.

Molina, Silvia. *Mi abuelita tiene ruedas.* Mexico City: CIDCLI: Consejo Nacional para la Cultura y las Artes, 2000.

Montejo, Victor. and Rafael Yockteng. *Blanca Flor: Una princesa maya.* Toronto: Groundwood, 2005.

Montes, Marisa, and Joe Cepeda. *Juan Bobo busca trabajo: Un cuento tradicional puertorriqueño.* New York: Rayo/HarperCollins, 2006.

Mora, Pat, Raul Colón, and Teresa Mlawer. *Doña Flor: Un cuento de un mujer gigante con un gran corazón.* New York: Dragonfly Books, 2005.

Mora, Pat, and Domi. *La carerra de sapo y venado*. Toronto: Groundwood, 2007.

———. *La noche que se cayó la luna: Mito Maya*. Toronto: Groundwood, 2000.

Morales, Yuyi. *Nochecita*. New York: Roaring Brook Press, 2007.

Moreno Hentz, Pedro, and Alma Velasco. *Mi primer diccionario de flora de México*. Mexico City: SM de Ediciones, 2004.

Morozumi, Atsuko. *Mi amigo gorila*. New York: Farrar, Straus and Giroux, 1999.

Morvillo, Mabel, Susana Garcia, Cecilla Pisos, and Vicky Ramos. *Poemas con sol y son*. Heredia, Costa Rica: Ediciones Farben, 2000.

Núñez, Alonso. *Y la luna siempre es una*. Mexico City: CIDCLI, 2006.

Olmos, Gabriela. *Pintores mexicanos de la A a la Z*. Mexico City: Artes de México: Consejo Nacional para la Cultura y las Artes, 2008.

———. *Cómo bailan los monstruos*. Mexico City: Artes de México, 2007.

———. *El juego de las miradas: A descubrir el arte!* Mexico City: Artes de México: Consejo Nacional para la Cultura y las Artes, 2007.

Oppenheim, Joanne, and Fabian Negrin. *El milagro de la primera flor de Nochebuena: Un cuento mexicano sobre la Navidad*. Cambridge, MA: Barefoot Books, 2003.

Páez, Indira. *Los poderes de Oriana*. Caracas, Venezuela: Camelia Ediciones, 2007.

Page, Jason. *El fútbol*. Princeton, NJ: Two-Can, 2001.

Palavicini, Teresa. *Palabras de fuego*. Mexico City: Editorial Serpentina, 2006.

Peña Muñoz, Manuel. *Del pellejo de una pulga y otros versos para jugar*. Mexico City: Alfaguara/Santillana, 2005.

Rathmann, Peggy. *Buenas noches gorila*. Colección Ponte Poronte. Caracas, Venezuela: Ediciones Ekaré, 2001.

Robleda Moguel, Margarita. *Trabalenguas, colmos, tantanes, refranes, y un pilón*. San Marcos, Mexico City: Sitesa, 1989.

Ryan, Pam Muñoz, and Claudia Rueda. *Nacho y Lolita*. New York: Scholastic en Español, 2005.

Secretaría de Educación Pública. *Lo mejor de México desconocido*. Mexico City: Libros de Rincón, 1999.

Sendak, Maurice. *Donde viven los monstruos*. New York: HarperTrophy, 1996.

Serrano, Esteban. *Leonidas y su perro Luis*. Montevideo, Uruguay: Nicanitasantiago, 2004.

Soto, Gary. *Qué montón de tamales!* New York: Penguin Putnam, 1996.

Stuart, Kelly. *Canción de cuna de la Virgen de Guadalupe*. Houston: Bright Sky Press, 2002.

Thaae, Soren. *Navidad de papel*. Mexico City: CIDCLI, 2008.

Uribe, Véronica. *Diego y la gran cometa voladora.* Caracas, Venezuela: Ediciones Ekaré, 2002.

Urrutia, Ma C. *La batalla del 5 de Mayo: ayer y hoy.* Mexico City: Ediciones Tecolote, 1996.

Waddell, Martin. *Las lechucitas.* Translated by Andrea Bermúdes. Compton, CA: Santillana Publishing, 1994.

Walsh, Ellen Stoll. *Cuenta ratones.* San Diego, CA: Harcourt Brace Jovanovich, 1995.

———. *Pinta ratones.* Mexico City: Fondo de Cultura Económica, 1992.

———. *Salta y brinca.* Translated by Alma Flor Ada and F. Isabel Campoy. San Diego, CA: Libros Viajeros, Harcourt Brace, 1996.

Walsh, María Elena. *El reino del revés.* Mexico City: Alfaguara, 2007.

Wood, Audrey. *La casa adormecida.* Translated by Alma Flor Ada and F. Isabel Campoy. San Diego, CA: Harcourt Brace, 1995.

Yolen, Jane. *¿Como dan las buenos noches los dinosaurios?* New York: Scholastic, 2000.

Zepeda, Monique. *Nicolas dos veces.* Mexico City: Ediciones El Naranjo, 2008.

Intermediate Age Books—Fiction and Informational

Anza, Ana L. C., and Eddie Martinez Gomez. *Amigos del otro lado.* Mexico City: Ediciones Castillo, 2000.

Bierhorst, John, ed. *Cuentos folklóricos latinoamericanos: Fábulas de las tradiciones hispanas e indígenas* Millers Falls, MA: Vintage, 2003.

Bravo-Villasante, Carmen. *Cuentos populares de Iberoamérica.* Madrid, Spain: Ediciones Gaviota, 1988.

Delacre, Lulu. *De oro y esmeraldas: Mitos, leyendas y cuentos populares de latinoamérica.* New York: Scholastic en Español, 1996.

Estrada, Jorge A. *Cuentos para una noche de insomnio.* Mexico City: Nostra Ediciones, 2008.

Forcada, Alberto. *La imaginación al poder.* Mexico City: Centro de Información y Desarrollo de la Comunicación y la Literatura Infantiles CIDCLI, 2007.

Gerson, Mary-Joan, and Maya Christina Gonzalez. *Fiesta femenina: Homenaje a las mujeres a través de historias tradicionales mexicanas.* Cambridge, MA: Barefoot Books, 2003.

Guerra, Sergio. *Ernesto Che Guevara.* Caracas, Venezuela: Los Libros de El Nacional, 2007.

Hiriart, Berta. *En Días de Muertos.* Mexico City: Everest, 2001.

Lázaro León, Georgina, and María Sánchez. *José.* New York: Lectorum, 2007.

León Portilla, Miguel. *Animales del nuevo mundo = yancuic cemanahuac iyolcahuan.* Mexico City: Nostra Ediciones, 2007.

Libura, Krystyna, M., and Gabriel López Garza. *Sorpresas en palabras.* Mexico City: Ediciones Tecolote, 2006.

Mansour, Vivian. *El enmascarado de Lata.* Mexico City: Fondo de Cultura Económica, 2006.

Morán, Paola. *El porfiriato, 1876–1910.* Mexico City: Nostra Ediciones, 2007.

Orejel, Alfonso. *El sendero de los gatos apachurra dos.* Mexico City: CIDCLI, 2008.

Paz-Castillo, María Fernanda. *Muertos de susto: Leyendas de acá y del más allá.* Bogotá, Colombia: Alfaguara, 2006.

Quino. *Toda mafalda.* Buenos Aires, Argentina: Ediciones de la Flor, 2008.

Ramos, Juan Antonio. *El príncipe de blancanieves.* Bogotá, Colombia: Grupo Editorial Norma, 1997.

Rincón, Valentín. *Trabalengüero.* Mexico City: Nostra Ediciones, S.A. de C.V, 2005.

———. *Ajedrecero.* Mexico City: Nostra Ediciones, 2008.

Rincón, Valentín, and A. Magallanes. *Acertijero.* Mexico City: Nostra Ediciones, 2008.

Rincón, Valentín, and Cuca Serratos. *Adivinancero.* Mexico City: Nostra Ediciones, 2003.

Robleda, Margarita. *Paco: Un niño latino en Estados Unidos.* Miami, FL: Santillana, 2004.

Rosas, Alejandro. *De Tenochtitlan a la Nueva España.* Mexico City: Nostra Ediciones, 2007.

Ruy Sánchez, Alberto. *Los demonios de la lengua.* Mexico City: Alfaguara, 1998.

Ryan, Pam Muñoz. *Esperanza renace.* New York: Scholastic, 2002.

Serrano, Francisco. *La virgen de Guadalupe.* Mexico City: CIDCLI, 1998.

Siemens, Sandra. *El último heliogábalo.* Bogotá, Colombia: Grupo Editorial Norma, 2008.

Silva, Carlos. *La posrevolución, 1917–1940.* Mexico City: Nostra Ediciones, 2007.

Uribe, Verònica. *Cuentos de espantos y aparecidos.* Caracas, Venezuela: Ediciones Ekare-Banco del Libro, 1984.

Vargas de González Carbonell, Gabriela, and Yordi Rosado. *Quiúbole con—tu cuerpo, el ligue, tu imagen, el sexo, las drogas y todo lo demás: Un libro para niñas, chavas, chicas o como quieras llamarles.* Mexico City: Aguilar, 2005.

Variana del Ángel, Gabriela L. *El juego de pelota Mixteca.* Mexico City: Ediciones Castillo, 2005.

Velando, Helen. *Una pulga interplanetaria*. Montevideo, Uruguay: Editorial Sudamericana Uruguaya, 2007.

Walsh, María. *Manuelita*. Buenos Aires, Argentina: Editorial Alfaguara, Colección AlfaWalsh (Pequeños Lectores), 2005.

High School Age Books—Fiction and Informational

Aguilera García, Flor. *Diario de un ostión*. Mexico City: Alfaguara/Santillana, 2005.

Aguirre, Sergio. *El misterio de crantock*. Buenos Aires, Argentina: Grupo Editorial Norma, 2004.

Agustín, José. *La panza del Tepozteco*. Mexico City: Alfaguara, 1992.

Birmajer, Marcelo. *El alma al diablo*. Bogotá, Colombia: Grupo Editorial Norma, 1994.

Cortázar, Julio. *Subidos de tono: Cuentos de amor*. Lima, Peru: Coedición Latinoamericana, 2003.

García Esperón, María. *Querida Alejandría*. Bogotá, Colombia: Grupo Editorial Norma, 2007.

Machado, Ana María. *Eso no me lo quita nadie*. Barcelona, Spain: Grupo Editorial Norma, 1998.

Monterroso, Augosto. *Obras completas: (y otros cuentos). su vida y obra*. Santafé de Bogotá, Colombia: Grupo Editorial Norma, 2004.

Rosero Diago, Evelio. *Los escapados*. Bogotá, Colombia: Grupo Editorial Norma, 2007.

Suárez Romero, Alfonso. *Zapatos de cocodrilo*. Mexico City: CONACULTA: Ediciones SM, 1999.

PROFESSIONAL RESOURCES FOR EVALUATING AND SELECTING LATINO CHILDREN'S MATERIALS

Allen, Virgina G. "Selecting Materials for the Reading Instruction of ESL Children." In *Kids Come in All Languages: Reading Instruction for ESL Students*, ed. by Karen Spangenberg-Urbschat and Robert Pritchard, 108–31. Newark, DE: International Reading Association, 1994.

Almerico, Gina M. "Identifying Award Winning Hispanic Children's Books for the Elementary Curriculum." *Journal of Early Education and Family Review* 10, no. 4 (2003): 30–34.

America Reads Spanish. "Essential Guide to Spanish Reading: Librarians' Selections"(cited December 29, 2009). Accessed at http://www.americareadsspanish.org/libro/pdf.pdf.

———. "Essential Guide to Spanish Reading for Children and Young Adults" (cited December 29, 2009). Accessed at http://www.americareadsspanish.org/libro/ARS_Essential_Guide_to_Spanish_Reading_for_Children_and_Young_Adults.pdf.

Dale, Doris. *Bilingual Children's Books in English and Spanish: An Annotated Bibliography, 1942–2001.* 2nd ed. Jefferson, NC: McFarland, 2003.

Day, Frances Ann. *Latina and Latino Voices in Literature: Lives and Works.* 2nd ed. Westport, CT: Greenwood Press, 2003.

Garza de Cortés, Oralia. "Developing the Spanish Children's Collection." In *Library Services to Latinos: An Anthology,* ed. by Salvador Güereña, 75–90. Jefferson, NC: McFarland, 2000.

Schon, Isabel. *The Best of Latino Heritage: A Guide to the Best Juvenile Books about Latino People.* Lanham, MD: Scarecrow Press, 1996.

———. *The Best of Latino Heritage, 1996–2002: A Guide to the Best Juvenile Books about Latino People.* Lanham, MD: Scarecrow Press, 2003.

———. *Recommended Books in Spanish for Children and Young Adults.* Lanham, MD: Scarecrow Press, 2000.

———. *Recommended Books in Spanish for Children and Young Adults: 2000–2004.* Lanham, MD: Scarecrow Press, 2004.

———. *Recommended Books in Spanish for Children and Young Adults: 2004–2008.* Lanham, MD: Scarecrow Press, 2008.

Wadham, Tim. *Libros Essenciales: Building, Marketing, and Programming a Core Collection of Spanish Language Children's Materials.* New York: Neal-Schuman, 2006.

York, Sherry. *Children's and Young Adult Literature by Latino Writers: A Guide for Librarians, Teachers, Parents, and Students.* Worthington, OH: Linworth, 2002.

———. *Picture Books by Latino Writers: A Guide for Librarians, Teachers, Parents, and Students.* Worthington, OH: Linworth, 2002.

PROFESSIONAL RESOURCES FOR INCLUDING LATINO CHILDREN'S LITERATURE IN CLASSROOMS AND CHILDCARE CENTERS

Ada, Alma Flor. *Alma Flor Ada and You: Volume One.* Westport, CT: Libraries Unlimited, 2005.

————. *Alma Flor Ada and You: Volume Two*. Westport, CT: Libraries Unlimited, 2008.

————. *A Magical Encounter: Latino Children's Literature in the Classroom*. 2nd ed. Boston: Allyn and Bacon, 2003.

Cronin, Sharon, and Carmen Sosa Massó. *Soy Bilingüe: Language, Culture, and Young Latino Children: A Manual for Bilingual, Bicultural, and Biliterate Early Childhood Educators*. Seattle, WA: The Center for Linguistic and Cultural Democracy, 2003.

Delgado Gaitan, Concha. *Involving Latino Families in Schools: Raising Student Achievement Through Home-School Partnerships*. Thousand Oaks, CA: Sage, 2004.

Dragan, Pat Barrett. *A How-To Guide for Teaching English Language Learners in the Primary Classroom*. Portsmouth, NH: Heinemann, 2005.

Dyson, Anne Haas, and Celia Genishi, eds. *The Need for Story: Cultural Diversity in Classroom and Community*. Urbana, IL: National Council of Teachers of English, 1994.

Eggers-Piérola, Costanza. *Connections and Commitments: Reflecting Latino Values in Early Childhood Programs*. Portsmouth, NH: Heinemann, 2005.

Flores, Judith LeBlanc. *Children of La Frontera: Binational Efforts to Serve Mexican Migrant and Immigrant Students*. Charleston, WV: ERIC, Clearinghouse on Rural and Small Schools, 1996.

Flores-Dueñas, Leila. "Reader Response, Culturally Familiar Literature, and Reading Comprehension: The Case of Four Latina(o) Students." In *Multicultural and Multilingual Literacy and Language: Contexts and Practices*, ed. by Fenice B. Boyd and Cynthia H. Brock, 180–206. New York: Guilford Press, 2004.

Freiband, Susan, and Consuelo Figueras. "Understanding Puerto Rican Culture: Using Puerto Rican Children's Literature." *Multicultural Review* 11, no. 2 (2002): 30–34.

Garzón Céspedes, Francisco. *El arte escénico de contar cuentos: La narracion oral escenica*. Madrid, Spain: Editorial Fraksan, 1991.

Hadaway, Nancy L., Sylvia M. Vardell, and Terrell A. Young. *Literature-Based Instruction with English Language Learners, K–12*. Boston: Allyn and Bacon, 2002.

Hill, Jane D., and Kathleen M. Flynn, *Classroom Instruction That Works with English Language Learners*. Alexandria, VA: Association for Supervision and Curriculum Development, 2006.

Isom, Bess A., and Carolyn P. Casteel. "Hispanic Literature: A Fiesta for Literacy Instruction." *Childhood Education* 74, no. 4 (1997): 83–89.

Kibler, John M. "Latino Voices in Children's Literature: Instructional Approaches for Developing Cultural Understanding in the Classroom." In *Children of La*

Frontera: Binational Efforts to Serve Mexican Migrant and Immigrant Students, ed. by Judith LeBlanc Flores, 239–68. Charleston, WV: ERIC, 1996.

King, K. A., and Alison Mackey. *The Bilingual Edge: Why, When, and How to Teach Your Child a Second Language*. New York: HarperCollins, 2007.

Kirmani, Mubina Hassanali. "Empowering Culturally and Linguistically Diverse Children and Families." *Young Children* 62, no. 6 (November 2007): 94–98.

Leavell, J. A., B. Hatcher, Jennifer Battle, and N. Ramos-Michail. "Exploring Hispanic Culture through Trade Books." *Social Education* 66, no. 4 (2002): 210–15.

Linse, Barbara, and Dick Judd. *Fiesta! Mexico and Central America: A Global Awareness Program for Children in Grades 2–5*. Torrance, CA: Fearon Teacher Aids, 1993.

Martínez-Roldán, Carmen. "Building Worlds and Identities: A Case Study of the Role of Narratives in Bilingual Literature Discussions." *Research in the Teaching of English*, 37 (2003): 491–526.

Nathenson-Mejia, Sally, and Kathy Escamilla. "Connecting with Latino Children: Bridging Cultural Gaps with Children's Literature." *Bilingual Research Journal* 27, no. 1 (2003): 101–16.

Páez, Mariela M., Patton O. Tabors, and Lisa M. López. "Dual Language and Literacy Development of Spanish-speaking Preschool Children." *Journal of Applied Developmental Psychology* 28, no. 2 (March 2007): 85–102.

Paquette, Kelli R., and Sue A. Rieg. "Using Music to Support the Literacy Development of Young English Language Learners." *Early Childhood Education Journal* 36, no. 3 (December 2008): 227–232.

Reid, Suzanne Elizabeth. *Book Bridges for ESL Students: Using Young Adult and Children's Literature to Teach ESL*. Lanham, MD: Scarecrow Press, 2002.

Ricken, Robert, and Michael Terc. *User-Friendly Schools for Latinos: A Model for All Immigrants*. Lanham, MD: Rowman & Littlefield Education, 2006.

Tabors, Patton O. *One Child, Two Languages: A Guide for Preschool Educators of Children Learning English as a Second Language*. Baltimore, MD: Paul H. Brookes, 1997.

Thorpe, Helen. *Just Like Us: The True Story of Four Mexican Girls Coming of Age in America*. New York: Scribner/Simon & Schuster, 2009.

Trousdale, Ann M., ed. *Give a Listen: Stories of Storytelling in School*. Urbana, IL: National Council of Teachers of English, 1994.

Valverde, Leonard A. *Improving Schools for Latinos: Creating Better Learning Environments*. Lanham, MD: Rowman & Littlefield Education, 2006.

Vigil, Angel. *¡Teatro! Hispanic Plays for Young People*. Englewood, CO: Teacher Idea Press, 1996.

Zentella, Ana Celia. *Growing Up Bilingual: Puerto Rican Children in New York.* Malden, MA: Blackwell, 1997.

———, ed. *Building on Strength: Language and Literacy in Latino Families and Communities.* New York: Teachers College Press, 2005.

PROFESSIONAL RESOURCES FOR LIBRARY PROGRAMS AND SERVICES TO LATINO CHILDREN AND THEIR FAMILIES

Alire, Camilla A., and Jacqueline Ayala. *Serving Latino Communities: A How-to-do-it Manual for Librarians.* 2nd ed. New York: Neal-Schuman, 2007.

Allen, Adela Artola. "The School Library Media Center and the Promotion of Literature for Hispanic Children." *Library Trends* 41, no. 3 (1993): 437–61.

Arquette, Kerry, Andrea Zocchi, and Jerry Vigil. *Day of the Dead Crafts: More than 24 Projects.* Hoboken, NJ: Wiley, 2008.

Avila, Salvador. *Crash Course in Serving Spanish-Speakers.* Westport, CT: Libraries Unlimited, 2008.

Ayala, John, and Salvador Güereña. *Pathways to Progress: Issues and Advances in Latino Librarianship.* Westport, CT: Libraries Unlimited, 2010.

Byrd, Susannah Mississippi. *¡Bienvenidos! ¡Welcome! A Handy Resource Guide for Marketing Your Library to Latinos.* Chicago: American Library Association, 2005.

Dame, Melvina Azar. *Serving Linguistically and Culturally Diverse Students: Strategies for the School Library Media Specialist.* New York: Neal-Schuman, 1993.

Diamont-Cohen, Betsy. *Early Literacy Programming en Español: Mother Goose on the Loose Programs for Bilingual Learners.* New York: Neal-Schuman, 2010.

Greene, Ellin, and Janice M. Del Negro. *Storytelling: Art and Technique.* 4th ed. Santa Barbara, CA: Libraries Unlimited, 2010.

Güereña, Salvador, ed. *Library Services to Latinos: An Anthology.* Jefferson, NC: McFarland, 2000.

Immroth, Barbara, and Kathleen de la Peña McCook. *Library Services to Youth of Hispanic Heritage.* Jefferson, NC: McFarland, 2000.

Kranwinkel, S., and M. H. Ekberg. *Spanish Piggyback Songs.* Everett, WA: Warren Pub. House, Inc., 1995.

Livo, Norman J., and Sandra A. Rietz. *Storytelling Folklore Sourcebook.* Westport, CT: Libraries Unlimited, 1991.

Lomas Garza, Carmen. *Making Magic Windows: Creating Papel Picado/Cut Paper Art with Carmen Lomas Garza.* San Francisco: Children's Book Press, 1999.

MacDonald, Margaret Read. *Twenty Tellable Tales: Audience Participation Tales for the Beginning Storyteller.* Chicago, IL: American Library Association, 2005.

Merrill, Yvonne Y., and Mary Simpson. *Hands-on Latin America: Art Activities for All Ages.* Salt Lake City, UT: Kits Publishing, 1998.

Moller, Sharon Chickering. *Library Services to Spanish Speaking Patrons: A Practical Guide.* Englewood, CO: Libraries Unlimited, 2001.

Naidoo, Jamie Campbell. "Informational Empowerment: Using Informational Books to Connect the Library Media Center with Sheltered Instruction." *School Libraries Worldwide,* 11 no. 2 (2005): 132–152.

Pavon, Ana-Elba, and Diana Borrego. *25 Latino Craft Projects.* Chicago: American Library Association, 2002.

Pellowski, Anne. *The World of Storytelling.* New York: H. W. Wilson, 1990.

Pérez, Elvia, Victor Francisco Hernández Mora, Margaret Read MacDonald, and Paula Martín. *From the Winds of Manguito: Cuban Folktales in English and Spanish/Desde los vientos de manguito: Cuentos folklóricos de Cuba, en inglés y español.* Westport, CT: Libraries Unlimited, 2004.

Perl, Lila, Victoria Bellinger, and Alma Flor Ada. *Piñatas and Paper Flowers: Holidays of the Americas in English and Spanish/Piñatas y flores de papel: fiestas de las Américas en ingles y español.* New York: Sandpiper, 1983.

Schiller, P. B., R. Lara-Alecio, and B. J. Irby. *The Bilingual Book of Rhymes, Songs, Stories, and Fingerplays/El libro bilingue de rimas, canciones, cuentos y juegos.* Beltsville, MD: Gryphon House, 2004.

Schon, Isabel. "Opening New Worlds for Latino Children." *American Libraries* 37, no. 5 (2006): 48–50.

Sierra, Judy, and Robert Kaminski. *Multicultural Folktales: Stories to Tell Young Children.* Phoenix, AZ: Oryx, 1991.

Thompson, Richard. *Frog's Riddle and other Draw-and-Tell Stories.* Toronto: Annick, 1990.

Tomás Rivera Policy Institute, Edward Flores, and Harry Pachon. "Latinos and Public Library Perceptions" (cited February 19, 2010). Available from http://www.webjunction.org/c/document_library/get_file?folderId=10860985&name=DLFE-2520003.pdf.

Treviño, Rose Z. *Read Me a Rhyme in Spanish and English/Léame una rima en español e inglés.* Chicago: American Library Association, 2009.

———. *The Pura Belpré Awards: Celebrating Latino Authors and Illustrators.* Chicago: American Library Association, 2006.

Turck, Mary C. *Mexico and Central America: A Fiesta of Cultures, Crafts, and Activities for Ages 8–12.* Chicago: Chicago Review Press, 2004.

U.S. Citizenship and Immigration Services. "Library Services for Immigrants: A Report on Current Practices" (cited December 29, 2009). Available from http://www.uscis.gov/files/nativedocuments/G-1112.pdf.

Wadham, Tim. *Programming with Latino Children's Materials: A How-to-Do-It Manual for Librarians*. New York: Neal-Schuman, 1999.

ONLINE RESOURCES

The Association of Library Service to Children (ALSC) has compiled a list of recommended children's books about "Growing Up in the Americas" which can be accessed at:
http://ala.org/ala/mgrps/divs/alsc/compubs/booklists/growingupwrld/americas.pdf

Barahona Center for Study of Books in Spanish for Children and Adolescents— This comprehensive Web site has many reviews of children's books either written in Spanish or written in English about Latinos. The site has a search engine that allows users to explore a database of Recommended Books in English About Latinos, as well as recommended Spanish titles. Users can limit the search to locate only books set in a specific country.
http://www.csusm.edu/csb/english/center.htm

La Bloga is a blog created by Rudy Garcia, Manuel Ramos, and Michael Sedano, which is dedicated to providing reviews, news, and interviews related to Latino publishing. Some of the information is related to Latino children's literature.
http://labloga.blogspot.com

Los Bloguitos is a Spanish-language blog, created by Latino authors and illustrators, which includes stories, songs, poems, etc. for children.
http://www.losbloguitos.com

Chiles: Children and Libraries en Español, created by Amanda Sharpe, is a blog with considerable information related to library services to Latino and Spanish-speaking children.
http://www.chil-es.org/home.

¡Colorín Colorado!—This reading program, produced by Reading Rockets, provides information on the importance of reading in the lives of English Language Learner (ELL) children. Activities and links are available concerning children's literature about Latinos, helping Latino families, how the school can help Latino families, etc. Librarians and educators could consider using the activities, the free 92 page booklet, and video clips in their programs and classrooms.
Available at: http://www.colorincolorado.org.

Críticas Magazine—Review resource examining books in Spanish for both children and adults. This publication provides various articles and recommendations for serving Spanish-speaking patrons.
http://www.criticasmagazine.com/csp/cms/sites/LJ/Reviews/Spanish/index.csp.

Cuentos y Más is a one-of-a-kind literacy program, produced in part by the Arlington Public Library, that promotes reading among both English and Spanish-speaking children. Think of a bilingual Reading Rainbow and you have Cuentos y Más. Free Webstreams of programs are available from:
http://arlington.granicus.com/ViewPublisher.php?view_id=13.

El día de los niños/El día de los libros (Day of the Child/Day of the Book) Toolkit is a 100 page online document describing booktalks, author visits, storytelling, and other programming ideas that can be used to celebrate El día de los niños/El día de los libros on April 30th. These suggestions can be used for library programs throughout the entire year! The comprehensive document is available at:
http://www.texasdia.org/toolkit.html.

El día de los niños/El día de los libros: A Celebration of Childhood and Bilingual Literacy—Created by the Texas State Library and Archives Commission, this Web site contains a variety of information related to planning a Día celebration including: fingerplays, downloadable Spanish/English rhymes and songs, suggested activities, bookmarks, a bibliography of recommended bilingual books and a list of helpful resources.
Available: http://www.tsl.state.tx.us/ld/projects/ninos.

Dígame un cuento / Tell Me A Story: Bilingual Library Programs for Children and Families—Created by the Texas State Library and Archives Commission, this useful online manual suggests bilingual story hour programs for Latino children and their families. Librarians can use this resource to plan activities using Latino children's books.
Available: http://www.tsl.state.tx.us/ld/pubs/bilingual/index.html.

¡Es divertido hablar dos idiomas!, created by Katie Cunningham, is a blog dedicated to sharing books, music, literacy techniques, and practical suggestions related to delivering bilingual storytimes.
http://www.bilingualchildrensprogramming.blogspot.com.

Imaginaria—Comprehensive Web site of recommended Spanish books for children and young adults (Web site is entirely written in Spanish)
http://www.imaginaria.com.ar.

¡Imagínense Libros! Celebrating Latino Children's Literature, Literacy and Libraries, created by Jamie Campbell Naidoo, is an evaluation blog of Latino children's literature and includes information about topics related to Latino children's

literature and literacy.
http://imaginenselibros.blogspot.com.

Latin Baby Book Club is a highly useful blog dedicated to highlighting Latino children's literature and providing interviews with notable Latino authors and illustrators.
http://www.latinbabybookclub.com.

Latino Children's and Young Adult Book Awards Web Sites:
Pura Belpré Award—http://www.ala.org/alsc/belpre.
Tomás Rivera Mexican-American Children's Book Award—http://www.education. txstate.edu/departments/Tomas-Rivera-Book-Award-Project-Link.html.
Américas Award—http://www4.uwm.edu/clacs/aa/index.cfm.

Lee y serás (Read and You Will Be)—Created with the support of Scholastic and Verizon, this program provides support for Latino parents with training about early literacy, offers educators resources that will create print-rich learning environments for Latino children, and supplies information to public agencies to support Latino literacy in the community. More information about the program is available at:
http://www.leeyseras.net/site/main.html or http://www.scholastic.com/aboutscholastic/communityleeyseras.htm.

Living To Tell the Story: The Authentic Latino Immigrant Experience in Picture Books, written by René Colato Laínez, this essay describes the importance of high-quality Latino children's literature in the lives of Latino children.
Available on the author's Web site: http://renecolatolainez.com.

National Latino Children's Literature Conference—This annual conference, directed by Jamie Campbell Naidoo, is designed to prepare librarians, teachers, and educators for the joys and opportunities in working with Latino children using authentic Latino children's literature. The conference highlights nationally-recognized scholars of Latino literacy as well as award-winning authors and illustrators of Latino children's books.
http://www.latinochildlitconf.org.

Official El día de los niños/El día de los libros (Day of the Child/Day of the Book) Web site: http://www.ala.org/dia.

Reading is Fundamental's Latino Outreach Initiative's Recommended Books (English Version):
http://www.rif.org/kids/leer/en/cuarto/libros_recomendados_english.htm.

REFORMA's Children's and Young Adults Services Committee Website offers many activities and resources for bilingual storytimes and programs. REFORMA, the National Association to Promote Library and Information Services to Latinos and the Spanish Speaking, is an affiliate of the American Library Association and the

forerunner in information for librarians serving Latino patrons.
http://www.reforma.org/CYASC.htm.

Spanish in Our Libraries and Public Libraries Using Spanish provides numerous resources for libraries serving Spanish-speaking populations including library signage in Spanish.
http://www.sol-plus.net.

Understanding Hispanic/Latino Culture and History Through the Use of Children's Literature, by Jean Sutherland, provides information on how to use Latino children's books in the classroom and lists several suggested children's books about the Latino people and subcultures.
http://www.yale.edu/ynhti/curriculum/units/1997/2/97.02.06.x.html.

Voces, created by Adriana Dominguez, is a blog covering Latino literature (children and adult), Spanish translations, and the Latino publishing industry.
http://adrianadominguez.blogspot.com.

WebJunction's Spanish Language Outreach Program contains information and free documents related to the various facets of serving Spanish-speaking patrons in the library. http://www.webjunction.org/spanish.

Selected Latino Author and Illustrator Web Sites

Inside the United States

Alma Flor Ada http://www.almaflorada.com

Francisco X. Alarcón http://www.colorincolorado.org/read/meet/alarcon

Julia Alvarez http://www.juliaalvarez.com

George Ancona http://www.georgeancona.com

Jorge Argueta http://jorgeargueta.com

Carmen "T" Bernier-Grand http://www.carmenberniergrand.com

Monica Brown http://www.monicabrown.net

F. Isabel Campoy http://www.isabelcampoy.com

Robert Casilla http://www.robertcasilla.com

Joe Cepeda http://www.joecepeda.com

Sandra Cisneros http://www.sandracisneros.com

Raúl Colón http://www.raulcolon.com

Felipe Dávalos http://felipedavalos.com

Carmen Agra Deedy http://carmendeedy.com

Lulu Delacre http://www.luludelacre.com

David Diaz http://www.rif.org/art/illustrators/diaz.mspx

Elizabeth Gomez http://www.elizabethgomezart.com

Lucía González http://www.luciagonzalezbooks.com/author/index.php

Maya Christina Gonzalez http://www.mayagonzalez.com and
http://www.reflectionpress.org

Susan Guevara http://susanguevara.com/index_flash.html

Juan Felipe Herrera http://www.juanfelipe.org/pageone.html

Francisco Jiménez http://www.scu.edu/cas/modernlanguages/facultystaff/
jimenezhomepage.cfm

Laura Lacámara http://www.lauralacamara.com/index.html

René Colato Laínez http://renecolatolainez.com

Carmen Lomas Garza http://www.carmenlomasgarza.com

Rafael López http://www.rafaellopez.com

Marisa Montes http://www.marisamontes.com

Pat Mora http://www.patmora.com

Yuyi Morales http://www.yuyimorales.com

José-Luis Orozco http://www.joseluisorozco.com

John Parra http://www.johnparraart.com

Amada Irma Pérez http://www.amadairmaperez.com

Luis J. Rodriguiez http://www.luisjrodriguez.com

Pam Muñoz Ryan http://www.pammunozryan.com

René Saldaña, Jr. http://renesaldanajr.blogspot.com

Alex Sanchez http://www.alexsanchez.com

Esmeralda Santiago http://www.esmeraldasantiago.com

Simon Silva http://www.simonsilva.com

Gary Soto http://www.garysoto.com

Carmen Tafolla http://www.carmentafolla.com

Alisa Valdes-Rodriguez http://www.alisavaldesrodriguez.com

Beatriz Vidal http://www.beatrizvidal.com

INTERNATIONAL

Ivar Da Coll http://www.ivardacoll.com

Silvia Dubovoy http://www.silviadubovoy.com

Ana María Machado http://www.anamariamachado.com

Luis Pescetti http://www.luispescetti.com

Carmen Posadas http://www.carmenposadas.net/obra-home.php

Margarita Robleda http://www.margaritarobleda.com

Common Small Press Publishers/Distributors of Latino Books

Children's Book Press—http://www.childrensbookpress.org/our-books/latino

Cinco Puntos Press—http://www.cincopuntos.com

Del Sol Books—http://www.delsolbooks.com

Groundwood Books—http://www.groundwoodbooks.com/gw_latino.cfm

Lectorum—http://www.lectorum.com

Lee & Low—http://www.leeandlow.com

Piñata Books—http://www.latinoteca.com/arte-publico-press/pinata-books

Santillana USA—http://www.santillanausa.com

University of New Mexico Press—http://www.unmpress.com/unmpress.php

Celebrating Cuentos: Programs & Materials for Latino Children In-Service Bingo Sheet

What is the name of a recommended Latino picture book?	Give an example of a book with a Latino stereotype or a stereotype found in Latino books for children.	What is the name of the Puerto Rican Librarian from New York who wrote Latino children's books?	How can a librarian or educator make a learning environment (classroom or library) "Latino Friendly"?	What year was the Américas Award Created?
How many major awards for Latino children's literature currently exist?	Who is the Latina author/illustrator that never saw herself in her picture books as a child and subsequently created picture books when she grew up?	Describe one of the National Latino Literacy Outreach Programs.	What is the name of the person who creates numerous CDs of Latino children's music?	List an electronic resource for locating Latino children's books.
List a print resource for planning library programs for Latinos.	List 2 publishers of Latino children's books.	FREE	List 3 recommended Latino or Latina authors and/or illustrators of Latino children's books.	How can Noche de Cuentos @ mi biblioteca bring Latino families to the library?
What is an intergenerational program and why is this type of program good for libraries serving Latino children?	List one recommended Latino folktale or storytelling resource.	Why is it important for Latino and non-Latino children to see positive images of Latino cultures in children's media and books?	What is El día de los niños/El día de los libros?	What is the name of the library association that serves Latinos and Spanish-speaking patrons?
List a resource that contains information on library services to Latinos.	What is one think to consider when selecting bilingual books in Spanish?	If a librarian or educator does not speak Spanish but wants to help Spanish-speaking children and their families, what can she/he do?	How can a library or school reach out to the local Latino community?	Explain why all Latinos do not have a "Latin Look" of dark hair and eyes accompanied by brown skin.

DETAILED EVALUATION SHEET FOR EVALUATING LATINO CHILDREN'S BOOKS

Title of Book:		Publication Date:		Publisher:	
Author:		**Illustrator:**			

BOOK CHARACTERISTICS: Please Circle ONE Answer

1.	What is the genre of the book?	Fiction		Nonfiction	
2.	What is the format of the book?	Picture Book	Novel	Other	
3.	Is the author of the book Latino or non-Latino?	Latino		Non-Latino	
4.	Is the illustrator of the book Latino or non-Latino?	Latino		Non-Latino	
5.	Is the text of the book bilingual, interlingual, or written only in English?	Bilingual	Interlingual	English Only	
6.	What supplemental linguistic features are present in the text? **Select all that apply.**	Glossary	Pronunciation Guide	Author Notes	None
7.	Which children's book award(s) did the book receive? **Select all that apply.**	Américas Award/ Honor/ Commended	Tomás Rivera Award	Pura Belpré Award/ Honor	None / Other

CHARACTERIZATION IN NARRATIVE & ILLUSTRATIONS: Please Circle ONE Answer

1.	Overall, are female Latino characters depicted in minor or major roles in the *narrative* (text)?	Minor Roles	Major Roles	No Female Characters
2.	Overall, are male Latino characters depicted in minor or major roles in the narrative?	Minor Roles	Major Roles	No Male Characters
3.	Which gender of Latino character appears more often in the *narrative*?	Female	Male	Equal Representation
4.	Which gender of Latino character appears more often in the *illustrations*?	Female	Male	Equal Representation
5.	Overall in the narrative, are female Latino characters portrayed in gender stereotyped roles such as house wife, maid, cook, mother of many children, sweet and submissive girl?	Yes	No	N/A
6.	Overall in the narrative, are male Latino characters portrayed in gender stereotyped roles such as bread-winner of the family, man full of machismo, superior boy?	Yes	No	N/A

7. Do Latinos have a primary or secondary role in the narrative?	Primary Role		Secondary Role	
8. What is the socioeconomic status of Latino characters in the story? (Make your best assumption based on the text and illustrations)	Low	Middle		High

9. Which Latino culture is represented? (Please select ONE of the following and list the country under the category heading. If a culture is not specified, select the Generic Latino category. If a culture is given but not a specific country, indicate the culture only, leaving the area underneath blank.).	Puerto Rican:	Mexican/ Mex. Amer.:	Cuban:	Central American:
	South American:	Caribbean (non-Puerto Rican or Cuban):	Generic Latino	

10. Are Latino characters with disabilities represented in the story or illustrations?	Yes	No	
11. Are there gay or lesbian Latino characters represented in the story or illustrations?	Yes	No	
12. Do *all* Latino characters have a "Latin Look" of brown skins, brown eyes, and dark hair?	Yes	No	

13. If Latinos without a "Latin Look" are represented, what is the other look? **Select all that apply.**	Black (African)	White (Non-Anglo)	Asian	Other, Please Specify:	N/A (All have Latin Look)

14. Are any of the Latino characters described as being of mixed race?	Yes	No	
15. Are there *any* elderly Latino characters in the story or illustrations?	Yes	No	
16. If elderly Latino characters are present, are they depicted as frail and feeble-minded?	Yes	No	N/A
17. Do the Latino characters in the book include an extended family of Aunts (Tias), Uncles (Tios), grandparents (Abuelas or Abuelos), or cousins?	Yes	No	
18. Do any of the Latino characters have a role as community leaders?	Yes	No	
19. Are the Latino characters in the story recently-arrived immigrants?	Yes	No	

20. Are the main "Latino" characters animal or human?	Animals		Humans	

SETTING & PLOT: — **Please Circle ONE Answer**

1. Does the story have a contemporary or historical setting?	Contemporary Setting (1980-Pres)		Historical Setting (Pre-1980)
2. Is the story set in the United States/Puerto Rico or in another country?	U.S. Setting/ Puerto Rico	Non-U.S. Setting	Not Addressed in Narrative
3. Is the overall mood of the story upbeat and positive or full of despair and negative?	Positive Mood		Negative Mood
4. Do Latino characters of the story face common, everyday problems such as bilingualism, immigration, family relationships, social relationships, etc?	Yes		No
5. Is the English language a barrier to the Latino characters?	Yes	No	N/A because Native Country
6. If the story is about a contemporary Latino child, does he/she face issues with racism at school or in society?	Yes	No	N/A
7. Does the book's narrative imply that Latino people are unable to solve their own problems without the help of Anglos?	Yes		No
8. Does the narrative or illustrations contain magical realism?	Yes		No

THEME: — **Please Circle ONE Answer**

	Celebrations/ Festivals	Immigration/ Migrant Workers	Family Traditions
1. Which *one* of the following themes best represents the theme of the book?	Foods/ Customs	Growing Up & Gaining Confidence	Important Latino Figure/Role Model
	Other, Please specify:		

CULTURAL AUTHENTICITY: — **Please Circle ONE Answer**

1. Is the use of Spanish accurate and authentic or does it contain errors?	Accurate	Errors	N/A
2. Is the character's use of Spanish natural or does it seem forced/contrived?	Natural	Contrived	N/A
3. Do Latino characters decide to give up some aspect of their root culture in order to achieve happiness or success?	Yes		No

4. Is the Latino subculture trivialized by limiting to fiestas, piñata parties, foods, patron saints, etc.?	Yes	No
5. Are Latino cultural factors communicated, such as strong sense of family relationships, sense of humor, respect for elders, responsibility for communal welfare?	Yes	No

ILLUSTRATIONS: (If applicable)   **Please Circle ONE Answer**

1. Are the illustrations in color or black-and-white?	Color		Black-and-White	
2. Are the illustrations photographs or media based (drawings, paintings, computer generated, etc.)?	Photographs	Media Based	Both	
3. Do the illustrations extend the story, adding further information?	Yes		No	
4. Do the illustrations contain cultural "props," such as sombreros, burros, and cacti that seem employed to add a *cultural flavor* to the story?	Yes		No	
5. How are barrios (Latino neighborhoods) portrayed?	Charming/ Post-Card Appearance	Dirty and Crime-filled	Natural, Every-day Environments	N/A
6. Do Latino characters wear period or peasant clothes in settings where they would ordinarily wear contemporary clothing?	Yes		No	
7. Are females shown outdoors and active in the illustrations?	Yes	No	N/A	

Additional Observations or Comments Regarding the Book's depiction of Latinos and/or the Spanish Language of the Text:

✿ INDEX

✸ ABOUT THE EDITOR AND CONTRIBUTORS

DR. MARÍA E. ARROYO is an educator for Lexington (South Carolina) School District One's Parent Information and Resource Center Bilingual Program. She is certified in both Parent-As-Teachers and Parent-Child Home Programs, and is also a Community Scholar Graduate. María presents at conferences around the United States on the advantages of biculturalism in an ever-changing society.

DR. JENNIFER BATTLE is a professor of literacy at Texas State University–San Marcos. She was a founding contributor to and subsequent director of the Tomás Rivera Mexican American Children's Book Award sponsored by the College of Education. Her teaching, scholarship, and service are interconnected with her own cultural heritage and her interests in Latino children's literature, literacy, and bilingualism.

HOPE CRANDALL is the school librarian at Washington Elementary, a two-way bilingual school in Woodburn, Oregon. Her passions are getting the right book for each reader and family literacy. She is a member of several library associations in Oregon as well as the American Library Association and REFORMA, the National Association to Promote Library and Information Services to Latinos and the Spanish Speaking (an affiliate of the American Library Association).

KATIE CUNNINGHAM is the children's librarian at the uniquely bilingual Village Branch of the Lexington (Kentucky) Public Library system. She has been conducting Bilingual Family Storytime programs and serving Latino and Spanish-speaking families through libraries for several years. Katie reviews Spanish and Latino children's books for REFORMA.

ORALIA GARZA DE CORTÉS is an ardent advocate of equity in library services for Latino children and families. A past president of REFORMA, Garza de Cortés co-founded the Pura Belpré Award. She led REFORMA and the library community in implementing *El día de los niños/El día de los libros*, a now annual national literacy event that celebrates children, books, languages, and cultures throughout the United States. She is also a co-founder of the *Noche de Cuentos* family literacy initiative.

LUCÍA M. GONZÁLEZ is an award-winning author, storyteller, and librarian raised in both Havana, Cuba, and Miami, Florida. Her books celebrate her Cuban heritage and the outreach work of Latina librarian Pura Belpré. Lucía is the president of REFORMA and co-creator of the *Noche de Cuentos* family literacy initiative. She has also served as chair of the Pura Belpré Awards committee and as the coordinator of the Pura Belpré Awards *celebracíon* for several years.

MAYA CHRISTINA GONZALEZ is a bilingual artist, illustrator, author, and art educator of Mexican and German descent who currently resides in California. Her distinctive art is suffused with elements of magical realism and Chicano culture. Maya is a strong advocate of Latino children's need to see their faces represented in their books. Her children's book illustrations have received numerous distinctions, including the Américas, Pura Belpré, and the Tomás Rivera Awards.

DR. CARMEN M. MARTÍNEZ-ROLDÁN is a professor in the Bilingual Bicultural Education Program at the University of Texas, Austin. Her research addresses bilingual students' literacy development in two languages (Spanish/English) and the use of children's literature to support Latino students' literacy and learning. Her work has been published in numerous national and international literacy journals.

DR. CARMEN L. MEDINA is an assistant professor of literacy, culture, and language education at the Indiana University School of Education. Her research focuses on the responses of Latino children to books representing their diverse cultural perspectives as well as the use of drama in literacy instruction. She has also served as a member of the Américas Award Committee.

YUYI MORALES is an award-winning author and illustrator, puppet-maker, and storyteller from Veracruz, Mexico. A multiple winner of the Pura Belpré, Américas, and Tomás Rivera awards for Latino children's literature, she has created several books for children that celebrate the richness and beauty within the Latino cultures. Yuyi currently resides in California with her dear friend Señor Calavera.

DR. JAMIE CAMPBELL NAIDOO is an endowed assistant professor at the University of Alabama School of Library and Information Studies and director/founder of the National Latino Children's Literature Conference. He teaches and researches in the areas of early childhood literacy, culturally diverse children's literature, and library services to Latino families. He is co-chair of the Children's and Young Adult Services Committee of REFORMA, children's book review editor for REFORMA, and has chaired both the Pura Belpré and Américas Award committees.

AMY OLSON is a children's and teen librarian who has worked extensively with Latino and Spanish-speaking populations. While Amy has previously worked in public libraries, she is currently working throughout the Fayette County School System of Lexington, Kentucky, as a literacy-based bilingual programming specialist. Amy reviews Spanish and Latino children's books for REFORMA.

IRANIA MACÍAS PATTERSON is a storyteller and bilingual children's specialist for the Public Library of Charlotte and Mecklenburg County. An award-winning Latina children's author, she has also worked within the field of children's literature in Spain and Venezuela. Irania is a frequent reviewer of Spanish and Latino children's books for REFORMA.

DR. RUTH E. QUIROA is assistant professor of language arts and children's literature at National-Louis University. She has written articles focusing on trends and issues in Mexican American-themed children's literature and on the use of Spanish in English-based Latino literature. Her research interests include investigating the responses of Latino students to children's literature with Latino themes and the impact of teachers' cultural and linguistic awareness on literacy instruction for ELL students.

DR. ROBERT K. REAM is an associate professor in the Graduate School of Education at the University of California, Riverside. His research addresses educational inequality, social capital, and Latino social demography.

GUILLERMINA "GIGI" TOWERS is a parent educator for Lexington (South Carolina) School District One's Parent Information and Resource Center Bilingual Program. She has served on the board of several literacy organizations including First Steps at Lexington County and the South Carolina Hispanic/Latino Advisory Committee.

LILLIA VAZQUEZ is a graduate student in School of Education at the University of California, Riverside. Under the direction of Dr. Robert Ream, she has been exploring her interests in the equity of education for Latino children in schools throughout the United States.